RABBI AKIBA'S MESSIAH

The Origins of Rabbinic Authority

DANIEL GRUBER

© Daniel Gruber, 1999

ELIJAH PUBLISHING
PO Box 776
Hanover, NH 03755
603 643-4151

TABLE OF CONTENTS

INTRODUCTION	1

THE REVOLT

1. HISTORICAL SETTING	4
From the Maccabees to Roman Dominance	4
From Roman Dominance to the Great Revolt	6
The Great Revolt	8
From the Great Revolt to the Bar Kokhba Rebellion	9
"Judaisms"	10
2. THE SOURCES	12
Rabbinic Sources	12
Non-rabbinic Sources	13
Modern Sources	14
3. THE COURSE OF THE REBELLION	16
4. SIMEON BEN KOSIBA	21
National Unity	22

THE REVOLUTION

5. AKIBA BEN JOSEPH	24
Akiba's Life	26
6. WHAT IS A RABBI?	29
In the Talmud	30

The Battle for Torah

7. TANAKH AND THE ORAL LAW	33
The First Talmudic Claim	34
The Record of the Torah	34
The Record from Moses to the Exile	38
The Record in the Exile and in the Return	43
Additional Testimony	46
8. THE ORAL LAW AS INTERPRETATION	49
The Second Talmudic Claim	49
The Talmud to the Contrary	49
9. *TORAH SHE'B'AL PE*	53
Al Pe and *B'Yad Moshe*	57
History to the Contrary	58
The Development of the Doctrine of the Oral Law	60
10. CONFRONTING THE SCRIPTURES	62
Additional Impact on the Scriptures	68

11. TALMUDIC REVISIONISM	73
The People in the Bible	73
The Teachings of the Bible	75
The God of the Bible	76
Replacement and Substitution	77
12. UPROOTING THE SCRIPTURES	80
13. A FENCE AROUND THE TORAH	85
The Third Talmudic Claim	85

Adversaries

14. CONFLICT WITH THE PRIESTS, BACKGROUND	88
The Priests and the Empire	92
15. THE RABBIS DISPLACE THE PRIESTS	94
Akiba's Role	97
16. SILENCING THE TRADITIONAL RABBIS	101
The Conflict with R. Eliezer Ben Hyrcanus	103
The Creation of Tradition	106
17. IT IS NOT IN HEAVEN	111
The *Bath Kol*	114
18. THE RABBIS REPLACE THE PROPHETS	121
Prophecy in the Talmud	122
The Rabbinic Interpretation of Dreams	123
Authoritative Citation vs. "the Word of the Lord"	124

Enforcement

19. THE SANHEDRIN	126
The Nature of the Sanhedrin	127
Saved at the Cost of their Lives	128
20. THE REBELLIOUS ELDER	131
The *Mesith* and Others	133
21. *AM HA'ARETZ*	135

THE MESSIAH

22. THE FIRST CENTURY CONCEPT OF MESSIAH	140
Government and Righteousness	140
Torah	142
The Supernatural	143
Common Messianic Expectation Evidenced in the Gospels	144
23. YESHUA, THE PHARISEES AND THE RABBIS	146
24. THE *MINIM*	150
The Threat of *Minuth*	151
R. Akiba vs. the *Minim*	152
A Time to Act	155
25. THE ROMAN TRIALS	159

26. "THIS IS THE KING MESSIAH"	165
Akiba's Role in the Revolt	169
27. *MILHEMET MITZVAH*	172
28. THE TRIAL	175
Bethar	177

THE CONSEQUENCES OF THE REBELLION

29. THE END OF THE REVOLT	181
The Loss of Life	181
The Exile and Slavery	182
"Judea" Becomes "Palestine"	183
30. THE FINAL SPLIT	184
31. RABBI AKIBA'S MARTYRDOM	187
A Theology of Suffering	188
32. SOME CONCLUDING REMARKS	191

APPENDICES

APPENDIX A:	
The Rabbis, the Messiah, and the Majority	194
APPENDIX B:	
Maimonides' Concept of the Messiah	199
CHAPTER NOTES	204
BIBLIOGRAPHY	277

INTRODUCTION

"In Jewish tradition the fall of Bethar [the headquarters of the Bar Kokhba Revolt] was a disaster equal to the destruction of the First and Second Temples."[1]

The First Temple was destroyed in Jerusalem in 586 B.C. by King Nebuchadnezzar of Babylon. King Zedekiah of Judah had rebelled against his rule. The rebellion was crushed. Jeremiah, who prophesied during this time, wrote "Lamentations" to mourn the disaster that befell the people and the land - the death, suffering, and exile to Babylon. The Midrash, the traditional rabbinic commentary, on Lamentations is a source for much of the information on the Bar Kokhba Rebellion.

Jeremiah's prophecy that the Babylonian exile would end after seventy years was fulfilled. In time, the city and the Temple were rebuilt.

The Second Temple was destroyed at the end of the Great Revolt of 66-70 C.E. The Great Revolt, led by the Zealots, was an unsuccessful attempt to throw off the yoke of the Roman Empire. As Vespasian and Titus put down the revolt, one million Jews died from starvation and violence. Others were led away into exile and slavery. Josephus records the events from beginning to end in The Wars of the Jews.

The Bar Kokhba Revolt against Roman rule in the time of the Emperor Hadrian equalled, or surpassed, these previous two tragedies in the numbers who were killed, starved to death, or led into exile and slavery. In other ways, the Bar Kokhba Rebellion was a greater tragedy than either the destruction of the First or the Second Temple.

In long-term consequences, the Bar Kokhba Rebellion of 132-135 C.E., "the Last Revolt" against Roman rule, may well have been the greatest disaster in Jewish history, bar none. The Babylonian destruction and exile were eclipsed by the return to the land seventy years later. The failure of the Great Revolt brought the destruction of Jerusalem and the Second Temple, but Jews were still permitted to remain in the land. Following the Bar Kokhba Rebellion, Jews were forbidden to inhabit the land of Judea. That legal prohibition and the exile it mandated lasted for eighteen centuries. The Romans changed the name of the land to "Palestine" to demonstrate that it would never again be a Jewish land.

The Bar Kokhba Revolt also witnessed a final, violent split between the followers of Jesus and the followers of the Rabbis. It generated great hostility on both sides. The homeless wanderings of the Jews soon became the hostile reproach and incitement of an imperial Church. In a way that neither the destruction of the First nor of the Second Temple did, the Bar Kokhba Rebellion set the stage for what became an endless procession of Jewish suffering down to, including, and beyond the Holocaust.

The disaster was further compounded by the fact that Rabbi Akiba, the father of rabbinic Judaism, had proclaimed Bar Kokhba, the leader of the rebellion, to be God's Anointed, the Messiah. In the eighteen hundred and fifty years since, as students of history and various religious persuasions have studied the sparse and sometimes conflicting evidence, one puzzling question always emerges. As Franz Rosenzweig expressed it, "Why did even the wisest teacher of his age fall for the false messiah, Bar Kochba, in the time of Hadrian?"[2]

There seems to be general, almost universal, agreement as to the character of both Bar Kokhba and Rabbi Akiba. In fact, it is the striking differences between the two that have caused much of the puzzlement. How could these apparent opposites have found any common ground for working together? What could Akiba have seen in Bar Kokhba?

To this day, no one has been able to convincingly answer the question "Why?" I think we can do that here, by piecing together the odd-shaped parts of the puzzle to form a very striking picture.

In examining the character, motivation, and method of Rabbi Akiba, I believe I have found the reason for his proclamation. It appears to be a well-reasoned decision that was completely consistent with the whole thrust of Akiba's life from the time he became a rabbi up until the day he was martyred by the victorious Romans. There is much in the evidence that would confirm this conclusion, nothing that would contradict it, and no satisfactory alternative explanation.

Since Rabbi Akiba ben Joseph played such a major role in the formation of rabbinic Judaism, his character can be seen throughout the rabbinic writings - in his own words, those of his contemporaries, and those of his disciples. Additionally, there are the views of various historians and religious scholars from that time to this.

Bar Kokhba's character is described in various rabbinic and church writings. In 1960, 15 of Bar Kokhba's personal military dispatches were discovered in some caves which had been the last refuge for some of his supporters. This correspondence verifies beyond doubt the traditional view of his character presented in both the rabbinic and the church writings.

Primary sources, especially the Talmud, provide the basic

evidence.[3] Later sources are used to affirm the way in which the basic evidence is understood. The underlying assumption is that examining the evidence is always better than prejudging a case.

I am well aware that there are those who, for different reasons, will not like some of the conclusions I reach. I agree. I personally am not pleased with these conclusions, but the question I have continually asked is, "What does the evidence show?" Even more than that, "Does the evidence lead inescapably to these conclusions?" I am convinced that it does. You may judge for yourself.

"Truth is hard enough for historians to discover and convey in their writings, but some readers resent their going to the trouble. Anatole France said 'if you present history in an unexpected aspect you surprise the reader, but he does not like to be surprised. If you try to instruct him, you only humiliate and anger him....As a result, an original historical view is an universal object of suspicion and disgust.' "[4]

I hope you do not resent the trouble to which I have gone.

THE REVOLT

1. THE HISTORICAL SETTING

Carl Degler suggested that the historian "is guided less by 'covering laws' that are presumed to be true in all times and places than by 'participant-sources' — that is, contemporary evidence. Thus the historian might think it plausible that the American Revolution was caused by high taxes or the navigation laws, but if he finds no evidence for that in the contemporary literature he has to abandon the thesis; conversely, if he finds other reasons given at the time he has to take them seriously, however strange they may seem to him. 'The careful historian,' Degler concluded, 'tries to think as his subjects did, and within their system of values.'"[1]

In the first and second centuries in Judea, people did not view religion and politics as separate, much less antagonistic, spheres. In the modern Western world, it does not seem difficult to distinguish between Church (or Synagogue) and State, even though their activities sometimes overlap. After all, they have a different polity, structure, and purpose.

To some extent, these Western distinctions are misleading. "Religion" and "politics" are different names for essentially the same thing. They cover the same territory: the determination of values and standards, permitted and prohibited behavior, justice and injustice, individual and community welfare, the proper and improper use of authority and power, the rights and responsibilities of wealth and property, and the proper training of future generations. In sum, they are about the correct purpose and course of human society.[2] For ancient Romans, Jews, and Christians, religion and politics were inseparable.

From the Maccabees to Roman Dominance

From the destruction of the First Temple in 586 B.C. to the Maccabean revolt in 167 B.C., the Jewish people and their land were subject to the domination of various empires — the Babylonian, the Medo-Persian, the Macedonian (Greek) and its Ptolemaic and Seleucid successors. But during those 420 years, as far as we know, there were no revolts against foreign rule. That is amazing, especially considering what happened during the following 300 years from 167 B.C.E. to 135 C.E.

In part, but only in part, the 420 years without revolt were due to the power and tolerance of the ruling empire. "The Hellenistic rulers, as well as the Romans later, were usually tolerant of other religions, as polytheistic religions usually were, unless some religion threatened its very existence or constituted a menace to the civil order."[3]

There was another very important reason for the lack of revolt. There was no Biblical justification for it. The exile was seen as the judgment of God. The return was facilitated by Cyrus the king of Persia, whom the Lord prophetically called "His Anointed".[4] The rebuilding of the Temple was facilitated by Cyrus and later Persian kings.

Centuries after that, according to Josephus, God told the High Priest Jaddua not to fight against Alexander the Great, but to open the gates of Jerusalem to him. God had previously given Alexander a prophetic dream in which Jaddua counseled him concerning the conquest of Persia. When Alexander saw Jaddua, he recognized him as the man in his dream, and greatly honored him and the Jews.[5]

So throughout the centuries which followed the destruction of Jerusalem, the Jewish people had lived with the assurance, though not necessarily one they appreciated, that God was working through the foreign empires which ruled over them. Consequently, there was no platform for revolt.

Following Alexander, "both Ptolemaic and Seleucid rulers, as well as various usurpers, usually treated the Jews as they treated other nationalities within their spheres of influence, but with greater tolerance, for the Jews were exempted from putting a royal cult in their Temple and public places."[6]

Greater tolerance was usually the case, but not always. Antiochus Epiphanes became the Seleucid ruler in 175 B.C. On his return from defeating Egypt in battle, he sacked Jerusalem, defiled the Temple, massacred the people, and fortified his own troops in the city. In 167 B.C., he desecrated the altar, and sought to destroy all those who still clung to the Law of the Lord.[7]

Mattathias and his five sons rose up in rebellion, and others joined with them. They suffered some defeats, but also won some victories and began to drive the forces of Antiochus out of the land.

Mattathias and his sons were priests. That meant they were chosen by God as leaders in Israel. The raison d'être of their revolt was the need to be faithful to God and His covenant.[8]

The Maccabees saw their own actions as comparable to those of the heroes of the Bible. Because the Maccabean revolt was eventually successful in delivering Israel from Seleucid dominance, it became the measure and the appeal of future revolts.

The rule of their descendants in Israel was tumultuous, characterized by intrigue, factionalism, and "a three-cornered struggle for power among the king, the high priest, and the Pharisaic scholars."[9] "The Pharisees were willing to allow power to the king and the priests, but only on condition that they ruled in accordance with the Pharisaic interpretation of the Law."[10]

The different factions violently fought and intrigued against one another. In 64 B.C.E., appeal was made to Pompey, the Roman emperor, to settle a struggle between two brothers, Hyrcanus and Aristobulus, over who would be king.[11] The appeal to Pompey was fatal. Rome came in as peacemaker, and stayed as lord.[12]

Though without a human king, the Jews of the time still viewed their polity as a kingdom, properly ruled by its priests. The Temple was the house of the Great King, where the priests served Him, and from which they were to govern the people.

Even Jews living in the Diaspora showed great allegiance to the land, to Jerusalem, and to the Temple. There was a strong sense of peoplehood and responsibility for other Jews. Though there were great divisions, there was also a strong sense of oneness.[13]

From Roman Dominance to the Great Revolt

"Gabinius in 57 B.C.E. was the second to shatter the concept of Palestine as one territorial entity: as a punishment for the recent uprising of Aristobulus II against Roman rule in Palestine, he divided the country into five districts and put them under the governorship of five *synhedria* (councils), instead of a central one in Jerusalem. This act was meant to be symbolic as well as administrative. The Jews remained on their territory no longer as owners and rulers, but as tenants and subjects. The Land of Israel had become a partitioned territory."[14]

For the Jews of the time, the Land itself was still holy. The only legitimate foundation for rule over it was God's Law. Though there were different spheres of operation, there was no separation of religion and politics. Government was to be run in obedience to Torah.

The Roman emperors viewed themselves, rather than the God of Israel, as worthy of worship and as the supreme authority in matters of governance. The God of Israel, however, commanded absolute allegiance and obedience. This was a great source of conflict, both between the Jews and the Romans,[15] and beween different Jewish factions.

For at least 200 years, from 64 B.C. to 135 A.D, the Pharisees fought to gain national authority and power. Josephus, a Pharisee, gives us the most contemporaneous or near-contemporaneous information on the state of the Pharisees from the end of the Maccabean period to the Great Revolt.

He tells us that towards the end of the Maccabean period, the ruler Hyrcanus left "the party of the Pharisees, and abolish[ed] the decrees they had imposed on the people, and punish[ed] those that observed them."[16] Hyrcanus's daughter-in-law, Alexandra, later took control and gave the Pharisees great power, which they used to kill those political enemies who had previously killed many of them.[17]

Josephus presents the Pharisees as a strong political force who did not hesitate to resort to violence to promote their vision and insure their power. Sometimes the violence was directed against the Romans.[18]

The Romans, on their part, sought native political rulers who would keep the people subservient enough to Rome to ensure tax revenue and dominion. Herod was such a man who understood his position and role.

"During Herod's reign the Temple became more of a religious and spiritual center for believing Jews. By lowering the profile of the Temple as a political center, Herod was true to his masters, the Romans, who wanted to eliminate any political power from native temples. The effect of Herod's reducing the status and importance of the priesthood was to enhance the status of the sages, who thus occupied a place of leadership."[19]

Describing the Pharisees during the time of Herod Antipater, Josephus says, "there was a certain sect of men that were Jews, who valued themselves highly upon the exact skill they had in the law of their fathers, and made men believe they were highly favoured by God...These are those that are called the sect of the Pharisees, who were in a capacity of greatly opposing kings. A cunning sect they were, and soon elevated to a pitch of open fighting and doing mischief. Accordingly, when all the people of the Jews gave assurance of their good-will to Caesar, and to the king's government, these very men did not swear, being above six thousand..."[20]

The power of the Pharisees grew during the reign of the different Herods. How great it was at any particular time before, during, and after the Great Revolt is a matter under dispute.[21] The Saducean priesthood formed the normal locus of power, and ruled in the councils, *sanhedria*, which the Romans had set up.

Among the Pharisees before the Great Revolt, there were different schools of interpretation which fought each other for supremacy.[22] Beit Hillel and Beit Shammai were the two major Pharisaic sects. In the Talmud, the views of Beth Hillel prevail, but the views of Beit Shammai had been dominant and remained so until Rabbi Akiba.[23]

Besides the Pharisees and the Sadducees, there were other Jewish groups who competed for the allegiance of the people. It was normal for each group to claim divine sanction and support, to present itself as the only group who spoke for God.

There were "the Covenanters of Damascus, the Pharisees at Jerusalem, the Sons of light from the Dead Sea, and in a place unknown those who composed and recited the 'Odes of Solomon'. Neither is that all. We know at least of two or three more groups of Jewish sectarians. There are first the Therapeutae, whom Philo described in his discourse 'On the contemplative life'; and there are secondly the Essenes, about whom both Philo and Josephus give more or less understandable reports."[24]

There was also "the Fourth Philosophy." According to Josephus, they were extreme Pharisees who refused to submit to any sovereign but God.[25] Perhaps these were the Zealots, or, more likely, they were *Sicarii*. From about 30 C.E. on, there were also the *Talmidei Yeshua*, the Jewish disciples of Jesus.

The march of time leaves some groups in the dust of insignificance, but that does not tell us their actual influence during their day. We should try to avoid reading their history only from the "victor's" point of view.

The Great Revolt

In 66 C.E., a group of *Sicarii* took Masada by deceit, and killed the Roman garrison there. Others in Jerusalem put a stop to the customary sacrifice that had been offered on behalf of Caesar in the Temple.[26] This was followed by factional fighting in Jerusalem, which then spread throughout the country.

As the high priests and the leading Pharisees had predicted, the cessation of the sacrifice offered for Caesar brought Roman reprisal. It was more than an insult. It was a theopolitical act of rebellion against the supreme authority of Caesar.

The Romans were able to stop the revolt first in Galilee. Fighting through Judea, they besieged Jerusalem. Finally, the city and the Temple fell. Masada, where the revolt began, was the last stronghold to fall.

In Josephus' account, both the leading Pharisees and the high priests were opposed to the revolt from the start. The Talmud gives us the same picture, except that the priests are not mentioned, and the leading Pharisees are replaced by "the Rabbis."[27]

An apparently dead Yohanan ben Zakkai was smuggled out of the city in a coffin. He prophetically greeted Vespasian, the Roman general, as king. At that point, a messenger arrived from Rome with the news that Vespasian had been made emperor. In response, Vespasian promised to grant Yohanan ben Zakkai's request to make Yavneh a place of religious authority.[28] The Talmudic account makes it clear that: 1) The Rabbis disassociated themselves from the Great Revolt; 2) The rabbinic rule which developed at Yavneh was approved by the Romans.

According to Josephus, the destruction of Jerusalem had been foretold in many ways. There had been a prophet who went throughout the city from four years before the rebellion began up until the beginning of the siege, warning of the coming destruction. There were many supernatural signs that also warned of the destruction.[29]

There is a range of opinions on how great a disaster the destruction of the Second Temple was.[30] From every point of view, however, it is agreed that institutions and relationships had to be worked through anew. The destruction of Jerusalem greatly changed the theopolitical environment.

From the Great Revolt to the Bar Kokhba Rebellion

"After 70 C.E., Rome reorganized the province and strenthened its pagan population by founding cities such as Flavia Neapolis and Flavia Ioppe, and in particular by imposing a heavy tax, the so-called *fiscus Iudaicus*, only on the Jews of Palestine and the Diaspora. The Romans also emphasized the Jewish subjugation by issuing coins that were in circulation all over the empire, but also in Palestine, bearing the inscriptions *'Iudaea capta'* [Judea captured] and *'Iudaea devicta '*[Judea defeated].'"[31]

To the Romans, the Emperor had proven himself more powerful in battle than the God of the Jews. The tax signified that sovereignty over Judea had passed from the God of the Temple to the head of the Capitol. As was their practice, the Romans continued to rule through a new, subservient, native leadership.[32]

The Temple had proven too dangerous; an impetus to rebellion against foreign domination.[33] The Romans strengthened their rule through Yohanan ben Zakkai and the group of Pharisees who followed him.[34]

The rabbinic institutions and the rationale for them grew under the Roman aegis after the destruction of the Temple. They developed into the national government under the Romans. Yavneh, "Jamnia" in Greek, became the center of rabbinic authority.[35]

Different cities served as the teaching and administrative centers for the different sects. They did not, for the most part, recognize each other's authority.

Following Johanan ben Zakkai, "...Gamaliel ii. was the head [*Nasi*] of the Academy at Jamnia....his family had kept close contacts [and good relations] with Rome and the Romans. He himself was no mean scholar not only in the Jewish sense, for he spoke Greek and Latin and was conversant with contemporary philosophy."[36]

Through Johanan ben Zakkai and Gamaliel II, Yavneh became the native administrative center for the Romans. That enabled those in charge there to gain supremacy over other competing Pharisaic groups and their academies.

Though they worked with and for the Romans, the Rabbis were never completely reconciled to Roman rule.[37] Roman historians seem to have felt that the Jews in particular were historically unappreciative of Roman beneficence. From 90 C.E. on, there were different incidents and locations of Jewish unrest and rebellion.[38]

"Judaisms"

"G. F. Moore (1927-30) characterized rabbinic Judaism as 'normative' Judaism... The Dead Sea Scrolls and further detailed research on the apocrypha, the pseudepigrapha, and other early sources as well as archaeological finds have convinced scholars of the diversity within Judaism (at least) before the destruction of the Temple in 70 C.E."[39] In the First Century, there was no normative or orthodox Judaism. There were several competing varieties.

For many years before the Great Revolt, there had been numerous groups which condemned the priesthood. Some rejected their authority outright. After the Great Revolt, the power of the priesthood dissipated significantly.

Stuart Cohen described the immense changes that began: "From a polity centred on Temple and state, Jewry was on the way to becoming a conglomeration of communities unified by their shared fidelity to the rabbinic definitions of law (*halakhah*). Equally seismic was the parallel shift in the identity of the nation's authoritative agents of indigenous government. Gone (until the coming of the Messiah) were the days when Israel was ruled by kings, priests, or prophets. Instead, if their own testimony is to believed, by the sixth century C.E. it was the early rabbis and their disciples who had propelled themselves to positions of
cases undivided — communal authority throughout \
world.

"...[T]he eventual hegemony of rabbinic Judaism, as thus portrayed, was not inevitable. Neither was there anything haphazard about the process whereby it occurred. In the political arena, as in others, the rabbis had to struggle for the realisation of their ambitions — often from positions of intrinsic constitutional inferiority. If the enormity of their achievement is to be properly assessed, appropriate note must be taken of the persistence with which they pursued an essentially political campaign. Their avowed purpose was to confound the contrary aspirations of rival contestants, some sacerdotal, others civil, for whatever communal authority native Jewish agencies could still claim to command."[40]

Very little remains of the literature and arguments of almost all non-rabbinic groups. "Especially is it important to realize that our Rabbinic sources represent the triumph of the Pharisean party, and moreover of a 'party' within the Pharisean party as it were, that of Johanan ben Zakkai. Pharisean opinions alone are recorded; parties, movements and opinions contrary to these were naturally excluded. Thus, for example as Danby points out, 'in the Mishnah the Sadducees figure only as an insignificant, discredited and heretical sect' although we know that they played a large part both in first-century and earlier Judaism. It is almost certain therefore...that many aspects of first-century Judaism find no place in our Rabbinic sources, and that that Judaism was much more variegated than such sources would lead us to expect."[41]

The Talmud is testimony to the achieved dominance of a particular sect of Pharisees.[42] That sect achieved dominance through an extended battle against its many opponents.

The relevant materials that we have, rabbinic or otherwise, were written by people who had a story to tell - their story. They give their version for their reasons. They were not seeking to be fair or impartial. If we understand that, we can work with what they wrote. All sources have their limitations.

2. THE SOURCES

The American Revolution took place a mere two hundred years ago. It is amply documented, continually studied, and endlessly analyzed. Despite that, or perhaps because of that, there is great disagreement over its cause and nature.

The Bar Kokhba Rebellion took place thirteen hundred years before the invention of the printing press.[1] The participants in the rebellion were almost totally annihilated. Their possessions and whatever they might have recorded were almost totally destroyed.

The contemporary and historically close accounts are both sparse and contradictory, often reflecting the particular prejudices of their authors, but to what extent we cannot be sure. There is no "history" of the Bar Kokhba Rebellion *per se*, but only a few references scattered in time and space. There is no biography of Bar Kokhba, and only a few modern attempts for Rabbi Akiba based upon the incomplete, ancient records, which made no pretense of being biographical.

Rabbinic Sources

Israeli scholars Benjamin Isaac and Aharon Oppenheimer summed up the caution necessary in using the Talmud: "The evaluation of the Talmud as an historical source is problematic in general, and this is particularly true of the evidence relating to the revolt. The character of talmudic literature is such that historical facts are mentioned incidentally only. The aim of the Talmud is not historiography. It concentrates on legislation (*halakhah*) and on theological didactics (*aggadah*). One may find there in juxtaposition sources from the period of the revolt itself; sources dating to the years after the revolt showing the deep impression made by failure and defeat; anachronistic descriptions of historical situations clearly reflecting a later period; sources which attempt to solve in a historiosophic manner problems connected with the revolt. All these are bound to have been distorted by later editors for whom the revolt was a nebulous event which took place in ancient history."[2]

Everyone who seeks to use the early rabbinic writings to gain historical understanding of the first and second centuries comes to a similar conclusion. Stuart Cohen put it like this: "Composed and edited by men who were jurists and mystics (sometimes both), they comprise internally consistent repositories of belief systems, not sequential statements of fact. Even when they do claim to recount historical events, the materials tend to deploy their data in a way more likely to create rabbinic myths and/or confirm rabbinic dogma than to transmit verifiable and objective information."³

Anthony Saldarini notes that, "In addition, evidence for rabbinic Judaism is derived from collections that date from 200 C.E. and later. Stories, anecdotes, halakic and historical statements may also be suspected of anachronism or distortion by later experience and have become increasingly uncertain as sources for the reconstruction of *early* rabbinic Judaism. It is very likely that the antecedents of Mishna, Midrash, the schools, and the rabbis were very different from their later mature progeny and that they underwent a complex development in varied social and historical settings and in response to important human and theological needs and tendencies. These antecedents are masked by the tendency of later sources to treat all statements and interpretations as part of a dialectically related whole rather than a series of historically related stages."⁴

The Talmud and the related rabbinic writings provide an historical record of the views of those who wrote them, or at least the public justification they wished to give. The Rabbi Akiba presented in that literature, whatever his relationship to any particular historical figure, is still the only Rabbi Akiba we know. It is this Akiba who is the father of rabbinic Judaism, and this Akiba who proclaimed Bar Kokhba the Messiah. We do not have a neutral data base, but these writings, especially the Talmud, present the most relevant reality for understanding Akiba's motivation.

Non-Rabbinic Sources

The Roman sources we have are Dio Cassius, the *Historia Augusta*, Fronto, and Pausanias. They do not agree with each other. Each has a bias and is, from our perspective, sometimes historically unreliable.

"These sources contain partial and isolated statements only, sometimes contradictory and often tendentious, which must then be interpreted in combination with the archaeological evidence. However, all the available combined information still does not produce a clear picture of the course of the revolt, and essential problems cannot be solved, such as the geographical scope of the rising, the question of whether Jerusalem was conquered by the rebels, and if so whether the Temple was rebuilt."⁵

"Fronto refers to the great number of Roman soldiers killed under Hadrian in Britain (c. AD 118) and in the Jewish rebellion....Pausanias, however, another contemporary of Hadrian, mentions the Jewish war as the only event to disturb the peace in

Hadrian's reign."[6]

For the Romans, the Jews had a history of and a reputation for rebellion, not being content to be under the yoke of any other nation. In that light, the Bar Kokhba Rebellion was simply one revolt among many, and, as such, received little attention.[7] It was, however, the last one.

"Christian sources are remote in time and antagonistic towards the Jews, yet it cannot be denied that they and the Jewish sources have features in common which they do not share with Dio: references to Bar Kokhba, Tineius Rufus and the fall of Bethar, as opposed to the statement regarding Julius Severus in the latter source. This may partly be explained by the circumstance that Jewish and Christian sources are, in fact, local sources, while Dio presumably based himself on Roman material. However, it is also possible that Talmudic literature and the Church fathers reflect, to a certain extent, a common tradition, even though they have no common sympathy. We have, altogether, four contemporary references to the war. Three are isolated sentences (Appianus, Fronto and Pausanias). The fourth does not even mention the revolt specifically (Apollodorus of Damascus). Our sources are deficient, however they are interpreted."[8]

The Christian sources give their version of the story, from their perspective, for their reasons. Eusebius, for example, was an apologist for Constantine and the Church of the Empire. Consequently, in his theology, the Church replaced the Jews as the covenant people of God. So Eusebius sought to portray the Jews in as bad a light as possible.

Modern Sources

When it comes to modern sources, we are still dealing with biases, blindnesses, and misunderstandings. G.F. Moore's "normative Judaism," though totally inaccurate and misleading, was scholarly orthodoxy for fifty years.

In a similar way, "Historians used to assume that the Jewish diaspora began after the destruction of the Second Temple. This view was determined by a theological concept, for in the nineteenth century and the beginning of the twentieth scholars wished to represent the destruction of the Second Temple as divine punishment of the people of Israel since they saw the rise of Christianity as the true continuation of Judaism."[9]

This negated the importance of the Bar Kokhba Rebellion, since "the issue" had already been decided in 70 C.E. The theological conclusion distorted the history.

This continues on both sides of the schism between Jews and

Christians, generating a variety of misconceptions and partisan assertions. Theological bias often affirms itself through bias in language, making it sometimes difficult to find appropriate neutral terms.

Even as there are factual discrepancies in the ancient sources, so there are discrepancies in interpretation among modern scholars. Sometimes the discrepancies are due to differences in perception, sometimes to a variety of assumptions or biases.

"Once scholars turned their attention to the Bar Kokhba revolt, they depicted it in various ways, depending to a large extent on personal conceptions of the Roman empire, the Jewish people, Greek and Roman culture, and Jewish religion. We find in scholarly literature discussions which wholly identify with a presumed Roman point of view or, conversely, with that of the Jews. A third group attempts to understand historical reality by giving both the supposed Roman and Jewish perspectives. Roman actions are described as basically benevolent but shortsighted; Jewish resistance as comprehensible."[10]

From a clinical point of view, the condition of the sources is not that promising. A definitive history of the revolt is impossible.[12] We do not have enough facts, and the facts we do have contradict one another.

"One should bear in mind, however, that every historical evaluation of any given period in history is an evaluation of what others have transmitted. When writing history we are in fact relating the history as it was preserved in the historical consciousness of certain authors with certain biases."[11]

We do not need a definitive history to enable us to determine the likely motive for Rabbi Akiba's Messianic proclamation. The sources may prove quite sufficient for that.

3. THE COURSE OF THE REBELLION

According to the first book of Maccabees, one of the hostile measures of Antiochus Epiphanes was a ban on circumcision. That ban and the other anti-Torah decrees of Antiochus are clearly presented as the cause of the Maccabean revolt.

The *Historia Augusta* explicitly states the immediate cause of the Bar Kokhba rebellion to have been a ban on circumcision instituted by the Emperor Hadrian.[1] The statement is explicit, but it is probably untrue. As Isaac and Oppenheimer note, "...the *Historia Augusta* is... the only source to mention a ban on circumcision preceding the revolt. The *Historia Augusta* is, of course, a most unreliable and problematic work."[2]

The Talmud says that the anti-Torah measures followed the revolt.[3] If the ban on circumcision had preceded and caused the revolt, there is every reason to believe that the Talmud would have emphasized that fact, just as the books of the Maccabees did. The Talmud emphasizes every anti-Torah decree.

Other sources say that the cause was Hadrian's decision to build a pagan temple on the Temple mount, rename Jerusalem accordingly, and/or the carrying out of these decrees.[4] Despite the contradictory testimony of the ancient sources, we can be relatively certain that Hadrian's decree to rebuild and rename Jerusalem preceded the revolt. A coin with the marking of "*Aelia Capitolina*" was found among Bar Kokhba coins in an underground refuge of the rebels.[5] Hadrian's decree, and the coin minted to honor it, must have taken place before the end of the rebellion, and most likely before the start.

It seems that the "honor" Hadrian gave, to make Jerusalem a rival to Antioch, was the likely cause of the rebellion. The Emperor's decision, and the impending desecration of the Temple Mount which it foretold, would have served as a catalyst for popular opposition.[6]

We know with assurance that the Jews were never content under Roman rule.[7] There had been earlier revolts among the Diaspora Jews in Cyrenaica, Egypt, Cyprus, and Mesopotamia, even in the decade prior to the Bar Kokhba rebellion.[8] Ever since the return of a remnant from Babylonian exile, the Jews in Israel had longed for freedom from foreign domination. Israeli scholar Hugo Mantel concluded, "Simeon Bar Kochba was merely an heir and disciple of the rebels in the days of the Temple, and the rebels and Zealots, in turn, continued to fight for the cause of the Hasmoneans..."[9] The rebellion was another effort to re-establish Jewish sovereignty.[10]

Hadrian must certainly have known the history of the province of Judea, including the Hasmonean/Maccabbean revolt that followed Antiochus Epiphanes' anti-Torah decrees. He must have known of the later willingness of the Jewish leaders and people to let themselves be slaughtered rather than endure the idolatrous Roman eagle in Jerusalem. He would have had every reason to expect some kind of rebellious response to an *"Aelia Capitolina"* proclamation.

"Epigraphical and archaeological evidence has now shown that the Roman army in Judaea was reinforced...in 129/130, which may reflect a response to local unrest, or preparations for the suppression of anticipated hostilities, or both."[11]

Perhaps Hadrian sought to make prudent military preparations, but the sources indicate that the Romans were not prepared for the full-scale revolt that broke out in 132.

The attitude of Hadrian towards the Jews is a disputed topic. The Talmud records some earlier congenial conversations between rabbis and Hadrian, but the prevailing rabbinic view is that Hadrian developed an unreasonable hatred towards the Jews, and simply seized whatever excuses he could to persecute them.[12]

But Hugo Mantel disputes this characterization of Hadrian. He points out that, "Spartianus, Dio, and Pausanias praise him that 'he never began a war willingly' and Pausanias accuses 'the Hebrews' that they brought upon themselves evil through their revolt, apparently, according to his view, without any reason."[13]

Mantel goes on to fortify this view of Hadrian as a peaceful emperor, who was quite gracious to his dominions: "As is well known, this Emperor [Hadrian] relinquished the conquests of Trajan beyond the Euphrates. When the news of the political liberation of the Armenians, Parthians, and Assyrians had reached the Jews, the only reaction of the latter could be: 'if thus is the fate of those who violate His will, how much more of those who do His will!' Those are the very words which Rabbi Akiba uttered when he beheld the great city of Rome."[14]

Dio gives the most complete account of how the war began and what happened in the course of the fighting.[15] He says that the rebels secretly prepared weapons and waited until Hadrian and his forces were far away. Then they began a guerrilla war, using underground caves and passages.

The Romans suffered heavy losses, mostly in the beginning.[16] After the initial successes of the rebels, Hadrian sent his best generals and troops. With the Roman garrison reinforced by the legions from Britain and elsewhere on the borders of the empire, the overall Roman strategy became one of isolation and attrition rather than direct confrontation.[17]

The Romans had the experience of many wars against different enemies. Though they suffered some initial defeats and continued losses through the sudden raids of the Jews, they confidently and patiently tightened the net.[18]

Much of Dio's account has been confirmed by archaeological finds or other sources.[19] While all Judea joined in the revolt, Galilee seems to have remained uninvolved.[20]

Initially, the rebel forces surprised and pushed back the Romans.[21] "Appianus and Christian authors lend support to the view that the city fell into the hands of the Jews and was reconquered by Roman troops."[22]

There is also archaeological evidence consisting mainly of coins minted during the revolt with the legends "Jerusalem" and "For the Freedom of Jerusalem."[23] The liberation of Jerusalem was clearly their goal, and probably their temporary success.

Archaelogoists have also unearthed coins from the Great Revolt of 66-70. Since we have Josephus' historical account of that revolt, these coins are helpful in understanding the aspirations of those who took part in the Great Revolt.

"The slogans of war such as 'Freedom of Zion,' found on the coins of Years 2 and 3 (67-68 C.E.), show that these coins were struck at a time when there was still hope for victory over the Romans in battle. These inscriptions give way to slogans like 'For the Redemption of Zion,' found on coins of Year 4 after most of the country had been captured by the Romans and only Jerusalem was left to defend itself from the legions of Titus. The expression 'redemption' on these coins indicated the hope of the defenders for help from heaven, a hope that is mentioned by Josephus."[24]

After crushing the Great Revolt, the Romans produced a series of provincial '*Judea Capta*' coins. These were used in Judea as a constant reminder of Roman dominion. During the Bar Kokhba Revolt, these Roman coins were put to a new use. Bar Kokhba destroyed the Roman reminder and idolatrous symbols by overstriking them with a design of the Temple and his own symbols and slogans.[25]

"The coins of the first year are dated, 'Year 1 of the redemption of Israel.' The coins of the second year are dated 'Year 2 of the freedom of Israel.' All the later coins, struck during the third and fourth years, are undated and are inscribed 'For the freedom of Jerusalem.' The fact that the written documents of Bar Kokhba found in the Judean Desert caves do bear the dates 'Year 3' and 'Year 4' indicate that the counting of the years did not cease and its absence from the coins remains a mystery."[26]

Whatever the reasons for the different slogans and the absence of dates on the later coins, the Talmud indicates that the Rabbis were instrumental in preparing the coinage.[27] If the Rabbis were instrumental in preparing the coinage, the implication is that they were also instrumental in preparing the revolt.[28] "The Redemption of Jerusalem" is a Biblical, Messianic hope.

On the basis of the coins, the Roman accounts, Pausanias, the Christian sources, and rabbinic references, it seems likely that Jerusalem was captured by the rebels for a period of time. Knowing that there was rabbinic involvement in the revolt, the next question is, "Was the Temple rebuilt by Bar Kokhba?"

There has been much speculation on this question, and too little evidence to know with certainty.[29] Rebuilding the Temple would have been a priority of the rebels, but it would have required a major effort of manpower, material, and finances, at a time when the forces of Bar Kokhba were fighting against the powerful forces of the Roman Empire.

There are some references in the rabbinic writings to a Bar Kokhba temple. In the Talmudic tractate Ta'anith, we are told, "It has been taught: When Turnus Rufus the wicked destroyed the Temple, R. Gamaliel was condemned to death."[30] Turnus Rufus was one of Hadrian's officials. Unless Bar Kokhba had rebuilt the Temple, there would not have been one for Turnus Rufus to destroy.[31]

It is not, however, necessary for us to know whether or not Jerusalem was captured and the Temple rebuilt in order to determine why Rabbi Akiba proclaimed Bar Kokhba the Messiah. Nor is it even necessary to know the immediate cause of the rebellion.

The Jews of that time disagreed as to whether or not there was sufficient cause and hope for a revolt. What some saw as sufficient cause was bearable in the eyes of others.

More to the point, the Great Revolt and the different rebellions in the Diaspora had taken place without any messianic pretenders. No Jewish king in the Hasmonean period made public messianic pretensions, or was regarded as a messiah.

The Bar Kokhba Rebellion apparently began, and could have continued, without Rabbi Akiba's proclamation. There was, however, a great longing for Messiah, the Deliverer, to come.

Ever since the suppression of the Great Revolt, "The Jews had not ceased weeping and mourning for the loss of their Temple. 'The footstool of our God is burned with fire — and should we not cry?' (Makkot 24b) Neither did the Jews give up hoping that on the day on which the Temple was destroyed, the Messiah was born."[32]

The Great Revolt had been brutally crushed and the House of God destroyed, but maybe God had sent His Anointed One into the world on that very day. That was the hope that endured, a longing that awaited fulfillment. There was one who was presented as that fulfillment — Simeon ben Kosiba.

4. SIMEON BEN KOSIBA

Bar Kokhba's real name was Simeon ben Kosiba: Shimeon, son of Kosiba. In declaring him the Messiah, Rabbi Akiba changed one letter in his name to make it "Kokhba", substituted the Aramaic *"bar"* for the Hebrew *"ben"*, meaning "son", and called him, "Bar Kokhba", i.e. "son of a star". This was a messianic designation referring to Numbers 24:17. When the rebellion ended in disaster instead of the messianic age, later rabbis changed that same letter in Kosiba's name to make it "Bar (son of) Koziba (a lie)".

The Encyclopedia Judaica characterizes Bar Kokhba, "as a leader who, in charge of both the economy and the army, ruled imperiously, concerned himself even with minor details, and did not refrain from threatening senior officers of his army with punishment or even from inflicting deterrent punishment."[1] Because of the recent discovery in the Bar Kokhba caves of a packet of letters from Bar Kokhba to various individuals, we now know this characterization to be quite accurate.

One letter begins, "From Shimeon ben Kosiba to Yeshua ben Galgoula and to the men of the fort, peace. I take heaven to witness against me that unless you 'mobilize' ('destroy') [the Hebrew word is not clear] the Galileans who are with you, every man, I will put fetters on your feet as I did to ben Aphlul."[2]

Other letters contain these phrases: "and if you do not [do] accordingly, you shall be punished severely." "Concerning every man of Tekoa who will be found at your place — the houses in which they dwell will be burned and you (too) will be punished." "...and if you shall not send them, let it be known to you, that you will be punished." And, "the wheat and fruit should be confiscated and if any one opposes you, send him to me and I shall punish him."[3]

In another letter, he commands that certain items for the celebration of Sukkot be brought to him.[4] He seems to have considered public ritual important, but not the God who commanded it.

The Midrash tells us of Bar Kokhba's forces that, "When they went forth to battle they cried, '(O God,) neither help us nor discourage us!'"[5] During the Great Revolt, the Zealots, though equally brutal and arrogant, had believed that God would give them victory rather than abandon His people.[6] The battlecry of Bar Kokhba and his men indicates that they did not place their hope in divine assistance. They were confident of victory, if only God would stay out of the way.[7]

The passage in the Midrash about the revolt goes on to declare

Bar Kokhba's courage and strength — "He would catch the missiles from the enemy's catapults on one of his knees and hurl them back, killing many of the foe" — but it also continues to relate his brutality and contempt for the godly who got in his way.

R. Eleazar of Modim was a priest from the same town where Mattathias the priest and his five sons had started the Maccabean revolt. Apparently, R. Eleazar of Modim was also Bar Kokhba's uncle. Some scholars believe that he was the High Priest mentioned on the Bar Kokhba coins. The Midrash says that Bar Kokhba kicked him to death.[8]

National Unity

Bar Kokhba's forces won some initial military victories against the Roman soldiers garrisoned in the land. There had been similar victories in the Great Revolt, but in the Great Revolt, the different factions had fought against each other as much as, if not more than, against the Romans.[9]

A lot had changed since then. There seems to have been unity in the struggle against the Romans.[10] The breadth and depth of the unity should not, however, be overestimated. Nor should the means by which it was enforced be underestimated.

Bar Kokhba suppressed or destroyed any opposition. Brutality and terror are often used to compel submission. In every account we have of Bar Kokhba, including his own letters, he is presented as brutal and dictatorial.

The Midrash Lamentations says that, "Bar Koziba...had with him two hundred thousand men with an amputated finger. The Sages sent him the message, 'How long will you continue to make the men of Israel blemished?' He asked them, 'How else shall they be tested?' They answered, 'Let anyone who cannot uproot a cedar from Lebanon be refused enrollment in your army.' He thereupon had two hundred thousand men of each class.'"[11] The account is interesting in that it portrays both Bar Kokhba's violent character and his submissive response to the sages.

The goal of Bar Kokhba's rebellion - freedom from Rome - if not the way in which he pursued it, had the sympathy of all the people. For, "He revived ancient traditions and established a new commonwealth as a theocratic state which had the support of the whole country...he worked in close cooperation with Rabbi Akiba, the outstanding scholar of his day."[12]

Maimonides says that, "Rabbi Akiva was a great sage, one of the authors of the Mishnah, yet he was the right-hand man of Ben Koziva, the ruler, whom he thought to be King Messiah. He and all the sages of his generation imagined Bar Kokhba to be King

Messiah until he was slain unfortunately. Once he was slain, it dawned on them that he was not [Messiah]."[13]

Maimonides may have had additional sources available to him which we do not have. Our sources do not explicitly identify Akiba as Bar Kokhba's "right-hand man" or aide-de-camp. The sources we do have clearly indicate that R. Akiba supported Bar Kokhba and his rebellion. As we have already seen, the contemporary sources indicate that the Rabbis as a whole were involved in the planning, preparation, and conduct of the revolt.

Since the sages exercised civil authority under Roman aegis, they had considerable power and knowledge. They would have known, at least, the general outline of Roman activities and plans. They would also have known the popular mood and intentions.

The Romans would have expected them to provide any information necessary to maintain the public order. The Rabbis could determine for themselves whether to provide the Romans with accurate information or to intentionally mislead them.

Whatever the details may have been, the people were seething under Roman rule. Once the rebellion began, they overwhelmingly supported it. Along with the sages, Bar Kokhba established a governmental authority independent of the Romans, but apparently modelled after them.

"In effect, Bar Kochba regarded himself as holding the authority of the Roman emperor and transferred the lands of liberated Judea to his own possession. His orders concerning leases, sales, and confiscations were grounded on a juridical succession to Roman rule, by virtue of which he was empowered to exercize control over the lands of Judea and confiscate property for the public good."[14]

Judging from his letters, he did not distinguish the public good from anything that furthered his own efforts. Whatever wealth he could confiscate would further his own efforts. So would the killing of any internal opponents.

THE REVOLUTION

5. AKIBA BEN JOSEPH

"A full history of Akiba, based upon authentic sources, will probably never be written, although he, to a degree beyond any other, deserves to be called the father of rabbinic Judaism."[1] Gershom Bader expresses the view of many when he says, "The **highest** place of honor **among all** of our national heroes **undoubtedly** belongs to **Rabbi Akiba ben Joseph**."[2] [emphasis added] Higher than David. Higher than Moses. Higher than Abraham.

Throughout the Talmud, Rabbi Akiba is given the highest praise. Rabbi Tarfon exclaimed, "Akiba! whoever departs from thee is as though he departed from life!."[3]

For the Rabbis, the greatest mystical knowledge was only to be found by entering the 'Garden.' Of those who tried to enter, only four succeeded. "Our Rabbis taught: ....Ben 'Azzai cast a look and died....Ben Zoma looked and became demented....Aher mutilated the shoots. [I.e., he became a heretic.] R. Akiba departed unhurt."[4]

"It was said that R. Akiba had twelve thousand pairs of disciples…The world remained desolate until R. Akiba came to our Masters in the South and taught the Torah to them. These were R. Meir, R. Judah, R. Jose, R. Simeon and R. Eleazar b. Shammua; and it was they who revived the Torah at that time."[5]

To say that "R. Akiba had twelve thousand [12 x 1000] pairs of disciples" is to say that **all** who came after him were his disciples. They have all been taught by him. To say that "the world remained desolate until R. Akiba" is to compare his creative work with that of God in the beginning. To say that his disciples "revived the Torah" is to say that they breathed life back into God's dying revelation.

The Talmud regards the death of Akiba as a loss almost beyond measure. "When R. Akiba died, the glory of the Torah ceased."[6] "When R. Akiba died, the arms of the Torah ceased and the fountains of wisdom were stopped up."[7]

Why is Rabbi Akiba so highly praised? Louis Ginzberg explained in <u>The Jewish Encyclopedia</u>: "The greatest *tannaim* [scholars and teachers] of the middle of the second century came from Akiba's school, notably Meir, Judah ben Ilai, Simeon ben

Yohai, Jose ben Halafta, Eleazar ben Shammai, and Nehemiah. Akiba's true genius, however, is shown in his work in the domain of the *Halakah*; both in his systematization of its traditional material, and in its further development.

"...Our Mishnah comes directly from Rabbi Meir, the Tosefta from R. Nehemiah, the Sifra from R. Judah, and the Sifre from R.Simon; but they all took Akiba for a model in their works and followed him. (Sanh.86a)"[8] We are told that, "All are taught according to the views of R. Akiba."[9]

Wherever an anonymous authority is quoted, we are to understand the view to be, through one channel or another, that of R. Akiba. As it says in Megillah 2a, "This rule follows the ruling of R. Akiba the anonymous authority." His anonymous rulings are authoritative, since, "It is a general principle that an anonymous Mishnah states the *halachah*."[10]

"...According to a tradition which has historical confirmation, it was Akiba who **systematized** and brought into methodic arangement the MISHNAH, or *Halakah* codex [the basic oral law]; the MIDRASH, or the exegesis of the *Halakah*; and the HALAKOT, the logical amplification of the *Halakah*...Akiba was the one who definitely fixed the canon of the Old Testament books."[11]

The Encyclopedia Judaica adds that he also "inspired his disciple Aquila, a convert, to write a Greek translation of the Bible in the spirit of his teachings (Jerome to Isa.7:14). A careful examination of the translation...shows that it follows Akiba's exegesis. The standard Aramaic translation of the Pentateuch, Targum Onkelos, invariably reflects Akiba's halakhic rulings...

"...In time, Akiba came to be regarded as 'one of the fathers of the world' (Tal.Jer., Shek.3:1,47b). He is credited with **systematizing** the Midrash, *halakhot* and *aggadot* (or, the principles on which they were built)."[12] Others added content, but only with the framework which Akiba devised.

Louis Finkelstein wrote that, "The later talmudists rated these achievements so high that they declared Akiba had saved the Torah from oblivion. They ranked his work with the discovery of the Law in the days of Josiah and Ezra. 'Had not Shaphan arisen in his time, and Ezra in his time, and Akiba in his time,' a homilist of the next century remarks, 'would not the Law have been forgotten in Israel.'"[13]

"In a wider sense, the contour of western thought generally has also been affected by Akiba's philosophy. His ideas molded those of Maimonides, Gersonides, and Hasdai Crescas. The influence of these men was felt by a whole series of Latin writers from Thomas Aquinas to Spinoza, who in turn laid the foundations of modern thought."[14]

There is no "authorized biography" of Akiba. The Rabbis did not consider themselves historians, but rather teachers and preservers of Israel's wealth of moral teaching. Nevertheless, because of the magnitude of Akiba's work, there are sufficient texts and quotations by him, and sufficient rabbinic references to him, to give a clear, consistent picture of the man, his motivation, and his method.

Akiba's Life

Akiba ben Joseph was born about 40 C.E. In his early life, as a poor, illiterate shepherd, he was not interested in studies of any kind. More than that, he was hostile towards those who engaged in them.

He later recalled, "When I was an *am ha-aretz* [an unlearned man] I said: 'I would that I had a scholar (before me) and I would maul him like an ass.' Said his disciples to him 'Rabbi, say "like a dog!"' 'The former bites and breaks the bones, while the latter bites but does not break the bones,' he answered them."[15]

In those days, scholarly disputes were heated and sometimes violent affairs.[16] We have already seen that in the accounts of Josephus.

These struggles were not merely verbal or academic. Religious practices and decisions were not simply a private, personal affair, devoid of public interest or consequence. Israel, in every aspect of life, was seen as a theocracy — a theocracy under a God who rewarded or punished men and nations according to their deeds. Amplifying, therefore, the human tendency to quarrel and contend for one's own position, were the important and public consequences of right teaching and action. There was no place for modern concepts of "religious tolerance" and "separation of church and state."

"Before Akiba was 30 years old, the ultranationalists of Judea, maddened by the oppression of the Roman procurators, had persuaded their brethren to undertake a hopeless rebellion which culminated in the capture of Jerusalem and the burning of the Temple (70 C.E.)."[17] Out of that siege of Jerusalem, Rabbi Johanan ben Zakkai was smuggled in a coffin to Vespasian. When Vespasian was proclaimed emperor a few days later, he gave Johanan ben Zakkai permission to begin the all-important academy at Yavneh.

It was to that academy that Akiba later came, when he had become hungry for learning.[18] The Talmud says that Akiba was a shepherd when he decided to give his life to study. His betrothed waited for him for 24 years while he studied at the Academy. There he became the most exalted of rabbis.[19]

Before Akiba attained such an exalted position, he had to fight tenaciously with all who opposed his vision of what Judaism should be. It is in relationship and conflict with his contemporaries that the character of Rabbi Akiba is revealed.

One of Akiba's marked characteristics was his persistence in pursuit of what he thought was correct. He was not intimidated by the position, stature, or power of his opposition. Nor was he silenced by punishment. This comes out clearly in his confrontations with Rabban Gamaliel.

Akiba was persuasive as well as persistent. He was a man of vision, with an organized, comprehensive view of what needed to be done, and how. The Talmud says, "To what may Akiba be compared? To a peddler who goes about from farm to farm. Here he obtains wheat, there barley, and in a third place, spelt. When he comes home he arranges them all in their respective bins. So Akiba went about from scholar to scholar, getting all the traditions he could; and then he proceeded to arrange them in an orderly granary."[20]

He systematically picked and chose from what was available. Akiba knew what he was looking for, recognized it when he found it, and appropriated it for his purposes. He had a single driving motivation in life: to create a Judaism in accordance with his vision of what it should be. To do that, he formed alliances, made disciples instilled with his vision, and fought against any and all who held to competing definitions of Judaism.

In doing that, Akiba earned the title of "the father of rabbinic Judaism." He, more than anyone else, created rabbinic Judaism. Before him there were many Judaisms, but after him there was only one. Before him there was precedent, and after him there was further development, but he is the one who put the new system together.

Before Akiba, there were rabbis and synagogues in Israel and the Diaspora, but Akiba was the one who produced the framework and the justification for a comprehensive rabbinic religion. He presented the justification for the change to rabbinic authority.

He was the compiler and editor of what went before, and his disciples completed the work with what came later. Their work, the whole Talmud, is a natural extension of the purpose, system, and procedure that he put together. **Structurally and programmatically, the Talmud is a declaration of rabbinic authority.**

There was a battle to determine who would formulate the identity, polity, and policy of the Jewish people. In Akiba's struggles, he used the means that seemed appropriate in his context, not the ones that seem appropriate in ours. His struggles reveal his character, methods, and motivation. They also clarify why he declared Bar Kokhba the Messiah.

There were certain historical and social circumstances which made Akiba's innovations attractive to many. Others wanted some of the end results for which he provided the rationale. There were circumstances that gave his program a natural constituency.

The magnitude of the accomplishments of "the father of rabbinic Judaism" can be seen if we ask the question, "What is a rabbi? and then compare the answer found in Tanakh to that found in the Talmud.

6. WHAT IS A RABBI?

The earliest *"zugoth,"* the pairs of ancient teachers recorded in the Talmud, appear about 250 years after the last period described in the Hebrew Scriptures, i.e. Tanakh. Jose b. Jo'ezer of Zeredah and Jose b. Johanan of Jerusalem taught in the early Maccabean period, somewhat less than two hundred years before Akiba was born. They "formed the beginning of the *Zugoth* (duumvirate) which governed Jewish religious life until Hillel and Shammai. It may be observed that the title 'Rabbi' is not prefixed to their names: the famous letter of Sherira Gaon to Jacob b. Nissim, quoted by Nathan b. Jehiel in the Aruk (s.v. אבי״) declares that this title dates from the time of R. Johanan b. Zakkai only."[1] Philo and Josephus do not seem to use the term.

In the Talmud, these earlier teachers are not called "rabbis," indicating that they were not called "Rabbi" during their lifetimes. I.e., the title was not yet in use. R. Johanan b. Zakkai became a pre-eminent leader after the destruction of the Jerusalem in 70 C.E.

In Tanakh, the word "Rabbi" does not appear. The various leaders of Israel were identified with designations like judge, prophet, priest, king, or redeemer. The Rabbis themselves speak of some of the great leaders in Israel's past, like Moses and Ezra, as rabbis, but they are never identified that way in Tanakh. Moses was a Levite; his brother Aaron was the first high priest. "Scribe" is used to describe Ezra four times, but each time, he is first described immediately before as a priest.[2]

The word "Rab" is used in Tanakh, but it is used to describe "Nebuzaradan the captain [*rab*] of the guard of the king of Babylon"; and "Daniel...ruler over the whole province of Babylon and chief [*rab*] prefect over all the wise men of Babylon"; and "the captain [*rab*]" of the ship on which Jonah fled.[3]

There are about 150 references in Tanakh to "being wise," "wise men," or "sages." However, none of these references mention anything that would specifically designate a rabbi. The term is used for gentiles as well as Jews, including the wise men of Egypt, those of Babylon, and those of Persia. It is also used for skilled artisans of different types, those considered wise in heart or learned in the law of God, whether king or counsellor, son or servant.[4] For that matter, Elihu the son of Barachel tells Job, "It is not the great [*rabbim*/רבים] that are wise [*yekhcamu*/יחכמו], nor the aged that discern judgment."[5]

In short, there is neither place, position, nor authority for the Rabbis in the Bible. They are not even mentioned. Stuart Cohen sums it up, "As a group, rabbis were unable to claim a historically sanctioned *locus standi* within any of the traditional frameworks of Jewish government."[6]

In the Talmud

In rabbinic Judaism, the Rabbis stand at the opposite pole. Here the Rabbis themselves, at least the leading scholars among them, are the judges, prophets, priests, redeemers, and lawgivers. They exercise authority over the king. They have ultimate authority, an authority which even extends to the world to come. Not even God can contradict them.

They are to be the most honored and the most obeyed. Failure to honor the Rabbis leads to excommunication from the community of Israel, destruction, and eternal punishment.

The Talmud speaks very clearly on rabbinic authority and position. For example, it speaks of a descending scale which determines the importance of different individuals in life or death situations, or in situations of lesser danger: "A scholar takes precedence over a king of Israel, for if a scholar dies there is none to replace him while if a king of Israel dies, all Israel are eligible for kingship. A king takes precedence over a High Priest...A High Priest takes precedence over a prophet...

"A priest takes precedence over a Levite, a Levite over an Israelite, an Israelite over a bastard, a bastard over a *Nathin* [a descendant of the Gibeonites], a *nathin* over a proselyte, and a proselyte over an emancipated slave. This order of precedence applies only when all these were in other respects equal. If the bastard, however, was a scholar and the high priest an ignoramus, the learned bastard takes precedence over the ignorant High Priest."[7]

"Any man who marries his daughter to a scholar, or carries on a trade on behalf of scholars, or benefits scholars from his estate is regarded by Scripture as if he had clung to the divine presence."[8]

"R. Hiyya b. Abba also said in R. Johanan's name: All the prophets prophesied only in respect of him who marries his daughter to a scholar, or engages in business on behalf of a scholar, or benefits a scholar with his possessions."[9]

There is greater reward for one who feeds and supports a scholar than for one who houses the ark of the Tabernacle.[10] "For R. Johanan said: Whoever casts merchandise into the pockets of scholars will be privileged to sit in the Heavenly Academy."[11]

Those who did not honor the Rabbis or accept their teachings were part of the despised *am ha'aretz* — the ignorant, common people. "Our Rabbis taught: ...Even if one has learnt Scripture and Mishnah, if he has not ministered to the disciples of the wise, he is an *'am ha-arez.*"[12]

"A rabbinical scholar may assert, I am a rabbinical scholar; let my business receive first attention..."[13] "A rabbinical scholar may declare, I will not pay poll-tax, . . ."[14] "A Rabbinic scholar may strip men of their cloaks? But we do not attend to his case....A scholar, if he has obtained his money by force from the debtor, is allowed to retain it; but an ordinary person is compelled by the court to return it."[15] "The Rabbis have power to expropriate."[16]

That is so because, "The disciples of the sages increase peace throughout the world..."[17] "Thus, the masters of the Talmud were, so to speak, as essential to Israel as bread itself."[18] They sustained life in this world, and their teachings provided the way of entry into the world to come. "It was taught in the Tanna debe Eliyyahu: 'Whoever repeats *halachoth* may rest assured that he is destined for the future world, as it says, His goings [*halikoth*] are to eternity. Read not *halikoth* but *halachoth*'."[19]

Because of the greater importance assigned to the lives of certain rabbis, protecting or prospering them could even guarantee an individual a place in the world to come. Such great rabbis could provide the guarantee themselves.

"R. Gamaliel was condemned to death....Thereupon the officer went up secretly to him and said, 'If I save you will you bring me into the world to come?' He replied: 'Yes.' He then asked him, 'Will you swear it unto me?' And the latter took an oath. The officer then mounted the roof and threw himself down and died. Now there was a tradition [amongst the Romans] that when a decree is made and one of their own [leaders] dies, then that decree is annulled. Thereupon a Voice from Heaven was heard declaring, This high officer is destined to enter into the world to come."[20]

The greatest possible blessings in this world and in the world to come are gained by serving the Rabbis. Likewise, the greatest possible misfortunes or curses come from not serving them.

"R. Joshua b. Levi further said: In twenty-four places we find that the Beth din inflicted excommunication for an insult to a teacher, and they are all recorded in the Mishnah."[21] "Has not R. Papa said: A certain man made derogatory remarks about Mar Samuel and a log fell from the roof and broke his skull?...R. Joshua b. Levi said: Whoever makes derogatory remarks about scholars after their death is cast into Gehinnom."[22]

At the end of an halachic discussion, "R. Tarfon remained silent, and at once the face of Judah b. Nehemiah brightened with joy. Thereupon R. Akiba said to him, 'Judah, your face has brightened with joy because you have refuted the Sage; I wonder whether you will live long' — Said R. Judah b. Ila'i, 'This happened a fortnight before the Passover, and when I came up for the 'Azereth festival I enquired after Judah b. Nehemiah and was told that he had passed away'."[23]

"R. Eliezer, furthermore, had a disciple who once gave a legal decision in his presence. 'I wonder', remarked R. Eliezer to his wife, Imma Shalom, 'whether this man will live through the year'; and he actually did not live through the year. 'Are you', she asked him, 'a prophet?' 'I', he replied: 'am neither a prophet nor the son of a prophet, but I have this tradition: Whosoever gives a legal decision in the presence of his Master incurs the penalty of death'."[24]

"Has it not been taught: Why were the bazaars of Beth Hini destroyed? Because they based their actions upon Scripture, [disregarding Rabbinical law.]"[25]

"Every man who forgets a single word of his mishnah (i.e. what he has learned [from the Rabbis]), Scripture accounts it unto him as if he had forfeited his soul!"[26]

"Rab Judah said: Jerusalem was destroyed only because scholars were despised therein: for it is said, *but they mocked the messengers of God, and despised his words, and scoffed at his prophets, until the wrath of the Lord arose against his people, till there was no remedy.* What does *'till there was no remedy'* intimate? He who despises a scholar, has no remedy for his wounds."[27] "The sword comes to the world...on account of those who interpret the Torah not in accordance with the accepted law."[28]

The preeminent role assigned to the Rabbis and to the system that surrounded and supported that role must be attributed to Akiba. Under Akiba's leadership, the Rabbis became an elite revolutionary party which transformed itself from a group of unauthorized outsiders into the holders and/or guardians of all authority in heaven and earth.

The Battle for Torah

7. TANAKH AND THE ORAL LAW

Biblical Law, i.e. Torah, is not a set of religious guidelines for those who believe. Torah is national law, governing Israel — both the land and the people, whether or not they are in the land. It includes both civil statutes and criminal code. The determination of what Torah is, therefore, is the determination of what individual behavior is permitted or prohibited, and what national goals and policy are to be embraced or shunned.

Since there are no rabbis in Torah or Tanakh, it can only be the oral law that appoints them the authorized interpreters and guardians of Torah. It can only be the oral law that establishes their place and authority.

What establishes the authority of the oral law? To answer that, we need to know where it came from and when it appeared. The origin and the purpose of the oral law are inseparable one from the other. The better we understand the one, the better we will understand the other. Knowing the origin and purpose enables us to identify its source.

If the oral law was in some way given at Sinai, then rabbinic Judaism would be a continuation of God's revelation at that time. On the other hand, if the oral law was not given at Sinai, then it was established at a later date by a different means. If it did not appear until the first and second century, then Rabbi Akiba would be rightly recognized as its founder.

To determine when the oral law first appeared, we need to know exactly what it is. In the Talmud, there are three related, but significantly different and distinct claims concerning the oral law:

1. The oral law is a separate divine revelation to Moses at Sinai.

2. The oral law is an extended interpretation and elaboration of the written Torah which was given to Moses. [*Or*, it was present as a seed in the written Torah, but later grew and flourished.]

3. The oral law is a fence around the written Torah.

We will examine each of these claims in turn. The Scriptures provided the form and content of the Law accepted by all groups in Akiba's day, even though there was as yet no standardized text.

So we will examine the Scriptures first to see what they say about the oral law.

The First Talmudic Claim: The Oral Law is a separate divine revelation given by God to Moses at Sinai.

"Moses received the Torah at Sinai and transmitted it to Joshua, Joshua to the elders, and the elders to the prophets, and the prophets to the men of the great synagogue." Avoth 1.1

"Our Rabbis learned: What was the procedure of the instruction in the oral law? Moses learned from the mouth of the Omnipotent [משה למד מפי הגבורה]. Then Aaron entered and Moses taught him his lesson. Aaron then moved aside and sat down on Moses' left. Thereupon Aaron's sons entered and Moses taught them their lesson. His sons then moved aside, Eleazar taking his seat on Moses' right and Ithamar on Aaron's left. R. Judah stated: Aaron was always on Moses right. Thereupon the elders entered and Moses taught them their lesson, and when the elders moved aside all the people entered and Moses taught them their lesson. It thus followed that Aaron heard the lesson four times, his sons heard it three times, the elders twice and all the people once. At this stage Moses departed and Aaron taught them his lesson. Then Aaron departed and his sons taught them their lesson. His sons then departed and the elders taught them their lesson. It thus followed that everybody heard the lesson four times."[1]

In this scenario, all Israel was taught the unwritten law that God had spoken to Moses at Sinai. Understanding language in the variety of its normal usages, does Tanakh support, permit, or preclude this claim?

The Record of the Torah

The scriptural incident that inspired the Talmudic account may have been the battle against Amalek. Amalek attacked Israel in the wilderness, but Israel triumphed in this first encounter. "Then the LORD said to Moses, 'Write this on a scroll as something to be remembered and put it in the ears of Joshua, because I will completely blot out the remembrance of Amalek from under heaven.'"[2]

This differs from the Talmudic scenario in that what was put in the ears of Joshua was written down first. It was written down so that it might be remembered. God wrote the words of the covenant on stone tablets for the same reason.

When Moses initially presented to the people the covenant of the Law which he had received from the Lord, the people accepted it. "Moses then wrote down all the words of the LORD....Then he took the Book of the Covenant and read it to the people. They responded, "We will do everything the LORD has said; we will obey.'

"Moses then took the blood, sprinkled it on the people and said, 'This is the blood of the covenant that the LORD has made with you in accordance with all these words.'"[3]

On the basis of what Moses wrote and then read to the people - i.e. "everything the LORD had said" - the people responded, "We will do everything the LORD has said; we will obey." They committed themselves to the covenant which Moses had written and then read to them. It is that covenant that was "cut" in the blood of the sacrifice.

Then, "The LORD said to Moses, 'Come up to Me on the mountain and stay here, and I will give you the tablets of stone with the law and commands I have written for their instruction.'"[4] Israel was to be instructed by what was written. Covenants were put in writing to fix their text and make their terms binding.

At the conclusion of Leviticus, we are told, "These are the statutes, the laws and the ordinances that the LORD established on Mount Sinai between Himself and the Israelites through Moses."[5] At the conclusion of Numbers, we are told, "These are the commandments and ordinances the LORD gave through Moses to the Israelites on the plains of Moab by the Jordan across from Jericho."[6] What the Lord added on the plains of Moab to the covenant He gave Israel on Mt. Sinai was also recorded in written form.

When Moses neared the end of his life, he told the people what the law would be concerning the king that they would one day want to rule over them. Kings are particularly susceptible to certain sins. Every king of Israel, therefore, is to guard himself from such sins, so that he can faithfully lead the people as the Lord's servant.

"When he takes the throne of his kingdom, he is to write for himself on a scroll a copy of this law, taken from that of the priests, who are Levites. It is to be with him, and he is to read it all the days of his life so that he may learn to revere the LORD his God and follow carefully all the words of this law and these decrees and not consider himself better than his brothers and turn from the law to the right or to the left. Then he and his descendants will reign a long time over his kingdom in Israel."[7]

The priests would have a written scroll of the law of the Lord which had been given through Moses. That is because the Lord charged Aaron, "you must teach the Israelites all the decrees the LORD has given them through Moses."[8]

The king is to personally "write for himself on a scroll a copy of this law...and he is to read it all the days of his life." He is not to "turn from the law [which he has copied] to the right or to the left." It is the written law that is to guide and judge the king.

Just before his death, and before Israel was to enter the promised land, Moses instructed the generation which had grown up in the wilderness about what the Lord required of them. He told them to bind themselves to an oath to carry out the law of the Lord. He gave them these preliminary instructions:

"When you have crossed the Jordan into the land the LORD your God is giving you, set up some large stones and coat them with plaster. Write on them all the words of this law when you have crossed over to enter the land the LORD your God is giving you...And you shall write very clearly all the words of this law on these stones you have set up."[9]

It is "all the words of this law" which the people write on the stones. It is to what they have written that they are to bind themselves, saying, "'Cursed is the man who does not uphold the words of this law by carrying them out.' Then all the people shall say, 'Amen!'"[10]

Obedience to "all the words of this law" which are written will bring blessing. Disobedience will bring curses.

"If you do not carefully follow all the words of this law, which are written in this book...the LORD will send fearful plagues on you and your descendants, harsh and prolonged disasters, and severe and lingering illnesses. He will bring upon you all the diseases of Egypt that you dreaded, and they will cling to you. The LORD will also bring on you every kind of sickness and disaster not recorded in this Book of the Law, until you are destroyed. You who were as numerous as the stars in the sky will be left but few in number, because you did not obey the LORD your God."[11]

It is obedience to the written law that determines whether Israel will be blessed or cursed. Moses stated explicitly that the written laws he was commanding the people that day were also part of their covenant with the Lord. "These are the terms of the covenant the LORD commanded Moses to make with the Israelites in Moab, in addition to the covenant He had made with them at Horeb."[12]

The words of the covenant were written down, and the blessings and curses were written down. Israel was told, "Carefully follow the terms of this covenant, so that you may prosper in everything you do."[13]

If a person's heart turned away from following the Lord, "The LORD will never be willing to forgive him; His wrath and zeal will burn against that man. All the curses written in this book will fall upon him, and the LORD will blot out his name from under heaven. The LORD will single him out from all the tribes of Israel for disaster, according to all the curses of the covenant written in this Book of the Law."[14]

The covenant was written down. The curses for turning away from it were also written down. The name of the one who turned away from what was written would be be blotted out. The only thing not written down were "every kind of sickness and disaster not recorded in this Book of the Law" which the Lord would bring on those who disobeyed what was written.

Moses prophesied that Israel would turn away from the written covenant of the Lord. He detailed the horrors that would follow such a turning away, especially the horrors that would take place in exile. Even the land of Israel itself would be severely afflicted, so that "All the nations will ask: 'Why has the LORD done this to this land? Why this fierce, burning anger?'

"And the answer will be: 'It is because this people abandoned the covenant of the LORD, the God of their fathers, the covenant He made with them when He brought them out of Egypt. They went off and worshiped other gods and bowed down to them, gods they did not know, gods He had not given them. Therefore the LORD's anger burned against this land, so that He brought on it all the curses written in this book...'"[15]

The covenant was written down for instruction. The curses were given as a warning. They were also written down as a future witness for the day when Israel would break the written covenant.

Moses then prophesied that after all these curses, there would be a turning back to the Lord. This turning back would bring restoration from the Lord, a restoration that would be conditional upon obeying the written covenant.

"You will again obey the LORD and follow all His commands I am giving you today. Then the LORD your God will make you most prosperous in all the work of your hands and in the fruit of your womb, the young of your livestock and the crops of your land. The LORD will again delight in you and make you prosperous, just as He delighted in your fathers, if you obey the LORD your God and keep His commands and decrees that are written in this Book of the Law and turn to the LORD your God with all your heart and with all your soul."[16]

"So Moses wrote down this law and gave it to the priests, the sons of Levi, who carried the ark of the covenant of the LORD, and to all the elders of Israel. Then Moses commanded them: 'At the end of every seven years, in the year for canceling debts, during the Feast of Tabernacles, when all Israel comes to appear before the LORD your God at the place He will choose, you shall read this law before them in their hearing. Assemble the people — men, women and children, and the aliens living in your towns — so they can listen and learn to fear the LORD your God and follow carefully all the words of this law. Their children, who do not know this law, must hear it and learn to fear the LORD your God as long as you live in the land you are crossing the Jordan to possess.'"[17]

Future generations were to live and worship in accordance with the written Law of the Lord. Every seven years, all Israel was to assemble to hear the Law read to them. The priests were responsible for reading the law to the people. The written law was to instruct the children of each generation so that they would "learn to fear the Lord."

In addition to the written law itself, God gave Moses and Israel a song to testify in the future of His faithfulness and Israel's unfaithfulness. "Now write down for yourselves this song and teach it to the Israelites and put it in their mouths, so that it may be a witness for Me against them."[18] The law was written, and the witness of the law was written.

"After Moses finished writing in a book the words of this law from beginning to end, he gave this command to the Levites who carried the ark of the covenant of the LORD: 'Take this Book of the Law and place it beside the ark of the covenant of the LORD your God. There it will remain as a witness against you.'"[19] Moses wrote all the words of the law "from beginning to end." The written "Book of the Law" would be a witness against the Levites and Israel for their future unfaithfulness.

According to the Torah, it is the written law that comprised God's covenant with Israel. It is the written law that is the guide to proper governance, and the standard by which those who govern will be judged. It is disobedience to the written law that will bring judgment and exile. It is obedience to the written law that will bring restoration. It is the written law that is to be taught to future generations.

There is no mention of an oral law.

The Record from Moses to the Exile

After the death of Moses, the Lord spoke to Joshua: "Be strong and very courageous. Be careful to obey all the law My servant Moses gave you; do not turn from it to the right or to the left, that you may be successful wherever you go. Do not let this Book of the Law depart from your mouth; meditate on it day and night, so that you may be careful to do everything written in it. Then you will be prosperous and successful."[20]

Joshua was commanded to meditate on the Book of the Law day and night to insure that he would obey all the law that Moses had given him. What was written in The Book of the Law was to be in his mouth. He was to be "careful to do everything written in it." Doing what was written in the Book of the Law would make him "prosperous and successful."

On Mt. Ebal, Joshua renewed the covenant between Israel and the Lord. He built an altar "as Moses the servant of the LORD had commanded the Israelites. He built it according to what is written in the Book of the Law of Moses — an altar of uncut stones, on which no iron tool had been used. On it they offered to the LORD burnt offerings and sacrificed peace-offerings. There, in the presence of all Israel, Joshua wrote on the stones the copy of the law of Moses, which he had written....

"Afterward, Joshua read all the words of the law - the blessings and the curses - just as it is written in the Book of the Law. There was not a word of all that Moses had commanded that Joshua did not read to the whole assembly of Israel, including the women and children, and the aliens who lived among them."[21]

The words translated "copy of the law" are *Mishneh Torat* [משנה תורת], the words which the Rabbis used to designate the Oral Law. In Torah, they refer to a copy of the written law which was read to all the people, rather than to a different law recited by memory to a select group.

It was the written Book of the Law that determined how the altar was to be built. When the altar was ready, "Joshua wrote on the stones the copy of the law of Moses, which he [Moses] had written." All that Moses commanded was written before all the people.

Then, "Joshua read all the words of the law...just as it is written in the Book of the Law. There was not a word of all that Moses had commanded that Joshua did not read to the whole assembly of Israel." Joshua read every word of all that Moses had commanded. Every word that Moses had commanded had been written down.

Before Joshua died, he "summoned all Israel — their elders, leaders, judges and officials — and said to them: '...Be very strong; be careful to obey all that is written in the Book of the Law of Moses, without turning aside to the right or to the left.'"[22]

Just as Moses had charged Joshua and his generation, so Joshua charged the next generation: "obey all that is written in the Book of the Law of Moses." Their response to what was written would determine their fate.

Joshua gathered the people one more time at Shechem. "On that day Joshua made a covenant for the people, and there at Shechem he drew up for them decrees and laws. And Joshua recorded these things in the Book of the Law of God..."[23] Joshua recorded the confirmation of the covenant and the added decrees and laws.

As we previously noted, the Law of Moses requires each king of Israel to write out a personal copy of the Law. From the behavior of many of the kings, it can certainly be doubted that they ever wrote it or read it. They did not follow the Law of the Lord.

For most of David's life, he was careful to follow the Law of the Lord. For example, "David left Zadok the priest and his fellow priests before the tabernacle of the LORD at the high place in Gibeon to present burnt offerings to the LORD on the altar of burnt offering regularly, morning and evening, in accordance with everything written in the Law of the LORD, which He had given Israel."[24] The sacrifices were to be offered "in accordance with everything written in the Law of the LORD." What was written was determinative.

"When the time drew near for David to die, he gave a charge to Solomon his son. 'I am about to go the way of all the earth,' he said. 'So be strong, show yourself a man, and observe what the LORD your God requires: Walk in His ways, and keep His statutes and commandments, His laws and requirements, as written in the Law of Moses, so that you may prosper in all you do and wherever you go, and that the LORD may keep his promise to me: *If your descendants watch how they live, and if they walk faithfully before Me with all their heart and soul, you will never fail to have a man on the throne of Israel.*'"[25]

David charged Solomon to keep the decrees, commands, laws, and requirements "as written in the Law of Moses." That would guarantee prosperity in every area of his life and the continuity of the Davidic kingdom. Obeying what was "written in the Law of Moses" was equated with walking faithfully before the Lord.

King Joash of Judah was assassinated by some of his own officials. His son Amaziah became king after him. "After the kingdom was firmly in his grasp, he executed the officials who had murdered his father the king. Yet he did not put the sons of the assassins to death, in accordance with what is written in the Book of the Law of Moses where the LORD commanded: '*Fathers shall not be put to death for their children, nor children put to death for their fathers; each is to die for his own sins.*'"[26]

Amaziah was a righteous king. He governed according to what was "written in the Book of the Law of Moses."

When King Ahaziah of Judah was killed, his mother, Athaliah, usurped the throne by murdering all but one of her son's children. The one, Joash, was hidden by his aunt and uncle, who was the priest Jehoiada. Seven years later, Jehoiada planned and performed the coronation and anointing of Joash, the child king.

"Then Jehoiada placed the oversight of the Temple of the LORD in the hands of the priests, who were Levites, to whom David had made assignments in the Temple, to present the burnt offerings of the LORD as written in the Law of Moses, with rejoicing and singing, as David had ordered."[27]

The burnt offerings were presented according to what was "written in the Law of Moses." That was the guide for offering the sacrifices properly.

Likewise, when King Hezekiah wanted to bring Judah back to the Lord, "They decided to send a proclamation throughout Israel, from Beersheba to Dan, calling the people to come to Jerusalem and celebrate the Passover to the LORD, the God of Israel. It had not been celebrated in large numbers according to what was written....Although most of the many people who came from Ephraim, Manasseh, Issachar and Zebulun had not purified themselves, yet they ate the Passover, contrary to what was written."[28]

Passover was to be celebrated "according to what was written." Those who celebrated "contrary to what was written" were guilty before the Lord.

The priests, however, were careful to consecrate themselves according to the Law. "Then they took up their regular positions as prescribed in the Law of Moses the man of God. The priests sprinkled the blood handed to them by the Levites."[29]

Hezekiah also sought to cleanse the land of idolatry and reinstitute the proper worship of the Lord. Accordingly, "The king contributed from his own possessions for the morning and evening burnt offerings and for the burnt offerings on the Sabbaths, New Moons and appointed feasts as written in the Law of the LORD."[30]

All the sacrifices were to be offered according to what was "written in the Law of the LORD." All the feasts were to be celebrated according to what was "written in the Law of the LORD."

In the days of Josiah, a similar revival took place. When Josiah the king first heard the words of the Law, he tore his robes. Then he ordered his servants: "Go and inquire of the LORD for me and for the people and for all Judah about what is written in this book that has been found. Great is the LORD's anger that burns against us because our fathers have not obeyed the words of this book;

they have not acted in accordance with all that is written there concerning us."[31]

It was the words written in the book of the Law that moved Josiah to repentance. It was the failure to observe what was written in the book that had brought judgment on Judah.

God confirmed Josiah's assessment of the situation: "This is what the LORD says: 'I am going to bring disaster on this place and its people, according to everything written in the book the king of Judah has read.'"[32] God held the people accountable for what was written in the covenant.

In response, Josiah "went up to the temple of the LORD with the men of Judah, the people of Jerusalem, the priests and the prophets - all the people from the least to the greatest. He read in their hearing all the words of the Book of the Covenant, which had been found in the temple of the LORD. The king stood by the pillar and renewed the covenant in the presence of the LORD — to follow the LORD and keep His commands, regulations and decrees with all his heart and all his soul, thus confirming the words of the covenant written in this book. Then all the people pledged themselves to the covenant."[33]

Josiah read "all the words of the Book of the Covenant." That is the covenant he then renewed. He confirmed "the words of the covenant written in this book." It was the written covenant to which "all the people pledged themselves."

Then Josiah set about cleansing the land and people of all their abominations. He set about restoring the proper worship of the Lord. "The king gave this order to all the people: 'Celebrate the Passover to the LORD your God, as it is written in this Book of the Covenant.'"[34]

"They set aside the burnt offerings to give them to the subdivisions of the families of the people to offer to the LORD, as is written in the Book of Moses."[35] The guide for proper worship and celebration was what was "written in this Book of the Covenant," i.e. "the Book of Moses."

"Furthermore, Josiah got rid of the mediums and spiritists, the household gods, the idols and all the other detestable things seen in Judah and Jerusalem. This he did to fulfill the requirements of the law written in the book that Hilkiah the priest had discovered in the temple of the LORD. Neither before nor after Josiah was there a king like him who turned to the LORD as he did — with all his heart and with all his soul and with all his strength, in accordance with all the Law of Moses."[36]

Josiah sought only "to fulfill the requirements of the law written in the book." For that, he is highly commended. The Law of Moses was what was written in the book.

To summarize the record of Tanakh concerning the time from Moses to the exile, it was the written law that was to be the object of meditation and the guide for those - whether general, priest, or king - who governed and lead in Israel. It was the written law that defined individual and corporate fidelity or infidelity to the Lord.

It was the written law that was followed in building the altar and in offering the sacrifices. It was obedience to the written law that would bring prosperity and success. It was the written law that was to be taught to future generations. According to Tanakh, concerning the time from Moses to the exile, not one word of all of the Law of Moses was unwritten.

The Record in the Exile and in the Return

In the Torah, God promised to send Israel into exile for disobedience to what was written in His Law. In exile in Babylon, Daniel the prophet read in the book of Jeremiah that "the desolation of Jerusalem [would last] 70 years."[37] Those 70 years were coming to an end, and Daniel wrote, "So I turned to the Lord God and pleaded with him in prayer and petition, in fasting, and in sackcloth and ashes."[38]

In seeking the Lord's mercy and forgiveness, Daniel confessed the sins of Israel. "All Israel has transgressed Your law and turned away, refusing to obey You. Therefore the curses and sworn judgments written in the Law of Moses, the servant of God, have been poured out on us, because we have sinned against You....Just as it is written in the Law of Moses, all this disaster has come upon us, yet we have not sought the favor of the LORD our God by turning from our sins and giving attention to Your truth...."[39]

In Daniel's understanding, the curses, judgments, and exile which had been decreed and "written in the Law of Moses" had been fulfilled. That was what defined Israel's sin. He prayed in the expectation that the promise of restoration which was written in the Book of Jeremiah would also be fulfilled.

Ezra is the most important of the dozen scribes who are mentioned by name in Tanakh. He is the only scribe mentioned in Tanakh who was a leader in Israel. In the Talmud, Ezra is very important in the transmission of the oral law. What do the books of Ezra and Nehemiah say about the written and oral law? "For Ezra had devoted himself to the study and observance of the Law of the LORD, and to teaching its decrees and laws in Israel."[40]

"Jeshua son of Jozadak and his fellow priests and Zerubbabel son of Shealtiel and his associates began to build the altar of the God of Israel to sacrifice burnt offerings on it, in accordance with what is written in the Law of Moses the man of God....Then in accordance with what is written, they celebrated the Feast of Tabernacles with the required number of burnt offerings prescribed for each day."[41]

Jeshua and Zerubbabel were among the first group that returned to Israel from Babylon. During their time, the altar was built, the sacrifices were offered, and Sukkot was celebrated "in accordance with what is written in the Law of Moses."

"So the elders of the Jews continued to build and prosper under the preaching of Haggai the prophet and Zechariah, a descendant of Iddo. They finished building the temple according to the command of the God of Israel and the decrees of Cyrus, Darius, and Artaxerxes, kings of Persia....And they installed the priests in their divisions and the Levites in their groups for the service of God at Jerusalem, according to what is written in the Book of Moses."[42] In the time of Haggai and Zechariah, the guide for installing the priests was "what is written in the Book of Moses."

Ezra recorded those things about those who returned before him. What about the time of his own return, and his own teaching? Did Ezra teach the written law, the oral law, or both?

"...all the people assembled as one man in the square before the Water Gate. They told Ezra the scribe to bring out the Book of the Law of Moses, which the LORD had commanded for Israel. So on the first day of the seventh month Ezra the priest brought the Law before the assembly, which was made up of men and women and all who were able to understand. He read it aloud from daybreak till noon as he faced the square before the Water Gate in the presence of the men, women and others who could understand. And all the people listened attentively to the Book of the Law....

"Ezra opened the book...and as he opened it, the people all stood up....The Levites...instructed the people in the Law while the people were standing there. They read from the Book of the Law of God, making it clear and giving the meaning so that the people could understand what was being read [במקרא]."[43]

Ezra read to the people from the Book of the Law. The Levites did the same. Then they explained the written text because the ancient language was not clear to the people.

"On the second day of the month, the heads of all the families, along with the priests and the Levites, gathered around Ezra the scribe to give attention to the words of the Law. They found written in the Law, which the LORD had commanded through Moses, that the Israelites were to live in booths during the feast of the seventh month and that they should proclaim this word and spread it throughout their towns and in Jerusalem: 'Go out into the hill country and bring back branches from olive and wild olive trees, and from myrtles, palms and shade trees, to make booths' — as it is written."[44]

They sought to obey what they found written in the Law. So the people celebrated Sukkot in accordance with what was written in the Law. "Day after day, from the first day to the last, Ezra read from the Book of the Law of God. They celebrated the feast for seven days, and on the eighth day, in accordance with the regulation, there was an assembly."[45]

Later in the same month the people gathered again. "They stood where they were and read from the Book of the Law of the LORD their God for a quarter of the day, and spent another quarter in confession and in worshiping the LORD their God."[46] The people confessed their sins because of what they had heard read from the Book of the Law.

Among other sins, the people and their leaders had intermarried with the surrounding nations, in violation of the Law of Moses. When Ezra prayed and confessed the sins of the people, he referred directly to what was written in the Torah.

"But now, O our God, what can we say after this? For we have disregarded the commands you gave through your servants the prophets when you said: `The land you are entering to possess is a land polluted by the corruption of its peoples. By their detestable practices they have filled it with their impurity from one end to the other. [e.g. Lev.18:24-30] Therefore, do not give your daughters in marriage to their sons or take their daughters for your sons. [e.g. Ex.34:12-16] Do not seek a treaty of friendship with them at any time, that you may be strong and eat the good things of the land and leave it to your children as an everlasting inheritance. [e.g. Dt.7:1-13; 4:40] '"[47]

Nehemiah also recorded the occasion when the returned remnant "...separated themselves from the neighboring peoples for the sake of the Law of God, ...and bind themselves with a curse and an oath to follow the Law of God given through Moses the servant of God and to obey carefully all the commands, regulations and decrees of the LORD our Lord."[48]

They bound themselves to obey all the Law, and listed some of the specifics: not to intermarry, not to defile the Sabbath nor any holy day, to keep the Sabbatical year, to tax themselves for the service and offerings of the Temple, to give firstfruits of crops and flocks, and to tithe for the support of the Levites. All this they pledged to do "as it is written in the Law."[49]

Nehemiah encouraged the people in the rebuilding of the wall around Jerusalem. When the wall was finished, the people celebrated, offered sacrifices, and listened to the reading of the Torah. "On that day the Book of Moses was read aloud in the hearing of the people and there it was found written that no Ammonite or Moabite should ever be admitted into the assembly of God..."[50] Again, the people obeyed what was written.

There is no reference to an oral law in the books of Ezra and Nehemiah. Ezra read and taught from the written Law. The people sought to learn and obey what was written in the Law.

To summarize: The record of Tanakh concerning the time of the exile and the return is that judgment and restoration come according to what is written. Priests were installed, sacrifices were offered, and holy days were celebrated according to the written law. Ezra and the Levites taught the people what was written in the law. The people confessed their sins and repented according to what was written in the law. They bound themselves under an oath and a curse to obey the written law.

Additional Testimony to the Importance of a Covenant being in Writing

The importance of the written record is borne out in other ways as well. While Moses was receiving the tablets of the Law from the Lord, the people had built the Golden Calf, and had worshipped it as the god who brought them out of Egypt. Moses interceded with the Lord that He not blot out all of Israel from His book.

Moses destroyed the Calf and chastised the people. "The next day Moses said to the people, 'You have committed a great sin. But now I will go up to the LORD; perhaps I can make atonement for your sin.'"[51]

Then he interceded with the LORD: "...But now, please forgive their sin — but if not, then blot me out of the book you have written."[52] The implication is that God has written down those who are recorded for life. (This is repeated throughout Tanakh, e.g. Dan.12:1.) Moses was willing to have his own name blotted out of that book, if that would bring atonement for Israel's sin.

When Israel demanded a king, the Lord told Samuel to give them their desire, though they were rejecting Him from being King over them.[53] "Samuel explained to the people the regulations of the kingship. He wrote them down on a scroll and deposited it before the LORD. Then Samuel dismissed the people, each to his own home."[54] It was written down so that both the people and the king would be accountable.

During the return from exile, there was some confusion about the genealogy of some people. Nehemiah records, "So my God put it into my heart to assemble the nobles, the officials and the common people for registration by families. I found the genealogical record of those who had been the first to return. This is what I found written there..."[55] Ezra also wrote down those who returned with him (Ez.8). The written record was essential for determining the priesthood, inheritance, and other matters.

At that time, to demonstrate their determination to obey the written law, the people wrote an agreement of their own. "In view of all this, we are making a binding agreement, putting it in writing, and our leaders, our Levites and our priests are affixing their seals to it."[56] To make the decree clear, the people put it in writing. Nehemiah records the names of all those who signed the agreement.[57] To affirm that the decree was binding on all, the leaders affixed their names to the agreement. What was written was binding.

Time and again throughout the history of the kings of Judah and Israel, we are told about a certain king: "As for the other events of Rehoboam's reign, and all he did, are they not written in the book of the chronicles of the kings of Judah?"[58] We are told this about Abijah, Asa, Jehoshaphat, Jehoram, Joash, Amaziah, et al. in Judah. We are told this about Nadab, Baasha, Elah, Zimri, Omri, Ahab, et al. in Israel. The written record told the story of what the king had done.

God referred to the written prophetic record to demonstrate both His own righteousness and longsuffering as well as the unfaithfulness of the people. "I will bring upon that land all the things I have spoken against it, all that are written in this book and prophesied by Jeremiah against all the nations."[59]

A heavenly being visits Daniel the prophet and tells him events that will take place in the future. The visitor must depart quickly to engage in a battle in the heavenlies, but he tells Daniel, "first I will tell you what is written in the Book of Truth...."[60] The events that are to take place are already written in the Book of Truth. The fact that the events were already written down meant that they would surely happen.

The book of Malachi is chronologically the last in Tanakh. In that day, as throughout the history of Israel, there were those who served the Lord and those who did not. God promised that each would be called to account.

"Then those who feared the LORD talked with each other, and the LORD listened and heard. A scroll of remembrance was written in His presence concerning those who feared the LORD and honored His name."[61] Then the Lord promised that those who were written down would be remembered unto life. The Lord wrote down the names to signify His commitment to them.

Yaakov Elman notes some additional historical problems confronting the various views which claim an Oral Torah that comes from Sinai: "They also assume — as does Avot 1:1 — that Rabbinic values prevailed in Biblical times. However, the relative lack of importance assigned to learning, in the Rabbinic sense, in Biblical texts remains a serious problem, as do the instances of un- or counter-halakhic acts attributed to Biblical figures."[62]

That is to say that there is no Biblical record of anyone - Abraham, Moses, David, Ezra, or anyone else - studying or interpreting Torah as the Rabbis say it should be studied and interpreted. The Bible does record, however, incidents when such Biblical heroes did what the Rabbis say should not be done, without any indication of guilt or divine disapproval.

What then is the record of Tanakh concerning the oral law? On the basis of what is in the Law, the Writings, and the Prophets, was there, or could there have been, an oral law given by God to Moses at Sinai?

If there was an oral law which God gave to Moses, Moses never mentioned it, nor did Joshua, Ezra, or any other person in the Bible. If it existed, it was not part of God's covenant with Israel. Nor was it relevant to the blessing or judgment of God.

No prophet, priest, or king either mentions it or demonstrates any concern to know it or obey it. It was not relevant to the governance or required worship of Israel. Nor did it play any part in the instruction of the people or their children.

In other words, on the basis of what is recorded in Tanakh, there was no Oral Law given by God to Moses at Sinai.

8. THE ORAL LAW AS INTERPRETATION

The Second Talmudic Claim: The oral law is an extended interpretation and elaboration of the written Torah which was given to Moses. [*Or*, it was present as a seed in the written Torah, but later grew and flourished.]

"When Moses ascended on high he found the Holy One, blessed be He, engaged in affixing coronets to the letters. Said Moses, 'Lord of the Universe, Who stays Thy hand?' [*I.e., 'is there anything wanting in the Torah that these additions are necessary?'*] He answered, 'There will arise a man, at the end of many generations, Akiba b. Joseph by name, who will expound upon each tittle heaps and heaps of laws'. 'Lord of the Universe', said Moses; 'permit me to see him'. He replied, 'Turn thee round'. Moses went and sat down behind eight rows (and listened to the discourses upon the law). Not being able to follow their arguments he was ill at ease, but when they came to a certain subject and the disciples said to the master 'Whence do you know it?' and the latter replied 'It is a law given unto Moses at Sinai' he was comforted. Thereupon he returned to the Holy One, blessed be He, and said, 'Lord of the Universe, Thou hast such a man and Thou givest the Torah by me!' He replied, 'Be silent, for such is My decree'."[1]

The story makes several important points:
1. The *halakha* is an elaborate interpretation of the Torah - an infinite number of laws generated from the scribal ornamentation of individual letters.
2. Moses did not know the *halakha*. He did not recognize what Akiba taught.
3. Rabbi Akiba is credited by God as being the originator of the oral law.
4. Neither Akiba nor his disciples recognized Moses. They had no interest in what his understanding of the Torah might be.
5. Moses is inferior to Akiba. This is demonstrated by the response of Moses to the Holy One — "Thou hast such a man and Thou givest the Torah by me!" — and by the placement of Moses behind the eighth row.[2]

The Talmud to the Contrary

The Talmud often distinguishes between those halakhot that are based on Scripture and those that are not. The clearest expression of this appears in Hag. 10a: "[The laws concerning] the dissolution of vows hover in the air and have nought to rest on. The laws concerning the Sabbath, festal-offerings, acts of trespass are as mountains hanging by a hair, for they have scant scriptural basis but many laws. [The laws concerning] civil cases and [Temple] services, Levitical cleanness and uncleanness, and the forbidden relations have what to rest on, and it is they that are the essentials of the Torah."

Some of the halakhot rest upon the Scriptures. Others are simply rabbinic decrees. Entire portions of rabbinic law are presented without any basis in the written Torah.

Jacob Neusner comments: "Perhaps the exegetes took for granted that the bed-rock convictions of the laws also were assumed by the Scriptures. But they still have not shown us where, in Scripture, they locate those laws or principles, and I think the probable explanation is that they could not (and did not care to). That is why they remind us that *Ohalot* has much law but little Scripture."[3] Implicit in the doctrine of a parallel "Oral Law" given at Sinai is the recognition that much of halakhah cannot be tied to the written Torah in any way at all.

Neusner examined a few Talmudic tractates to determine the source of the different material they contained. He concluded that, "Neither *Kelim* nor *Ohalot* begins in the Priestly Code [i.e. Leviticus and related sections]. Neither tractate develops the lines laid out therein. Indeed, the most fundamental convictions of both tractates lie wholly outside of Scripture."[4] "Having carefully distinguished Mishnaic from Pentateuchal conceptions in respect to utensils and Tents, *Kelim* and *Ohalot*, we now see that there is virtually no fundamental and reciprocal relationship whatever."[5]

Often the Rabbis cited scripture without maintaining that the particular scripture cited was actually the source of the ruling. One verse, sometimes intentionally altered, could be "a hair" on which a "mountain" of rabbinic regulation was hung.

As Israel Abrahams noted: "Such textual changes are not to be regarded as serious Biblical emendations, but as part of the exegetical method of the Rabbis for the purpose of halachic and Haggadic deduction." Neusner says, "The authorities of Mishnah-Tosefta do not derive their laws from Scriptures. On occasion they do twist Scriptures to make them fit preconceived conclusions...."[6] Or as the Talmud puts it: "Rather, then, it is a Rabbinical ordinance and the Scriptural verse is merely a support."[7]

Rabbinic halakhot are often contrasted with the written Torah, rather than identified with it. Here are some examples:

"Is then the searching for leaven Scriptural; surely it is [only] Rabbinical, for by Scriptural law mere annulment is sufficient."[8]

"[G]ranted that food cannot defile food by Scriptural law, by Rabbinical law it can nevertheless defile."[9]

There are a variety of Talmudic phrases that indicate that the halakhot following them are the creation of the Rabbis, rather than an interpretation of the written Torah.

Sometimes the source of the halakhot is given simply as "the words of the sages," i.e. *divre soferim*. The law is authoritative because it has been decreed by the sages/scribes.

"In mKelim 13:7 (=mTebul Yom 4:6) we encounter another expression similar to *divre soferim*. There we read *davar hadas hiddesu soferim*, 'Scribes innovated a new law.'"[10] "Likewise, the exegetical tradition indicates that the formulae 'for the benefit of the altar' in mGittin 5:5, and 'for the sake of harmony' in mGittin 5:8 all designate *corpora* of man-made law."[11]

The Talmud says that the rabbinic decrees sometimes stand in opposition to the written Torah. "In mPesahim 6:2 'they enacted legislation to forbid' is modified by an adverbial phrase *missum sevut*. This expression, which is attested also in mShabbat 10:6; mEruvin 10:3, 15; mBesah 5:2 and mRosh ha-Shanah 4:8, designates a *corpus* of man-made law, which forbids on the Sabbath or festivals that which God permits."[12]

Rabbinic law also permits what the Bible forbids. The most well-known instance of this is the *"prozbul."* Biblically, loans could not be made for longer than 6 years. Every 7th year, the Sabbatical year, all loans expired. According to the Talmud, Hillel instituted a legal fiction, the *prozbul*, which was "a declaration made in court, to the effect that the law shall not apply to the loan transacted."[13]

"[A loan secured by] *prozbul* is not cancelled. This was one of the things instituted by Hillel the Elder; for when he observed people refraining from lending to one another, and thus transgressing what is written in the Law, 'Beware, lest there be a base thought in thy heart', he instituted the *prozbul*."[14]

Mayer Gruber concluded that, "Sufficient attention is paid in the Mishnah to the innovative legislation of such mortal figures as Hillel, Rabban Gamaliel the Elder, Rabban Yohanan b. Zakkai, and the unnamed Scribes and Sages to put to rest the notion that the 'Oral Torah' doctrine was the Mishnah's characteristic device for introducing change in Judaism."[15] They legislated without reference to Torah, written or oral.

In the Talmud, the Rabbis generally do not claim that their law is either a separate revelation given to Moses or that it is an interpretation of the written Torah. The Rabbis do claim, however, that they have the authority to forbid what the Torah permits, and to permit what the Torah forbids.

Torah is national law, understood as being given by God. In claiming authority over Torah, the Rabbis claimed sovereign authority over every aspect of life for all Israel.

Personally, we might welcome the changes they made, or we might recoil from them, but the relevant question is, "What was the basis for this claim of unlimited rabbinic authority?" We will seek to answer that question as we continue to examine the Talmudic claims about the Oral Law.

9. TORAH SHE'B'AL PE

"A certain gentile who came before Shammai asked him, 'How many Torahs do you have?' he replied, 'Two: a Written Torah and an Oral Torah.' 'I believe you with respect to the Written, but not with respect to the Oral Torah; make me a proselyte on condition that you teach me the Written Torah [only].' [But] he scolded and repulsed him in anger. When he went before Hillel, he accepted him as a proselyte. On the first day he taught him, *Alef, beth, gimmel, daleth*; the following day he reversed [them] to him. 'But yesterday you did not teach them to me thus,' he protested. 'Must you then not rely upon me? Then rely upon me with respect to the Oral [Torah] too.'"[1]

According to this passage, both Hillel and Shammai agreed that knowledge of the Oral Law was essential for a proselyte. They agreed that it was basic and fundamental. If that were so, then both Hillel and Shammai must have known and taught the Oral Law, and the Talmud, at least from their time on, would be filled with references to it. That is not the case.

"It is especially significant that the term 'Oral Torah', widely assumed to be a fundamental doctrine of the Babylonian Talmud, is attested in that document twice in the [above] anecdote in bShabbat 31a and only twice more, bYoma 28b and in bQiddushin 66a."[2] The Talmud was completed hundreds of years after Hillel and Shammai. It often refers to received tradition [*kabbalah*] and to the correct way [*halakha*], but it only mentions the "Oral Law" in three places.

The passages in Kiddushin and Yoma place the concept and use of the term "Oral Torah" farther back in time than Hillel and Shammai. The passage in Kid.66a places the term "Oral Torah" in the time of the Hasmoneans.

"Now, there was a man there, frivolous, evilhearted and worthless, named Eleazar son of Po'irah, who said to King Jannai. 'O King Jannai, the hearts of the Pharisees are against thee.' 'Then what shall I do?' ...'If thou wilt take my advice, trample them down.' 'But what shall happen with the Torah?' 'Behold, it is rolled up and lying in the corner. Whoever wishes to study, let him go and study!' Said R. Nahman b. Isaac: Immediately a spirit of heresy was instilled into him, for he should have replied. 'That is well for the Written Law; but what of the Oral Law?' Straightway, the evil burst forth through Eleazar son of Po'irah, all the Sages of Israel were massacred, and the world was desolate until Simeon b. Shetah came and restored the Torah to its pristine [glory]."

According to this passage, Elijah b. Po'irah counselled King

Jannai that the destruction of the Pharisees would not hinder the study of Torah. Whoever wanted to study Torah could read and study it unhindered, without the Pharisees. Centuries later, R. Nahman b. Isaac, a Babylonian Amora, agreed that the study of the Written Torah would not be hindered by the destruction of the Pharisees, but maintained that only the Pharisees could or would transmit the Oral Torah. No one else would. It was not in the possession of all Israel. With the destruction of the Pharisees, the world would be desolate, as it was before God gave it form. It would be without the Oral Torah.

Yoma 28b places the term "Oral Torah" even farther back in time. "Raba or R. Ashi said: Abraham, our father, kept even the law concerning the *'erub* of the dishes,' as it is said: 'My Torahs': one being the written Torah, the other the oral Torah."[3] Abraham lived several centuries before God gave the written Law at Sinai, and therefore several centuries before there could have been any oral law related to it.

In making man in His own image and likeness, God had given law to all men. Most disobeyed it, but God commended Abraham for keeping it.

Though these are the only three places in Talmud where the term "Oral Torah" (*Torah she'b'al pe*/תורה שבעל פה) actually appears, there are other related passages. Especially important is a passage in Gittin 60b.

"R. Judah b. Nahmani the public orator of R Simeon b. Lakish discoursed as follows: It is written, *Write thou these words* [Ex.34:27], and it is written, *For according to the mouth of these words*. What are we to make of this? - It means: The words which are written thou art not at liberty to say by heart, and the words transmitted orally thou art not at liberty to recite from writing. A Tanna of the school of R. Ishmael taught: [It is written] *These*: these thou mayest write, but thou mayest not write *halachoth*. R. Jochanan said: God made a covenant with Israel only for the sake of that which was transmitted orally, as it says, *For by the mouth of these words I have made a covenant with thee and with Israel*."[4]

There are several claims made here: 1. One is not permitted to say by heart the words of the Written Torah. 2. One is not permitted to recite from writing the words of the Oral Torah. 3. The halakha, or Oral Law, is the reason that God established a covenant relationship between Himself and Israel. Tanakh was an introduction to God's real purpose for Israel - obeying the Rabbis.

The first claim is interesting in light of the numerous scriptures like Dt.6:6-7: "And these words which I command you this day shall be upon your heart, and you shall teach them diligently to your children, speaking them when you sit in your house, when you walk by the way, when you lie down, and when you rise up."

All Israel was commanded to put the written commandments upon their hearts and then teach and speak of them in every aspect of life. This particular claim, however, is not pertinent to our discussion at this point.

We will look at the second claim later. The place to begin evaluating the third claim is Ex.34:27-28, the text on which it is based.

"Then the LORD said to Moses, 'Write down [כתב לך] these words [הדברים האלה], for in accordance with these words [על פי האלה הדברים] I have made a covenant with you and with Israel [כרתי אתך ברית ואת ישראל].' Moses was there with the LORD forty days and forty nights without eating bread or drinking water. And he wrote [ויכתב] on the tablets the words of the covenant [דברי הברית] —the Ten Commandments."[5]

The interpretation in Gittin 60b puts "these words" which must be written in opposition to "these words" which are the substance of the covenant. It claims that "these words" which are the substance of the covenant are not given in the book of Exodus or in the written Torah, i.e. the phrase points to an oral communication which is not in the text. The text itself says nothing about an oral law. It does say that Moses "**wrote** on the tablets the words of the covenant," precluding an unwritten covenant.

Other scriptures have been put forth as support for this claim. Baumgarten suggests that, "In view of the similar word-play reflected in the scholion to Megillat Ta'anit..., it is even more plausible to derive תורה שבעל פה from Deut. 17, 11 על פי התורה אשר יורוך, which passage serves, indeed, as the pentateuchal source for the authority of tradition; see Sifre ad locum and b. Sanhedrin 87a."[6]

The scholion of Megillat Ta'anit also alludes to other verses as being the Biblical source for the authority of the Oral Law. "The Sages said to them, Is it not written: '*According (*על פי*) to the Torah which they shall teach thee etc.*' (Deut.17,11), which verse indicates that one must not write halakhot in a book. According to another version, the Sages said to them, Is it not written: '*The Torah and the commandment which I have written to instruct them*' (Ex. 24,12)? This means the Torah which I have written and the commandment to instruct them orally. It is also written: '*And now write down this poem and teach it to the people of Israel, put it in their mouths*' (Deut. 31,19). '*Teach it to the people of Israel*' refers to Scripture, while '*Put it in their mouths*' refers to halakhot."[7]

Let us examine each of these verses, starting with Dt.17:11 in its context, to see if they provide a basis for the doctrine of an Oral Law. "If cases come before your courts that are too difficult for you to judge —whether bloodshed, lawsuits or assaults —take them to the place the LORD your God will choose. Go to the Levitical priests and to the judge [אל כהנים הלבים ואל השפט] who is in office at that time. Inquire of them and they will give you the verdict.

"You must act according to the decisions they give you at the place the LORD will choose. Be careful to do everything they direct you to do. Act according to the law they teach you [על פי התורה אשר יורוך] and the decisions they give you. Do not turn aside from what they tell you, to the right or to the left. The man who shows contempt for the judge or for the priest who stands ministering there to the LORD your God must be put to death. You must purge the evil from Israel."[8]

This section concerns future difficult individual civil or criminal cases when Israel is in the land. It does not refer in any way to a covenant or to an oral law, or to the institution of some system that would replace the written Law, most of which Israel had not yet even started to observe.

The decisions are to be made by the Levitical priests and/or a judge, like Gideon or Samuel. In a related portion in Dt.21:5, only the priests are mentioned. The text does not mention the Rabbis or Sages. It was written more than 1200 years before the first *zugoth*, the ancient Talmudic teachers.

The hearing and judgement are to be made at "the place the LORD your God will choose." Twenty times in Torah, all in Deuteronomy, reference is made to a place which the Lord will choose in the future.[9] These verses refer to Jerusalem, not to Yavneh or any other place.

Ex.24:12 says: "The LORD said to Moses, 'Come up to me on the mountain and stay here, and I will give you the tablets of stone, with the law and the commandment which I have written for their instruction [והתורה והמצוה אשר כתבתי להורתם].'" The claim in the scholion of Megillat Ta'anit is that, "This means the Torah which I have written and the commandment to instruct them orally."[10]

Grammatically, the text says, "the commandment which I have written." Both the law and the commandment are written on the tablets of stone. There is no reference here to an oral law, nor any grammatical place to insert one.

Deut. 31:19 is introductory to the Song of Moses in chapter 32. The verse itself says, "Now **write** down for yourselves this song and teach it to the children of Israel and put it in their mouths, so that this song may be a witness for me against the children of

Israel." The Rabbinic claim is, "'Teach it to the children of Israel' refers to Scripture, while 'Put it in their mouths' refers to *halakhot*."

The text refers to the song, which is to be first written down and then taught to the children of Israel. The song is to be a witness against their future apostasy from the written law. There is no grammatical place for reading in *halakhot*. There is no conceptual place for an oral law.

Al Pe and *B'Yad Moshe*

The phrase *Torah she'b'al pe*/תורה שבעל פה does not appear in these texts, nor anywhere else in Torah or Tanakh. There are, however, forty uses in Torah of the phrase "*al pe*/על פי," but none of these uses refers to, or even possibly could refer to, an oral law. The text of some of these, as in Ex.34:27, refers explicitly to something that is written.

Lev.24:12 refers to "the will of the LORD" which is written in Lev.24:14. Num.3:16,39,51 & 4:37,41,45,49 refer to the census and responsibilities of the Levites which are written in that section.

Num.33:2 says, "And Moses **wrote** the stages in their journey **at the mouth** of the LORD ...." Num. 36:5 says, "Moses commanded the children of Israel at the mouth of the LORD saying: 'What the tribe of the descendants of Joseph is saying is right.' " What Moses commanded at the mouth of the Lord was written down.

Ex.38:21 is the only verse in the Bible that uses the phrase - "at the mouth of Moses," i.e. *al pe Moshe*/על פי משה. It says, "These are the amounts of the materials used for the tabernacle, the tabernacle of the Testimony, which were **written** at the mouth of Moses [על פי משה] by the Levites under the direction of Ithamar son of Aaron, the priest."

"At the mouth of" is not set in opposition to "written." To the contrary, what was from the mouth of Moses was **written** by the Levites. "At the mouth of" indicates the source of the communication, not the way in which it is recorded.

In Torah, the phrase "*al pe*" does not indicate something, or some teaching, that is transmitted orally but not written. It usually refers to something that is written in the adjacent text. This is also evident in the book of Jeremiah, where Baruch the scribe "**wrote** from the mouth of Jeremiah all the words of the Lord."[11]

If the Scriptures had used "at the mouth of" to refer to something spoken but not written, then it would have followed that "by the hand of" would be used to refer to something written but not spoken. That also is not the case. Here are a few examples:

"So Pharaoh's heart was hard and he would not let the children of Israel go, just as the LORD had **said** by the hand of Moses."[12]

"And you must teach the children of Israel all the decrees the LORD has given them by the hand of Moses."[13]

"This was to remind the children of Israel that no one except a descendant of Aaron should come to burn incense before the LORD, or he would become like Korah and his followers, as the LORD said to him by the hand of Moses."[14]

Num.10:13 has the interesting phrase, *"al pe adonai b'yad Moshe"*/על פי יהוה ביד משה. The same words are spoken both "at the mouth of the Lord" and "by the hand of Moses." There is no opposition between the two. In fact, this is the phrase used in the traditional liturgy after the reading of the torah - *al pe adonai b'yad Moshe*.

In sum, the Rabbis made themselves the creators and administrators of an Oral Law claimed to be given to Moses. The basis of their claim is a peculiar interpretation of the phrase *al pe*/ על פי, one which is contradicted by the grammar, words, and teaching of the Torah. Neither Torah nor Tanakh as a whole provide any basis for the doctrine of an Oral Law.

History to the Contrary

The contemporary sources bear witness that there was a significant body of Pharisaic, and then rabbinic, law in the first century. The sources do not, however, indicate in any way that the Pharisees, and then the Rabbis, claimed at that time that this law came from Sinai or that it was solely an interpretation of the Torah.

The sources all speak in terms of tradition or an "oral tradition."[15] None of them speak of an "Oral Law." "We thus have indications that in the time of Josephus and Philo oral transmission was looked upon as the characteristic medium of Pharisaic tradition."[16] Though Josephus and Philo mention Pharisaic tradition, they do not mention an "Oral law."

The Pharisees did try to add weight to their tradition by placing its origin as far back in the past as they could. "Josephus brings this out when he says of the Jewish leaders, 'Their endeavour is to have everything they ordain believed to be very ancient.'"[17]

Josephus gives some of the political history of this tradition. He tells us, for example, about the reign of Alexandra towards the end of the Maccabean period. "So she made Hyrcanus [her son] high-priest because he was the elder, but much more because he cared not to meddle with politics, and permitted the Pharisees to do everything; to whom also she ordered the multitude to be obedient. She also restored again those practices which the Pharisees had introduced, according to the traditions of their forefathers, and which her father-in-law, Hyrcanus, had abrogated."[18]

In this account, the traditional practices of the Pharisees were enforced upon the people by the ruling governmental power. The extent of the common observance of Pharisaic traditions depended upon the extent of the Pharisees' political power.

The Sadducees had a different power base - the Temple and its institutions - and a different view of these traditions. Josephus tells us, "What I would now explain is this, that the Pharisees have delivered to the people a great many observances by succession from their fathers, which are not written in the law of Moses; and for that reason it is that the Sadducees reject them, and say that we are to esteem those observances to be obligatory which are in the written word, but are not to observe what are derived from the tradition of our forefathers..."[19]

"...Josephus not only characterizes the Pharisaic ordinances as 'unwritten', but as 'handed down by the fathers' (εχ πατερων διαδοχη)."[20] There was no claim that they came from Sinai or from God. "A similar expression παραδοσις των πρεσβυτερων (traditions of the elders) is used in the New Testament to designate the Pharisaic oral traditions.... Eusebius refers to the *agrafos paradosis* [αγραφοσ παραδοσις(unwritten traditions) of the Jews."[21]

The Dead Sea Scrolls reinforce the point. "In sum, the Qumran literature provides concrete and abundant examples of written halakhic texts from the pre-rabbinic period. It moreover lacks any trace of the distinction between Written Law and Oral Law which is characteristic of rabbinic sources and which serves as the basis of the contrasting forms of transmission."[22]

"Joseph M. Baumgarten and Lawrence H. Schiffman have likewise shown that the Qumran law books speak neither of an oral Torah nor of two Torahs....It should be no less significant than the absence of the term Oral Torah from Josephus' description of the Pharisees and from the Qumran law books that this term is similarly absent from the Mishnah and the Tosefta. Moreover, the term 'two Torahs' is also absent from the Mishnah while none of the three attestations of this term in the Tosefta refers to an Oral and a Written Torah. In tSanhedrin 2:5 'two Torahs' refers to the two scrolls of the pentateuch to be written by and for every king of Israel. In the two remaining cases - tHagigah 2:9 and tSotah 14:9 - 'two Torahs' is the term of disparagement applied to the controversies between the disciples of Hillel and Shammai, who, it is alleged, created their two separate doctrines because they failed to study carefully the single Torah which they all received from Hillel and Shammai."[23]

This teaching of Two Torahs also conflicts with Ex.12:49: "There shall be one Torah [תורה אחת] for the native-born and for the alien living among you." If 'Abraham kept My Torahs' is to be understood to mean a Written Torah and an Oral Torah, then "one Torah for the native-born and for the alien" would have to be understood to mean only a Written Torah.

These traditions and decrees were not called "Oral Law" in the first century. Nevertheless, they were of great importance for the Pharisees.[24]

The Development of the Doctrine of the Oral Law

Josephus wrote his <u>Antiquities of the Jews</u> in about 93 AD. The concept of an Oral Law received from Sinai, either directly or through authorized interpretation, had apparently not yet been put forth. The Pharisees claimed that their traditions gave the authoritative interpretation of Torah, but they did not claim to have a separately revealed oral law. "Hence, despite the insistence of the Pharisees on the validity of their ordinances, they never added them to the written canon."[25]

When then did the Rabbis begin to speak about an "Oral Law"? "As has been noted, the picture of Moses' oral formulation and transmission of traditions was certainly held by rabbinic masters from Judah b. Ilai onwards, hence ca. A.D. 150. So between ca. A.D. 100 and ca. 150 the process described in b. 'Eruvin 54b probably took shape."[26] "While the process may have begun with Joshua and Eliezer, it was probably 'Aqiba who fully developed them, for it was he who set forth the foundations of the Mishnah, and it was in his time that the institution of the *Tanna*, or reciter, is first referred to."[27]

"In a 4th century Palestinian midrash we read: 'R. Judah b. Shalom said: Moses desired the Mishnah to be also in writing, but the Holy One Blessed Be He foresaw that the nations of the world would translate the Torah, read it in Greek, and assert: 'We, too, are Israel.' The Holy One Blessed Be He thereupon said to Moses: 'Were I to write for thee the multitudes of my Torah then they would be considered as a stranger' (Hosea 8,12). Why so? Because the Mishnah is the *mysterium* of God which He transmits only to the righteous.'"[28] The Oral Torah became the rabbinic means of keeping their followers separated from the Gentiles, the Christians, and especially the *minim*, the Jewish heretics.

At least until the end of the first century, the Rabbis openly enacted new legislation, without maintaining that they were presenting an Oral Torah parallel to the written Torah given at

Sinai. "I.R.Weiss in his History of the Development of the Oral Law tells us that forty-two Halakoth are said to have been given 'to Moses from Sinai,' but that many, indeed the large majority, of them were not so entitled because the Rabbis thought they really had been given to Moses, but for other reasons..."[29]

Throughout the entire Talmud, only forty-two *halakhot* are distinguished as having been given "to Moses from Sinai." Whether that is understood to indicate a direct revelation given to Moses or to indicate an authorized interpretation of the written Torah, one thing is quite striking: No such claim is made for the overwhelming remainder of *halakhot*.

What then is *halakha* that was **not** given "to Moses at Sinai?" What is its source and its purpose?

Later Rabbis said that, "Oral Torah is what the sages of Israel and Keneset Yisra'el innovated by their own perception of heart and mind of the will of God, and that is the understanding that God apportioned to them according to the limits of their capacity."[30]

All the rabbinic innovations - including those that forbid what Torah permits, and permit what Torah forbids - were said to be still tied to the Written Torah.[31] That revelation even included "whatever an able student may in the future propound before his teacher."[32]

The Scriptures, with the normal use and meaning of language, offered no basis for the doctrine of an Oral Law, nor for the authority of the Rabbis. However, the rabbinic claims are not based upon the normal use and meaning of language. They are based upon Rabbi Akiba's unique method of interpretation.

10. CONFRONTING THE SCRIPTURES

When words have normal meaning and usage, there is no evidence in Tanakh of the existence of any rabbis or any oral law. The text actually precludes the possibility of there having been either authoritative rabbis or oral law throughout the time encompassed in the canon.

The Scriptures themselves denied to the Rabbis any legitimate authority or role. The Scriptures themselves were therefore the greatest barrier standing in the way of Rabbi Akiba and his desire to create a system of rabbinic authority.

From the outset, Rabbi Akiba faced many adversaries in his struggles, but the Scriptures themselves were the greatest of all. They had to be overcome first and foremost. To fight and defeat each of his adversaries, Akiba needed a high place to stand and a formidable weapon to employ. If he could somehow neutralize the opposition of the Scriptures or even turn them into his ally, then he would have both.

Akiba's method of attacking the Scriptures was contained in his unique system of interpretation. Some would question whether it should be called a "system" at all, since the rules were not fixed, but changed to fit the need of the moment. This method of interpretation is universally recognized as Akiba's greatest distinctive and achievement.

Louis Finkelstein commented extensively on it. [Emphasis added] "Akiba's mode of interpretation of Scripture is a development of that which he derived from his master Nahum of Gimzo. Superfluous letters, words, and verses were the meat whereon he thrived. By the use of them **he was able to read his whole juristic program into Scriptures.** But what he called superfluous words would hardly seem such to us. The juxtaposition of the various chapters had a meaning which must be discovered. **He rejected the old Hillelite principle** of inference by generalization from particulars, and replaced it with **a curious and complicated rule of his own invention** which he called 'Inclusion and Limitation.' **Neither rhetoric nor grammar offered a bar to his imaginative argument.** Indeed, were we to accept at face value the technical reasons he gave for his decisions, we should be forced to the conclusion that, far from being the greatest of the Talmudists, he was simply a brilliant example of extraordinary - but wasted - ingenuity. But the rules which he derived through his curious and intricate logic are so reasonable that when we examine them we are even more impressed with his judgment as a jurist than with his skill as debater. **It is obvious that he** considered the interpretation of the written law merely the form which had to be followed in the derivation of desirable rules from the biblical text.

"Akiba was trying to change the complexion of the inherited law. To accomplish this he had to find an authority superior to that of his predecessors and accepted by everyone. Only one instrument could fulfill those requirements - Scripture itself."[1]

Several of Finkelstein's observations are worth repeating:

1. Akiba had an agenda which he read into the Scriptures.

2. His method of interpretation rejected the logic and grammar of the text. Interpretation of scripture was only the form, not the reality.

3. He rejected the accepted methods of interpretation.

4. To accomplish his agenda - to change the law and its authorized interpreters and enforcers - he had to tie his agenda to the Scriptures.

The highest accepted authority in Israel was the Scriptures. Akiba therefore sought to use the form of Scripture, without regard to its content, as a means of deriving a new law and religion.

Akiba tied his own rulings to any peculiarity or verbal similarity in the Biblical text to attach the authority of the Scriptures to his views. Different verses, words, or even letters simply provided the pretext for him to introduce his own teaching, which otherwise could not be found in Tanakh.

Louis Ginzberg notes, "How little he cared for the letter of the Law whenever he conceives it to be antagonistic to the spirit of Judaism, is shown by his attitude towards the Samaritans."[2] For Akiba, the Scriptures themselves could "be antagonistic to the spirit of Judaism."

Obviously, the Scriptures were not antagonistic to the Judaism which they themselves created. They were, however, quite hostile to the spirit of the Judaism that Akiba was trying to create. To overcome this antagonism of the Scriptures, Akiba read his meaning into the text, rather than reading the plain meaning out of the text. The plain meaning of the text was of no use to him. It presented an insurmountable barrier to what he hoped to accomplish.

"As a result, Akiba became the foremost champion of *eisegesis*, while other scholars tried to stay (somewhat) closer to the actual meaning of the text as did R. Yishmael who maintained, 'The Torah speaks the language of the people,' i.e., seemingly superfluous text elements need not have a specific meaning. From the scientific point of view Ishmael was right, but Akiba's method was more useful and prevailed."[3] I.e., Akiba's method made no sense grammatically or logically, but there was an attractive utility to it. It was the only way to legitimize rabbinic authority.

Akiba used certain rules of interpretation when they suited his purpose, and disregarded them when they did not. "He used to say, 'Between a wide and a limited interpretation, choose the limited.' (Sifra Zabim, par 5.5, 79a; Yer. Yoma 2.5, 40a) It would be easy to show that he himself violated this rule frequently..."[4]

The only logic that governed Akiba was whatever would further his purpose. That was his overarching rule of interpretation. There was no other rule of interpretation which he consistently followed.

When the rules for interpretation are not fixed, the interpretation can be arbitrary and artificial. The Scriptures simply provide the pretext for asserting the desired conclusion. Though Akiba's interpretation is often arbitrary, it is never random. Perhaps from the outside it sometimes seems to be so, but from the inside it is deliberate and purposeful. The purpose was to bring Israel out from under the authority of the Scriptures, and place her firmly under the authority of the Rabbis.

"Aqiba's statement in Sifre Num §131 (H.169), that 'every Scripture passage which is close to another must be interpreted with respect to it' appears to say the same [as an argument from the context]; however, this principle frequently leads not to a natural exegesis of context but to often farfetched expositions based on the accidental proximity of two terms."[5]

"His new rules of hermeneutics, and his utter independence of tradition were freely attacked. 'Akiba,' Eleazar ben Azariah once shouted at him, 'even if you continue to repeat for a whole day that the superfluous word proves your point, we will not listen to you.'"[6] The traditional rabbis were both enraged and frustrated by Akiba's assertions.

Other rabbis were also said to have created ingenious interpretations of their own. "Thus, e.g., R. Ishmael directs the following critical words against R. Eliezer ben Hyrkanos: 'You say to the Scripture: Silence, while I interpret!'"[7]

Rabbi Ishmael is noted for his 13 rules of interpretation. His rules were fixed and logical. That is why he often found himself in conflict with Akiba.

In one skirmish, because of an extra Hebrew letter [*vav*] in the text, Akiba maintained that, "'A daughter of a priest who commits adultery should be executed by burning.' Rabbi Ishmael said to him: 'Shall we burn this woman because you must find an interpretation for your *vav*?'"[8]

"R. Ishmael, the great teacher of the generation before Bar

Kokhba, is regarded as the antagonist of Rabbi Aqiba especially in the area of Biblical interpretation. Over and against the forced interpretation of individual words he advances the principle, 'The Torah speaks in the language of men'."[9]

"Akiba created his own Midrash [commentary], by means of which he was able 'to discover things that were even unknown to Moses' (Pesik., Parah, ed. Buber, 39b). Akiba made the accumulated treasure of the oral law - which until his time was only a subject of knowledge and not of science - an inexhaustible mine from which, by the means he provided, new treasures might be continually extracted."[10]

"It was a mighty key that R. Akiba provided to unlock the Torah, so that a never-ending stream of *halakoth* could be derived from it....The written Torah, thanks to R. Akiba, kept its central place in Judaism without its hampering the development of the oral law....He supplied the principles for justifying this abandoning of absolute reliance on tradition without breaking with the alleged fount of all tradition."[11]

Rabbi Akiba kept the written Torah central, but made it irrelevant. He alleged obedience to the Torah, but transformed it into a powerless royal figurehead. Torah said whatever he wanted it to say.[12]

In this way, he accomplished something quite remarkable. The words of the Rabbis became the law that Israel had to obey. As Akiba wrote, "Blessed be God, the God of Israel, who has chosen the words of Torah and the words of the sages, for the words of the sages are established forever and to all eternity."[13] Since the words of the sages were the only means by which Israel could understand the words of the Torah, the words of the sages became the ultimate authority.

On one notable occasion, two witness came to Yavneh and claimed to have seen the new moon. The men who claimed to have seen the new moon had not really seen it. Rabban Gamaliel, accepting their testimony, erroneously proclaimed the new moon.

Rabbi Dosa b. Harkinas and R. Joshua recognized that the new moon had really not yet come, and they said so. "Thereupon Rabban Gamaliel sent to him [R. Joshua] to say, I enjoin upon you to appear before me with your staff and your money on the day which according to your reckoning should be the day of atonement."[14]

Rather than admit his error and change his ruling, Rabban Gamaliel decided to compel everyone to affirm his error. He commanded R. Joshua to transgress the regulations of the actual day of atonement, the holiest day of the year. Rabban Gamaliel was compelling him to honor instead what would be the day of atonement according to Gamaliel's mistaken reckoning.

Biblically, such transgression would bring the gravest consequences. "For any soul who does not humble himself in that same day, he shall be cut off from his people. And any soul who does any work in that same day, I will destroy that soul from among his people."[15]

R. Joshua was in a predicament. He could obey the Scriptures or he could obey Rabban Gamliel. He could not obey both. To obey Gamaliel would mean being cut off by God. To obey the Scriptures would mean being excommunicated by Gamliel.

That the nature of this predicament was genuine is borne out by *The Book of Jubilees*. "The angel of the presence relates to Moses that 'on the heavenly tables the division of days is ordained' (6,35; cf. also 16, 28-30). Use of any other calendar means that its adherents will '...make an abominable (day) the day of testimony, and an unclean day a feast day, and they will confound all the days, the holy with the unclean, and the unclean day with the holy....'"[16]

R. Akiba, with his unique manner of interpretation, convinced R. Joshua to obey Rabban Gamliel. "R. Akiba went and found R. Joshua while he was in great distress. He said to him, *Master, why are you in distress?* He replied: *Akiba, it were better for a man to be on a sick-bed for twelve months than that such an injunction should be laid on him.* He said to him, *[Master,] will you allow me to tell you something which you yourself have taught me?* He said to him, *Speak*. He then said to him: *The text says, 'you', 'you', 'you', three times, to indicate that 'you'* [may fix the festivals] *even if you err inadvertently, 'you', even if you err deliberately, 'you', even if you are misled*. He replied to him in these words: *'Akiba, you have comforted me, you have comforted me'*."[17]

How did R. Akiba come up with his comforting interpretation? To begin with, he changed the Biblical text. "The word אתם (them) in Lev. XXII, 31, XXIII, 2 and XXIII,4 is read אתם (you) for homiletic purposes."[18] In the text, the word in question ["them"] refers to "the appointed seasons of the Lord." R. Akiba changed the word to make it refer to the Rabbis ["you"].

Then, having discarded the original text, Akiba assigned the meaning he wanted to the text he had created. Even so, the changed text still provided no basis for the meaning he invented. Yet in this way, we are told, he comforted R. Joshua, convincing him that whether or not the sages were right was irrelevant.

One more extreme example of Akiba's method of interpretation will suffice. The issue under discussion was the rabbinic ruling that there must be four portions of scripture in the *tefillin*, in four separate compartments. (The oldest known tefillin, which are from Qumran, contain more than four portions.) How did the Rabbis derive their ruling from scripture?

"Our Rabbis taught: It is written, *Letotefeth, letotefeth*, and *letotafoth*, making four in all. So R. Ishmael. R. Akiba says, There is no need of that interpretation, for *'tot'* means two in Katpi [perhaps the Coptic language] and *'foth'* means two in Afriki [the language of N. Africa]."[19]

The interpretation of the Rabbis, and specifically of R. Ishmael, is a little tenuous. "The word לטטפת [*Letotefeth*] (frontlets, i.e., the tefillin) occurs three times in the Torah, twice (Deut. VI, 8, and XI, 18) defectively written, לטטפת [*Letotefeth*] so that in each instance the word might be read in the singular, and once (Ex.XIII, 16) written *plene*, לטטפות [*Letotafoth*], which indicates the plural number, thus making a total of four."[20]

Perhaps R. Ishmael was stretching the limits of "interpretation." R. Akiba, on the other hand, departed from the realm of rational discourse. Akiba was not actually maintaining that *"letotafoth"* was etymologically derived from a combination of one particular Coptic word with another particular North African word. He was simply demonstrating that his method of "interpretation" provided ingenious ways of obtaining any desired result. In "interpretation" of this kind, the possibilities are truly endless.[21]

But Akiba's method of interpretation should not be looked upon as an eccentric aberration. It was purposeful and necessary. Without it, there was no way to tie rabbinic authority to the Scriptures. Other rabbis found the method helpful for establishing the Scriptural derivation of their own decrees.

For example: "We have now deduced [the law relating to] a priest's daughter; whence, however, is this deduced in respect of the daughter of a Levite or an Israelite? — As R. Abba stated in the name of Rab [that deduction is made from the Scriptural use of] 'But a daughter' [where only] 'daughter' [could have been used]. so here also [deduction is made from the use of] 'and a daughter' [where only] 'daughter' [could have been used]. In accordance with whose view? Is it only in accordance with that of R. Akiba who bases expositions on [superfluous] *Vavin!*"[22]

Another example: R. Meir derived a certain rabbinic decree concerning the sacrifices in one way. "And the Rabbis? They derive it from the dot [above the word]."[23]

Often the Rabbis, following Akiba's example, disregarded the actual text, and pretended that it said something else. Then they would argue about how to interpret their creation as though it were actually the text itself.

Once the Rabbis have changed the text to support their ruling, the actual text is no longer relevant. There is a clear example of this in a passage in Yebamoth:

"The question, however, arises on the view of the Rabbis: Does the Scriptural text...also bear its ordinary meaning, or since it was once torn away [from its ordinary meaning] it must in all respects so remain? Others say: According to the Rabbis no question arises, for since the text has once been torn away [from its ordinary meaning] it must in all respects so remain."[24]

Eliezer Berkovits has a simple comment on this example and procedure. "In this case, on the strength of a *S'bara*, because of logical argument, a new meaning was forced upon the biblical text, violating its linguistic content."[25] What the text actually said was not relevant to the discussion.

Berkovits summarizes the Rabbinic rule: "Sound reasoning overrules an authoritative text."[26] This, though direct, is somewhat circular in that someone must first establish what the basis of "sound reasoning" is.

What was sound reasoning to Akiba was often nonsense to other rabbis. His "interpretation" was not limited by grammar, word meaning, logic, or any of the rules of language. There were others for whom sound reasoning demanded a relationship between the text and the interpretation.

Additional Impact on the Scriptures

There are three additional ways in which Rabbi Akiba exerted his influence over the written Torah. We do not have sufficient evidence to judge how significant this influence was, but these efforts certainly deserve mention.

1) R. Akiba played a significant role in fixing the canon and, most likely, the text of Tanakh.

Ginzberg concluded that, "Akiba was the one who definitely fixed the canon of the Old Testament books."[27] Almost all of the included books were already recognized as having been given by God. There were some books, however, that some people would have included but Akiba did not; and some books that some people would not have included but Akiba did.

Without question, community consensus was a guiding constraint and played a major role in Akiba's determination. He was not acting with a free hand, but he apparently did make decisions. In fixing the canon, R. Akiba made a final determination of what books would be included in "the Holy Scriptures" and what books would be excluded.

In making that determination, Akiba made the judgments that he thought were best, in light of the evidence and purpose that he had. The declaration of the completion of the canon was a doctrinal decision. It was a declaration that the contemporary revelations of other groups of Jews (including those at Qumran and the *Talmidei Yeshua*) were not divinely inspired or sanctioned. Since the Rabbis held political power at that time, the decision strengthened their position. Their interpretations and writings were presented as the only divinely authorized additions to Tanakh. Without being formally added to Tanakh, the Talmud became canonical in its own right.

"The relationship between canonization and oral tradition in Pharisaic doctrine can be discerned from rabbinic sources. In harmony with the Pentateuch itself, which underlines the uniqueness and finality of the prophecy of Moses (Deut. 34,10), a tannaitic principle declares that henceforth 'no prophet has the authority to introduce any (halakhic) innovations.' [Sifra, Behuqotai, 13; b. Temuirah 16a] The statement that the Torah was not in the heavens (Deut. 30,12) was homiletically interpreted as a caution against the notion that 'another Moses might arise and bring another Torah from the heavens'. Moreover, with Haggai, Zechariah, and Malachi prophecy is said to have departed from Israel. [n1 Sanh 11a; T. Sotah 13,2] This belief, already reflected in 1 Maccabees and the writings of Josephus, resulted in an increasing emphasis on interpretive tradition: 'From now on bend your ear and hearken to the words of the Sages'."[28] Akiba, however, as we have seen, was considered another Moses, another lawgiver greater than the first.

Once the canon was fixed, it became possible to endeavor to fix the text of the different books that were included. We have no explicit evidence indicating that it was R. Akiba who standardized the text.[29] It is a conjecture, but one that is consistent with the historical circumstances and with Akiba's characteristic procedure of inclusion and exclusion. Akiba focused on bringing in and ruling out. That applied to interpretations, traditions, methods, and groups. He was the dominant rabbi, the leader, of the time.

"[P]rior to the standardization of the consonantal text at Jamnia there probably existed more versions and recensions of the Old Testament than are now extant, as the discoveries at Qumran seem to indicate."[30] As Harry Orlinsky points out, "the rabbinic literature itself, in quotations from the Bible, exhibits more frequently than is generally realized readings that differ from those preserved in our so-called 'masoretic' texts, readings that are not due to faulty memory and that crop up in Hebrew manuscripts and/or biblical quotations in Mechilta, Sifra, Sifre, the Gemara, the grammatical works of ibn Janah, etc."[31]

The standardization of the text, to whatever extent that occurred, offered an opportunity for those doing the "standardizing" to choose those variations which were most in accord with their own beliefs.[32] It then led to seeing that all other versions were eliminated. It is not likely that this was an impartial, disinterested exercise. The Rabbis and their followers were a minority sect seeking power. They freely changed the text they kept.

Whatever the exact text was which R. Akiba fixed, it was still somewhat different from the Masoretic texts in use today. For example, in the Talmudic discussion noted above concerning the proper number of compartments in tefillin, the argument of the Rabbis is based on a different text than we have today. "It must be noted that this Talmudic statement does not agree with the Masoretic text, for לטטפות, written *plene,* is not to be found at all in our versions."[33]

Likewise, there is evidence that the Masoretic texts do not always follow what had previously been recognized as the traditional text. "The Haggadah text begins with the text *Avadim Havinu* and includes the phrase *uvizroa netuya* (Deut. 6:21) which is not Masoretic but accords with the Septuagint. Likewise the wise son asks (in all texts up to the 13th century) *Ma haeduth* (Deut. 6:20) and includes the word *othanu* in accordance with the Septuagint in opposition to M.T. *ethchem.*"[34]

2) R. Akiba authorized a new Greek translation to replace the Septuagint.

The Septuagint had been universally used throughout the Diaspora for centuries. Greek was the common language of the people. The Greek version of Tanakh was necessary for many, if not most, of the Jews living outside the land of Israel.

Greek was also used in the land. "Palestine was dominated since 333 B.C. by the Greeks and from 63 B.C. by the Romans. This domination was not merely political. Under the Seleucids (198-168 B.C.) Palestine was subjected to a definite propaganda for its Hellenization, and throughout our period it was open to strong Hellenizing influences. Thus it came about that, although the common people spoke Aramaic, Greek was also known at least to the learned, so that Palestine was bilingual. Greek terms were used to designate such essentially Jewish institutions as the Sanhedrin, and it has been claimed that more than 1100 Greek terms are used in the Talmud."[35] "Synagogue" is also a Greek word.

An additional factor to consider is that the *Talmidei Yeshua* often cited the Septuagint in their proclamation of Yeshua as the Messiah. As we will see in greater detail later, R. Akiba struggled intently and intensely to overcome the alternative they presented to rabbinic authority.

Ginzberg maintains that, "To the same motive underlying his [Akiba's] antagonism to the Apocrypha, namely, the desire to disarm Christians - especially Jewish Christians - who drew their 'proofs' from the Apocrypha, must also be attributed his wish to emancipate the Jews of the Dispersion from the domination of the Septuagint, the errors and inaccuracies in which frequently distorted the true meaning of Scripture, and were even used as arguments against the Jews by the Christians. Aquila was a man after Akiba's own heart; under Akiba's guidance, he gave the Greek-speaking Jews a rabbinical Bible (Jerome on Isa.viii.14, Yer. Kid. i.59a)...thus Judaizing the Bible, as it were, in opposition to the Christians."[36]

Though Ginzberg is probably correct in his estimation of Akiba's motivation, his phrasing of the issue is inaccurate. First, from our perspective today, we can speak of errors and inaccuracies in the Septuagint, but that is because we have had (almost) a fixed, standardized text for many centuries. That was not the case in the first century. There were many variants in circulation in the first century, and no "received text" by which to judge all the others. There was no accepted standard by which to judge the Septuagint, or any other version. In fact, the Septuagint was probably the text used by more Jews than any other.

Second, there is reason to believe that in some cases the Septuagint is more accurate than the Masoretic. Orlinsky points out, as an example, "the Septuagint of Samuel...not only fails to coincide with our preserved, so-called masoretic text, but is often clearly superior to it."[37] As previously noted, the traditional Haggadda agrees with the Septuagint, not the Masoretic.

Third, whatever arguments took place before the Bar Kokhba Revolt - such as those recorded in the "New Testament" and the Talmud - they were basically between Jews and Jews. Both the *Talmidei Yeshua* and the *Rabbanim v'Talmideihon* (the Rabbis and their disciples) claimed to be "the true Jews." So did the Qumran community. The issue then was not what eighteen and a half centuries of history have made it today.

Fourth, if Aquila did produce "a rabbinical Bible," it differed from all the previous texts. The previous texts were all written before there were rabbis. Aquila's, or Akiba's, version, was not more "Jewish" than the other texts, for they were all written and used by Jews. Aquila's version would simply have been one newly produced to support the teachings of his own particular sect. As Ginzberg pointed out, it was Akiba's idea, and "A careful examination of the translation...shows that it follows Akiba's exegesis."[38] Akiba's exegesis did not follow the text of Tanakh.

3) R. Akiba authorized a new Targum of the Scriptures.

The Jews living in the land in the first century did not readily understand the ancient Hebrew of Tanakh. Even in the time of Ezra, it had been necessary to explain the language of Torah to the people.[39]

The purpose of a written Targum was to give the people the sense of the text in their own contemporary language. Paraphrasing the old language in the new required a certain amount of interpretation. Such interpretation also provided an opportunity to push a certain perspective.

"The standard Aramaic translation of the Pentateuch, Targum Onkelos, invariably reflects Akiba's halakhic rulings."[40] Akiba's halakhic rulings do not follow the Biblical text.

So while we do not have all the necessary before-and-after documents to accurately gauge the extent of Akiba's influence on the text of Tanakh, it is fair to say that it was significant. To some extent, he fixed the canon and most likely "standardized" the Hebrew text itself. He authorized a new Greek translation and a new Aramaic Targum of his own text. In whatever language a Jew read or heard the Scriptures, he would be hearing from Akiba.

11. TALMUDIC REVISIONISM

"'Who controls the past,' ran the Party slogan, 'controls the future: who controls the present controls the past.'"[1]

Fixing the canon, "standardizing" the text, and authorizing new translations for both those in the land and those in Diaspora provided mechanical ways of affecting what Israel would read in Tanakh. These were powerful but limited ways.

The problem was immense. The Rabbis, their disciples, and their authority were not found in the text of Tanakh. They did not exist during the times when Tanakh was written. To establish and authorize the Rabbis as rulers in Israel, it was necessary to revise the way that Israel understood the text. It was necessary to read rabbinic authority back into Tanakh.

There was a need for a powerful way, unlimited in scope and effect, to change the evidence against rabbinic authority. R. Akiba's method of interpretation provided the key. Talmudic revisionism did the rest.

Revisionism does not change the text, it changes the way the text is perceived. It is like placing an optical lens between the reader and the text. The lens refracts and/or colors the textual image that reaches the mind and heart. Once the lens is implanted, EVERYTHING must pass through it.

The one who looks through the lens thinks that everything he sees is in the text. He does not know that the lens is there. In fact, if the lens were to be taken away, he would think that the true image he is seeing is a gross distortion.

There is such a lens in the Talmud. Talmudic revisionism places the Rabbis, and especially R. Akiba, in the forefront of all of God's activity from the time of Adam on.

The People in the Bible

Through this rabbinic lens, everyone in Tanakh is always thinking about the Rabbis and their ordinances. They are read into every situation. A seemingly straightforward verse that introduces the descendants of Adam to the time of Noah is turned into Adam's exaltaltion of the uniqueness of R. Akiba and his learning.

"What is the meaning of the verse, 'This is the book of the generations of Adam?' It is to intimate that the Holy One, blessed be He, showed him [Adam] every generation and its thinkers, every generation and its sages. When he came to the generation of Rabbi Akiba, he [Adam] rejoiced at his learning but was grieved at his death, and said: How weighty are Thy friends to me, O

God."[2]

All of God's work from Creation on is said to have reached its glory in Akiba. The descendants of Noah after the flood are said to have studied the rabbinic writings. "What does [the name] *Babel* connote? — R. Johanan answered: [That the study of] Scripture, Mishnah and Talmud was intermingled [therein]."[3]

At the time of the Tower of Babel, the "Scripture" could only have consisted of the first 10 chapters of Genesis. Nothing else had happened yet. Abraham was not born. Moses would not be born for another 600 years. It would be 700 years before the covenant of the Law was given at Sinai. It would be more than 2000 years before the first rabbi appeared.

What Mishnah and Talmud (i.e. Gemara) could there have been? If it was given at Sinai seven centuries later, how could it have been orally handed down backwards from Moses? Who among that generation which rebelled against God at Babel would have been studying it? The revisionist effort makes no sense in terms of the text, but it does serve to redirect Israel's focus to rabbinic teaching.

An ordinary plural is said to reveal Abraham's obedience to rabbinic decrees. We have already encountered the statement in Yoma 28b: "Raba or R. Ashi said: Abraham, our father, kept even the law concerning the *'erub* of the dishes,' as it is said: 'My Torahs': one being the written Torah, the other the oral Torah."[4]

Even the rabbinic academy was inserted into the time of Abraham. "Eliezer, the servant of Abraham was an elder and a member of the scholars' council, as it is said: And Abraham said unto his servant, the elder of his house, that ruled over all he had, which R. Eleazar explained to mean that he ruled over [knew, controlled] the Torah of his master."[5]

Moses and the prophets were continually created anew in the image of the Rabbis. "The Rabbis did not consider the Pharisees as a new group but as the successors of the prophets. For them Moses and the Israelites were followers of Pharisaism even if they did not use the term. They referred to Moses as 'our Rabbi' completely blurring any distinction in the Judaism of the bible and that of their own day."[6]

Biblical heroes were changed into rabbinic disciples. "David exclaimed before the Holy One, blessed be He, 'Sovereign of the Universe! Thou knowest full well that had they torn my flesh, my blood would not have poured forth to the earth. Moreover, when they are engaged in studying "Leprosies" and "Tents" they jeer at me, saying, *"David! what is the death penalty of him who seduces a married woman?"* I reply to them, *"He is executed by strangulation, yet has he a portion in the world to come. But he who publicly puts his neighbour to shame has no portion in the world to come."'* "7

"David represented the Messianic model. The Rabbis transferred the personality of David to that of a veritable Pharisee of Pharisees."[8]

We are told that other kings besides David held the Rabbis in great esteem. *"'He honoureth them that fear the Lord;'* that was Jehoshaphat king of Judah, who every time he beheld a scholar-disciple rose from his throne, and embraced and kissed him, calling him 'Father, Father; Rabbi, Rabbi; *Mari, Mari!'"*[9] "*Mari* is the Aramaic equivalent of Rabbi, my Master or lord."[10]

We are told that the prophets also were greatly attracted to the teaching of the Rabbis. "Elijah used to frequent Rabbi's academy."[11]

The Talmud claims that long before Alexander and the Greeks, the Sanhedrin was supreme. *"For Mordecai the Jew was next unto king Ahasuerus, and great among the Jews and accepted of the majority of his brethren*. Of the majority of his brethren but not of all his brethren; this informs us that some members of the Sanhedrin separated from him."[12]

"For Esther did the commandment of Mordecai. R. Jeremiah said: [This means] that she used to show the blood of her impurity to the Sages."[13]

Just as the Rabbis revised the past, so they revised the future. "Even of more relevance to the Rabbis was the role of the Messiah as Pharisee par excellence. He would unravel their problems and interpret Biblical verses with clarity and precision."[14] When Messiah came, he would come in their image and likeness.

The Teachings of the Bible

In a similar way, the Rabbis approached the teachings of the Scriptures. They wrote themselves in wherever they could. "Our Rabbis taught: *Justice, justice shalt thou follow*: this means, Follow the scholars to their academies."[15]

"Rab Judah said in Rab's name: What is meant by, *Touch not mine anointed, and do my prophets no harm*? Touch not mine anointed' refers to school children; 'and do my prophets no harm', to disciples of the Sages."[16]

They found hidden references to the whole range of their teachings. "Resh Lakish said, What is meant by the verse, *and there shall be faith in thy times, strength, salvation, wisdom and knowledge*? 'Faith' refers to the Order of Seeds; thy times, the Order of Festivals; strength, the Order of Women; salvation, the Order of Nezikin; wisdom, the Order of Sacrifices; and knowledge, to the Order of

Purity."[17]

"He hath made me to dwell in dark places like those that have been long dead. [Lam.3:6] This, said R. Jeremiah, refers to the Babylonian Talmud."[18]

"And R. Judah? - [Scripture states:] *According to the Torah which they shall teach thee*, intimating that both the Torah and their [the Scribes'] teaching must be involved."[19]

This revisionism developed to such a point that the Midrash Rabbah claimed Scriptural proof that all that the Rabbis had decreed, and all that they and their disciples might one day decree, was all sanctioned in the Scriptures. To make the claim, Akiba's method of attaching immense importance to a single Hebrew letter was used.

"R. Nehemiah expounded: '*And the superfluities of the earth are included*' [Eccl.v,8] means that even things which appear to you additions to the actual Revelation - for example, the laws of fringes, of phylacteries and of *mezuzah* - are also included in the Revelation, as may be inferred from the fact that it says, *And the Lord delivered unto me the two tables of stone written with the finger of God; and on them was written according to all the words* (Deut. IX,10). R. Joshua b. Levi explained: It says, '*On them...according to all* (kekol) *the words* (haddebarim),' and it is also written, *All* (kol) *the commandments* (hammizwah) *which I command thee* (ib. VIII,1). Instead of the expression *kol* the expression '*kekol*' is used, instead of *debarim*, '*hadebbarim*' is used, implying that Scripture, Mishnah, *Halachoth*, Talmud, *Tosefoth, Haggadoth*, and even what a faithful disciple would in the future say in the presence of his master, were all communicated to Moses on Sinai; for it says, *Is there a thing whereof it is said: See, this is new* (Eccl. I,10)? and the other part of the verse provides the reply to this: *It hath been already* (ib.)."[20]

Ultimately, the Rabbis taught that Torah itself recognized the indispensable superiority of halakha. (cf. Baba Metzia 33a) They taught that God would have destroyed Israel for rejecting the Oral Law.[21] They considered rejecting the Oral Law to be the same as rejecting God. [page 76 correction]

the true God".

The God of the Bible

Even God Himself is transformed by the Rabbis and placed under their authority. He is depicted in the image and likeness of the Rabbis: "God keeps the commandments of the Torah, written and oral. T.B. Rosh ha-Shanah 17b depicts God in His Tallith prayer-shawl teaching Moses the order of the prayers.

"T.B. Sanh. 39a tells how God, after burying Moses, became defiled and purified Himself, not with water, but by fire. God kept the first Sabbath (Pirke de R. Eliezer, ch. XIX). God wears phylacteries (T.B. Ber.7a). In the T.B. 'Abodah Zarah 3b Rab shows how God occupies Himself every day. He studies Torah; He judges the world; He feeds all living things from the smallest to the biggest; He plays with leviathan. In T.B. Ber. 8a the opinion was expressed by R. Hiyya bar Abba that since the destruction of the Temple there is only 4 cubits [72 inches] of the *Halakah* left to God. In Gen. R. LXIV 4 R. Berekiah gave the teaching of R. Judah b. Ezekiel that there is no day without a new teaching (on the Law) produced by God in His Beth ha-Midrash [House of Study/Commentary] in Heaven. In T.B. Gittin 6b R. Abiathar and R. Jonathan gave different interpretations of Jud. 19:2 (the concubine of Gibeah). R. Abiathar met Elijah and enquired of him what God was doing then. Elijah told him that God was studying the subject of the concubine of Gibeah. On being asked what God said about it, Elijah reported: 'He (God) says: "My son Abiathar says so, and My son Jonathan says so."' 'What!' exclaimed the other, 'Is there any doubt with Heaven (God)!' 'No,' said Elijah, but both utter the words of the living God.' "[22]

As Talmudically revised, God Himself studies the teachings of the Rabbis, for sometimes they are wiser than He. He is *"Ribbono shel Olam,"* the Master or Rabbi of the world. But as *"Ribbono shel Olam,"* God is only one rabbi among many. In matters of *halakha*, He must follow the majority. He submits to them, and learns from them.

Each day he learns something new about the Law He has given. Apparently He is not omniscient.

The teaching that God was defiled is a monumental departure from "Holy, holy, holy is the Lord of hosts...."[23] In this revision, God Himself is no longer the standard of holiness. There is an external standard to which He must submit.

None of these claims for rabbinic authority can be seen in the text of Tanakh without the revisionist lens. Where even that is not sufficient, the rabbinic teaching becomes a tradition which is granted equal authority with Torah. Even more, whereas Torah is limited to what the Rabbis say it says, their teaching has no limits. Talmudic revisionism is the means by which the Rabbis attain the legitimacy and authority that Scripture denies them, but that only Scripture can bestow.

Replacement and Substitution

Another important aspect of Talmudic Revisionism is the consistent pattern of replacement and substitution. Rabbinic practices and decrees were substituted for Biblical ones. Usually these were related to the void created by the destruction of the Temple and the cessation of the sacrifices. Where would Israel find atonement?

The Rabbis presented numerous alternative means of atonement. Among them were circumcision, exile, death, burial, and giving to the Rabbis. Even hospitality was said to bring atonement. Looking to the description of the future Temple presented in Ezekiel, R. Johanan and Resh Lakish noted the proximity of the altar and the table. From this they concluded: "At the time when the Temple stood, the altar used to make atonement for a person; now a person's table makes atonement for him."[24]

The most prominent substitutes were study and prayer. "R. Huna said: 'If you study the laws about sacrifice, that is to me as if you had offered them.'"[25] "Whoever occupies himself with the study of the torah needs no burnt offering nor sin-offering, no meal offering nor guilt offering."[26]

Reading the scriptures on sacrifices was equivalent to offering the sacrifices. "R. Jacob b. Aha said in the name of R. Assi;...Abraham then continued: Master of the Universe! This holds good whilst the Temple remains in being, but when the Temple will no longer be what will become of them? (God) replied: I have already long ago provided for them in the Torah the order of sacrifices and whenever they read it I will deem it as if they had offered them before me and I will grant them pardon for all their iniquities."[27]

The atoning nature of rabbinically ordained prayer was said both to have originated in the earliest beginnings of the Jewish people and also to have begun almost 2000 years later. "R. Jose son of R. Hanina said: The Tefillahs [the 3 daily times of prayer] were instituted by the Patriarchs. R. Joshua b. Levi says: The Tefillahs were instituted to replace the daily sacrifices. It has been taught in accordance with R. Jose b. Hanina, and it has been taught in accordance with R. Joshua b. Levi. It has been taught in accordance with R. Jose b. Hanina: Abraham instituted the morning Tefillah...Isaac instituted the afternoon Tefillah...Jacob instituted the evening prayer..."[28]

The daily sacrifices began to be offered when the covenant at Sinai was given. That was several centuries after the Patriarchs. The daily sacrifices ceased after the destruction of the First Temple and then again after the destruction of the Second. If the Patriarchs instituted the times of prayer, they could not have instituted them to replace the daily sacrifices. The daily sacrifices had not yet been offered for the first time.

Daniel did pray three times a day[29], and it is certainly possible that others did as well. So the practice may have been quite old. According to Abraham Idelsohn, "These three services were made obligatory in the Adademy at Jamnia, ca. 100 C.E."[30] Whatever the case of their origin may be, there is no implication that Daniel's prayers, or those of anyone else, replaced the sacrifices.

Additionally, there were only two daily offerings in the Temple. The commandment was, "Prepare one lamb in the morning and the other between the two evenings."[31] The time of evening prayer could not have been a substitute for the evening sacrifice, "for there was no corresponding evening offering. It is for this reason that the obligatory status of this worship service was always questionable and a matter of dispute."[32]

Other times of rabbinically prescribed prayer were also substituted for the Temple sacrifices. "R. Hisda said in Mar 'Ukba's name: He who prays on the eve of the Sabbath and recites 'and [the heaven and the earth] were finished', the two ministering angels who accompany man place their hands on his head and say to him, *and thine iniquity is taken away, and thy sin purged.*"[33]

The rabbinic house of study became a substitute for the Temple.[34] For this form of atonement, the Rabbis replaced the priests.

"The pursuit of scholarship, in fact, possesses the power to induce supernatural redemption - particularly when allied with other forms of communal service. Hence: 'If a man occupies himself with the study of the torah, works of charity, and prays with the community', says God, 'I account it to him as if he had redeemed Me and My children from among the nations of the world' (TB Berakhot 8a). In an extended sense, popular study could even be described as a form of atonement."[35]

More than that, simply attributing a rabbinic teaching to its proper author could do what all the sacrifices of the Temple had no power to do. "He who quotes a statement by name brings redemption to the world."[36]

12. UPROOTING THE SCRIPTURES

Sometimes, the Rabbis were unable to read their teachings into the Scriptures by any means. So they simply annulled the decrees of Torah.

The most well-known instance of this concerns the *"prosbul."* "The *prosbul* was a deed whereby a creditor transferred his debts to the Beth din, which were then regarded as though already collected from the debtor, so that the seventh year did not cancel them. This was done only if the debtor possessed land."[1]

The Torah says, "At the end of every seven years you must cancel debts. This is how it is to be done: Every creditor shall cancel the loan he has made to his fellow Israelite. He shall not require payment from his fellow Israelite or brother, because the LORD's time for canceling debts has been proclaimed....Be careful not to harbor this wicked thought: 'The seventh year, the year for canceling debts, is near,' so that you do not show ill will toward your needy brother and give him nothing. He may then appeal to the LORD against you, and you will be found guilty of sin."[2]

"Hillel instituted the *prosbul*....For he saw that people were unwilling to lend money to one another and disregarded the precept laid down in the Torah. *Beware that there be not a base thought in thine heart saying*, etc. He therefore decided to institute the prosbul."[3]

Apparently, in the time of Hillel, poor Israelites were unable to attain needed loans before the Sabbatical year, because their better-off brothers were not obeying the Torah, not fearing that the Lord would find them "guilty of sin." Hillel reasoned that, because of the people's disobedience, annulling the Torah would produce a greater good than following it.

Some would agree. Others would not. What matters here is the rabbinic claim of authority to annul the Law. Where did Hillel get the authority to annul this part of Torah?

Hillel was not the only one. Annulling, or "uprooting," a Biblical law is an essential component of the rabbinic system.

Herbert Basser said that, "The medieval Tosafists showed how radical the Rabbis were. For social and political reasons they alleviated many problems by subtly contravening Biblical law. They only resorted to such methods if the prohibited act could be made to 'appear legal'. The Gospels are not altogether wrong in claiming the Pharisees breached Biblical law by appeal to certain 'traditions' of the fathers. The Talmud also admits that *halakha* uprooted some Biblical laws and the implication is certain that non-Biblical practices were current in Pharisaic times."[4]

"In many instances where greater transgressions were to be prevented, or for the sake of the glory of God, or the honor of man, certain Mosaic laws were abrogated or temporarily dispensed with by the Rabbis (Mishnah Ber. ix.5, 54a, 63a; Yoma 69a; compare also Yeb. 90b)."[5]

There are numerous other cases recorded and discussed in the Talmud where this rabbinic authority to "uproot" and overthrow the Torah is asserted.

"Cannot the Beth din lay down a condition which would cause the abrogation of a law of the Torah?...At all events it was here stated, 'He is entitled to be her heir'; but, surely, by Pentateuchal law it is her father who should here be her legal heir, and yet it is the husband who is heir in accordance with a Rabbinical ordinance!

"...'*He may defile himself for her*'. But, surely, by Pentateuchal law it is her father who may here defile himself for her, and yet it is the husband who by a Rabbinical law was allowed to defile himself for her!"[6]

These examples are followed by a discussion of other cases where, because rabbinic law conflicted with that of Torah, the Rabbis simply annulled the Torah. "Now, according to Pentateuchal law, it is here undoubtedly accepted...and yet the Rabbis ruled that 'it is not accepted'."[7]

"Where a man remarried his divorced wife after she had been married, she and her rival are to perform *halizah*."[8] The Torah explicitly forbids a man to remarry his wife after she has remarried.[9] The Rabbis permitted what the Torah forbid, and then enacted conditions for the forbidden act.

"When murderers multiplied, the ceremony of breaking a heifer's neck was discontinued....When adulterers multiplied, the ceremony of the bitter waters was discontinued..."[10]

Jonathan Sacks summed up some of the different categories that the Rabbis used for annulling the laws of Scripture: "Another set of concepts, which include *horaat shaah* (a temporary decision), *le-migdar milta* (to improve a particular matter), *laasot seyag la Torah* (to create a protective boundary for the Torah), and *eit laasot la-Shem* (a time to act for God), concern the relationship of *halakha* to time: specifically to unusual circumstances. Here policy overrides principle. An act or rule that could not normally be mandated is permitted on consequentialist grounds. In exceptional circumstances, the consequences of temporarily suspending a rule are overwhelmingly more beneficial within the terms of the halakhic system than those of maintaining it. In such cases, its temporary suspension may be justified. These are the cases to which *horaat shaah* are directed."[11]

When they deemed it necessary, the Rabbis altered, suspended, or overruled the Torah. In the principle of *keivan*, "the sages have the power to uproot something from the Written Law by reference to a similar category."[12] "[T]he principle of *'lo plug'* is a patent excuse for uprooting."[13]

The Jewish Encyclopedia defines "Rabbinical Authority" as "The power or right of deciding the Law, in dubious cases, or of interpreting, modifying, or amplifying, and occasionally of abrogating it, as vested in the Rabbis as its teachers and expounders."[14]

This power or right belonged to the Rabbis alone. As for anyone else, even a prophet, who dared to uproot the written Law, "Our Rabbis taught: If one prophesies so as to eradicate a law of the Torah, he is liable (to death)...If one prophesies so as to uproot a law of the Torah, all agree that he is strangled...If one prophesies to uproot an injunction of the Torah, whether idolatry or any other precept, he is liable...."[15]

What then is the source of rabbinic authority to annul the Torah? "Rab maintains that...**the Sages have imparted to their enactments the same force as that of Pentateuchal laws.**"[16]

The Rabbis are the source of their own authority to annul the Torah. They gave this power to themselves. They gave to their own laws the same binding power as the laws of Torah. Actually, they ascribed greater authority to their own laws than to the laws of Torah, for they claimed that their laws took precedence over what is written in Torah.[17]

Baumgarten summed up the Talmudic position: "'Wherever a man makes a condition which is contrary to what is written in the Torah, his condition is null and void,' [Kid.19b] but not wherever a Rabbinic scholar makes such a condition."[18] The Rabbis could establish conditions and practices that contradicted and even nullified the Torah.

According to the Rabbis, God Himself would obey whatever they decided. Related to the issue of the inaccurate announcement of the new moon which we looked at earlier is the claim that, "Heaven itself yields to the authority of the earthly court of justice as to the fixing of the calendar and the festival days."[19] Setting the dates of the calendar, which regulated personal and national life, was of major importance.

"Though there were probably several reasons why the original priestly members of the Qumran sect left the temple community in Jerusalem, the group's literature permits one to isolate a calendrical dispute as one of the most significant factors. In this respect the Essenes resembled many other Jewish dissident movements from the time of Jeroboam I to the Middle Ages. The system of festivals in Judaism involves all adherents of the faith; the cultic calendar is therefore an important practical as well as theoretical matter. Control of it was essential, during the second-temple period, for any group or person who desired to wield supreme religious authority in the community."[20]

In every area of life, one had to be more careful to obey rabbinic law than to obey Torah. As the Talmud says, "The sages have applied to their enactments higher restrictions than to those of the Torah."[21] "In truth, it is Rabbinical, but the Sages made their law even stricter than Scripture."[22]

"There is greater stringency in respect to the teachings of the scribes than in respect to the Torah. (Thus,) if one (a rebellious elder) says, there is no precept of tefillin, so that a Biblical law may be transgressed, he is exempt. (But if he rules that the tefillin must contain) five compartments, thus adding to the words of the Scribes, he is liable [to death]."[23]

The Rabbis claimed the sanction of Torah for whatever they decreed, even if it was the uprooting of Torah. "R. Yohanan and R. Yudan b. R. Simeon [had a dispute over the proper interpretation of Exod. 34:27]: One of them said, 'If you observe [laws that are transmitted] orally and if you observe [laws that are transmitted] in writing, I shall establish a covenant with you. But if not, I shall not establish a covenant with you.' [According to this view, the two types of laws are of equal weight.] The other said, '[My covenant is established with you because of these orally transmitted words.] [But] if you not only observe that which is transmitted orally, but also uphold that which is transmitted in writing, [then in addition to the covenant,] you will receive a reward. But if not, you will receive no reward.' [According to this view, the laws transmitted orally are more weighty, because their observance leads to the establishment of God's covenant.]"[24]

This was more than the assertion of a different "religious" system. The Torah governs every aspect of the life of Israel. By governing the Torah, the Rabbis would govern Israel.

This applied to the most intimate of relationships and to the most indispensable of activities. "In matrimonial matters the principle adopted is that, since marriages are, as a rule, contracted in accordance with the rabbinical statutes, the Rabbis have the right to annul any marriage which is not in conformity with their ruling (Yeb.90b). In money matters the Rabbis claimed the same right of confiscation in cases when their ruling was disregarded as was exercised by Ezra (see Ezra x.8; Git.36b)."[26]

The objective was to bring Israel under the rule of the Rabbis.

If the Scriptures stood in the way, the Scriptures had to be uprooted.

"R. Hanina once sat in the presence of R. Jannai when he stated: The *halachah* is in agreement with R. Eleazar b. Azariah. [The Master] said to him, 'Go out, read your Biblical verses outside; the *halachah* is not in agreement with R. Eleazar b. Azariah'."[27]

R. Jannai was being threatened with excommunication. He was being told, 'If you and your Scriptures are unwilling to submit to the decision of the Rabbis, then take them and be cut off from Israel.'

13. A FENCE AROUND THE TORAH

"Moses received the Torah at Sinai and transmitted it to Joshua, Joshua to the elders, and the elders to the prophets, and the prophets to the men of the Great Synagogue.
"The latter used to say...make a fence round the Torah." Aboth 1.1

The Third Talmudic Claim: The oral law is a fence around the written Torah.

Why does the Torah need a fence around it? Because "The Torah is conceived as a garden and its precepts as precious plants. Such a garden is fenced round for the purpose of obviating wilful or even unintended damage. Likewise, the precepts of the Torah were to be 'fenced' round with additional inhibitions that should have the effect of preserving the original commandments from trespass."[1]

This explanation is affirmed in different places in the Talmud, e.g. "The Rabbis erected a safeguard for a Scriptural law."[2] "R.Eliezer b. Jacob said: I have heard that the Beth Din may impose flagellation and pronounce [death] sentences even where not [warranted] by the Torah; yet not with the intention of disregarding the Torah but to make a fence around it."[3] Though the actions of the Rabbis are not sanctioned by the Torah, they are done to protect the Torah.

This is the common understanding of how the Oral Law serves as a fence around the Torah, but there is a serious problem with it. The Rabbis were not seeking to "preserve the original commandments from trespass." Had they done that, they and their laws would have been left without any authority. After all, the original commandments did not authorize the Rabbis to build a fence or do anything else.

There was a radical and irreconcilable conflict between the Torah and the Rabbis as to the basis and structure of authority, as well as its source and administration. That is why the Rabbis gave themselves the right to alter, revise, trespass, and uproot the original commandments.

Nevertheless, there is a real sense in which the Oral Law is a fence around the Torah, a fence that serves a different purpose. Robert Frost speaks to the point in his poem, "Mending Wall:"

"Before I built a wall I'd ask to know
What I was walling in or walling out,
And to whom I was like to give offense."

A fence protects by restricting access. What it surrounds can only be seen through the fence or approached by permission of the owner. When something is fenced in, someone is fenced out.

To obscure the fact that they had no Biblical authority, the Rabbis built a fence around Torah. The fence both obscures Torah and keeps the people from Torah. "Our Rabbis taught: They who occupy themselves with the Bible are but of indifferent merit; with Mishnah, are indeed meritorious, and are rewarded for it; with Gemara — there can be nothing more meritorious; yet run always to the Mishnah more than to the Gemara."[4]

Studying the Bible was said to be of no great importance. Studying the rabbinic writings brought great reward. Israel was told to trust in the Rabbis.

Above all, a fence indicates ownership. The Talmud explains that erecting a fence is a means of asserting ownership over something one didn't own before.

"In the case, however, where land is presented as a gift, or of brothers dividing an inheritance, or of one who seizes the property of a proselyte, ownership can be claimed as soon as the first step has been taken towards making a door or a fence or an opening."[5] "If he does anything at all in the way of setting up a door or making a fence or an opening, this constitutes a title of ownership."[6]

This Talmudic portion is followed by a section discussing what actions constitute 'taking possession' of a particular piece of property. One means for taking possession is to increase the height of a fence. "If a man raises a fence already existing to ten handbreadths, ...this constitutes effective occupation."[7]

"R. Akiba said:...Tradition is a fence to the Torah.'"[8] In saying this, Akiba agreed with Josephus and the gospels, though their view of placing torah behind tradition was negative. The contemporary sources indicate that the appearance of "tradition" before Akiba was as a small fence with great gaps in it.

That allowed too much free access. "The All Merciful taught Moses thus: 'Thou must not allow the greater part of a fence to consist of gaps'. R. Huna the son of R. Joshua ruled, 'it is forbidden for it is this that the All Merciful taught Moses: 'Its greater part [must be] fence'."[9] Akiba raised the fence and closed the gaps to assert ownership of the Torah, according to the rabbinic principle of *labud*. [10]

R. Akiba sought to fence the people off from the Torah and from all other influences that would have challenged rabbinic interpretation and authority.[11] In the system he erected, no one else had the right to interpret Torah. Not the *am ha'aretz*, nor the priests, nor the prophets, nor the Sadducees, the Qumran Covenanters, the *Talmidei Yeshua*, nor anyone else. Not even God.

This was the continuing theme of the rabbinic writings. "The apologetic function of the midrash is not only to denigrate the translation of Scripture, but to establish *the* exclusive authority of the Pharisaic tradition as the legitimate recipient and interpretation of divine revelation."[12]

Only the Rabbis could give the authorized interpretation. Who said so? They themselves. As a fence, the Oral Law is a means to assert and entrench rabbinic hegemony. Without it, nothing needs rabbinic approval. With it, everything does.

Adversaries

14. CONFLICT WITH THE PRIESTS: BACKGROUND

Torah Judaism is a priestly religion. The Temple in Jerusalem, where the priests performed their office, was the center of religious and civil life. Every male of age was required to come to the Temple on three occasions every year, or be cut off from his people. Everyone was required to support, through their tithes and offerings, the ministry of the priests and the Levites in the Temple.

The priests, however, like everyone else, were not always what they were supposed to be. During the time preceding the Babylonian exile, the priesthood was particularly corrupt.

Jeremiah grieved that, "From the least to the greatest, all are greedy for gain; prophets and priests alike, all practice deceit."[1] "The prophets prophesy lies, the priests rule by their own authority, and my people love it this way. But what will you do in the end?"[2]

The Lord told Ezekiel of the iniquity of Jerusalem: "Her priests do violence to My law and profane My holy things; they do not distinguish between the holy and the common; they teach that there is no difference between the unclean and the clean; and they shut their eyes to the keeping of My Sabbaths, so that I am profaned among them."[3]

Consequently, Jerusalem and the First Temple were destroyed, "because of the sins of her prophets and the iniquities of her priests, who shed within her the blood of the righteous."[4] The destruction of the First Temple became the archetypal symbol of the failure of the priests.

2 Baruch, written after the destruction of the second Temple, looked back at the fall of the first. "You, priests, take the keys of the sanctuary, and cast them to the highest heaven and give them to the Lord and say, 'Guard your house yourself, because, behold, we have been found to be false stewards.'"[5]

This was later echoed and embellished in the Talmud: "Our Rabbis have taught: When the First Temple was about to be destroyed, bands upon bands of young priests with the keys of the Temple in their hands assembled and mounted the roof of the Temple and exclaimed, 'Master of the Universe, as we did not have the merit to be faithful treasurers these keys are handed back into Thy keeping.' They then threw the keys up towards heaven.

And there emerged the figure of a hand and received the keys from them. Whereupon they jumped and fell into the fire."[6]

The destruction of the First Temple, followed by the Babylonian exile, put the priests out of their element. With no Temple, they were unable to fully perform their ministry. After 70 years of Babylonian captivity, a remnant of Jews returned to the land of Israel and sought to rebuild the Temple.

When that was accomplished, Nehemiah records that the people joined "with their kinsmen, their nobles, and are taking upon themselves a curse and an oath to walk in God's law, which was given through Moses, God's servant, and to keep and to observe all the commandments of God our Lord, and His ordinances and His statutes..."[7] Almost all the conditions of this covenant into which the people entered concern the support of the Temple, the priests, and the Levites, who helped the priests.

With the rebuilding of the Temple, and the faithful tithing of the people, the priests were able to resume their duties. Unfortunately, they also resumed the neglect of their duties. It was not long before Malachi delivered the rebuke of the Lord.

"'A son honors his father, and a servant his master. If I am a father, where is the honor due Me? If I am a master, where is the respect due Me?' says the LORD Almighty. 'It is you, O priests, who show contempt for My name. But you ask, *How have we shown contempt for Your name?*...'Oh, that one of you would shut the temple doors, so that you would not light useless fires on My altar! I am not pleased with you,' says the LORD Almighty, 'and I will accept no offering from your hands.'"[8]

The centuries that followed did not witness a change for the better. From the Babylonian exile to the Bar Kokhba Rebellion, except for a century of chaotic Hasmonean rule, Israel was governed by foreign powers. Those foreign powers installed subservient local rulers who would serve the purposes of the empire. Consequently, the people could no longer look to civil governmental institutions as the locus for national identity.[9]

The foreign empires sought to control the national priesthood to reduce the likelihood of revolt. They often appointed the High Priest, choosing one who would serve their interests.[10]

During the century of Hasmonean rule, the priests resumed their position of national authority. They competed with the kings for political control. "The Hasmonean high priests increasingly became political figures and were acknowledged as such by many powers, both in the region and outside it."[11]

Sometimes a leader such as Aristobulus would seek to hold both the kingship and the High Priesthood. "He knew perfectly well, like many political figures later, that control of the Temple and its priests who practiced the daily cult meant control of the nation."[12]

The Romans made Herod the Great King of Judea, and reduced the political role of the priesthood.[13] A priesthood and temple that had only "religious" meaning did not threaten Roman dominion.[14] Like the previous empires, however, Rome knew that a subservient high priest would play an important role in keeping the people quiescent.

"The high priesthood, which had been abused for a long time, was frequently held by people who were thieves such as Jason and Menelaus, and was not given to the legitimate Zadokite house already from Hasmonean times. The position was granted to people as a reward for certain deeds by Herod, his successors, and the Romans."[15]

By the time of the Great Revolt, there was widespread dissatisfaction with the conduct of some of the priests, and especially the High Priestly families. On this, the Talmud, Josephus, and the gospels agree. These High Priests are described as violent, greedy, gluttonous men; and the cause, at least partially, of the destruction of Jerusalem in the Great Revolt.

The Talmud speaks of how the High Priests robbed the common priests of their due, and disregarded all appeals to restrain themselves. For example, the skins of the animals sacrificed at the Temple were traditionally divided among all the priests who served. These particular high priests violently took all the skins for themselves, depriving the common priests of a significant part of their livelihood.

They were entreated to consider the needs of others, "Yet the chief priests still seized (them) by force...Abba Saul b. Bothnith said in the Name of Abba Joseph b. Hanin: 'Woe is me because of the house of Boethus; woe is me because of their staves! [with which they beat the people.] Woe is me because of the house of Kathros; woe is me because of their pens! [with which they wrote their evil decrees.] Woe is me because of the house of Ishmael the son of Phabi; woe is me because of their fists! For they are High Priests and their sons are Temple treasurers and their sons-in-law are trustees and their servants beat the people with staves!

"Our Rabbis taught: Four cries did the Temple Court cry out. The first: 'Depart hence, ye children of Eli,' for they defiled the Temple of the Lord..."[16]

Eli was the High Priest when Samuel, who later anointed Saul and then David as Israel's kings, was a boy. In this first cry of the Temple Court the Rabbis called the High Priestly families, "children [sons] of Eli." What they meant is clear from the Scriptures. "Now the sons of Eli were worthless men; they did not know the Lord."[17] They robbed the people of their sacrifices, and "they lay with the women who served at the doorway of the tent of meeting."[18]

Josephus remarks, "As for the high priest Ananias, he increased in glory every day, and this to a great degree, and had obtained the favour and esteem of the citizens in a signal manner; for he was a great hoarder up of money: he therefore cultivated the friendship of Albinus, and of the high priest (Jesus), by making them presents; he also had servants who were very wicked, who joined themselves to the boldest sort of the people, and went to the thrashing-floors, and took away the tithes that belonged to the priests by violence, and did not refrain from beating such as would not give these tithes to them. So the other high priests acted in the like manner, as did those his servants, without any one being able to prohibit them; so that (some of the) priests, that of old were wont to be supported with those tithes, died for want of food..."[19]

This High Priestly family enriched themselves through their commerce in the Temple: "This (Temple) market was what in Rabbinic writings is styled 'the bazaars of the sons of Annas' (*Chanuyoth beney Chanan*), the sons of that High-Priest Annas, who is so infamous in New Testament history... From the unrighteousness of the traffic carried on in these Bazaars, and the greed of the owners, the 'Temple-market' was at the time most unpopular. This appears, not only from the conduct and words of the patriarch Simeon [the grandson of Hillel, cf. Ker. i.7] and of Baba ben Buta... [Jerus. Chag. 78a], but from the fact that popular indignation, three years before the destruction of Jerusalem, swept away the Bazaars of the family of Annas, and this, as expressly stated, on account of the sinful greed which characterized their dealings."[20]

The high priestly families joined with the Roman rulers in intrigue and murder, sometimes even in the Temple itself. "Josephus comments that this outrageous behavior was why, in his opinion, 'even God himself, for loathing of their impiety, turned away from our city and, because He deemed the Temple to be no longer a clean dwelling place for Him, brought the Romans upon us and purification by fire upon the city, while He inflicted slavery upon us together, with our wives and children; for He wished to chasten us by these calamities. With such pollution did the deeds of the brigands infect the city'."[21]

The Pharisees, the predecessors of the Rabbis, were major

opponents of the priestly Sadducees. The Talmud records a number of confrontations between the two groups.

On one occasion, the Pharisees deliberately made a priest unclean so that, according to the teaching of the Sadducees, he would be unable to offer the necessary sacrifice.[22] On another, a priest who did not perform the water libation ceremony according to Pharisaic prescriptions was pelted with fruit.[23] In another account, a priest sums up the situation for his son, "My son, although we are Sadducees, we are afraid of the Pharisees."[24]

The Pharisees rejected many of the Temple practices of the Sadducean priests. They had their own traditions concerning the Temple practices.

The Priests and the Empire

Richard Horsley has examined the political role of the high priests under Roman rule, and the dynamics of their position. "[T]he imperial government held the provincial aristocrats accountable not simply for the steady flow of tax revenues but also (under the authority and supervision of the Roman governor) for maintenance of order in their society. This apparently included accountability for breaches of public order by those supposedly under their control - just as a Roman governor was held responsible for outbreaks of disorder in the territory subject to his authority."[25]

"In the years leading up to the Revolt of 66-70, while ostensibly using their authority 'in the interests of order,' the high priests and royalists actually contributed to the breakdown of social order through their own aggressive, even violent, predatory actions....

"The Jewish aristocracy, ostensibly placed in a situation of conflict between representing the Jewish people on the one hand and maintaining the imperial system on the other, appear to have pursued their own political-economic interest as collaborators with the Roman government....

"As the ostensible leaders of the Palestinian Jewish people, the High Priests were supposedly responsible for the guidance and protection of the interests of Jewish society as a whole. But as the leaders of the Jewish aristocracy in particular, they were expected by Rome to control Jewish society in the interest of the imperial order, and they were dependent on Roman power for the maintenance of their own position of power."[26]

"The provincial upper classes were by and large loyal to the imperial regime that guaranteed their own position. The aristocracies apparently preferred to enjoy their wealth and power rather than to risk the drastic penalties they knew would result from any unsuccessful revolt for independence."[27]

They could bring charges to Rome against the appointed governors. Sometimes the governor was recalled. "[I]n the large majority of known cases the accused governors were convicted - or committed suicide before the trial."[28]

The High Priests had position, with a covering of Biblical legitimacy despite their appointment by the Romans. They had power and wealth, and no scruples about using what they had to get what they wanted. They were the natural ruling aristocracy in Israel.

15. THE RABBIS DISPLACE THE PRIESTS

With the destruction of the Second Temple in 70 A.D., the priests were again out of their element. Only this time they encountered competition for their authority. In 70 more years, their authority would be in the hands of the Rabbis.

Throughout the Biblical history of Israel, the kings occasionally instructed the people. The prophets often did. Generally, however, the teaching function was exercised by the priests and Levites.

The Lord said of the faithful priest: "True instruction was in his mouth, and unrighteousness was not found on his lips; he walked with Me in peace and uprightness, and he turned many back from iniquity. For the lips of a priest should preserve knowledge, and men should seek instruction from his mouth; for he is the messenger of the Lord of hosts."[1]

The priest was the one to decide questions of purity and religious law. "They are to teach My people the difference between the holy and the common and show them how to distinguish between the unclean and the clean. In any dispute, the priests are to serve as judges and decide it according to My ordinances. They are to keep My laws and My decrees for all My appointed feasts, and they are to keep My Sabbaths holy."[2]

The Lord rebuked Jerusalem because, "Her priests have done violence to My law and have profaned My holy things; they have made no distinction between the holy and the profane, and they have not taught the difference between the unclean and the clean; and they hide their eyes from My sabbaths, and I am profaned among them."[3] These were priestly functions.

When the Second Temple was destroyed, during Akiba's young adulthood, the religious leaders among the people naturally sought to provide a way for the people to continue their religious life. The Pharisees had an ambitious program.

Rabban Johanan ben Zakkai had been given imperial permission to found an academy at Yavneh. Others in the Jewish community challenged the function and authority of this academy. There arose a dispute concerning Rosh HaShanah, the Biblical Feast of Trumpets and the civil New Year.

The Biblical ordinance is: "Now in the seventh month, on the first day of the month, you shall also have a holy convocation; you shall do no laborious work. It will be to you a day for blowing trumpets."[4] "When convening the assembly, however, you shall blow without sounding an alarm. The priestly sons of Aaron, moreover, shall blow the trumpets; and this shall be for you a perpetual statute throughout your generations."[5]

The dispute that arose concerned the blowing of the trumpets on Rosh HaShanah when it fell on Shabbat. On one side, the *Bene Bathyra* maintained that only the priests in the Temple could blow the trumpets in such a case. The Mishnah says, "If the festive day of New Year fell on a Sabbath, they used to blow the shofar in the Temple but not in the country: After the destruction of the Temple, Rabban Johanan ben Zaccai ordained that it should be blown (on Sabbath) in every place where there was a Beth Din."[6]

The discussion which follows says, "Our Rabbis taught: Once New Year fell on a Sabbath (and all towns assembled), and Rabban Johanan said to the *Bene Bathyra*, 'Let us blow the shofar. They said to him, 'Let us discuss the matter.' He said to them, 'Let us blow and afterwards discuss.' After they had blown they said to him, 'Let us now discuss the question.' He replied: 'The horn has already been heard in Jabneh, and what has been done is no longer open to discussion.'"[7]

The *Bene Bathyra* "were the religious heads of Palestine at the time of [Hillel]."[8] They are praised elsewhere in the Talmud as being exceptionally humble.[9] At Yavneh, they were apparently seeking to maintain the traditional priestly role, regulation, and authority laid out in Torah.

Rabban Johanan ben Zakkai's action and subsequent declaration that the matter was closed were a novel assertion of rabbinic authority in the domain of the priests. He was claiming that the Rabbis, not the priests, had the authority to decide such issues. He had other encounters on this same general issue.

Stuart Cohen examined the conflicts in the revolutionary rabbinic seizure of power from the priests and the king. "More often than not, they were generated by issues which champions of the *keter kehunah* [authority/crown of the priesthood] must conventionally have regarded to fall fair and square within their own domain's terms of reference. Yohanan [ben Zakkai] ...challenged priestly and/or Saducean traditions on the status of rulings handed down by the municipal courts in cases which concerned civil law and commercial transactions (Mishnah, Ketubot 13:1,2); he oppposed them on specific details relevant to the laws of uncleanliness (the *tevul yom*; Tosefta', Parah 3:8) and the precise dating of the Pentecost festival (TB Menahot 65a). He also questioned priestly rights to consume certain parts of the sacred offerings; passed judgement on the validity of certain women to be considered permitted marriage partners for priests (Mishnah, 'Eduyyot 8:3) and insisted on the priestly obligation to pay the Temple dues prescribed in Exodus 30:13 (Mishnah, Sheqalim 1:4).

"Quite as important as the formal substance of those debates is the acerbic tone in which the retrospective records remembered them to have been conducted. Altogether, Yohanan emerges from the relevant sources as a testy personality possessed of both a sharp tongue and an almost volcanic disposition....Moreover, and in order to get his way, he was not above sharp practice and (on at least one occasion, Tosefta', Parah 3:8) physical molestation. Quite apart from greatly embittering relations between the Pharisees and Sadducees, ...at the very least, it served notice of the lengths to which the spokesmen for the former were now prepared to go in order to assert the dominance of their domain over the entire Jewish polity."[10]

"By assuming a prerogative to legislate for the continued performance of actions which had previously been dependent on the sacrificial cult and its timing, Yohanan was in effect heralding a seismic shift in the very axis of Jewish religious observance as well as the auspices under which its practice was to be determined.

"...In effect, he was also proclaiming the right of the *keter torah* [the Rabbis] to legislate for the entire Jewish polity, and not simply for that section of the population which had already accepted the rigours of Pharisaic discipline."[11]

The rabbinic writings contain detailed commentary on the various sacrifices and offerings.[12] Many have supposed that the Rabbis, writing after the destruction of the Second Temple, wanted to insure that nothing would be forgotten. That supposition, however, misses the crucial issue of authority.

The rabbinic writings contain only the views of the Rabbis on how the sacrifices and offerings were to be conducted. They do not contain the views of the priests who had conducted them. The Rabbis rejected all Saducean views, and the priests were primarily Saducees.

The rabbinic writings are a *de facto* declaration that the Rabbis are the ones with the authority. If the Temple were ever rebuilt, the priests would have to operate under rabbinic law.

A truly Jewish kingdom had to focus on the Temple. A rebuilt Temple would mean an active priesthood. The Rabbis needed a way to keep an active priesthood from reasserting its natural, Biblical authority. The purpose of the rabbinic writings on the priestly domain was not to preserve a cherished system, but rather to create a radically different one.

For example, the first of the six orders of the Talmud, *Zera'im*, contains 11 tractates. All of them could be considered to be in the domain of the priests. Here are examples of the area they cover:

"*Demai*: ...produce concerning which there is a doubt whether or not the tithes have been set aside from it...

"*Kil'ayim*: ...the prohibition of mixture in plants, animals and garments...

"*Terumoth*: ...the laws regarding the portion of the harvest assigned to the priest...

"*Ma'aseroth*: ...the 'first tithe' which must be given annually to the levite from the produce of the harvest...

"*Hallah*: ...the portion of the dough which must be given to the priest...

"*Bikkurim*: ...the offering of the first fruits in the Temple... and includes an account of the accompanying ceremony..."[13]

In fact, much of the entire Talmud deals with areas, such as ritual purity, holiness, holy days, and sacrifices, which in the Bible are clearly the domain of the priests. The Pharisees had already rejected some of the priestly practices. The Rabbis laid down the law for the priests.

This was a major transformation. Even during the time of the Great Revolt, the priests were recognized as the only authority in such matters. When the conflict arose over accepting or refusing the Emperor's sacrifice, Josephus records that, "And as they said these things, they produced those priests that were skilful in the customs of their country, who made the report, that all their forefathers had received the sacrifices from foreign nations."[14]

If the Temple were not rebuilt, the Rabbis had prepared a new religious framework which had no place at all in it for the priests. "The daily synagogue service, which had originated quite independently of the Temple, probably without the consent of the priesthood, had been transformed into substitutes for the abolished services."[15]

Whatever need there had been before for priests was now met within a rabbinic context. Whatever priestly functions were not taken over by the Rabbis could only henceforth be conducted under rabbinic regulation. This became the rabbinic pattern for dealing with all existing Jewish authorities.

Akiba's Role

Johanan ben Zakkai is only mentioned by rabbinic writers, not by Josephus or any other contemporary writers. In the rabbinic writings, Johanan ben Zakkai's escape from the city and the consequent Imperial authorization to begin the academy at Yavneh are highly significant events.

Josephus gives great detail concerning all that befell the Jews in the war and as a result of it. We would certainly expect him to have known of these pivotal events and the role that Johanan ben

Zakkai played in them. Why he does not mention them we do not know.

We do know that Akiba is the one primarily responsible for determining what was to be mentioned in the Talmud. He was the one who determined its scope, direction, and emphasis. The character, interests, and strategy that the Talmud ascribes to Johanan ben Zakkai are remarkably similar to those of Akiba himself. When it comes to the incidents concerning Rabban Johanan and the priests, there is reason to believe that Akiba may have projected some of his own struggles, at least by emphasis, back into Rabban Johanan's time.

Yohanan ben Zakkai's encounter with the Bene Bathyra produced a specific decision for a particular situation, but it had broad implications. Not long afterwards, in the time of Akiba, a conflict arose as to whether this newfound rabbinic authority applied only to the gathering in Yavneh, or also to everywhere there was, or would be, a Beth Din.

"R. Eliezer said: 'Rabban Johanan ben Zaccai laid down this rule for Jabneh only.' They said to him: 'It applies equally to Jabneh and to any place where there is a Beth Din.'"[16] R. Eliezer was a disciple of Rabban Johanan ben Zakkai.[17] If anyone were to know what the extent of Johanan ben Zakkai's ruling had been, it would have been R. Eliezer. He claimed that "Rabban Johanan ben Zaccai laid down this rule for Jabneh only." If that were the case, then Rabban Johanan ben Zakkai played a much lesser role in this pivotal shift of power than the Talmud ascribes to him.

Overruling R. Eliezer, "They" extended rabbinic authority from the initial emergency situation at Yavneh after the destruction of the Second Temple to ordinary daily life, anytime and any place there was a Beth Din. The Rabbis were on their way to taking over the authority of the priesthood. As we will see in the next chapter, Akiba was Eliezer's primary opponent.

Neusner claims that, "...nearly the whole of Holy Things, on how things *are* done in the cult, demonstrably is put together after 140, when there was no possibility of conducting a sacrificial cult in Jerusalem at all."[18] That would indicate that the framework for the rabbinic assertion of authority over the priests was established well after the lifetime of Johanan ben Zakkai. That would agree with Rabbi Eliezer's position. Rabbi Akiba, of course, was the preeminent rabbinic leader during that later period.

There is enough material in Akiba's own name to clearly identify his own attitude towards the priests. Ginzberg notes that, "Akiba comes near abolishing the Biblical ordinance of *kilaim*; nearly every chapter in the treatise of that name contains a mitigation by Akiba. Love for the Holy Land, which he as a genuine nationalist frequently and warmly expressed (see Ab.R.N.xxvi), was so powerful with him that he would have exempted agriculture from much of the rigor of the Law."[19]

Kila'im concerns the Biblical prohibition against mixing different kinds of things, as expressed in Leviticus.[20] The book of Leviticus takes its name from the fact that it is mostly concerned with regulations concerning the Levitical priests, their duties and their support. The *kilaim* commands are not explicitly placed under the authority of the priests, but the Biblical teaching is that the priests were to make decisions as to what is prohibited and what is permitted, what is clean and what is unclean.

"Thus says the Lord of hosts, 'Ask now the priests for a ruling [lit. "law"]: *If a man carries holy meat in the fold of his garment, and touches bread with this fold, or cooked food, wine, oil, or any other food, will it become holy?* And the priests answered and said, 'No.' Then Haggai said, 'If one who is unclean from a corpse touches any of these, will the latter become unclean?' And the priests answered and said, 'It will become unclean.'"[21] The priests were the ones to be asked for such a ruling.

Akiba put the Rabbis in the place of the priests. That Akiba loved the Holy Land is not to be doubted, but others with different opinions did as well. His decisions, however, effectively appropriated the priestly authority and nullified the law of the tithe which provided for their support.

As Finkelstein noted, "While therefore earlier teachers urged the people to gather in their harvest early so as to have the tithe ready betimes, Akiba ruled that grain which has not been garnered in time is free from the tithe. (Mish. Ma'aserot 3.5) He went further and maintained that the grain is free from tithes unless it is stored in a protected barn. If it is stored in a court to which two people have keys, it is unprotected and free from tithes. (Mish. Ma'aser Sheni 4.8) These interpretations effectually abolished the whole system of tithes."[22] Abolishing the whole system of tithes effectually eliminated the livelihood of the priests, which effectually eliminated priestly Judaism as a competitor for authority.

The priests, while the Temple stood, were also sustained by offerings which the people brought from their flocks. "The Shammaites had held that only priests may eat the flesh of the firstling (unfit for sacrifice); and the earlier Hillelites who disagreed with them, had insisted that any Israelite might partake of it. But Akiba had said that there was no limitation in the matter at all. Even a pagan might eat of the firstling."[23] Akiba went beyond the earlier Hillelites in order to strip the priests of a distinction which helped them to live.[24]

Had the purpose of including the priestly regulations in the rabbinic writings been to guard against the day when they might be forgotten, the priests would have been the natural source for them. Indeed, "An attempt was made to collect priestly traditions of Temple practice but Akiba, with his exegetical methods, could improve on tradition. And the Law, as interpreted by him, was as it always had been or should have been."[25]

Much of the Talmud deals with subjects which were clearly the domain of the priests. Much of it deals with affairs that would be presumed to be the domain of the priests. In this way, Akiba was able to firmly establish his own Judaism over that of the priests - to make the Torah what it "should have been."

"...Although meticulous in their acknowledgement of the dignity owing to the priesthood as an institution, the rabbis made no bones about their disapproval of priests as individuals. On the contrary, the denigration of *kohanim* became something of a favoured motif in early rabbinic literature, leaving an imprint on virtually every one of its various strata.

"...Only the most illiterate, one suspects, might have been insensitive to the innuendoes behind rabbinic reconstructions of Biblical stories, several of which suggest that moral failings are in some way a congenital fault of the priestly breed. For those who may still have been ignorant of the message being conveyed, there was the resort of more explicit language. Random talmudic passages indicate that priestly deportment was altogether to be considered a byword for arrogance, a posture made particularly objectionable by the alleged fact that several priests were neglectful of some *miswot* [commandments] and downright ignorant of others."[26]

16. SILENCING THE TRADITIONAL RABBIS

Opposition to the High Priests and their abuses was widespread among all the Jewish groups of the first century. Each group determined for itself the direction and course of action that opposition would take.

Among the Rabbis, there were differences of opinion. Akiba wanted revolution. That brought him into conflict with the traditional rabbis who wanted only reform.

There were other issues that brought Akiba into conflict with the traditional rabbis. The conflict was long and bitter. Though some of them could occasionally defeat Akiba in a particular battle, there were none who could meet and defeat him on all fronts in the relentless war he waged. His most notable conflicts were first with Rabban Gamaliel, and later with Rabbi Eliezer ben Hyrcanus.

Gamaliel II was a priest, and the Nasi, i.e. the head of the academy at Yavneh. The Talmud portrays him as a strong, intemperate ruler. He was on good terms with the Romans, and his position as Nasi gave him the decisive voice in admitting or expelling different rabbis.[1]

Up until Akiba's triumph, that power determined the course the religious leadership would follow; and that course, backed by Roman authority, determined the course the nation would follow. The conflicts between Gamaliel and Akiba, as between all national parties, were over who would control the nation.

Louis Finkelstein characterized those conflicts in this way: "Gamaliel's prejudices derived from the traditions of his class; he therefore considered it sacred and, like all partisans, he claimed to speak for the people as a whole...the fact is that both Akiba and Gamaliel wanted national unity; but each on his own terms."[2]

That is normal political behavior. Each presented his own program as the only basis for national unity. For the good of the nation, the other side must relinquish its beliefs and goals. The call for unity is simply a way to advance one's own agenda.

As Nasi, Gamaliel appointed supervisors to report to him offenses of members of the academy. "Johanan ben Nuri reports that he had frequent occasion to complain to Gamaliel of Akiba and that he [ben Nuri] caused him [Akiba] to be publicly flogged five times!"[3]

The conflict became so intense that Gamaliel kicked Akiba out of the academy, but later invited him, unchanged and unrepentant, to return. "His (Akiba's) determination did not blind him to the need for strategy; he bided his time for the opportunity to inflict a decisive defeat on the patrician rulers of the academy."[4] Akiba was patient, determined, and continually ready for battle. He carefully prepared his plan of attack.

Because Akiba was so persuasive, he was often able to convince a majority of rabbis in the academy. That is probably why Gamaliel decided to kick him out. It is also probably why Gamaliel had to take him back in again.

As the confrontations with Gamaliel continued, Akiba's views began to prevail. "It was only occasionally that Akiba was outvoted in the academy. Johanan ben Nuri sorrowfully admitted this to his fellow-Galilean, Halafta, whom he visited. Twice in the course of their discussion of various legal matters he remarked, 'I agree with you on this point, but what can be done, since Akiba opposes us?'"[5] Johanan ben Nuri is the one who had earlier caused Akiba to be publicly flogged five times.

On more than one occasion, Rabban Gamaliel angrily challenged Akiba, "'Akiba, why do you look for quarrels?' Akiba replied, 'You have taught us that the decision of the majority is binding, and the majority agrees with me in this.'"[6]

Akiba used different issues to bring the majority in the academy against Gamaliel. "It seems that Akiba made several journeys throughout all the East of the Empire, Palestine, Syria, probably even Asia Minor, for the purpose of collecting funds and the distribution of comforts amongst the distressed, similar to Gamaliel's famous journey to Rome. His travels seem to have gained for him the moral support necessary to sway the Academy of Jamnia to passing a vote of no confidence in the Patriarch."[7]

The struggle with Gamaliel seems to have reached its climax in the famous conflict concerning R. Joshua and the two men who falsely claimed to have seen the new moon. (R. Joshua had been one of Akiba's teachers.)

"Two witnesses came and said, 'We saw it at its proper time,' but on the night which should have been new moon it was not seen, and Rabban Gamaliel [had already] accepted their evidence. Rabbi Dosa b. Harkinas said: 'They are false witnesses. How can men testify that a woman has born a child when on the next day we see her belly still swollen?'

"Said R. Joshua to him: 'I see [the force of] your argument.' Thereupon Rabban Gamaliel sent to him to say, 'I enjoin upon you to appear before me with your staff and your money on the day which according to your reckoning should be the Day of Atonement.'

"...R. Akiba went and found R. Joshua while he was in great distress. He said to him, 'Master, why are you in distress?' He replied: 'Akiba, it were better for a man to be on a sick-bed for twelve months than that such an injunction should be laid on him. He said to him, '[Master,] will you allow me to tell you something which you yourself have taught me?' He said to him, 'Speak.' He then said to him: 'The text says, *'you'*, *'you'*, *'you'*, three times, to indicate that *'you'* [may fix the festivals] even if you err inadvertently, *'you'*, even if you err deliberately, *'you'*, even if you are misled.' He replied to him in these words: 'Akiba, you have comforted me, you have comforted me'."[8]

There are several dynamics to this conflict. "It is clear that whether the initial phase of the moon appeared or not is a question of fact, not one of either law or definition. It is a matter that can normally be resolved by observation, that is, by empirical procedures. Notwithstanding, when Rabbi Joshua consulted Rabbi Akiva, the latter declared that it was ultimately a matter of law - for the act of consecrating the new month does not depend on the fact of the moon's appearance, but on the decision of the court to which the Torah explicitly gave the power to make this determination."[9]

Akiba, by asserting that the Scriptures said something other than what they actually did say, used the incident to assert the supremacy of rabbinic authority over both the Torah and natural phenomena. In doing so, he temporarily supported Rabban Gamaliel, without losing sight of his long term goal. The incident became a strategic stepping-stone on the path to removing Gamaliel.

"They then said: How long is he [Rabban Gamaliel] to go on insulting him [R. Joshua]? On New Year last year he insulted him; he insulted him in the matter of the firstborn in the affair of R. Zadok; now he insults him again! Come, let us depose him!"[10] Akiba used compromises and coalitions as temporary steps towards attaining full power.

The removal of Gamaliel required a majority vote from the members of the academy. Gamaliel had plenty of supporters. Just to ensure the correct outcome, "Said R. Akiba to the Rabbis: Lock the doors so that the servants of Rabban Gamaliel should not come and upset the Rabbis."[11] With Gamaliel's supporters locked out of the academy, Akiba's choice, R. Eleazar b. Azariah, was voted in as the new Nasi.

The Conflict with R. Eliezer ben Hyrcanus

Rabbi Eliezer ben Hyrcanus had been one of the faithful, trusted disciples of Rabban Yohanan ben Zakkai. He helped Rabban Yohanan to escape in a coffin from the Zealots and the destruction they had brought upon Jerusalem. "Rabban Johanan b.

Zakkai...used to say: If all the sages of Israel were in one scale of the balance and Eliezer b. Hyrcanus in the other scale, he would outweigh them all."[12]

Rabbi Eliezer was a very learned, respected man. In the Talmud, he is called Rabbi Eliezer the Great.[13] He is the very first Rabbi quoted in the Talmud, in the very first Mishnah of the very first tractate. The entire Talmud begins with the words of R. Eliezer.

Rabbi Eliezer was also a priest. He knew the way that Temple affairs were to be conducted. That had been part of his training and service.

He is presented as a humble man, open to learn from his own disciples, or from anyone who might have something to teach. We are told that he talked with the *minim*, i.e. the *Talmidei Yeshua*, and appreciated some of their teachings.[14]

Rabbi Eliezer was also the brother-in-law of Rabban Gamaliel, and one of the leading rabbis of the school of Shammai. At that time, Pharisaic scholars tended to follow the teachings of either Hillel or Shammai, the two great earlier sages.

At some time after Johanan ben Zakkai, the School of Shammai lost its power. The logical point for that to have taken place was when Rabban Gamaliel was deposed.

"R. Abba stated in the name of Samuel: For three years there was a dispute between Beth Shammai and Beth Hillel, the former asserting, 'The halachah is in agreement with our views' and the latter contending, 'The halachah is in agreement with our views'. Then a bath kol issued announcing, '[The utterances of] both are the words of the living God, but the halachah is in agreement with the rulings of Beth Hillel'. Since, however, 'both are the words of the living God' what was it that entitled Beth Hillel to have the halachah fixed in agreement with their rulings? Because they were kindly and modest, they studied their own rulings and those of Beth Shammai, and were even so [humble] as to mention the actions of Beth Shammai before theirs..."[15]

The School of Hillel had gained power, but they needed to make some kind of concession to the opposition. Their condemnation of the school of Shammai appears clearly in other sections.

"R. Nahman b. Isaac said: One who follows the rule of Beth Shammai makes his life forfeit, as we have learnt: R. Tarfon said: I was once walking by the way and I reclined to recite the Shema in the manner prescribed by Beth Shammai and I incurred danger from robbers. They said to him: You deserved to come to harm, because you acted against the opinion of Beth Hillel."[16]

R. Dosa b. Harkinas, of Beth Hillel, called his younger brother, who followed Beth Shammai, "the first-born of Satan."[17] To follow the views of Beth Shammai was to invite death and damnation.

"These also are the words of the living God" was a creative political accomodation. It honored the views of Beth Shammai, but rejected them and relegated them to irrelevance. Anyone who held to the views of Shammai was excommunicated.

Despite Rabbi Eliezer's knowledge, heritage, proven service, and disposition, that is what awaited him. His views are often cited in the Talmud in opposition to "the sages," or to Akiba and his disciples.[18]

Sometimes, Akiba seems to oppose him only for the purpose of opposing him, but Akiba continually opposed Eliezer because of all the things that Eliezer was. Eliezer stood in the way of all that Akiba wanted to do. "'Akiba!' said R. Eliezer to him, 'you would erase what is written in the Torah.'"[19]

Akiba spent years in preparation. Then one day, in the midst of the academy, he successfully challenged a position that Rabbi Eliezer espoused. Finkelstein suggests that, "Both Akiba and Eliezer must have realized that this discussion was only an opening skirmish in the long-drawn out battle which life was forcing upon them. With unwearying persistence, Akiba returned to the struggle each day, lying in wait for any expression of Shammaitic opinion which he might need to refute."[20]

There is an interesting confrontation between Rabbi Eliezer and Rabbi Akiba, which became the means for excommunicating Rabbi Eliezer. Since it presents some of the pivotal issues so clearly, we will look at it in detail later.

"This incident is significant as it brought to a head the tension between the older type of Pharisaic rabbinism typified by the traditionalist par excellence, Rabbi Eliezer ben Hyrcanus, and Rabbi Akiba who stressed his exegesis as more important than tradition. Rabbi Eliezer was the greatest exponent of traditional oral law at the end of the first century A.D. But he refused to extend the scope of the oral law. Akiba could and did extend the oral law to cover all contingencies by his own method of exegesis, while at the same time claiming that it was not new but a rediscovery of an alleged oral law in its totality as given to Moses on Sinai along with the written law. The written law was not enough by itself. The oral law was the Law to be obeyed, and it was aimed at bringing all life under the aegis of that Law.

"If Eliezer ben Hyrcanus were asked a halakic point on which he had not tradition, he had to say that he had nothing to say. Whereas Rabbi Akiba by his hermeneutics could give a halakic ruling and at the same time relate his ruling to some dictum in the Law."[21]

"The centrality of the oral Torah, the view of the rabbi as the new priest and of study of Torah as the new cult, the definition of piety as the imitation of Moses 'our rabbi' and the conception of God as a rabbi, the organization of the Jewish community under rabbinic rule and by rabbinic law, and the goal of turning all Israel into a vast academy for the study of the (rabbinic) Torah - none of these motifs characteristic of later rabbinism occurs at all [in Eliezer's legislation].

"Since by the end of the Yavnean period the main outlines of rabbinism were clear, we may postulate that the transition from Pharisaism to rabbinism, or the union of the two, took place in the time of Eliezer himself. But he does not seem to have been among those who generated the new viewpoints; he appears as a reformer of the old ones. His solution to the problem of the cessation of the cult was not to replace the old piety with a new one but, rather, to preserve and refine the rules governing the old in the certain expectation of its restoration in a better form than ever. Others, who were his contemporaries and successors, developed the rabbinic idea of the (interim) substitution of study for sacrifice, the rabbi for the priest, and the oral Torah of Moses 'our rabbi' for the piety of the old cult."[22]

The "transition from Pharisaism to rabbinism" took place in the time of Eliezer, but it took place in spite of him. He was the leading opponent of Akiba's innovations. That is why Akiba had to get rid of him.

The Creation of Tradition

Once the conflict was in full swing, Akiba used several means to overcome his traditional rabbinic contemporaries. We have already examined his unique method of interpreting the scripture. Akiba used this **First** and foremost, his most powerful weapon against all competitors.

In this, he was opposed by many of his contemporaries, such as Rabban Gamaliel, R. Jose the Galilean, R. Eliezer ben Hyrcanus, and R. Ishmael ben Elisha. "One of his [Ishmael ben Elisha's] foremost principles from the beginning of his studies had been that the Torah must be interpreted like any other literary document, and he had therefore opposed the new and ingenious rules of hermeneutics introduced by Nahum of Gimzo and Akiba."[23]

As we have already seen, these "new and ingenious rules" of interpretation were so remarkable and flexible that Akiba was able to use them for whatever his particular purpose happened to be at the moment. They enabled him to effectively use the Scriptures to support whatever view he held. He controlled the debate by controlling the language.

Second: Akiba made the decision to put the rabbinic traditions he favored in writing. In so doing, he put the traditionalists in the midst of a dilemma. In order to defend their traditions and successfully oppose Akiba's innovations, they would have to put their own traditions in writing, which was contrary to their tradition. Akiba changed the groundrules and used the changes to ensure that what was to be Judaism would be according to his definition.

Prior to Akiba, "These works were not put into writing, for it was a cardinal principle of Pharisaism at the time that rabbinic traditions must be preserved orally. They were handed down from generation to generation by a special class of professional memorizers."[24]

Saul Liberman notes that, "Since in the entire Talmudic literature we do not find that a book of the Mishnah was ever consulted in case of controversies or doubt concerning a particular reading, we may safely conclude that the compilation was not published in writing."[25]

"R. Yishma'el said "these (the words of the Torah) you are to write, but not halakhot.' R. Yohanan b. Nappaha taught that 'those who commit halakhot to writing are considered as if they burnt the Torah.'"[26]

"The dictum of R. Johanan parallels the wording of a similar baraita (b. Shabbat 115b and Tos. Shabbat 13,4) with regard to the writing of blessings: 'Those who write down blessings are considered as if they burnt the Torah', the technical reason being that such writings, though they contained scriptural quotations, would not be evacuated from a fire on the Sabbath."[27]

The written Talmud records the traditional admonition: "'My son, take heed of the words of the Scribes (דברי סופרים) more than of the words of the Torah...Should you ask, 'If they have substance, why were they not written?' Scripture says: *'Of making many books there is no end.'*"[28]

To be faithful to their traditions and understanding of Torah, the traditional rabbis could not write down their traditions. If they did not write them down, then their traditions would be replaced by R. Akiba's. Akiba was not creating an impartial history, he was pursuing a radical agenda. He abolished the foundation of the oral tradition.

Third: Akiba recorded the traditions with which he agreed, and discarded the others. Akiba was the editor who determined what was written and what was thrown out. "Having decided on the method which he would follow in the arrangement of his material, Akiba even more boldly replaced ancient norms with others which represented his own opinions. Such, however, was the authority he came to enjoy that within a generation the rejected material was almost unknown."[29]

"Akiba's *Halakhoth* are several times contrasted with the *Mishnah Reshonah*, the 'old law' [or 'first law'] meaning that he introduced new laws to replace corresponding old laws."[30] What fit into his vision he kept, and what did not he replaced. Akiba's "authority" lay in his all-encompassing vision for what Judaism should be; and in his ability to gain support from a majority of rabbis in the Academy.

The Talmud contains a number of references to this creative activity of Akiba. For example, "R. Jose said: This is [the text of] R. Akiba's Mishnah; but the First Mishnah..."[31]

"R. Huna said: There is no contradiction; one teaching is from the older Mishnah and the other from the later Mishnah.'"[32]

"One text speaks of offences committed by a man against God, the other of offences committed by a man against his fellow man. [This explanation was generally accepted] until R. Akiba came and taught..."[33]

"The early Sages ruled: That means that she must not rouge nor paint nor adorn herself in dyed garments; until R. Akiba came and taught..."[34]

"He objected to the ancient tradition which forbade women to adorn themselves during their menstrual periods. 'Such a rule,' he said, 'can only lead to loss of marital love, and divorce!' ...We may observe that Akiba had no authority whatever for this change in what was, at the time, a fundamental principle of ceremonial law."[35]

Akiba was actually the greatest opponent of traditional Pharisaic Judaism. He opposed the teachings of Shammai, which had been authoritative. He put the oral tradition in writing. He rejected any and all traditions with which he disagreed. How could he have done so if those authoritative rulings had been the correct interpretation of Torah or if they had been given as a separate revelation at Sinai?

"Of further significance in this direction was Akiba's endeavor to establish the correct view of traditions and to reduce the number of divergent practices and views by giving in most cases only one opinion."[36] An editor who is going to give only one opinion is going to give his own, or, what amounts to the same thing, the one with which he agrees.

Here, as with the text of Tanakh, Akiba seems to have formulated a comprehensive strategy. With Tanakh, Akiba authorized a new Targum for those who spoke Aramaic, and a new Greek translation for those who did not. No matter what language a person used, Akiba established the authority.

He did the same with the oral tradition. He put it in writing to increase his leverage against the traditional rabbis, but he knew that he had to formulate a plan for the transitional period. So he gave some of his disciples a new official mission. They would be the official reciters of the "correct" oral tradition.

"The authority of the college-*Tanna* ('a word apparently first used for college-reciter in the time of 'Aqiba...) was that of a published book...'The *Tanna* ("repeater") committed to memory the text of certain portions of the Mishnah, which he subsequently recited in the college in the presence of the great masters of the Law."[37]

Prior to Akiba, each individual remembered the traditions which he had heard. The testimony of non-scholars, as to what they had heard scholars teach, was acceptable. By creating a new official position, that of *Tanna*, Akiba could control what memory and what tradition was acceptable. Only the *Tannaim* were allowed to remember tradition. They only committed to memory what was officially acceptable. During "the time of Akiba," only Akiba had the power to make such a change.

Fourth: Rabbi Akiba is the recognized source for anonymous citations. "R. Johanan said: (The author of) an anonymous Mishnah is R. Meir; of an anonymous Tosefta, R. Nehemiah; of an anonymous (dictum in the) Sifra, R. Judah; in the Sifre, R. Simeon; and all are taught according to the views of R. Akiba."[38]

Jacob Neusner says, "In those tractates on which the work is done, Kelim and Ohalot, I know of not a single unassigned saying which cannot be shown to depend upon an assumption or principle demonstrably later than 70."[39] "And when we do know the name of the Yavnean responsible for the most fruitful developments in the law, it is, time and again, Aqiva."[40]

When a statement, Mishnah, or *halakha* is anonymous, it means that it cannot be attributed to any rabbi, or any early sage. According to the tradition, a tradition that cannot be attributed cannot be *halakha*. "Hillel himself had a discussion with other teachers for a whole day, and until he thought of saying that he had been taught so by his teachers, Shemaiah and Abtalion, he was not believed."[41]

Akiba rejected the tradition that established the authority of all traditions. He made anonymous traditions acceptable. An accepted anonymous Mishnah can only be attributed to Akiba. And in the system that Akiba set up, "It is a general principle that an anonymous Mishnah states the *halachah*."[42]

Fifth: Akiba was the primary architect of the structure and form of rabbinic Judaism. He determined the agenda. The rest is commentary, and development.

Akiba took the primary and predominant role in ordering and selecting what was to go into the written oral law. Not only that, but his authority became such that he could silence all discussion and, therefore, support of contrary views.

"They told R. Akiba that R. Eliezer used to say, *A hide that has been smeared with oil of the seventh year must be burnt*. He replied: 'Hold your peace; for I will not divulge to you what R. Eliezer actually said in this connection.'"[43]

"They also told him [R. Akiba] that R. Eliezer said: 'He who eats bread (baked) by Samaritans is like one who eats the flesh of a pig. (To this, too) his reply was: 'Hold your peace; for I will not divulge to you what R. Eliezer really did say in this connection'."[44]

Samaritans had been strictly excluded from the congregation of Israel by Ezra and Nehemiah. Some in the academy told Rabbi Akiba that Rabbi Eliezer had maintained that, therefore, whoever eats their bread is eating forbidden food. Rabbi Akiba's response indicates his view that their tradition is not accurate, or that at any rate, whatever Rabbi Eliezer had said should not be known or discussed. "R. Eliezer b. Hyrcanus was under a ban (v. B.M. 59b), and was forbidden to participate in the discussions and decisions of the court; Yad. IV, 3."[45] Consequently, whatever Rabbi Eliezer's view had been, it could not be a source for *halakha*.

The incident used to excommunicate R. Eliezer epitomizes the radical nature of the rabbinic system that Akiba was establishing. We therefore turn to that incident.

17. "IT IS NOT IN HEAVEN"

The issue in dispute was whether or not a certain earthen oven, the *tanoor Akhnai*, could be considered unclean. R. Eliezer said it could not. The other rabbis disagreed.

"On that day R. Eliezer brought forward every imaginable argument, but they did not accept them. Said he to them: 'If the halachah agrees with me, let this carob-tree prove it!' Thereupon the carob-tree was torn a hundred cubits out of its place - others affirm, four hundred cubits. 'No proof can be brought from a carob-tree,' they retorted. Again he said to them: 'If the halachah agrees with me, let the stream of water prove it!' Whereupon the stream of water flowed backwards. 'No proof can be brought from a stream of water,' they rejoined. Again he urged: 'If the halachah agrees with me, let the walls of the schoolhouse prove it,' whereupon the walls inclined to fall. But R. Joshua rebuked them, saying: 'When scholars are engaged in a halachic dispute, what have ye to interfere?' Hence they did not fall, in honour of R. Joshua, nor did they resume the upright, in honour of R. Eliezer; and they are still standing thus inclined. Again he said to them: 'If the halachah agrees with me, let it be proved from Heaven!' Whereupon a Heavenly Voice cried out: 'Why do ye dispute with R. Eliezer, seeing that in all matters the halachah agrees with him!' But R. Joshua arose and exclaimed: 'It is not in heaven.' What did he mean by this? - Said R. Jeremiah: That the Torah had already been given at Mount Sinai; we pay no attention to a Heavenly Voice, because Thou hast long since written in the Torah at Mount Sinai, *After the majority must one incline.*

""R. Nathan met Elijah and asked him: 'What did the Holy One, Blessed be He, do in that hour?' - 'He laughed (with joy),' he replied, 'saying, *My sons have defeated Me, My sons have defeated Me.*' It was said: On that day all objects which R. Eliezer had declared clean were brought and burnt in fire. Then they took a vote and excommunicated him. Said they, 'Who shall go and inform him?' 'I will go,' answered R. Akiba, 'lest an unsuitable person go and inform him, and thus destroy the whole world.'"[1]

In this passage, as throughout the Talmud, the historical or physical accuracy of the account is not crucial. It is what the account teaches that matters. There are five major lessons conveyed:

1. The Rabbis do not accept the miraculous in determining the correctness of a position.

2. The Rabbis pay no attention to a Heavenly Voice after Sinai.

3. The authority to determine what is acceptable and what is not does not rest with God, but rather with the majority of the

leading Rabbis.
4. God laughs when men outwit Him.
5. **The Rabbis will excommunicate anyone who will not submit to their decisions.**

Each of these points constitutes a radical departure from the teaching of Torah, all in the same direction. Each is part of Akiba's quest for rabbinic power.

1. The Rabbis do not accept the miraculous in determining the correctness of a position.

The Bible teaches that not all miracles are from God. Pharaoh's magicians, for example, were able to duplicate some of the miracles that Moses performed.

There is also the explicit admonition in Deuteronomy: "If a prophet or a dreamer of dreams arises among you and gives you a sign or a wonder, and the sign or the wonder comes true, concerning which he spoke to you, saying, 'Let us go after other gods (whom you have not known) and let us serve them,' you shall not listen to the words of that prophet or that dreamer of dreams; for the Lord your God is testing you to find out if you love the Lord your God with all your heart and with all your soul."[2]

The incident with R. Eliezer is in a different category. As the story is related, the miracles were legitimate confirmations of the correctness of R. Eliezer's position. So the question was not one of idolatry, but rather authority: 'Can proof be brought from a carob-tree? a stream of water? or the walls of a building?'

Torah answers that question differently than the Rabbis do. Torah teaches that some miracles are signs from God that must be believed. The LORD sent Moses to deliver Israel, affirming the divine source of his mission with three signs - Aaron's staff becoming a snake and then becoming a rod of wood again; the hand of Moses becoming first leprous and then healthy again; and the water from the Nile becoming blood.

"If they do not believe you or pay attention to the first miraculous sign, they may believe the second. But if they do not believe these two signs or listen to you, take some water from the Nile and pour it on the dry ground. The water you take from the river will become blood on the ground."[3]

Israel was supposed to accept each of these three signs as proof that Moses was sent by God. It is interesting that these three signs can be related to the three signs in the story of R. Eliezer's excommunication.

Aaron's staff, of course, came from a tree. Israel was to accept its sign as proof. Later, following the rebellion of Korah which challenged the authority of Moses and Aaron, the rod again provided proof of God's choice. God told Moses to gather a rod from each of the 12 tribes, and write the name of the leading prince of each tribe upon the rod from that tribe. Aaron's name was written on the rod of the tribe of Levi.

The Lord said, "'The staff belonging to the man I choose will sprout, and I will rid myself of this constant grumbling against you by the Israelites.' So Moses spoke to the Israelites, and their leaders gave him twelve staffs, one for the leader of each of their ancestral tribes, and Aaron's staff was among them. Moses placed the staffs before the LORD in the Tent of the Testimony.

"The next day Moses entered the Tent of the Testimony and saw that Aaron's staff, which represented the house of Levi, had not only sprouted but had budded, blossomed and produced almonds. Then Moses brought out all the staffs from the LORD's presence to all the Israelites. They looked at them, and each man took his own staff.

"The LORD said to Moses, 'Put back Aaron's staff in front of the Testimony, to be kept as a sign to the rebellious. This will put an end to their grumbling against me, so that they will not die.'"[4] According to Torah, proof can be brought from an almond-tree.

The second sign concerned the appearance and disappearance of leprosy on the hand of Moses. After the deliverance from Egypt, in the wilderness of Sinai, God gave regulations for discerning and dealing with leprosy in humans, articles, and buildings. One such instance is pertinent in considering R. Joshua's claims.

"The LORD said to Moses and Aaron, "When you enter the land of Canaan, which I am giving you as your possession, and I put the plague of leprosy in a house in that land...[the priest] is to examine the plague on the walls, and if it has greenish or reddish depressions that appear to be deeper than the surface of the wall, the priest shall go out the doorway of the house and close it up for seven days.

"On the seventh day the priest shall return to inspect the house. If the plague has spread on the walls, he is to order that the contaminated stones be torn out and thrown into an unclean place outside the town."[5] According to Torah, proof can be brought from the walls of a building.

The third sign was to follow a rejection of the first two. This sign promised judgment, and had to be accepted. Water from the Nile became blood upon the land. According to Torah, proof can be brought from a stream of water.

2. The Rabbis pay no attention to a Heavenly Voice after Sinai.
God continued to speak authoritatively to Israel after Sinai. Sometimes He spoke through angelic messengers from heaven.

Sometimes He spoke through chosen men on the earth.

"Thus saith the Lord,..." or "The word of the Lord came to..." are common phrases in both the historical and the prophetic books. God often corrected and rebuked prophets, priests, kings, and people. This forms the context of Rabbi Eliezer's appeal, even though, in Tanakh, God did not usually speak in a voice from heaven. (In the next chapter, we will examine the rabbinic stance toward the prophetic voice.)

The phenomenon of a Heavenly Voice appears occasionally in the gospels, more often in the apocalyptic literature, and perhaps most often in rabbinic literature. The Rabbis call such a heavenly voice a *"Bath Kol."*

The Bath Kol

In several places, the Talmud maintains that, "After the later prophets Haggai, Zechariah, and Malachi had died, the Holy Spirit departed from Israel, but they still availed themselves of the Bath Kol."[6] I.e., after Sinai, Israel still paid attention to a Heavenly Voice.

"R. Eleazar said: The Holy Spirit manifested itself in three places; at the Tribunal of Shem, at the Tribunal of Samuel of Ramah, and at the Tribunal of Solomon. At the Tribunal of Shem, as it is written, *And Judah acknowledged them, and he said, 'She is right, it is from me.'* How did he know [for certain]? Maybe, just as he had come to [consort with] her, some other man had come to [consort with] her? [But] it was a Bath Kol that came forth and said, 'She is right, constrained by Me these things came about.'

"'At the Tribunal of Samuel,' — as it is written, *Here I am; witness against me before the Lord and before His anointed, whose ox have I taken? or whose ass . . . and they said, Thou hast not defrauded us nor oppressed us, neither hast thou taken aught of any man's hand. And he said unto them, The Lord is witness against you and His anointed is witness this day that ye have not found aught in my hand,' and He said, [He is] witness.* 'And He said'; should it not be 'And they said'? [But] it was a Bath Kol that came forth and said, 'I am witness in this matter.'

"'At the Tribunal of Solomon,' — as it is said, *And the king answered and said, 'Give her the living child, and in no wise slay it; she is his mother'*: 'She is his mother'; whence knew he [for certain]? Maybe, she had been acting craftily? [But] it was a Bath Kol that came forth and said, 'She is his mother'."[7]

In each of these incidents the *Bath Kol* is accepted as authoritative. That is the normal message of the Talmud in a variety of circumstances.

"Come and hear: For R. Johanan b. Zakkai said: What answer

did the Bath Kol give that wicked man [Nebuchadnezzar] when he asserted, *'I will ascend above the heights of the clouds; I will be like the Most High'*? A Bath Kol came forth and rebuked him."[8]

In incidents involving the Sages, a *Bath Kol* was still considered decisive. A Heavenly Voice settled all questions.

"The Targum of the Prophets was composed by Jonathan ben Uzziel under the guidance of Haggai, Zechariah and Malachi, and the land of Israel [thereupon] quaked over an area of four hundred parasangs by four hundred parasangs, and a Bath Kol came forth and exclaimed, Who is this that has revealed My secrets to mankind? Jonathan b. Uzziel thereupon arose and said, 'It is I who have revealed Thy secrets to mankind. It is fully known to Thee that I have not done this for my own honour or for the honour of my father's house, but for Thy honour 1 have done it, that dissension may not increase in Israel.' He further sought to reveal [by] a targum [the inner meaning] of the Hagiographa, but a Bath Kol went forth and said, 'Enough!' What was the reason? — Because the date of the Messiah is foretold in it."[9]

In fact, it is by a *Bath Kol* that the whole tenor of *halakha* - the shift in authority from Beth Shammai to Beth Hillel - was fixed. "R. Abba stated in the name of Samuel: For three years there was a dispute between Beth Shammai and Beth Hillel, the former asserting, 'The halachah is in agreement with our views' and the latter contending, 'The halachah is in agreement with our views'. Then a bath kol issued announcing, '[The utterances of] both are the words of the living God, but the halachah is in agreement with the rulings of Beth Hillel'."[10]

This is a confrontation of major rabbinic significance. The accepted traditions were rejected and the rejected traditions were accepted. When it is suggested that the issue could have been decided without the *Bath Kol*, we are told that this is not the view of the Rabbis. It only "represents [the view of] R. Joshua who does not recognize the authority of a bath kol."[11]

When a Roman officer gave up his own life to save R. Gamaliel from death, it was a *Bath Kol* that declared, "This high officer is destined to enter into the world to come."[12]

In another incident involving R. Eliezer, a *Bath Kol* is accepted as decisive. "It is further related of R. Eliezer that once he stepped down before the Ark and recited the twenty-four benedictions [for fast days] and his prayer was not answered. R. Akiba stepped down after him and exclaimed: Our Father, our King, we have no King but Thee; our Father, our King, for Thy sake have mercy upon us; and rain fell. The Rabbis present suspected (R. Eliezer) [of being a heretic], whereupon a Heavenly Voice was heard proclaiming, '[The prayer of] this man [R. Akiba] was answered not because he is greater than the other man, but because he is ever forbearing and the other is not.' "[13]

R. Eliezer had friendly dealings with some of the *Talmidei Yeshua*. Because of this, some of the Rabbis suspected him of having heretical views. The Heavenly Voice settled the matter by proclaiming his innocence.

"R. Joshua b. Levi said: Every day a bath kol goes forth from Mount Horeb, and makes proclamation and says: Woe unto men on account of [their] contempt towards the Torah..."[14]

It was even a *Bath Kol* that twice declared R. Akiba's great heavenly reward. Following the defeat of the Bar Kokhba Revolt, "R. Akiba was arrested and thrown into prison...When R. Akiba was taken out for execution, it was the hour for the recital of the Shema'...He prolonged the word *ehad* until he expired while saying it. A bath kol went forth and proclaimed: Happy art thou, Akiba, that thy soul has departed with the word *ehad*! The ministering angels said before the Holy One, blessed be He: Such Torah, and such a reward? [He should have been] from them that die by Thy hand, O Lord. He replied to them: Their portion is in life. A bath kol went forth and proclaimed, Happy art thou, R. Akiba, that thou art destined for the life of the world to come.'"[15]

In the Talmud, a Heavenly Voice is **ALWAYS** accepted as authoritative, with one exception. The only case in which a Heavenly Voice is not accepted as authoritative is that which led to the excommunication of R. Eliezer. It is this one exception that most explicitly proclaims the supremacy of rabbinic authority over that of God Himself.

3. The authority to determine what is acceptable and what is not does not rest with God, but rather with the majority of the leading rabbis.

In his farewell discourse, Moses told the children of Israel, "For this commandment which I command you today is not too difficult for you, nor is it far off. It is not in heaven, that you should say, 'Who will go up to heaven for us to get it for us and make us hear it, that we may observe it?' Nor is it beyond the sea, that you should say, 'Who will cross the sea for us to get it for us and make us hear it, that we may observe it?' But the word is very near you, in your mouth and in your heart, that you may observe it."[16]

Rabbi Joshua's response to God - "It is not in heaven." - is taken from this portion in Deuteronomy. Rabbi Jeremiah explained Rabbi Joshua's response to mean that God gave His Law to Israel at Sinai, and now it is up to the majority of sages to determine what it means. In effect, it has become the property of the Rabbis. In support of this position, God was told, "Thou hast long since written in the Torah at Mount Sinai, *'After the majority must one incline.'"*

Actually, that phrase is not written in Torah at all, nor anywhere else in Tanakh. It is an inversion of what is written in Exodus 23:2: "You shall not follow a multitude [*rabbim*/רבים] to evil, nor shall you testify in a dispute so as to turn aside after a multitude [*rabbim*/רבים] in order to pervert justice."

The Talmud explains: "By the implications of the text, 'Thou shalt not follow a majority for evil,' I infer that I may follow them for good."[17] Aside from the problem of making God accountable for and subject to a rabbinic inference, this explanation bypasses the real issue in such cases.

How does one determine whether a particular majority is doing good or doing evil? Or even more directly, how does one determine what is good and what is evil? especially when God's "opinion" is not decisive?

"The principle of *lo ba-shamayim hi* [i.e., "it is not in heaven"] is that the Torah itself confers authority on the sages to interpret and apply its laws."[18] As we have seen, however, the Torah does not confer such authority on the sages.

In fact, in the *tanoor Akhnai* [unclean oven] passage, God is surprised to hear the rabbinic interpretation. God Himself did not know that at Sinai He had given up His authority to the sages.

In the Biblical history of Israel from Sinai on, there is not the slightest hint of a suggestion that God had submitted Himself to the authority of the Rabbis. It is the first time that God had heard of it.

R. Joshua dismissed the authority of the Heavenly Voice, claiming that God was contradicting Himself. The claim was that, "we pay no attention to a **Heavenly Voice**, because **Thou** hast long since **written in the Torah** at Mount Sinai..." In other words, what God was saying contradicted what God had written.

God had not, however, written in the Torah what R. Joshua quoted. The Rabbis claimed that their words had authority over what God had written. So if they said that God had written it, then God had written it. The meaning was clear: Do not listen to a Heavenly Voice, listen to the voice of the Rabbis.

How was one to know whether the Rabbis were the multitude to evil or the multitude to good? In their own eyes, of course, they themselves were the ones who defined the Law, i.e. the good. But how was anyone else to know?

"Thus R. Nissim b. Gerondi writes, in explication of *lo ba-shamayim hi*, 'All of the sages saw that the view of R. Eliezer was closer to the truth [*maskim el ha-emet*] than theirs, and that the signs he produced were honest and legitimate, and that Heaven itself had decided in his favour. Nonetheless they ruled in accordance with their consensus. For since their reason was inclined to declare the oven impure even though they knew that their decision was counter to the truth, they would not agree to declare it pure. Had they declared it pure, they would have been violating the Torah, since their reason guided them to declare it impure. For the determination of the law has been entrusted to the sages of each generation and what they decide is what God has commanded."[19]

There is an explicit Talmudic principle: "[In a dispute between] one individual and a majority the halachah is in agreement with the majority!"[20] That holds true whether the one is R. Eliezer or God Himself.

The Torah reads quite differently. In the Torah, it is difficult to find a place where the majority was not in opposition to the will of God. They were in Egypt. They were in the wilderness.

That is the Biblical reason for the wandering in the wilderness. The people would not believe Joshua and Caleb. They believed the majority of the spies.

Time after time, Moses stood alone against the majority of the people and the majority of the leaders; e.g., the Golden Calf and the waters of Meribah. In various supernatural ways, God made it clear that Moses was right. The rebellion of Korah is an instructive example because it arose concerning the same issues that put R. Eliezer in conflict with Akiba and the majority.

Korah, Dathan, Abiram, On, and 250 leaders of the people challenged the authority of the Aaronic priesthood and the leadership of Moses. These men were all "princes of the congregation, the elect men of the assembly, men of renown."[21] According to Rashi, Korah, in his rebellion, "drew the heads of the Sanhedrin among them...He arose and assembled two hundred and fifty, the heads of the Sanhedrin..."[22] Had the authority of the majority of the sages been established at that time, Moses would have been excommunicated or executed.[23]

4. God laughs when men outwit Him.

In the Talmudic story, God good-naturedly accedes to the interpretation and authority of the Rabbis when they point out how He had unwittingly contradicted Himself. This picture of God is significantly different from the Biblical one.

The primary and ultimate aspects of the nature of God in Tanakh are His omniscience and His sovereignty.[24] He does not need to give account to man. Certainly that is the gist of His response to Job.

There are very few occasions in Tanakh when God laughs. Whenever we do read of Him laughing, it is never because He has been outwitted by man. In Tanakh, that is not possible. On the contrary, when God laughs, it is always in derision of those men who think they have outwitted Him.

"See what they spew from their mouths — they spew out swords from their lips, and they say, 'Who can hear us?' But you, O LORD, laugh at them; you scoff at all those nations."[25]

"The wicked plot against the righteous and gnash their teeth at them; but the Lord laughs at the wicked, for he knows their day is coming."[26]

"Why do the nations conspire and the peoples plot in vain? The kings of the earth take their stand and the rulers gather together against the LORD and against his Anointed One. 'Let us break their chains,' they say, 'and throw off their fetters.'

"The One enthroned in heaven laughs; the Lord scoffs at them. Then he rebukes them in his anger and terrifies them in his wrath, saying, 'I have installed my King on Zion, my holy hill.'"[27]

"Wisdom calls aloud in the street, she raises her voice in the public squares; at the head of the noisy streets she cries out, in the gateways of the city she makes her speech: 'How long will you simple ones love your simple ways? How long will mockers delight in mockery and fools hate knowledge?

"'If you had responded to my rebuke, I would have poured out my heart to you and made my thoughts known to you. But since you rejected me when I called and no one gave heed when I stretched out my hand, since you ignored all my advice and would not accept my rebuke, I in turn will laugh at your disaster; I will mock when calamity overtakes you.'"[28]

The jovial, submissive God of the *Tanoor Akhnai* incident does not appear in the pages of Tanakh. To craft a radically different relationship between God and Israel, one where the Rabbis had the central role, it was necessary to change the nature and character of God.

5. The Rabbis will excommunicate anyone who will not submit to their decisions.

R. Nissim b. Gerondi stated the fundamental claim of Rabbinic authority quite clearly: "What they [the majority of the sages] decide is what God has commanded." There can be no dissent from this foundational principle. Without it, there is no rabbinic authority.

Such a claim is clearly a radical departure from every prior form of Judaism. It is, therefore, particularly appropriate that it was R. Eliezer the Great who was excommunicated.

Rabbi Eliezer was a traditional Pharisee, a disciple of Johanan ben Zakkai, who "received the oral tradition from Hillel and Shammai."[29] Eliezer was a scholar of what had been the dominant rabbinic school, the school of Shammai. He was the brother-in-law of Rabban Gamliel, and he is the very first rabbi quoted in the Talmud.

He was a priest who sought to retain the limits on rabbinic authority. He believed in a traditional interpretation of scripture. Rabbi Eliezer is the one whom Akiba first challenged, and the one he persistently sought to overthrow. It was, eventually, Rabbi Eliezer's views that Akiba refused to make known or discuss.

Akiba championed the position that 'the decision of the majority is binding.' He made it an instrument to overthrow the traditional authority. Akiba established the decision of the majority as the ultimate authority.

"R. Akiba came and taught: Thou shalt fear (*eth*) the Lord thy God, that is to include scholars."[30] It is Akiba who put the Rabbis in the place of "the Lord thy God." And Akiba is the editor, if not the recorder, of the account itself.

It was a change of inestimable significance. As Jonathan Sacks noted, "For *lo ba-shamayim hi* is - if I may be forgiven for using such terminology - an assertion of a 'Catholic' as against a 'Protestant' view of divine law. By it, interpretive authority is vested in the *ecclesia*, the community of the sages, as against the individual in lonely confrontation with the divine word."[31]

The system set up by Akiba placed ultimate authority neither in the hands of God nor in the hands of the majority of people, but rather in the hands of the majority of the Rabbis. It established an insular, self-contained, ruling Party. The Rabbis of the great Sanhedrin, i.e. the leading party members, would determine who else would be admitted to the ruling elite. There was no means of correction from outside, or from above.

As with all such parties, the Rabbis saw themselves in control for the good of the people. And as with all such parties, that "good" was defined as whatever the Rabbis chose it to be. The only other independent authority they recognized was a Gentile state ruling over them.

The picture of a self-appointed ruling elite as guardians of the will of God stands in marked contrast to the outcast prophet denouncing the sins of leaders and people alike. It was a system that would not allow a challenge to its authority. The source of its rulings was "not in heaven." Even as the voice of God from heaven had to be silenced, so did the voice of God on earth, the prophet.

18. THE RABBIS REPLACE THE PROPHETS

"R. Abdimi from Haifa said: 'Since the day when the Temple was destroyed, prophecy has been taken from the prophets and given to the wise [i.e., the Sages].'" Baba Batra 12a

It is often said that the Rabbis believed that prophecy had ceased. That is not correct. The rabbinic contention was not that prophecy had ceased, but rather that they alone could prophesy. Under the Rabbis, prophecy itself underwent radical changes.

Biblical prophecy is the result of a sovereign God speaking directly to men, through a man. The prophet was sent by God to deliver His message in the power of the Holy Spirit.

The message might be a blessing or a curse, encouragement or rebuke. It might bring forgiveness or condemnation, God's counsel or the annulment of the counsel of men. Whatever the message, it was not of the prophet's own choosing, and often not to his liking either.

As Amos responded to the palace official who told him to go prophesy somewhere else, "I was neither a prophet nor a prophet's son, but I was a shepherd, and I also took care of sycamore-fig trees. But the LORD took me from tending the flock and said to me, 'Go, prophesy to My people Israel.'"[1]

Often, the prophet was sent by God to rebuke the state and religious leaders. He came without credentials of genealogy or learning, wealth or position. He operated independently of, and unsubmitted to, any human authority. Usually an outsider, the prophet came alone and unarmed to a fortified, walled city, and commanded it to surrender.

From Moses to Malachi, God spoke to Israel through His prophets. From the time of Malachi to the destruction of the Second Temple and beyond, Jewish sources record prophetic utterances in a variety of circumstances. Some entire works, like 1 Enoch, were presented as prophecies.[2] Other works, like the Sybylline Oracle, contain prophecies scattered throughout.[3] The Pseudepigrapha, the writings of the Qumran community, the "New Testament," and Josephus all evidence a belief in the ongoing occurrence both of prophetic utterance and of prophets. So does the Talmud.

Josephus records the ordeal of a particular prophet before the destruction of Jerusalem. The rulers beat and whipped him, but he continued to prophesy, "Woe, Woe to Jerusalem!"[4] Josephus also speaks of "a false prophet" who was believed because he said what the leaders wanted to hear.[5] It is evident that the people did not believe that prophecy had ceased.

Neither the Rabbis nor anyone else believed that the Holy Spirit had completely departed from Israel after the later prophets. What the Rabbis actually maintained is that the Holy Spirit had departed from all of Israel except themselves. No one but they could prophesy.[6]

Prophecy in the Talmud

Statements to the effect that prophecy had ceased or that the Holy Spirit had departed were simply a way of saying that the Rabbis would, and everyone else should, disregard the prophecies of any unauthorized men, i.e. those who were not recognized sages. The Holy Spirit was limited to bringing forth prophecy through the inner circle of the Rabbis.

There are different kinds of prophecy or signs that are recorded in the Talmud. Some are minor. For example, "R. Johanan said: If at the moment of rising a text occurs to one, this is a minor kind of prophecy."[7] R. Johanan believed that God was speaking directly to the individual through a scriptural text, making this a minor kind of prophecy.

Then there are three major types of prophetic utterance or signs recognized in the Talmud. These are important because, in one way or another, they each demonstrate the radical nature of the new religion which Akiba was creating. They help to define the system of rabbinic authority.

The first is the *Bath Kol*. The second is the foretelling of specific future events, usually judgments. The third is the interpretation of dreams.

As we have seen, the *Bath Kol* was heard repeatedly. God spoke directly to an individual or a group. The *Bath Kol* was always authoritative, except when it stood in the way of rabbinic supremacy.

The foretelling of specific future events is not uncommon in the Talmud.[8] Rabban Yohanan ben Zakkai prophetically greeted Vespasian as the emperor. When that prophetic greeting became reality, Rabban Yohanan was given the right to found the Academy at Yavneh.

"Samuel the Little also said shortly before he passed away: 'Simeon and Ishmael will meet their death by the sword, and his friends will be executed; the rest of the people will be plundered, and many troubles will come upon the world.'"[9] He was prophesying the outcome of the Bar Kokhba Revolt. The "friends" who would then be executed were R. Akiba and R. Hanina b. Teradyon.[10]

When the revolt failed, later rabbis recognized Bar Kokhba as a false Messiah. They still expected the true Messiah to come. The time before Messiah's coming was prophesied to be a time of distress and trouble.[11]

Others prophesied that Messiah's coming would establish Israel as a holy people and a righteous nation.[12] From the founding of the Academy at Yavneh to the martyrdom of R. Akiba, and even to the end of the age, prophecy continued to have a place in rabbinic Judaism. But from the destruction of the Second Temple on, the Rabbis authorized themselves alone to prophesy.

The Rabbinic Interpretation of Dreams

The Talmud declares that "the dream follows the mouth." That is, whatever the interpreter of dreams declares the meaning of the dream to be, so it will be.

"R. Bana'ah [said]: There were twenty-four interpreters of dreams in Jerusalem. Once I dreamt a dream and I went round to all of them and they all gave different interpretations, and all were fulfilled, thus confirming that which is said: All dreams follow the mouth. Is the statement that all dreams follow the mouth Scriptural? Yes, as stated by R. Eleazar. For R. Eleazar said: Whence do we know that all dreams follow the mouth? Because it says, *and it came to pass, as he interpreted to us, so it was.*"[13]

R. Eleazar (not to be confused with R. Eliezer) was a disciple of R. Akiba. The scriptural proof he offered was another example of the utility of Akiba's manner of "interpretation." The word "mouth" does not actually appear in the Hebrew text of Gen.41:13, the verse cited.

The Biblical passage to which R. Eleazar appeals concerns Joseph in prison with the cupbearer and baker. On that occasion, "They said, 'We both had dreams, but there is no one to interpret them.' Then Joseph said to them, 'Do not interpretations belong to God? Tell me your dreams.'"[14]

Joseph gave them the same response that he later gave Pharaoh. "Pharaoh said to Joseph, 'I had a dream, and no one can interpret it. But I have heard it said of you that when you hear a dream you can interpret it.'

"'I cannot do it,' Joseph replied to Pharaoh, 'but, for the peace of Pharaoh, God will give an answer.'"[15] The interpretation had to come from God.

For the rabbinic interpretations of dreams, God was not needed. "Bar Hedya was an interpreter of dreams. To one who paid him he used to give a favourable interpretation, to one who did not pay him he gave an unfavourable interpretation. Abaye and Raba each had a dream. Abaye gave him a *zuz*, and Rab did not give him anything...."[16]

Abaye and Raba had an identical series of dreams. For each dream they told him, Bar Hedya gave Abaye an interpretation of prosperity and Raba an interpretation of disaster.[17]

The extended passage that follows makes three points. 1) The rabbinic interpreter of dreams functions independently of God. 2) He has the power not only to foretell the future, but also to determine it. 3) "A curse uttered by a sage, even when undeserved, comes to pass." Each point is an assertion of the ultimate supremacy of rabbinic authority.

In the Talmud, the meaning of a dream depends upon the rabbi who interprets it, not the Lord. So does the course of events, for better or for worse. God must bow to the will of the Rabbis. This is a radical departure from Tanakh.

"Daniel replied, 'No wise man, enchanter, magician or diviner can explain to the king the mystery he has asked about, but there is a God in heaven who reveals mysteries. He has shown King Nebuchadnezzar what will happen in days to come....As for me, this mystery has been revealed to me, not because I have greater wisdom than other living men, but so that you, O king, may know the interpretation and that you may understand what went through your mind.'"[18]

Balaam, who was hired to curse Israel, said, "'Even if Balak gave me his palace filled with silver and gold, I could not do anything of my own accord, good or bad, to go beyond the command [lit., the mouth] of the LORD — and I must say only what the LORD says.'"[19]

The rabbinic interpreter of dreams, on the other hand, is completely autonomous. He interprets without hearing from the Lord. Whatever he says, however, whether justified or not, determines the future.

Authoritative Citation vs. "the Word of the Lord"

The wisdom of the Rabbis replaced "the word of the Lord." The lone prophet had declared, with all the authority of God, "Thus saith the Lord..." That was replaced by, "When Rabin came he stated in the name of R. Simeon b. Pazzi in the name of R. Joshua b. Levi who had it from Bar Kappara..."[20] Or, "R. Bizna b. Zabda said in the name of R. Akiba who had it from R. Panda who had it from R. Nahum, who had it from R. Biryam reporting a certain elder — and who was this? R. Bana'ah..."[21]

The crucial question had been, "What is the Word of the Lord?" That was replaced by, "What is the law of the (majority of the) sages?" The *halakha*, the law under which the Rabbis contended that Israel should now live, followed the majority, not God.

"R. Eleazar further said in the name of R. Hanina: Whoever reports a saying in the name of its originator brings deliverance to the world..."[22] The words of the prophets, or the Word of the Lord, did not carry such power.[23]

Assigning the prophetic role to the Rabbis was important in establishing their supremacy. Consequently, it was not only the voice of present and future unauthorized prophets that needed to be silenced, but also, sometimes, the voice of past prophets. The Talmud tells us that Jonathan ben Uzziel "sought to reveal [by] a targum [the inner meaning] of the Hagiographa, but a Bath Kol went forth and said, Enough! What was the reason? — Because the date of the Messiah is foretold in it."[24]

The passage referred to in the Writings which foretells the date of the Messiah is Dan.9:24-25. There it states that the Temple will be destroyed after Messiah has come and been cut off. (cf.Naz.32b) That is why the Talmud also says, "Blasted be the bones of those who calculate the end. For they would say, since the predetermined time has arrived, and yet he has not come, he will never come."[25]

Some have seen this as a warning against speculation and date-setting. It is not. The stated reason for the prohibition is that proper calculation would lead to the conclusion that the time for Messiah to come has already passed. Therefore, since he has not come, he will not come. Or what was worse, those who calculate the time of Messiah's coming from Daniel's prophecy might say, "Messiah must have already come." That was too dangerous to permit.

Enforcement

19. THE SANHEDRIN

Torah was not given or understood to be "religious" law. It was national law. Inasmuch as the Rabbis presented their rulings as having equal or greater authority than Torah, rabbinic law was also never intended to be "religious" law. It too was presented as national law. Under Akiba's leadership, the Rabbis were asserting their right to determine the law and destiny of all Israel.[1]

In actual number, the Pharisees were never more than a small minority within Israel.[2] Those who followed Akiba in his desire and plan to make rabbinic authority supreme were a party within the Pharisaic movement. As such, they had to devise a means for consolidating their newly gained power and insuring national compliance with their rulings. The Sanhedrin was the means to that end.

The Great Sanhedrin in Jerusalem had become the repository of all the national authority that Rome allowed. Prior to the destruction of the Temple, the Sanhedrin had been controlled by the Sadducees. After the destruction of the Temple, the synagogue grew in religious importance. Increasingly, the Rabbis defined that importance. When Akiba gained control, the Academy at Yavneh became the legislative body for enacting rabbinic law and for controlling the membership of the Sanhedrin.

"Thus Jewish law, with regard to its sources, is essentially aristocratic, that is, rabbinic, not democratic, not emanating from the sovereignty of the people. This is equally true with regard to the administration of the law. Halakhic adjudication and halakhic interpretation in their traditional, classical forms have invariably been in the hands of rabbinical judges and rabbinical scholars.

"In view of the vital role of the rabbis, we are justified in calling Jewish law *divrei Soferim* (rabbinic law). Indeed, the halakhah of *lo tasur* — Thou shalt not turn aside from the sentence which they [the rabbis] shall teach thee (Deuteronomy 17:11), — and the theology of *Emunat Hakhamim* (faith in the sages) enunciated by the aggadic addition to the Sayings of the Fathers, take on fuller meaning: Jewish law without the rabbis — their erudition, their devotion, and their ethical sensitivity — is inconceivable."[3]

The Rabbis made the law. The Sanhedrin, or Beth Din, which they controlled, became the means of enforcing it.

The Nature of the Sanhedrin

Only the leading rabbis could qualify to serve on the Sanhedrin. "R. Johanan said: None are to be appointed members of the Sanhedrin, but men of stature, wisdom, good appearance, mature age, with a knowledge of sorcery, and who are conversant with all the seventy languages of mankind, in order that the court should have no need of an interpreter. Rab Judah said in Rab's name: None is to be given a seat on the Sanhedrin unless he is able to prove the cleanness of a reptile from Biblical texts."[4]

To qualify for the Sanhedrin, a rabbi had to be, literally, a "master of sorcery". In other words, he had to be a master of what the Torah expressly forbids: "Let no one be found among you who ...practices divination or sorcery, interprets omens, engages in witchcraft, or casts spells, or who is a medium or spiritist or who consults the dead. Anyone who does these things is detestable to the LORD, and because of these detestable practices the LORD your God will drive out those nations before you."[5]

To qualify for the Sanhedrin, a rabbi also had to know "all the seventy languages of mankind." That would necessitate knowing their culture and practices. Yohanan ben Zakkai is said to have also studied the language of the demons and that of the ministering angels.[6]

"A Sanhedrin must not be established in a city which does not contain [at least] two who can speak [the seventy languages] and one who understands them. In the city of Bethar there were three and in Jabneh four [who knew how to speak them]: [viz.,] R. Eliezer, R. Joshua, R. Akiba, and Simeon the Temanite..."[7] R. Akiba was a member of the Great Sanhedrin in Yavneh and in Bethar, the center of Bar Kokhba's power.

To qualify for the Sanhedrin, a rabbi also had to be able to prove from the Bible that reptiles — which the Bible explicitly declares to be unclean — are clean. In other words, he had to be able to use the Scriptures to prove the exact opposite of what they actually teach.

The entire rabbinic system was based upon the authority of the Rabbis to declare that 'right is left and left is right.'[8] "The terms 'bind' and 'loose' (*'asar we-hittir'*), employed by the Rabbis in their legal terminology, point indeed to a sort of supernatural power claimed by the Pharisees for their prohibitory or permissory decrees, probably because they could place both men and things under the ban, or '*herem.*'...Singularly enough, the abolition of the power of excommunication, under the influence of modern times and through the interference of the worldly government, marks the beginning of the decline of Rabbinical Authority in occidental

Judaism..."⁹

"On a biblical verse which instructs a Jew not to deviate from the decisions of the judges 'to the right or to the left,' Rashi comments, reflecting an interpretation of the Sifrei, 'Even if you are told that right is left or left is right.'

"...In sum, the Great Sanhedrin was assigned unqualified authority, by majority vote, to decide questions affecting the oral law and matters of legal definition."[10]

The Rabbis invested the Bet Din, i.e. House of Judgment, with absolute authority in every aspect of life. There was no appeal of its decisions.[11]

Saved at the Cost of their Lives

During the time of Rabban Simeon b. Gamaliel, the Sanhedrin was not an instrument for putting many people to death. That is not surprising, since the Sanhedrin did not then have the authority to put anyone to death.[12] Still, the death penalty was seen as judicially necessary to maintain civil order.

"A Sanhedrin that effects an execution once in seven years, is branded a destructive tribunal; R. Eliezer B. Azariah says: Once in seventy years. R. Tarfon and R. Akiba say: Were we members of a Sanhedrin, no person would ever be put to death. [Thereupon] Rabban Simeon b. Gamaliel remarked, [Yea] and they would also multiply shedders of blood in Israel!"[13]

During the time of Rabban Simeon b. Gamaliel, R. Akiba was not a member of the Sanhedrin. At that time, when he was continually challenging almost every position Gamaliel took, Akiba said that if he were a member of the Sanhedrin, "no person would ever be put to death." When Akiba did become a member of the Sanhedrin, his position changed.

He did not shy away from pronouncing the harshest death sentence for any offender. In one of his arguments with R. Ishmael, Akiba used an extra letter in the text to maintain that, "'A daughter of a priest who commits adultery should be executed by burning.' Rabbi Ishmael said to him: 'Shall we burn this woman because you must find an interpretation for your *vav*?'"[14]

"If a priest performed the Temple service whilst unclean, his brother priests do not charge him therewith at Beth Din, but the young priests take him out of the Temple Court and split his skull with clubs. A layman who performed the service in the Temple: R. Akiba said, He is strangled; The Sages say: [His death is] at the hands of Heaven."[15]

The other Sages left this particular matter in the hands of God, but Akiba taught that the Sages were in the place of God. That became the rule. "In the early rabbinic period the role of divine judgment as part of the human legal process is reduced. The Mishnah itself records that the suspected adulteress's ordeal by bitter waters has ceased to be practiced [Sot.9.9]; the Biblical oracle and curse in property offences are replaced by judicial oaths (for breach of which there are sanctions in human courts [Sheb.8.3] indeed the very word 'God' in these Biblical sources is sometimes interpreted by the Rabbis to mean 'judges'."[16]

The Rabbis took over from God the role of bringing judgment on men for certain offences. "...[T]hey ruled that flogging imposed by the court relieved the offender of the divine threat."[17]

Akiba's method of interpretation endowed the Sanhedrin with great powers of punishment. "Whence do we derive that his property may be forfeited? — From the text: *And whosoever come not within three days, according to the counsel of the princes and the elders, all his substance should be forfeited and himself separated from the congregation of the captivity.* Whence do we derive that we may quarrel [with an offender], curse him, smite him, pluck his hair and put on him an oath? — From the text: *And I contended with them, and cursed them, and smote certain of them and plucked off their hair and made them swear by God.* Whence do we derive that we may fetter, arrest and prosecute them? — From the text: [Let judgment be executed upon him with all diligence], *whether it be unto death, or to uprooting, or to confiscation of goods or to imprisonment.*"[18]

From the rabbinic point of view, all of these punishments, including death, were inflicted not just for the protection of society, but for the offender's own good. They were necessary to turn the offender from his sin, and thereby save his soul from death.

There were other circumstances that also required that a man die for his own good. Ben Dama, R. Ishmael's nephew, was dying from a snake bite. He wanted Jacob, a well-know *min*, to heal him. R. Ishmael forbid it, Ben Dama died and R. Ishmael rejoiced because being healed by a *min* would have destroyed Ben Dama's soul.[19]

In the eyes of the Rabbis, the *minim*, by influencing others to believe as they did, were committing a sin greater than murder. For his own good, anyone seeking to kill another would have to be killed, if he would not turn away from his sin. An anonymous Mishnah decrees that, "The following must be saved [from sinning] even at the cost of their lives: He who pursues after his neighbour to slay him..."[20]

The Rabbis were building a fence around the Torah, and the *minim* were breaking through that fence. They had to be stopped.

The Sanhedrin was the official means of enforcing rabbinic authority, especially in dangerous times.[21]

There were others, such as the *Zaken Mamre*, i.e. the Rebellious Elder, who rebelled against the authority of the Rabbis. For their own good and for the good of the community, they had to be put to death.

20. THE REBELLIOUS ELDER

Before his death, Moses gave Israel specific prescriptions for life in the land they would soon enter. Some of these had to do with resolving disputes. God had established a priesthood in Israel, and given them judicial responsibility. He would soon raise up judges like Gideon, Deborah, and Samuel. They would lead the people in battles and help decide disputes.

The Rabbis put themselves in the place of the priests and the judges, as we have already seen in their treatment of Dt.17:11. ("Do not turn aside from what they tell you, to the right or to the left.") The following verses say that, "The man who shows contempt for the judge or for the priest who stands ministering there to the LORD your God must be put to death. You must purge the evil from Israel. All the people will hear and be afraid, and will not be contemptuous again."[1]

The Rabbis applied this warning and judgment to any and all of their rulings. It was a means to command submission and conformity. Since the Rabbis had no Biblical authority, there were those unwilling to do that.

Sometimes there was even rebellion among the Rabbis themselves. That threatened the whole basis of rabbinic authority. An elder could not be allowed to do that. So the Rabbis formulated the law of the rebellious elder, based on their transformation of Dt.17:12-13.

Shaye Cohen makes the simple observation: "The law of the rebellious elder, a (deliberate?) distortion of Deut. 17:12, was discussed by Yavnean authorities."[2] Their discussion produced something quite different from what appears in Torah.

The Torah text calls the people to come with difficiult civil and criminal law cases to the priest or judge whom God had raised up. The Rabbis referred it to general obedience to their own decrees, and instituted a death sentence for any recalcitrant elder. The Torah text commands the parties to the dispute to obey exactly the judicial decision of the priest or judge. The Rabbis commanded all Israel to give unswerving obedience to any decision they made, whether it was right or wrong.

"Our Rabbis taught: A rebellious elder is liable only for a matter the deliberate transgression of which is punished by extinction, whilst the unwitting offence involves a sin offering: this is R. Meir's view. R. Judah said: For a matter of which the fundamental principle is Biblical, whilst its interpretation is by the Scribes. R. Simeon said: Even for a single detail arising out of the subtle interpretations of the Rabbis."[3]

The rebellious elder is one who deliberately rejects the teaching of the Rabbis. "Especially intriguing is the assertion in mSanhedrin 11:3, 'there is greater stringency with respect to Scribes' laws than with respect to laws of Torah....He who holds that there is no legal basis for tefillin so as to transgress laws of Torah is exempt from punishment while he who holds that there are five biblical passages to be included in the tefillin so as to amend Scribes' laws is liable for punishment.'

"The Mishnah here defends the right of Scribes to interdict the oldest tefillin now known to us [from Qumran], which contain more than four passages and include the decalogue."[4]

An elder could teach the people to transgress Torah without becoming guilty, but if he taught the people to transgress the words of the Rabbis he was brought before the Sanhedrin. If he would not submit, he was executed. A *Zaken Mamre*, a rebellious elder, was one who would not recognize the ultimate authority of the Rabbis over Scripture, prophets, priests, people, and God.

R. Eliezer the Great had refused to submit to the Rabbis, because even God Himself had said that he was correct. R. Eliezer was excommunicated. If the doctrine of the rebellious elder had been in place at that time, he would have been put to death.

R. Akiba was often flogged for refusing to submit to Gamaliel and his majority. If the doctrine of the rebellious elder had been in place at that time, Akiba would have been put to death. Moses would have been put to death by Korah and his majority. Most of the prophets would have been considered similarly rebellious.

"The crime of the rebellious elder, for which he was executed, consisted of his giving a practical decision opposed in the final ruling of one of the *Botte din* (plural of Beth din) in Jerusalem."[5] An anonymous Mishnah states that, "An elder rebelling against the ruling of Beth Din (is strangled)..."[6]

"He [the rebellious elder] was executed neither by his local Beth Din nor by the Beth Din at Jabneh, but was taken to the Great Beth Din in Jerusalem and kept there until the [next] festival and executed thereon, for it is written, 'And all the people shall hear and fear, and do no more presumptuously.' This is R. Akiba's opinion."[7]

Michael Sokol explains that, "The status of *Zaken Mamrei* (Z.M.), the rebellious elder who disputes the *pesak* of the Great Sanhedrin, is one of the best examples of this theme of authority. Ramban explains that the need to publicize the punishment of Z.M. (Sanhedrin 89a) follows from the fact that he is executed not because of the severity of his offense *per se* but because of its destructive impact. He is, after all, entitled to express his sincerely held halakhic convictions, but is put to death despite this as a result of his refusal to acquiesce, which threatens to undermine the very concept of uniform normative behavior crucial to any legal system. The fact that Z.M. is obligated to accept rabbinic authority and its procedures, even when they appear to be blatantly inaccurate — *af al yemin she-hu semol, ve-al semol she-hu yemin* (even if they declare right to be left and vice versa) — further underscores the significance of formal procedure and principles of *pesak*, which may even outweigh objective halakhic truth."[8]

The Rabbis would not tolerate any challenge to the position in which they had placed themselves.[9] Their primary concern was not "objective halakhic truth," nor objective Biblical truth, but rather the establishment and maintenance of their own power. If even one of their own were to challenge that self-proclaimed authority, he had to be killed.

The *Mesith* and Others

The Torah says, "If your very own brother, or your son or daughter, or the wife you love, or your closest friend secretly entices you [יסיתך] saying, 'Let us go and worship other gods' (gods that neither you nor your fathers have known, gods of the peoples around you, whether near or far, from one end of the land to the other), do not yield to him or listen to him. Show him no pity. Do not spare him or shield him.

"You must certainly put him to death. Your hand must be the first in putting him to death, and then the hands of all the people. Stone him to death, because he tried to turn you away from the LORD your God, who brought you out of Egypt, out of the land of slavery. Then all Israel will hear and be afraid, and no one among you will do such an evil thing again."[13]

A *Mesith* is one who seduces an individual or a town to turn away from the Lord and worship other gods. For such a person, the Torah commands death by stoning. The Rabbis authorized the Sanhedrin to convict people of this crime.

"IN CAPITAL CHARGES etc. Our Rabbis taught: Whence (do we infer) that if the accused leaves the Beth din guilty, and someone says: 'I have a statement to make in his favour,' he is to be brought back? — Scripture reads: *The guiltless slay thou not*. And whence (do we infer) that if he leaves the Beth din not guilty, and someone says: 'I have something to state against him,' he may not be brought back? — From the verse, *And the righteous, slay thou not*.

"R. Shimi b. Ashi said: It is the reverse in the case of a Mesith, for it is written: *Neither shalt thou spare, neither shalt thou conceal him*. R. Kahana derived it from the words: *But thou shalt surely kill him.*"[11]

"R. Hama b. Hanina said: I heard it said in a lecture by R. Hiyya b. Abba: A *Mesith* is different, because the Divine Law states, *Neither shall thine eyes pity him; neither shalt thou conceal him.*"[12]

In the gospels, the accusation the Sanhedrin brought to Pilate against Yeshua was that he was a *Mesith*. "We have found this man to be deceiving the people [את זה מצאנו מסית את העם]."[13] Pilate later responded, "You brought me this man as one who was deceiving the people [כמסית את העם]..."[14]

There were other similar crimes for which the Sanhedrin was also committed to sentence people to death.[15] "As to magianism, Rab and Samuel (differ thereon): one maintains that it is sorcery, the other, blasphemy. For R. Zutra b. Tobiah said in Rab's name: He who learns a single thing from a Magian is worthy of death."[16] The magi were the priests of ancient Persia.

The gospel of Matthew says, "After Jesus was born in Bethlehem in Judea, during the time of King Herod, Magi from the east came to Jerusalem and asked, 'Where is the one who has been born king of the Jews? We saw his star in the east and have come to worship him.'"[17] For the Rabbis, anyone who learned anything from magi was worthy of death.

There are related sections in the Talmud that speak of the attitude one should have towards anyone who transgressed the rabbinic interpretation of Torah or a rabbinic ruling. "Rabbah the son of R. Huna said: It is permissible to call 'wicked' any one who is insolent, as it is said, *A wicked man hardeneth his face*. R. Nahman the son of R. Isaac said: One may even hate him, as it is said, *And the boldness of his face is changed*. Do not read *yeshuneh* [changed] but *yesuneh* [hated]....One may call every impudent person a scoundrel and hate him."[18]

"Whoever commits a transgression, to hate that person is a meritorious work (mitzvah)."[19] Hatred is a very powerful force. It overrides mercy.

21. *AM HA-ARETZ*

" 'But now be strong, O Zerubbabel,' declares the LORD. 'Be strong, O Joshua son of Jehozadak, the high priest. Be strong, all you people of the land [וחזק כל עם הארץ],' declares the LORD, 'and work. For I am with you,' declares the LORD Almighty."[1]

"*Am ha'aretz*" literally means "people of the land," but in rabbinic writings it is a term of contempt for anyone who did not accept rabbinic authority. In the time leading up to the Bar Kokhba Revolt, the vast majority of Jews did not accept rabbinic authority.

"Rabbinic interpretations of normative Jewish religious behaviour carried little inherent authority immediately after the Destruction. Attached though most Jews may have been to the ancient rites of the Sabbath and circumcision, and steadfast though the majority were in the observance of the Biblical commandments affecting their diet and sexual relations, few were immediately predisposed to perform such practices in accordance with the rigid dictates of Pharisaic halakhah."[2]

"Our Rabbis taught: Who is an *'Am ha-arez*? Whoever does not recite the Shema morning and evening with its accompanying benedictions; such is the statement of R. Meir. The Sages say: Whoever does not put on the phylacteries. Ben Azzai says: Whoever has not the fringe upon his garment. R. Jonathan b. Joseph says: Whoever has sons and does not rear them to study Torah. Others say: Even if he learnt Scripture and Mishnah but did not attend upon Rabbinical scholars, he is an *'Am ha-arez*."[3]

For some of the Rabbis, only those who accepted their authority and gave financially or materially to their support escaped the contempt and stigma of the term, and the consequences.[4] Most people had no reason to accept or support the Rabbis.

"As a group, rabbis were unable to claim a historically sanctioned locus standing within any of the traditional frameworks of Jewish government.

"...Even amongst those Jews who were not pronounced *minim* (heretics), and hence outside the obvious orbit of rabbinic influence, the authority of the rabbis had to be asserted; it could not be automatically assumed. As the talmudic record frequently laments, non-rabbinic Jews had persistently to be wooed. The much maligned *'amei ha-'ares* of 'Eres Yisra'el, to take the most outstanding case, could not simply be brow-beaten; eventually, they had to be won over. To disregard that situation is both to telescope the length of the rabbinic enterprise and to miss much of its essentially political thrust."[5]

The Pharisees had used whatever power they had to eliminate oppositon and gain more power. The Rabbis did the same.

The position the Romans granted to Yohanan ben Zakkai gave the Rabbis some power with which to work. The Talmud shows the Rabbis using that power to disenfranchise everyone who would not accept their rule.

The Talmud says, "Greater is the hatred wherewith the *'amme ha-arez* hate the scholar than the hatred wherewith the heathens hate Israel, and their wives [hate even] more than they.... Our Rabbis taught: Six things were said of the *'amme ha-arez'*: We do not commit testimony to them; we do not accept testimony from them; we do not reveal a secret to them; we do not appoint them as guardians for orphans; we do not appoint them stewards over charity funds; and we must not join their company on the road. Some say, We do not proclaim their losses too."[6]

These are severe restrictions. The Sanhedrin would receive testimony against the *am ha'aretz*, but would not accept testimony from them. The *am ha'aretz* could not testify on their own behalf nor on the behalf of anyone else. They could not lodge accusations. They had no standing before the Sanhedrin.

If the children of the *am ha'aretz* were orphaned, the Rabbis would appoint guardians for them. If the relatives of the orphans did not accept rabbinic rule, they would not be appointed as their guardians.

Only followers of the Rabbis were put in charge of the distribution of charity funds. Only they would determine who received what we would today call humanitarian aid.

Not only did the Rabbis annul the legal rights of the *am ha'aretz*, they also publicly shunned them, and claimed the right to interfere in their most personal affairs. "In matrimonial matters the principle adopted is that, since marriages are, as a rule, contracted in accordance with the rabbinical statutes, the Rabbis have the right to annul any marriage which is not in conformity with their ruling (Yeb.90b). In money matters the Rabbis claimed the same right of confiscation in cases when their ruling was disregarded as was exercised by Ezra (see Ezra x.8; Git.36b)."[7]

For any man looking to marry, "Our Rabbis taught: ...let him not marry the daughter of an *'am ha-arez*, because they are detestable and their wives are vermin, and of their daughters it is said, *Cursed be he that lieth with any manner of beast*.

"...R. Meir used to say: Whoever marries his daughter to an *'am ha-arez* is as though he bound and laid her before a lion."[8]

Such characterizations of the *am ha'aretz* as being less than human reached some extremes. According to R. Eleazar, a disciple of R. Akiba, it was permitted to kill an *am ha'aretz*, even in the holiest of times, as though he were less than a beast.

"R. Eleazar said: An *'am ha-arez*, it is permitted to stab him (even) on the Day of Atonement which falls on the Sabbath. Said his disciples to him, Master, say *to slaughter him* (ritually). - He replied: This (ritual slaughter) requires a benediction, whereas that (stabbing) does not require a benediction.

"...R. Samuel b. Nahmai said in R. Johanan's name: One may tear an *'am ha-arez* like a fish! Said R. Samuel b. Isaac: And (this means) along his back."[9]

The extent of power which the Rabbis claimed and sought to exercise was designed to bring every aspect of life under their control. When possible, that power was exercised according to the dictum of R. Akiba: "'No pity is to be shown in a matter of law."[10] Those who did not accept rabbinic rule had no legal recourse when wronged.

Though the Rabbis gained in power after the Great Revolt, they still were far from having complete control. That was especially so in Galilee, which was geographically removed from the center of rabbinic power. The Galileans even refused to join the rabbinically sanctioned and commanded Bar Kokhba Revolt.

"Moved to the centre of Jewish life through the two wars with Rome, the Galilean peasants allowed themselves to be but little impressed by the religious demands and ideals of rabbis who had come into Galilee from Judea: the rigorous purity and tithe laws of these 'immigrant rabbis' could not be enforced in Galilee. 'Galileans, it seems, were not prepared to accede to the rabbis' demands, especially since the rabbis of the second century were on the whole artisans unaffected themselves by any of the agricultural laws that they tried to impose on the farmers'."[11]

The Talmud presents the Galileans as ignorant and backward. "Josephus, however, pictures Galilee as consisting mainly of Torah-true Jews and does not hint at all that Galilee spawned its own sort of assimilated Judaism."[12]

"The Targum's recurrent encomia of the rabbis...and of adhering to '*torah*' may, in large measure, reflect the centuries-long struggle of the rabbis to impose their authority on the masses of Jewry and on their institutions and practices. The length of this struggle can be ascertained from the fact there is virtually no evidence of popular acceptance of the binding character of rabbinic law and rabbinic institutions before the middle of the third century C.E."[13]

There was one additional serious problem which the Rabbis found with the *am ha'aretz*. More and more of them were either becoming *minim* or were sympathetic to the *minim*. They were looking with favor on a movement in irreconcileable conflict with rabbinic claims of authority.

We will soon look more closely at the *minim*, but here it is sufficient to note that the Jewish disciples of Jesus, the *Talmidei Yeshua*, were among those considered *minim*, perhaps the primary group so designated. Later we will delineate the issues in conflict, because Yeshua and his disciples are an important part of the Bar Kokhba-Akiba story.

According to the gospels, "the common people [i.e. the *am ha'aretz*] heard him [Jesus] gladly."[14] The following four sections from the gospels help frame the problems this caused for the Pharisees and the Rabbis after them.

1) "Jesus entered the temple courts, and, while he was teaching, the chief priests and the elders of the people came to him. 'By what authority are you doing these things?' they asked. 'And who gave you this authority?'

"Jesus replied, 'I will also ask you one question. If you answer me, I will tell you by what authority I am doing these things. The baptism of John - where did it come from? Was it from heaven, or from men?'

"They discussed it among themselves and said, 'If we say, *From heaven*, he will ask, *Then why didn't you believe him?* But if we say, *From men* - we are afraid of the people, for they all hold that John was a prophet.'"

"...When the chief priests and the Pharisees heard Jesus' parables, they knew he was talking about them. They looked for a way to arrest him, but they were afraid of the crowd because the people held that he was a prophet."[15]

Some of the common people believed that John the Baptist and Jesus were prophets, i.e. authorized by God alone. Mark and Luke both say that "the teachers of the law" were joined with the chief priests and the elders in this confrontation. In the eyes of this coalition, Yeshua had no authority - neither institutional, nor traditional, nor Pharisaic. They would have arrested him except for fear of the common people.

2) "Finally the temple guards went back to the chief priests and Pharisees, who asked them, 'Why didn't you bring him in?'

"'No one ever spoke the way this man does,' the guards declared.

"'You mean he has deceived you also?" the Pharisees retorted. Has any of the rulers or of the Pharisees believed in him? No! But this mob that knows nothing of the law - there is a curse on them."[16]

The Pharisees considered Yeshua a deceiver, i.e. a *mesith*. They cursed the common people for not knowing the law and for believing in Yeshua.

3) "So the Pharisees said to one another, "See, this is getting us nowhere. Look how the whole world has gone after him!"

"...Yet at the same time many even among the leaders believed in him. But because of the Pharisees they would not confess their faith for fear they would be put out of the synagogue [ἀποσυνάγωγοι]."[17]

The common people and some of the leaders, i.e. the elders, were believing in Yeshua. The Pharisees were excommunicating those who believed, placing them under the ban.

4) "Then the chief priests and the Pharisees called a meeting of the Sanhedrin. 'What are we accomplishing?' they asked. 'Here is this man performing many miraculous signs. If we let him go on like this, everyone will believe in him, and then the Romans will come and take away both our place and our nation.'

"Then one of them, named Caiaphas, who was high priest that year, spoke up, 'You know nothing at all! You do not realize that it is better for you that one man die for the people than that the whole nation perish.'"[18]

The am ha'aretz were believing in Yeshua. Because of the Messianic expectations surrounding him, that threatened the governmental role which the Romans had given to the Sanhedrin. In response, the Sanhedrin gathered to decide what to do. The counsel of Caiaphas was that Yeshua should be put to death for the good of the people.

All this brings us to the question: What were the common Messianic expectations in the time leading up to Rabbi Akiba's proclamation of Simeon ben Kosiba as the Messiah?

THE MESSIAH

22. THE FIRST CENTURY CONCEPT OF MESSIAH

R. Akiba saw something that convinced him to proclaim Simeon ben Kosiba the Messiah. What was it? The Talmud does not tell us. We can, however, determine what others at the time were expecting the Messiah to be and do. Then we can judge how ben Kosiba fit into those expectations.

In the first and second centuries, there was widespread anticipation of and desire for the appearance of Messiah. The different expectations of who Messiah would be and what he would do were derived from many different verses of Scripture, interpreted in many different ways.

"[T]he figure of the messiah that emerges from the literature written after the Roman conquest of Palestine takes two different shapes. First, there is the political figure of Messiah the son of David; and, second, there is the transcendental messiah, who is dissociated from any physical kingship."[1]

There were different mixes of expected changes that Messiah would bring in government, righteousness, and Torah. There were different expectations concerning changes in the natural order that would be brought with supernatural signs and wonders.

The various Judaisms of the time produced a variety of expectations. These are contained in the Apocalyptic/Pseudepigraphical works, the Dead Sea Scrolls, the Talmud, and the "New Testament."

Historical hindsight tends to spotlight the "winners," and relegate the "losers" to obscurity. That, however, gives us a distorted view of the conditions at the time. Some groups that faded into obscurity later were very significant in their day.

As James Charlesworth notes: "...the Pseudepigrapha is a major source for understanding the intertestamental period. These writings can no longer be discarded as documents from a fringe group of heterodox Jews. They must be recognized as containing many important ideas, concepts, expressions, and dreams that permeated the fabric of Hellenistic Judaism."[2]

Government and Righteousness

The "Psalms of Solomon" contain a variety of Messianic references. "They attest a belief in afterlife (3:12; 13:11; 14:3; 14:13;

16:1-3), but the primary focus of the eschatology is on the restoration of Jerusalem, which will be brought about by the Davidic messiah. The Psalms were written in the wake of Pompey's conquest of Jerusalem in 63 B.C....Because of their general theology the Psalms are usually ascribed to Pharisaic circles.

"The portrait of the messiah echoes the language of the canonical Psalms (especially Psalm 2) and Isaiah. He will at once subdue and save the nations."[3]

Similar views are expressed in 2 Baruch and in 4 Ezra, written during the second half of the first century.[4] The destruction of the wicked, the purging of Israel, and the bringing in of the righteous kingdom are all part of the envisioned endtime scenario which God brings about through Messiah. Messiah will destroy the unrighteous Gentiles, purify Jerusalem, deliver the remnant of Israel, and restore the Davidic kingdom.[5]

The Similitudes of Enoch focus on Messiah, the 'Chosen One,' 'the Son of Man.' "Righteousness is rather an attitude of rejecting this world and having faith in the Lord of Spirits and the Son of Man. Faith here involves both belief in the existence of the Lord of Spirits and the Son of Man and trust and dependence on them for salvation....

"In short, the human community of the elect and the righteous stands in very close association with the angelic world and will ultimately be merged with it. The righteous, elect 'Son of Man' figure is directly related to both the human and the heavenly righteous."[6]

Messiah is seen as the bridge between heaven and earth. He brings the righteousness of the kingdom of heaven to the earth. He brings God's salvation.

"Salvation" (ישע, ישועה) is actually a title of the Messiah in different Jewish writings of the time. It appears as such in "Jubilees," the Hymns of the Qumran community, the "Damascus Document," and in fragments like 4Q Florilegium. It is also found in rabbinic writings in the Talmudic tractate Berakoth and in the Testaments of the Twelve Patriarchs.[7]

The Dead Sea Scrolls and the Testaments of the Twelve Patriarchs speak of two Messiahs, one of whom is a priest.[8] There are scriptures that speak of Messiah as a priest, most notably Zechariah 6:13. "It is he who will build the temple of the LORD, and he will be clothed with majesty and will sit and rule on his throne. And he will be a priest on his throne. And there will be harmony between the two.'"

Whether one or two Messiahs are expected, his priestly function is to put away sin. His kingly function is to establish the rule of righteousness in the earth. The eighteenth Psalm of Solomon suggests two comings of Messiah: "May God cleanse Israel in the day of mercy and blessing, in the day of election when he brings back His Messiah."[9]

Messiah will bring cleansing from sin to Israel, which will bring the people back to God's Law. 2 Baruch speaks of the inclusion of Gentiles who observe God's law, and the exclusion of Jews who do not.[10]

Torah

In the "Rule of the Community" and other scrolls from Qumran, Messiah is presented as the final interpreter of God's Torah.[11] To some extent, this same role had also appeared in 1 Maccabees.[12]

The finalized written form of the Talmud belongs to the third, fourth, and fifth centuries. Without doubt, it contains first century material, but it is not always easy, or even possible, to determine which material that is. Appendix A looks at those aspects of the Talmudic portrayal of Messiah that seem to embody a response to the failure of the Bar Kokhba Revolt. Here we simply note that the Rabbis portrayed Messiah as the Interpreter of the Law.

"The Holy One, blessed be He, will sit in Paradise and give instruction (דורש), and all the righteous will sit before him and all the hosts (lit. family) of Heaven will stand on his right and the sun, and stars on His left; and the Holy One, blessed be he, interprets (דורש) to them the grounds of a new Torah (תורה חדשה) which the Holy One, blessed be He, will give to them by the hand of King Messiah."[13] This new Torah that Messiah brings is related to the Torah at Sinai, but different in some respects.

The Midrashim are written several centuries later, but they ascribe their views to Talmudic times. In the Midrash on Psalms, we are told that Torah will change in the days of Messiah. Unclean animals will be declared clean, but "some of the demands of the Law would be even more severe: thus marital relations would become stricter."[14]

Perhaps the most radical declaration of all is found in the Midrash on Ecclesiastes. "The Torah which a man learns in this world *is vanity*' in comparison with the Torah of the Messiah."[15] The reasoning seems to be that all things in this age are but form and appearance compared to the substance of the Messianic age and the kingdom of God on earth. According to the Rabbis, "In the days of the Messiah, bastards...will be pure."[16]

There is also the later equation of the new Torah that Messiah brings with the Oral Torah: "and this is the great hope (vouchsafed to the Jews) in Exile...for all is for good in order to (allow them) to merit *the light of the Messiah and the Oral Torah* which will be revealed through him."[17]

Messiah upholds Torah or brings a new Torah.[18] In any case, when he comes, he is to be obeyed. "Come and hear: *Unto him ye shall hearken*, even if he tells you, 'Transgress any of all the commandments of the Torah' as in the case, for instance, of Elijah on Mount Carmel, obey him in every respect in accordance with the needs of the hour!"[19]

The Supernatural

"The literature of Judaism evidences an expectation that in the Messianic Age the spirit of prophecy would be restored and prophetic figures would be prominent in the life of the nation....The inclusion of Deut. 18.18f. in the *testimonia* fragment discovered at Qumran indicates that in certain circles, at least, the appearance of a prophet 'like unto' Moses was an important feature in messianic expectations."[20]

The concluding words of Torah, which were understood to refer to the promised Messiah, emphasize the supernatural nature of the ministry of Moses. "Since then, no prophet has risen in Israel like Moses, whom the LORD knew face to face, who did all those miraculous signs and wonders the LORD sent him to do in Egypt —to Pharaoh and to all his officials and to his whole land. For no one has ever shown the mighty power or performed the awesome deeds that Moses did in the sight of all Israel."[21]

From Isaiah 11, Messiah's reign was believed by some to be eternal, and to bring changes in nature. "And wild beasts shall come from the forest and minister unto men. And asps and dragons shall come forth from their holes to submit themselves to a little child.

"And women shall no longer then have pain when they bear, Nor shall they suffer torment when they yield the fruit of the womb.'"[22]

Different scenarios present Messiah as a supernatural being. There is an eschatology "... presumed throughout 4 Ezra. First, the signs will come, then 'the hidden city' (presumably the heavenly Jerusalem) and the messiah will be revealed. ...The manner in which he slays his enemies with the breath of his mouth is paralleled in Revelation 19 ('the sword of his mouth') and evidently reflects apocalyptic traditions that were current at the end of the first century. In the interpretation the 'man' is explicitly identified as the messiah. He will gather the ten lost tribes."[23]

One of the Dead Sea Scrolls, referring to Isaiah 61:1, says that,

"The heavens and the earth will obey His Messiah...he will release the captives, make the blind see, and raise up the downtrodden...he will heal the sick, resurrect the dead, and announce glad tidings to the poor."[24]

Fragments from Qumran refer to the 'Son of God' and the 'Son of the Most High.'[25] The term "Son of God" appears in fifteen different texts from early Judaism. "The first group of texts dates from the second or early-first century B.C.E....In the second group are three documents that date from the late-first century B.C.E....In the third group are three documents from the first century C.E....In the final group are four documents that refer to an ideal person in Israel's history as God's son; they can be dated sometime around 100 C.E., give or take a quarter of a century...."[26]

In another text from Qumran, "we are told that the heavens and the earth shall obey (or serve) 'his Messiah'."[27] In the Similitudes of Enoch, Messiah is presented as a supernatural being. "As Sjoberg has remarked, he is not a man, at least not in the usual sense of the word, but is rather a heavenly being."[28]

Common Messianic Expectation Evidenced in the Gospels

In whatever form they circulated, the gospels were part of the mix of first and early second century concepts of the Messiah. They formed the faith of some Jews and probably influenced other Jews who did not believe in Jesus as Messiah. Most of the New Testament Messianic teachings appear in other earlier or later Jewish works.

Even the belief in the atoning death of Messiah is paralleled by the concept of Messiah as "salvation"; and in the cleansing from sin that his coming - sometimes understood to be a second coming after his death - was to bring. Sanhedrin 98b, the Targum, and the Midrash on Samuel all relate Isaiah 53 to Messiah. [See Appendix B.]

"2 Baruch presupposes an eschatological scenario similar to 4 Ezra. after a period of time (unspecified here) the messiah will 'return in glory.' This presumably corresponds to the death of the messiah in 4 Ezra, although it is characteristically put in a more positive way. The resurrection and judgment follow."[29]

Inasmuch as the New Testament presents the view of Jews who believe they have found their Messiah, most of it cannot properly be said to be expectation, for it is after the fact. The gospels themselves point this out: "At first his disciples did not understand all this. Only after Jesus was glorified did they realize that these things had been written about him and that they had done these things to him."[30] The disciples did not expect or even understand these things beforehand.

There is also evidence in the gospels of various, though sometimes conflicting, popular Messianic expectations. These need to be considered as part of the first century Messianic expectations.

Some people believed his origin was unknown,[31] others believed he was descended from David and came from Bethlehem, David's hometown.[32] His reign would be preceded by the coming of Elijah.[33] Elijah and/or Messiah would call Israel to a baptism, signifying cleansing and a new life.[34]

Messiah was expected to sit upon David's throne as king, and bring deliverance for Israel.[35] Messiah would establish a new government for Israel,[36] which would bring the rule of God on earth.[37] This new kingdom would be inaugurated by a sifting judgment, and characterized by the outpouring of the Holy Spirit.[38] It would in some way be universal, opening the eyes of the Gentiles to the true God.[39]

Messiah would perform miracles.[40] He would have supernatural knowledge,[41] and would prophesy.[42]

Messiah was seen as the Son of Man prophesied in Daniel 7.[43] Messiah was expected to be "the Holy One of God."[44] In a unique sense, he was to be the son of God.[45] Messiah was expected, as the son of God, His Chosen One, to have supernatural power to save and deliver himself and others.[46] He was expected to live forever, and, therefore, his kingdom was to be an eternal kingdom.[47]

We will later examine what Akiba saw that convinced him to proclaim Bar Kokhba the Messiah. At this point, we turn to the conflict between Yeshua and the Pharisees and Rabbis.

23. YESHUA, THE PHARISEES, AND THE RABBIS

Geza Vermes reminds us that, "In inter-testamental Judaism there existed a fundamental unity of exegetical tradition. This tradition, the basis of religious faith and life, was adopted and modified by its constituent groups, the Pharisees, the Qumran sectaries and the Judeo-Christians. We have, as a result, three cognate schools of exegesis of the one message recorded in the Bible, and it is the duty of the historian to emphasize that none of them can properly be understood independently of the others."[1]

On some issues, like divorce,[2] Yeshua and Beth Shammai, the dominant school at the time, held to the same position. On other issues his position could be likened to that of Beth Hillel. There are many issues — proselytes, the Sabbath, vows, sacrifices, etc. — that show both agreement and disagreement.

There was one underlying issue that gave rise to irreconcileable conflict: Authority.[3] Who was authorized by God to interpret the Scriptures and thereby define the life that all Jews should live? The Talmud and the gospels both make claims of absolute authority — mutually exclusive claims.[4]

Yeshua and the Rabbis both pointed to themselves as the supreme authority. One could not accept the claims of both. That is the reason for the intensity of the conflict presented in both the gospels and the Talmud.

"Then some Pharisees and teachers of the law came to Yeshua from Jerusalem and asked, 'Why do your disciples break the tradition of the elders? They don't wash their hands before they eat!'

"Yeshua replied, 'And why do you break the commandment of God for the sake of your tradition? You hypocrites! Isaiah was right when he prophesied about you: *These people honor me with their lips, but their hearts are far from me. They worship me in vain; their teachings are but rules taught by men.*' "

"Then the disciples came to him and asked, 'Do you know that the Pharisees were offended when they heard this?'

"He replied, 'Every plant that my heavenly Father has not planted will be pulled up by the roots. Leave them; they are blind guides. If a blind man leads a blind man, both will fall into a pit.' "[5]

On their side, the Rabbis called Yeshua a sorcerer and deceiver, a *mesith*. They called him Balaam[6] (a corrupted prophet) and Haman (an enemy of the Jews).

"It was taught: On the eve of the Passover *Yeshu* (Ms. M[unich] adds 'the Nasarean'.) was hanged. For forty days before the execution took place, a herald went forth and cried, 'He is going forth to be stoned because he has practised sorcery and enticed Israel to apostacy. Any one who can say anything in his favour, let him come forward and plead on his behalf.' But since nothing was brought forward in his favour he was hanged on the eve of the Passover! — 'Ulla retorted: Do you suppose that he was one for whom a defence could be made? Was he not a *Mesith*, concerning whom Scripture says, Neither shalt thou spare, neither shalt thou conceal him?"[7]

On his side, Yeshua did not have much good to say about the teachers of the law, i.e. the Sages or soferim, and the Pharisees. His public condemnation of them reached its greatest intensity in the famous "Seven Woes" of Matthew 23.

"They love the place of honor at banquets and the most important seats in the synagogues; they love to be greeted in the marketplaces and to have men call them `Rabbi.' But you are not to be called `Rabbi,' for you have only one Master and you are all brothers. Nor are you to be called `teacher,' for you have one Teacher, the Messiah....

"Woe to you, teachers of the law and Pharisees, you hypocrites! You shut the kingdom of heaven in men's faces. You yourselves do not enter, nor will you let those enter who are trying to.

"Woe to you, teachers of the law and Pharisees, you hypocrites! You travel over land and sea to win a single convert, and when he becomes one, you make him twice as much a son of hell as you are.

"Woe to you, blind guides! You say, 'If anyone swears by the temple, it means nothing; but if anyone swears by the gold of the temple, he is bound by his oath.'...

"Woe to you, teachers of the law and Pharisees, you hypocrites! You give a tenth of your spices—mint, dill and cummin. But you have neglected the more important matters of the law — justice, mercy and faithfulness. You should have practiced the latter, without neglecting the former. You blind guides! You strain out a gnat but swallow a camel.

"Woe to you, teachers of the law and Pharisees, you hypocrites! You clean the outside of the cup and dish, but inside they are full of greed and self-indulgence....

"Woe to you, teachers of the law and Pharisees, you hypocrites! You are like whitewashed tombs, which look beautiful on the outside but on the inside are full of dead men's bones and everything unclean. In the same way, on the outside you appear to people as righteous but on the inside you are full of hypocrisy and wickedness.

"Woe to you, teachers of the law and Pharisees, you hypocrites!

You build tombs for the prophets and decorate the graves of the righteous. And you say, 'If we had lived in the days of our forefathers, we would not have taken part with them in shedding the blood of the prophets.' So you testify against yourselves that you are the descendants of those who murdered the prophets. Fill up, then, the measure of the sin of your forefathers!

"You snakes! You brood of vipers! How will you escape being condemned to hell?"[8]

In whatever form the Pharisees and their heirs encountered such sayings, the meaning was clear. The lines were drawn. There was no possibility of accomodation.

The rabbinic designation for Yeshua became *"Yeshu."* This name was used in the early centuries, retained throughout the Middle Ages, and is still used today. It is a parody of "Yeshua." "The three consonants j, s (shin), v, with which the name of Jeshu was written, are explained as being the first letters of the three words *'Jimmach sh'mo w'zikhro'* ('May his name and his memory be blotted out!')"[9] In the eyes of the Rabbis, that was necessary for the preservation of Israel.

"For it has been taught: If a man said, 'Come and worship me,' R. Meir declared him liable to death [as any other seducer], but R. Judah ruled that he is not. Now if they [his listeners] did actually worship him, all agree that he is executed, for it is written, Thou shalt not make unto thee any idol."[10]

This passage is followed by a lengthy discussion of idolatry and seduction to idolatry. In it, discussing those guilty unto death, there is a mnemonic: *"ebed yistahaveh lemoshiah...* like Haman." The meaning of the mnemonic is literally, "the servant shall bow down to the anointed one the Messiah [*"moshiah"*; like Haman before Mordechai]... S. Funk... sees in this mnemonic an allusion to the Christians' acceptance of Jesus, 'the servant' being the title claimed by those who worship him as the Messiah."[11]

The reference to Haman is interesting. The book of Esther is unique in that it is the only book in the Bible that does not mention God, although His working behind the scenes is apparent. The story focuses on Esther and her uncle Mordecai who pleaded with the king of Persia to spare the Jews from the total annihilation that Haman had planned for them.

In granting their request, the king ordered Haman hung on a tree (literal), and his ten sons were later put to death. In the rabbinic writings, it is said that "Haman was hung in Nisan (15th according to the Midrash Esther Rabbah 5:11). How early the crucifixion of Jesus and [the hanging of] Haman were compared by the Jews is uncertain. Certainly the Esther Targum Sheni makes a direct comparison by making Haman ask for a superinscription over his gallows to say that he was king, and an indirect comparison by saying that Haman and Ben Pandora (i.e. Jesus) shared the same lodging."[12]

The fifteenth of Nisan is the date for Passover, the date on which Jesus was hung on a tree. Haman was hung on a tree in the month of Nisan, but not on the fifteenth.[13]

Haman was hung on the gallows by royal decree, and his ten sons were put to death. That brings us to the disciples of Yeshua and how they were perceived by the Rabbis.

24. THE *MINIM*

Examining the rabbinic passages that relate encounters between the Rabbis and the disciples of Yeshua is not a straightforward task. "It is a fact well known, alike to Jewish and Christian students of Hebrew literature, that certain passages of the Talmud have been erased by the 'censure.'...The Amsterdam edition of the year 1644 is the last which contains a considerable portion of the passages in question."[1]

In the Middle Ages, the Church had burned and censored the rabbinic writings for their "blasphemous" comments about Jesus, the disciples, and Christianity. The medieval rabbis, for their own safety and that of the Jewish community, had also censored the text. As a result, the passages that remain are camouflaged to facilitate their survival.

Generally, the teaching of those the Rabbis considered heretics, especially the *Talmidei Yeshua*, was called *"minuth."*[2] Those who engaged in *minuth* were called *"minim."* This view is confirmed by explicit statements in some of the uncensored texts.

"While it may be true that the term *'Minim'* may indeed describe more than one type of sectarian, the subjects discussed in many a *Ma'aseh* about the *Minim*, or encounters with them, seem clearly to point to Jewish Christians...T.B. Hag. 5b tells us that when R. Joshua b. Hananiah died it was said: 'Who will now defend our cause against the *Minim*?' (Rashi explains that the *Minim* referred to were the disciples of Jesus [*Talmide Yeshu*] who do not believe in the words of the wise.)"[3]

It may be that *"minim"* is a shortened, derogatory form of *"ma'aminim,"* i.e. believers, a designation for the *Talmidei Yeshua*. The Hebrew word *"minim"* means "kinds," "types," or "genders," as in "they brought forth after their kind." There are many ways in which the Rabbis could have derogatorily applied the term to the Talmidei Yeshua. If that is what was done, the word *"minim"* would be another example of R. Akiba's way with words, although not necessarily attributable to him personally.

The Rabbis spoke of the gospels in that way. The Greek word for "gospel" is *"evangelion,"* i.e. good news. "R. Meir called it *Aven gilyon*, R. Johanan called it *Avon gilyon*. *'Aven gilyon'* means 'a worthless thing of a book (roll),' or, since *'Aven'* in the Old Testament generally has some reference to idolatry, 'a book of idolatry.' In like manner, *Avon gilyon* may be rendered 'a book of iniquity.' R. Meir's...teachers were R. Aqiba, whom we have already met with as a fierce opponent of Christianity, and Elisha ben Abuja..."[4]

150

The Threat of *Minuth*

It was not Elisha ben Abuyah who instilled this hostile attitude in R. Meir, for "it seems highly probably that Elisha ben Abuyah himself became a Christian. Later Rabbis, for this reason, did not quote him by name, but called him Acher, the other one, because his name had been struck from the book of the living.'"[5] "It is told of Aher that when he used to rise [to go] from the schoolhouse, many books of *Minim* used to fall from his lap."[6]

"Aher mutilated the shoots....Perhaps, - God forfend! - there are two divinities!...Permission was [then] given...to strike out the merits of Aher. A Bath Kol went forth and said: Return, ye backsliding children - except Aher."[7] This is followed by various examples of Aher breaking the Sabbath, which was the primary charge of the Pharisees against Yeshua in the gospels.

Only four Rabbis ever succeeded in entering the "Garden," the place where the greatest mystical knowledge is revealed. One died instantly. Another went insane. That left only Akiba and Elisha ben Abuyah. Elisha ben Abuyah became a *min*.

About 60 A.D., Jacob, the brother of Yeshua and leader of the Talmidei Yeshua in Jerusalem, told the Apostle Paul, "You see, brother, how many myriads there are among the Jews of those who have believed, and they are all zealous for the Torah."[8] Jacob was speaking of those in Jerusalem alone. The number throughout Israel and the Diaspora was much greater, and continued to increase. They were aggressive and persuasive.

"It therefore happened sometimes that even some notable Jews were led to the new sect. Midrash Koheleth tells us that Chanina, Rabbi Joshua ben Chananiah's nephew, narrowly escaped apostasy. Only his uncle saved him. And Chanina was one of the great men of his time, of whom it was said when he afterwards went to Babylon that there was no one like him left in the Holy Land. Midrash Koheleth gives several more such examples, showing how dangerous contact with the new sect was even to men of great learning and wisdom."[9]

R. Eliezer b. Hyrcanus talked with and appreciated some of the teaching of the *minim*, i.e. *minuth*. He was suspected by some of the Rabbis of *minuth*, and was even brought before the Roman court on that charge.[10] R. Akiba convinced R. Eliezer to admit his sin and turn from it.

The Apostle Paul had been a Pharisee, "educated at the feet of Gamaliel [I], strictly according to the law of our fathers..."[11] In his own words, he had been "extremely zealous for the traditions of my fathers."[12] In his zeal, he had actively persecuted the *Talmidei*

Yeshua. But then he had become one of them.

In Avodah Zarah, i.e. "Strange Worship," everyone is warned to stay away from the minim. "'No man should have any dealings with *Minim*, nor is it allowed to be healed by them even [in risking] an hour's life. It once happened to Ben Dama the son of R. Ishmael's sister that he was bitten by a serpent and Jacob, a native of Kefar Sekaniah, came to heal him but R. Ishmael did not let him; whereupon Ben Dama said, 'My brother R. Ishmael, let him, so that I may be healed by him: I will even cite a verse from the Torah that he is to be permitted'; but he did not manage to complete his saying, when his soul departed and he died. Whereupon R. Ishmael exclaimed, 'Happy art thou Ben Dama for thou wert pure in body and thy soul likewise left thee in purity; nor hast thou transgressed the words of thy colleagues, who said, He who breaketh through a fence, a serpent shall bite him.' — It is different with the teaching of *Minim*, for it draws, and one [having dealings with them] may be drawn after them.

"The Master said: 'Nor hast thou transgressed the words of thy colleagues who have said, He who breaketh through a fence, a serpent shall bite him.' But a serpent did indeed sting him! — The bite of the serpent of the Rabbis is such as can never be cured."[13]

This Jacob of Kefar Sekaniah was the same *min* whose sayings pleased Rabbi Eliezer, causing him to be accused of *minuth*. The Rabbis recognized that healings could come from the *minim*, but maintained that such a healing would make one unclean. The Rabbis attributed the healings at the hands of the *minim* to magic or sorcery.

In order to protect Israel from the *minim*, the sages erected a fence against them. The Rabbinic law was the fence. Obedience to the words of the Rabbis led to life. Breaking through that fence led to death. To listen to the teachings of the *minim* was to break through the rabbinic fence. Since the teaching of the *minim* were said to defile the soul, it was better for a man to die than to receive such teaching.

R. Akiba vs. the *Minim*

In some Talmudic portions, Lud (Lydda), Akiba's city, is said to be the place where Jesus was crucified, rather than Jerusalem.[14] The time that had elapsed since the crucifixion of Jesus was too short for there to have been any real confusion as to where it had taken place, but the purpose of the rabbinic writings was not to record history per se, but to teach lessons. In this regard, the Talmudic peculiarity is quite interesting.

Gustav Dalman, in his comprehensive analysis of the various rabbinic passages, commented: "Lud became for the Jews a center for accounts of Jesus, i.e. nowhere was there more related about Jesus than at Lud, so that later generations received the impression that these occurrences, the accounts of which were derived from thence, took place in Lud itself. The circumstance that R. Akiba was a teacher at Lud supports the view that Lud is really to be looked upon as the source of several accounts of Jesus; for as to R. Akiba we know what great celebrity he possessed as a Rabbi, as well as also what passionate hatred of Jesus dwelt within this admirer of Bar Kokh'ba...For to say that Jesus was crucified in Lud means nothing else than that He was crucified in Akiba's city."[15]

R. Travers Herford also wrote a comprehensive analysis of the various rabbinic passages. He concluded, "R. Aqiba also is said to have been a particularly zealous opponent of the Christians. Indeed, according to one of the two conflicting opinions represented in the Talmud, Jesus was actually a contemporary of Aqiba, an anachronism which finds its best explanation in a pronounced hostility on the part of Akiba towards the Christians."[16]

What then is the meaning of the anomaly? It is a type of humor similar to what we have encountered before. I.e., "If you think that Jesus was crucified in Jerusalem, you should have seen what Rabbi Akiba did to him in Lud!"[17]

In its hostility, R. Meir's attitude towards the gospels - "*Avon Gilyon*" - did not reflect the attitude of his teacher Elisha ben Abuyah, but it did reflect that of his other teacher, R. Akiba. At a time when rabbinic Judaism was in its nascent form, Akiba made great efforts to eliminate every challenge to rabbinic authority, including the message of the *Talmidei Yeshua*.[18]

Akiba's opposition to the *Talmidei Yeshua* led him to sponsor a rabbinical Greek Bible and a rabbinical, colloquial Targum.[19] It also led him to alter Pharisaic tradition.[20] In his efforts to bring Jewish life under rabbinic authority, Akiba was consistent and relentless. Sometimes Akiba intentionally held to certain doctrines just to contradict the beliefs of the *Talmidei Yeshua*, as he had done in his struggle against Gamaliel.[21]

Other Jews were hearing, reading, and believing the message of the *Talmidei Yeshua*. To further isolate them, Akiba forbade the reading of such books. A Mishnah in Sanhedrin begins, "All Israel has a part in the world to come," and then enumerates exceptions. "R. Akiba added, 'He who reads in external books, also he who whispers over a wound, and says, *None of the diseases which I sent in Egypt will I lay upon thee, I am the Lord thy healer.'* "22

"Rabbi Akiba decided, apparently while the war of Bar Kokhba was still going on, that 'whoever is reading in 'outside' books (the Babylonian gemara explains this as meaning 'in the books of the *Minim'*) and whoever whispers over a wound (as the Judaeo-Christians were doing while healing by faith) has no share in the world to come.'"23

There were other rabbis who contended with the *minim*, but Akiba was a commander-in-chief with an overall strategy. He had provided the decisive weapon — his interpretation and manipulation of the Scriptures. "After all, this was indeed the major issue to be debated by Jews and Jewish Christians in the years leading up to the Bar Kokhba Revolt. Both communities accepted the same Scriptures as canonical. They disagreed, however, on how those Scriptures were to be interpreted."24

Akiba's method of interpretation, as well as his claim of rabbinic supremacy, effectively excluded the Jews who believed in Yeshua. It gave authority for any further Divine Revelation after Sinai to the Rabbis alone. The *Talmidei Yeshua* claimed the same authority for Yeshua and the writings of the apostles.25 There was no room on either side for compromise.

In the incident which led to the excommunication of Rabbi Eliezer, Rabbi Joshua cited Deuteronomy 30:11-14 — "It is not in heaven" — to argue for rabbinic authority. Those same verses had been cited by the Apostle Paul to refer to faith in Yeshua.26 There was a battle going on over whose interpretation of Scripture was authorized by God.

Rabbi Eliezer had been excommunicated when his last witness, the Heavenly Voice, was rejected. The gospels place great importance upon obeying the Heavenly Voice, even as the Rabbis did in every other instance. The identity of Yeshua as the Messiah was confirmed in this way.27

In the Letter to the Hebrews, there are two examples that serve to demonstrate how diametrically opposed the views of the *Talmidei Yeshua* and the Rabbis were. Both examples cite Tanakh. "See to it that you do not refuse Him who is speaking. For if those did not escape when they refused him who warned on earth, much less shall we escape who turn away from Him who warns from heaven. And His voice shook the earth then, but now He has promised, saying, *'Yet once more I will shake not only the earth, but also the heaven.'* [Haggai 2:6]"28

"Therefore, just as the Holy Spirit says, *'Today if you hear His voice, do not harden your hearts as when they provoked Me, as in the day of trial in the wilderness where your fathers tried Me by testing Me, and saw My works for forty years.'* [Ps.95:7-9]"[29] Was a *Bath Kol* to be considered authoritative or not?[30]

The major role that Akiba played in the struggle against these *minim* and their beliefs is perhaps best captured in the way each side treats Isaiah 53:12. This verse says, "Therefore will I divide him a portion among the great, and he shall divide the spoil with the mighty, because he poured out his soul unto death, and was numbered with the transgressors. For he bore the sin of many and made intercession for the transgressors." The *Talmidei Yeshua* applied this verse and the entire chapter to Yeshua.

The Rabbis applied it to Akiba. "Said R. Jonah, it is written (Is.53:12), 'Therefore will I divide him a portion among the great, and he shall divide the spoil with the mighty.' This is Rabbi Akiba who arranged Midrash, Halakhoth and Aggadoth."[31]

The gospels had presented Yeshua as the savior of the Jews, because of his atoning death. The Rabbis presented Akiba as the savior of the Jews, because he saved them from Yeshua.

In rabbinic law, a man should not be executed on a holy day, such as Passover, as Yeshua was, but, "In the view of R. Akiba, 'the instigator and inciter' is put to death on a festival."[32] Akiba considered the death of such a one so great a service to God that it could be and should be publicly performed on a festival, a holy day.

A Time to Act

The teaching of the *minim* "draws, and one may be drawn after them." Even great rabbinic scholars were drawn to it. The teaching of the *minim* broke through the fence which the Rabbis, led by Akiba, were building around the Torah. The teaching of the *minim* constituted a major obstacle to the establishment of rabbinic authority as supreme for all Israel.

The Rabbis employed a variety of methods to cut off and isolate the *minim*. "The Johannine community had apparently been expelled from the synagogue. The term *aposunagogos* appears three times in John (9:22, 12:42, 16:2) ...it means that members of the Johannine community had been thrown out (*apo*) of the synagogue (*sunagogos*)."[33]

The Pharisees had been able to expel the *Talmidei Yeshua* from some synagogues. The Rabbis sought to complete the work.

According to the Talmud, God had wanted the *Talmidei Yeshua* to be permitted to remain, but the angels had protested. "The descendants of Haman studied Torah in Benai Berak. The Holy One, blessed be He, purposed to lead the descendants of that wicked man too under the Wings of the Shechinah, but the ministering Angels protested before Him, 'Sovereign of the Universe! Shalt Thou bring him under the wings of the Shechinah who laid Thy House in ruins, and burnt Thy Temple?'"[34]

Yeshua is elsewhere rabbinically identified with Haman. Haman never came to Jerusalem. He had nothing to do with the destruction of the Temple. His descendants never studied Torah. Yeshua, on the other hand, came to Jerusalem and prophesied its destruction.[35] His disciples studied Torah, and were the one major group to be expelled from the synagogue.

The Rabbis formulated a specific curse, called the "*Birkat* (Blessing of) *ha-Minim.*"[36] It was to be recited daily in every synagogue. The purpose was twofold: 1. To weed out unknown *Minim* and their sympathizers, through their unwillingness to recite the curse; and 2. To inculcate a popular hatred of them.

The content of that "blessing" was not known for certain until "...1925 when the question was settled by the discovery of Genizah fragments containing portions of the liturgy according to the ancient Palestinian rite. In these versions, *Birkat ha-Minim* reads like this: 'May the apostates have no hope, unless they return to Thy Torah, and may the Nazarenes and the *Minim* disappear in a moment. May they be erased from the book of life, and not be inscribed with the righteous.'...The editor notes that his manuscript contains a marginal note: '*Birkat ha-Minim* was introduced after Yeshua ben Pandera, when heretics became numerous.'"[37]

In heaven, the angels convinced God to withdraw His mercy and exclude the *Talmidei Yeshua* from His kingdom in Israel. On earth, the Rabbis enforced that decision.

The purpose of some rabbinic traditions is explicitly said to be to separate all those under the authority of the Rabbis from the minim.[38] To keep people from reading the books of the minim, the Rabbis declared that they made a person unclean. But since there are places where the sacred Name of God (*azkarot*) appeared in these books, the question arose, "Should they be saved from a fire?"

"Come and hear: The blank spaces and the Books of the *Minim* may not be saved from a fire, but they must be burnt in their place, they and the Divine Names occurring in them. Now surely it means the blank portions of a Scroll of the Law? No: the blank spaces in the Books of *Minim*. Seeing that we may not save the Books of *Minim* themselves, need their blank spaces be stated? — This is its meaning: And the Books of *Minim* are like blank spaces."[39]

"R. Ishmael said: (One can reason) *a minori*: If in order to make peace between man and wife the Torah decreed, Let my Name, written in sanctity, be blotted out in water [Num.5:11-31], these, who stir up jealousy, enmity, and wrath between Israel and their Father in Heaven, how much more so; and of them David said, *Do not I hate them, O Lord, that hate thee? And am I not grieved with those that rise up against thee? I hate then with perfect hatred: I count them mine enemies.* And just as we may not rescue them from a fire, so may we not rescue them from a collapse [of debris] or from water or from anything that may destroy them."[40]

To the Rabbis, other Jews had to be kept from reading the gospels. It was so important that not only should such books not be saved from a fire, but the Rabbis also decreed that they should be intentionally burned. "R. Ishmael says: The way to deal with the books of the *Minim* is this: one cuts out the *azkarot* and burns the rest. R. Akiba says: One burns the whole thing, because it was not written in holiness."[41]

The Rabbis decreed that even a Torah scroll should be burned if it had been written by a *min*. "R. Nahman said: We have it on tradition that a scroll of the Law which has been written by a *Min* should be burnt, and one written by a heathen should be stored away."[42]

Burning books is one way to prevent others from reading and believing what is in them. But what about those who have already read and believed them? R. Akiba declared that whoever did read them had no portion in the world to come.[43] As for life in this world, the Rabbis formulated "the law of casting down into a pit."

In Tanakh, there are two instances of a living person being thrown into a pit. Joseph was thrown into a pit by his brothers.[44] Jeremiah was thrown into a pit by the officials of King Zedekiah.[45] Inasmuch as both Joseph and Jeremiah had been chosen by God, neither of these cases would seem to provide a good basis for the rabbinic law.

"R. Abbahu recited to R. Johanan: 'Idolaters and [Jewish] shepherds of small cattle need not be brought up though they must not be cast in, but *minim*, informers, and apostates may be cast in, and need not be brought up.'"[46]

"But surely, if what is slaughtered by a *min* who is an Israelite is prohibited, it goes without saying that what is slaughtered by a gentile *min* is prohibited! Do you then say it applies to the law of 'casting down into a pit'? But surely, if a *min* who is an Israelite may be cast down, it goes without saying that a gentile *min* may be cast down!"[47]

The *minim*, and all that they touched, were to be strictly and completely avoided. "'Slaughtering by a *Min* is idolatry; their bread is Samaritan bread, their wine is wine offered to idols; their fruits are not tithed, their books are books of witchcraft, and their sons are bastards. One does not sell to them or receive from them or take from them or give to them. One does not teach their sons trades, and does not obtain healing from them, either healing of property or healing of lives'."[48]

The *Talmidei Yeshua* were to be hated, and treated as defiling outcasts who had no place in this world, and no share in the world to come.[49] Their books were to be burned. Their businesses were to be boycotted. They were to be publicly ostracized. It was legal to throw them into a pit to die. Their children were not to be taught.

In the rabbinic references, the *minim* are accused of immorality, magic, and enchantment, and of seducing Israel to follow other gods. The *minim* were not teachable, submissive, or repentant, and had to be dealt with accordingly. The Rabbis are not reticent to present themselves as violent attackers of the *minim*. They considered such action to be a defense of the faith.

The Midrash Rabbah on Ecclesiastes tells us that: "The *minim* used to have dealings with R. Judah b. Nakosa. They used constantly to ask him questions which he was always able to answer. He said to them, 'In vain you bring your trifling arguments. Let us agree among ourselves that whoever overcomes his opponent (in debate) shall split his head open with a mallet.' He defeated them and rained blows on their heads until they were filled with cracks."[50]

The *minim* were considered idolators, blasphemers, and wizards who should all be put to death. Under Roman rule, however, the Rabbis themselves did not have the authority to do that.

25. THE ROMAN TRIALS

During the time of Rome's power, all her subjects were required to honor her gods. Cicero lists the "Law from the Twelve Tables", about 450 B.C., as including, "Let no one have gods on his own, neither new ones nor strange ones, but only those instituted by the State."[1]

The State authorized those gods amenable to its purposes, because the gods were the servants of the State.[2] Therefore, "Maecenas counselled Augustus: 'Honor the gods according to the custom of our ancestors, and compel others to worship them. Hate and punish those who bring in strange gods.'"[3]

Opposition to the State religion was opposition to the State. That was rebellion, and the punishment was severe. Julius Paulus, a second century jurist, recorded the following decree: "Of those people who introduce new religions with unknown customs or methods by which the minds of men could be disturbed, those of the upper classes shall be deported, those of the lower classes shall be put to death."[4]

Of all Rome's subject people, only the Jews found it impossible to obey these laws. Concerning other gods, the God of Israel had commanded: "You shall not bow down to them or worship them; for I, the LORD your God, am a jealous God, punishing the children for the sin of the fathers to the third and fourth generation of those who hate me, but showing love to a thousand generations of those who love me and keep my commandments."[5]

On numerous occasions, Jews had chosen to fight or let themselves be slaughtered rather than bow down to the gods of those who ruled over them. The Romans found this incomprehensible, but were for the most part willing to make an accomodation.[6] In general, so long as loyalty to the Emperor could be assured, it was counterproductive to provoke such religious zeal.

"Thus, after Augustus, when the worship of the Roman emperors became an imperial religion and was cultivated with obsequious zeal in the provinces, the Jews, and they alone, were not required to manifest their loyalty in any of the usual forms of adoration such as burning incense before the image of the emperor, or to take oath by the emperors. In strictness this exemption would have extended only to peregrine Jews, not to such as acquired the status of Roman citizens, and particularly not to freedmen, who in law were bound to worship the *sacra* of their former masters. But here also an exception was made in their favor, and various other privileges were accorded to them."[7]

Those rights and privileges belonged only to those who were Jewish by birth. If a proselyte did not worship the gods, he made himself liable to prosecution for 'atheism.'

The followers of Yeshua consisted of Jews and also Gentiles who had joined themselves to the sect. The first great State persecution of Christians, mostly Gentiles, took place under Nero, without trials. Rome had burned in 64 A.D., and the populace suspected the emperor of having started the blaze. He needed a scapegoat.[8] He chose the Christians.

In 66 A.D., the Great Revolt broke out in Judea. Prior to that, and for forty years following, there does not seem to have been any concerted Roman persecution of the *Talmidei Yeshua* in Judea. There, as throughout the empire, the Romans seemed content to work through the local leadership they had empowered.

When the leaders of the Sanhedrin brought Yeshua to Pilate, around 30 A.D., "Pilate came out to them and asked, 'What charges are you bringing against this man?'

"'**If he were not a criminal,**' they replied, '**we would not have handed him over to you.**'

"Pilate said, 'Take him yourselves and judge him by your own law.'

"'**But we have no right to execute anyone**,' the Jewish leaders objected."[9]

The response of the leaders of the Sanhedrin - "If he were not a criminal, we would not have handed him over to you" - shows that they expected and were accustomed to the cooperation and compliance of the procurator.[10] Their own power to punish Yeshua or his disciples was limited. Sometime before 30 A.D., Rome took away the authority of the Sanhedrin to put anyone to death.[11]

The high priests and the leaders of the Sanhedrin were politically appointed, but they needed the procurator's assistance to legally execute Yeshua or anyone else. Occasionally they ignored this Roman limitation, but they endangered their own position when they did so.[12]

Paul said of himself, "I too was convinced that I ought to do all that was possible to oppose the name of Yeshua of Nazareth. And that is just what I did in Jerusalem. On the authority of the chief priests I put many of the saints in prison, and when they were put to death, I cast my vote against them. Many a time I went from one synagogue to another...to imprison and beat [them],...and I tried to force them to blaspheme. In my obsession against them, I even went to foreign cities to persecute them."[13]

In Judea as elsewhere, individuals who brought a message that challenged those in power did so at the risk of their lives. Josephus records the account of one Jesus, the son of Ananus, who prophesied the destruction of Jerusalem four years before the war began. The leaders had him scourged, but he continued to prophesy.

"Hereupon our rulers supposing, as the case proved to be, that this was a sort of divine fury in the man, brought him to the Roman procurator - where he was whipped till his bones were laid bare..."[14] The Roman procurator enforced the judgment of the Sanhedrin.

Initially, in some synagogues, the Pharisees had excommunicated the *Talmidei Yeshua*.[15] Before the Great Revolt, being put out of the synagogue was not in itself life-threatening. The Temple was still the center of Jewish worship and identity.

The Temple was the base of Priestly and Sadducean power. They had no teaching or construct for excluding Jews from the Temple.

With the destruction of Jerusalem and the Temple, the synagogue became the center of Jewish worship and religious identity. The Romans had empowered Yohanan ben Zakkai and the rabbinic academy. The Rabbis had both teaching and construct for excluding other Jews. From that point on, being kicked out of the synagogue carried the danger of being considered no longer a Jew.

The Romans were not interested in theological disputes.[16] They were interested in control. Rome related to those it had placed in power.

"Now so long as Christianity was regarded by the Romans as a mere sect of Judaism, it shared the hatred and contempt [of the Romans towards the Jews], indeed, but also the legal protection bestowed on that ancient national religion...So soon as it was understood as a new religion, and as, in fact, claiming universal validity and acceptance, it was set down as unlawful and treasonable, a *religio illicita*; and it was the constant reproach of Christians: 'You have no right to exist.'"[17]

When the *Talmidei Yeshua* were kicked out of the synagogue by the Rabbis, they could no longer legally establish before the Romans the Jewishness of their religion. That put them on trial for their lives.

"Any Judaeo-Christian who was expelled from the Jewish community was by law bound to sacrifice to the emperor and to take his part in idolatrous practices. If he refused, he was punished as an 'atheist'."[18]

Part of the Roman accomodation had been a special tax on the Jews, in place of sacrifice to the emperor. Some emperors were more zealous than others in collecting the tax. Many Gentiles had adopted Jewish customs and the observance of some Biblical laws.[19]

"Domitian's energetic collection of the special poll-tax on Jews, the *fiscus Judaicus*, which was exacted from those who without openly professing their adhesion to Judaism lived like Jews, as well as from born Jews who concealed their race, gave occupation to the informers whom he encouraged; and their denunciations probably included some more highly placed in society than the mass of Roman Jewry."[20]

Domitian became emperor in 81 A.D. The Roman tax collectors worked hand-in-hand with his network of informers. This turned into a powerful weapon that was used against the *Talmidei Yeshua*.

They had continued to increase in number. Dio records that in 95 A.D., "Domitian slew among many others Flavius Clemens the consul, though he was a cousin and had to wife Flavia Domitilla, who was also a relative of the emperor's. The complaint brought against them both was that of atheism, under which many others who drifted into Jewish ways were condemned. Some of these were killed and the remainder were at least deprived of their property."[21]

Gaius Pliny, Governor in Asia Minor, wrote to the Emperor Trajan, as to the correct procedure in trying and executing Christians: "...Meanwhile I have followed this procedure with those who were denounced to me as Christians: I asked them whether they were Christians. If they confessed I repeated the question a second and third time and, moreover, under threat of the death penalty. If they persisted I had them led away to their death, for I had no doubt that, whatever it was that they confessed, their stubbornness and inflexible obstinacy certainly deserved to be punished...

"The matter seems to me worthy of consultation especially because of the large number of those imperiled. For many of all ages, of every rank, and of both sexes are already in danger, and many more will come into danger. The contagion of this superstitition has spread not only in the cities but even to the villages and to the country districts. Yet I still feel it is possible to check it and set it right..."[22]

The letter was written in 112 A.D., about the time of Rabbi Eliezer's trial for *minuth*. "That he was arrested for *Minuth* is, of course, the Jewish way of describing the affair. The Roman government knew nothing of *Minim* as such, but only of adherents of Jesus, as distinct from Jews, with whom they did not interfere."[23]

"When he came home, his disciples called on him to console

him, but he would accept no consolation. Said R. Akiba to him, 'Master, wilt thou permit me to say one thing of what you have taught me?' He replied, 'Say it.' 'Master,' said he, 'perhaps some of the teaching of the *Minim* had been transmitted to you and you approved of it and because of that you were arrested?'"[24]

R. Eliezer then remembered that he had approved of something which Jacob of Kefar Sekaniah, a well-known Jewish disciple of Yeshua, had told him. The Talmudic account is not presented as a transcript, but rather as a lesson from an historical occurrence.

The lesson? No matter how wise a man is, approving of, or even listening to the teaching of the *minim* could cost him his life.

Someone had gone to the Romans and accused R. Eliezer of living outside what the acceptable definition of a Jew was. The charge made no sense. R. Eliezer the Great, the first rabbi quoted in the Talmud, was the trusted disciple of Yohanan ben Zakkai, the one who defined post-Temple Judaism. Eliezer was the embodiment of a Pharisaic Jew.

Who could have made such a charge credible to the Roman authorities? Who had the standing before the Romans to define Judaism in a way that excluded R. Eliezer?

On at least one occasion, other rabbis believed Eliezer to be guilty of *minuth*. A *Bath Kol* had declared him to be innocent.[25]

At the trial, no one from the Academy went to R. Eliezer's defense. A simple word from the Rabbis that such an accusation was absurd would have ended the matter. After all, they, being so authorized by the Romans, had the power of inclusion and exclusion. R. Eliezer's later excommunication was a declaration that he had crossed the line which the Rabbis had drawn.

R. Eliezer's disciples sought to console him on his return from the court. R. Akiba did not. He sought to show R. Eliezer his guilt.

The Rabbis had a category of offenses for which the guilty party was turned over to the ruling power to be put to death. That included murderers and the inhabitants of a seduced city.[26]

A murderer is one who kills or comes to kill an innocent other. That was the rabbinic estimation of the *minim*.

A seduced city is a community that follows a *mesith*. "The inhabitants of a seduced city have no portion in the world to come...In this (the penalty) of individuals is severer than (that of) a multitude, for individuals are stoned, therefore their property is saved; but multitudes are decapitated; hence their possessions are destroyed."[27]

Those guilty of *minuth* followed a deceiver. Therefore, the members of such a community were to be handed over to the Roman government to be put to death.

The early followers of Yeshua were all Jews. They claimed that "the Iudaioi/Ιυδαιοι" took a zealous part in bringing accusations to the Romans and in doing everything they could to stir up public hostility against the *Talmidei Yeshua*. The primary meaning of Iudaioi is "Jews," but sometimes "Judeans," and in these contexts the term generally meant the religious authorities. Specifically, the *Talmidei Yeshua* blamed the synagogue, where the Rabbis exerted their authority.

"Tertullian's famous remark: 'the synagogues, the sources of the persecutions' is...clear. A reference which is even more impressive, because it is an aside, lies in the attack of an anonymous author upon the Montanists. When he disallows their right to be called Christians, because they and their women prophets have neither been scourged in the synagogues of the Jews nor stoned by them, he is clearly implying that such treatment was, to some extent at least, the lot of the orthodox Christians. Finally, Origen, in commenting upon the thirty-seventh psalm, remarks that 'the Jews do not vent their wrath on the Gentiles who worship idols and blaspheme God, and they neither hate them nor rage against them. But against the Christians they rage with an insatiable fury'."[28]

"It is, however, one of the most serious charges made by Tertullian and Origen that the Jews stirred up the pagans against the Christians. The former makes the general statement that the synagogues were 'the seed-plot of all the calumny against us.' Origen is much more explicit and says that Celsus has acted 'like the Jews, who when Christianity first began to be preached, scattered abroad false reports of the Gospel, and such as that Christians offered up an infant in sacrifice, and partook of its flesh, and again that the professors of Christianity wishing to do the works of darkness used to extinguish the lights, and each one to have sexual intercourse with any woman he chanced to meet.'"[29]

Gamliel had taken a wait and see attitude towards the new sect.[30] A century later, despite expulsion from the synagogue and the Roman trials, many more Jews were following Yeshua. More, it seems, than were following the Rabbis. It was time to act.

26. "THIS IS THE KING MESSIAH!"

Many Jews in the first and second centuries believed that Numbers 24:17 prophesied the coming of Messiah.[1] "I see him, but not now; I behold him, but not near. A star will come out of Jacob; a scepter will rise out of Israel. He will crush the foreheads of Moab, the skulls of all the sons of Sheth."

"R. Johanan said: Rabbi used to expound 'There shall step forth a star out of Jacob, thus: read not '*kokab*' (star) but '*kozab*' (lie). When R. Akiba beheld Bar Koziba he exclaimed, 'This is the king Messiah!' R. Johanan b. Tortha retorted: 'Akiba, grass will grow in your cheeks and he will still not have come!'"[2]

Rabbi Akiba declared Simeon ben Kosiba the Messiah.[3] He used the Aramaic "*bar*" instead of the Hebrew "*ben*," and changed one letter of "Kosiba" to make him bar Kokhba, the messianic "Son of a Star." Later rabbis changed the same letter to make him bar Koziba, the "son of a lie."

The Messianic title "Son of a Star" is taken from the Scriptures, but we have no indication of why Simeon ben Kosiba should or could have been called that. Nor are we told of any other prophetic scriptures or popular expectations that he fulfilled. The Talmud does tells us of prophecy that he did not fulfill. Isaiah prophesied that Messiah would have supernatural discernment. According to the Rabbis, Bar Kokhba did not.[4]

We know there were other rabbis who supported the revolt, but there is no record of any others who believed that Bar Kokhba was the Messiah. R. Johanan b. Tortha, an otherwise unknown rabbi, is recorded as mocking Akiba's declaration. Yet it was Akiba's declaration that prevailed. That indicates the influence that Akiba had, especially considering how he had earlier been rebuked for his Messianic views.

Akiba was rebuked for his interpretation of a vision of Daniel the prophet. Daniel wrote: "As I looked, thrones were set in place, and the Ancient of Days took his seat. His clothing was as white as snow; the hair of his head was white like wool. His throne was flaming with fire, and its wheels were all ablaze. A river of fire was flowing, coming out from before him. Thousands upon thousands attended him; ten thousand times ten thousand stood before him. The court was seated, and the books were opened....

"In my vision at night I looked, and there before me was one like a son of man, coming with the clouds of heaven. He approached the Ancient of Days and was led into his presence. He was given authority, glory and sovereign power; all peoples, nations and men of every language worshiped him. His dominion is an everlasting dominion that will not pass away, and his kingdom is one that will never be destroyed."[5]

The passage refers to a "Son of Man" to whom God gives universal and eternal dominion. R. Joshua taught that these verses referred to Messiah.[6] The Similitudes of Enoch and 1 Enoch taught the same.

In the Talmud, we read: "One passage says: *His **throne** was fiery flames*; and another passage says: *Till **thrones** were placed, and One that was ancient of days did sit*! - There is no contradiction one (throne) for Him, and one for David; this is the view of R. Akiba. Said R. Jose the Galilean to him: Akiba, how long wilt thou treat the Divine Presence as profane! ...Said R. Eleazar b. Azariah to him: Akiba, what hast thou to do with *Aggadah*? Cease thy talk, and turn to (the laws concerning defilement through) leprosy-signs and tent-coverings!"[7]

Akiba had also understood these verses in Daniel to be referring to Messiah. Both Jose the Galilean and Eleazar b. Azariah rebuked him, the latter claiming that Akiba was not qualified to interpret nonlegal matters.

The sharpness of the rebukes of Jose the Galilean and Eleazar b. Azariah are more understandable against the backdrop of the gospels. In the gospels, Yeshua applied these verses in Daniel to himself as Messiah.[8] Akiba also understood the prophecy to speak of Messiah, enthroned next to God.

The Talmud tells us that Akiba accepted the rebuke of his interpretation, but not the denial of his ability to comment on *aggadah* or on the Messiah. In fact, seeing the danger of his previous views, he went further to build a fence around the Messianic prophecies.

Akiba redefined the Messianic Age. He separated it from the World to Come. In so doing, he eliminated the supernatural and the exceptional from the Messianic Age and from the role of Messiah.[9] It was no longer necessary for God to demonstrate through signs and wonders who His Anointed was, because "No proof can be brought from a carob-tree." This stands in marked contrast to the declaration of Yeshua: "...the very [miraculous] works that I do, bear witness of Me, that the Father has sent Me."[10]

With this redefinition, Akiba declared Bar Kokhba the Messiah. What convinced him?

Louis Finkelstein urged that, "Akiba himself did not long resist the contagion of Messianism. When he saw Roman legions yield to untrained Judean youths, new hope blossomed in his heart."[11] This seems, almost by default, to be the view of others. There are, however, six serious problems with this view.

1) We have no evidence that there was any Messianism surrounding Bar Kokhba, other than Akiba's own declaration. There is no historical record of widespread belief that Bar Kokhba was the Messiah, not even after Akiba's declaration. In fact, the ONLY record of such belief that we have is Akiba's declaration.

R. Johanan b. Tortha, who rebuked Akiba, was certainly not swept away by any Messianism. Akiba resisted the Messianism of the common people expressed in popular Messianic expectations. Akiba resisted the Messianism of the *Talmidei Yeshua*.

2) No one ever characterized Akiba as one who was swept along by emotion, his own or that of others. He was patient, systematic, calculating, and relentless.

3) In the Great Revolt, Roman legions also yielded to untrained Judean youths who had no Messiah. Akiba was a young man then, and knew well what total devastation had followed the initial successes.

4) A few military victories do not signal the advent of the Messiah; not for Akiba or anyone else. Though there was commonly understood to be a military aspect to Messiah's deliverance, military success alone did not qualify a man to be the Messiah. It was certainly possible to rejoice in the victories and support the revolt, as others did, without declaring ben Kosiba the Messiah.

The Midrash, written centuries later, does say that after he saw Bar Kokhba "catch the missiles from the enemy's catapults on one of his knees and hurl them back, killing many of the foe...Rabbi Akiba declared him the Messiah."[12] Eusebius, two centuries after the Revolt, said that fire proceeded from Bar Kokhba's mouth. The statements are not given much weight since the accounts are so fanciful, but even if ben Kosiba had displayed supernatural ability, these feats alone would not make him the Messiah - especially since it was Rabbi Akiba who eliminated the supernatural from the role and reign of Messiah.

5) Akiba was not a fervent anti-Roman. He had travelled to Rome and different parts of the empire. He knew the breadth and depth of Roman achievements and power. His hope was not for immediate political independence, but rather for a new Judaism. That was the whole thrust of his life.

6) Akiba was warned by others that the revolt would fail. In fact, he himself had prophesied the same thing.

"In vain did such patriots as Gamaliel and Eliezer, and such pacifists as Joshua and Samuel the Little warn leaders and followers of the folly of the enterprise."[13] "They all looked at Samuel the Little; and when he died, they lamented over him,

'Alas, the humble man! Alas, the pious man! Disciple of Hillel!' At the time of his death he also prophesied, 'Simeon and Ishmael [are destined] for the sword and their colleagues for death, and the rest of the people for spoliation, and great distress will come upon the nation.'"[14]

At the graves of Rabbis Ishmael and Simeon, who were ardent nationalists, Akiba himself had warned: "'Prepare yourselves for suffering,' he cried to the weeping multitude. 'If happiness were destined to come in our times, none deserved better to share in it than Rabbi Simeon and Rabbi Ishmael. But God, knowing what distress is in store for us, removed them from our midst, as it is written, *the righteous is taken away from the evil to come.*' (Is. 57:1)"[15]

Dio Cassius says that the people had other supernatural warnings. "Thus nearly the whole of Judaea was made desolate, an event of which the people had had indications even before the war. The tomb of Solomon, which these men regarded as one of their sacred objects, fell to pieces of itself and collapsed and many wolves and hyenas rushed howling into their cities."[16]

As Rabbi Akiba knew, Johanan ben Zakkai had tried to warn the people before the Great Revolt. His warning went unheeded.[17]

Rabbi Akiba had ample reasons to believe that the Bar Kokhba Rebellion would also fail. He had prophesied that the outcome would be great distress. He knew that Simeon ben Kosiba would not deliver Israel from the Romans, but still chose to anoint and crown him.

Akiba's position was such that his declaration became the banner of the revolt,[18] led by his Messianic "Son of a Star", i.e Bar Kokhba. Compared to the Great Revolt, where factions and gangs in Jerusalem fought against each other at least as much as against the Romans, the Bar Kokhba Revolt seems to have been marked by exceptional unity.

As Isaac and Oppenheimer remark, "It is no coincidence that the revolt of Bar Kokhba was the only Jewish war fought against foreign rule in antiquity to have been named after one leader, for a major contribution to the impact of the rising was the unity of the rebels under Bar Kokhba's leadership. In talmudic sources he is given the title 'Nasi and Messiah', and the years of his reign are described as kingship."[19]

The extent of that unity needs to be qualified. Bar Kokhba's own letters indicate that he perceived a lack of obedience to his commands, at least as the Revolt began to crumble.[20] Only the most violent threats seemed adequate to insure compliance. Apparently, the Galileans did not join in the Revolt at all; or if they did, they did not long support it.[21]

Why did the Rabbis support Akiba's Messiah? Simeon ben Kosiba did not fulfill the recorded rabbinic qualifications for the Messiah.

The range of rabbinic messianic expectation included much of the mix of other groups. The Rabbis stressed in particular the role of Messiah as the Interpreter of the Torah, or the bringer of a new Torah. As the Jerusalem Talmud says: "And (the Torah) will not again return to its (uncontroversial) place until the son of David (i.e., the Messiah) will come."[22]

Oppenheimer observed that, "The main question that arises in regard to Bar Kokhba's leadership revolves around the traits and qualifications that enabled him to achieve the lofty status of a messiah king. For while it is known that after the destruction of the Second Temple the leadership of the nation was in the hands of sages, there is no evidence that Bar Kokhba was a scholar, and no rulings, laws or interpretations are attributed to him."[23]

Nor is there any evidence that he fulfilled any of the varied aspects of the first and early second century concepts of Messiah. He did not qualify in any normative way.

Akiba's Role in the Revolt

In Tanakh, there are five basic ways in which kings are appointed:

1) Self-appointment through military victory, as with Baasha;

2) Appointment by a conquering foreign power, as with Eliakim at the hand of Pharaoh Neco;

3) Hereditary appointment either through explicit choice, as with Solomon, or through succession upon death, as with Uzziah;

4) Prophetic appointment, as with David at the hand of Samuel; and

5) Priestly appointment, as with Joash at the hand of Jehoida.[24]

Messiah is "the Anointed One." It would therefore be expected that he would be anointed as king by either prophet, priest, or both, since only these would anoint. In order to proclaim Solomon king, over the claim of his half-brother Adonijah, King David said, "And let Zadok the priest and Nathan the prophet anoint him there as king over Israel, and blow the trumpet and say, 'Long live King Solomon!'"[25]

Who anointed Bar Kokhba? By his oral declaration, Rabbi Akiba asserted a rabbinic prerogative in the place of priest and prophet. For Simeon ben Kosiba to be proclaimed "the Anointed One," someone first had to anoint him. The only candidate we have for that task is Rabbi Akiba.

In so doing, he asserted rabbinic authority over the kingship.

The one who has the power to appoint also has the power to withhold or withdraw appointment; or to issue decrees, as Samuel did to Saul.

The extent of Akiba's involvement in the revolt itself cannot be unequivocably established. Some say that he merely approved of it; others, that he participated in it; others that he instigated it. Herford called him "the apostle of the insurrection." Others claim he was the "soul of the revolt."[26]

Maimonides said Akiba was an aide-de-camp of the king.[27] Given the rabbinic view on the applicability of spiritual discernment to temporal government, that would have made sense. The Rabbis believed that only they were qualified to govern.[28]

Gershom Bader said, perhaps a bit imaginatively, "The revolt was prepared during the famous 'Seder' night which is mentioned in the Hagada. Several Tanaim met in the home of Rabbi Akiba in Bnei Brak. ...This 'debate' lasted all night while crowds of impatient people stood outside and waited for the decision of the scholars... A ray of light penetrated the house and the scholars together with their disciples began to chant the old hymn of revenge, 'Pour out Thy wrath upon the nations that have not known You.' The echo of the chant resounded from the hills of Judea. Like one man the people arose from Gilead to Bashan to cast off the yoke of the Romans."[29]

Inasmuch as the evidence we have shows that the Jews of Galilee did not participate in the revolt, Bader has exaggerated the unity, but the suggestion that the revolt was planned and instigated by the Rabbis at "the home of Rabbi Akiba in Bnei Brak" is an interesting possibility.[30]

Whatever the extent of Akiba's involvement in the commencement of the revolt, it offered a near perfect vehicle, if properly utilized, for the establishment of rabbinic authority. We are told that Akiba was like a peddler who knew when he saw something whether or not he could make use of it. When he got what he wanted, he already knew where it belonged and what its use would be.

Here was the possibility of establishing the precedent of rabbinic authority in choosing the king, and in regulating the government, worship, and life of the people. That would firmly establish the supremacy of rabbinic authority over every competitor. It would insure that the priests could not regain their former prominence and power. It would put an end to the influence of the *Talmidei Yeshua*.

The precedent of a state that operated according to Akiba's

version of rabbinic law would end all discussion. "Doubtless he saw the oral law (as developed and expounded by him) as the constitution of the Messianic Age."[31] As Johanan ben Zakkai had said earlier, "The shofar has been heard in Jabneh, and what has been done is no longer open to discussion."

What did Akiba see in Simeon ben Kosiba? Probably he saw the same that we see as we read ben Kosiba's military correspondence or the rabbinic accounts. He saw an arrogant strongman with some religious inclinations, a man who was prone to great violence and brutality when his orders were not obeyed. Such a man would be quick to get rid of those who would not obey his orders or the orders of the religious authority that appointed and supported him.

From all the source material we have, Bar Kokhba did not qualify in any way as the Messiah, by anyone's standard. No claim was made that he did. The unwarranted Messianic declaration insured Bar Kokhba's support of Akiba. Akiba proclaimed Bar Kokhba the Messiah for the same reason that he did everything else: To establish ultimate rabbinic authority over the life of Israel. Bar Kokhba was quite useful to that end.

27. MILHEMET MITZVAH

The Torah provides for certain cases when men are exempted from participating in battle.[1] The Rabbis determined that, "These rules apply to a war of choice (*milhemet reshat*); but in a commanded war (*milhemet mitzvah*) all go forth, even the bridegroom from his chamber and the bride from her huppah."[2]

That made it necessary to decide when participation in a war was commanded, and when it was optional. "Raba said: The wars waged by Joshua to conquer [Canaan] were obligatory in the opinion of all; the wars waged by the House of David for territorial expansion were voluntary in the opinion of all; where they differ is with regard to [wars] against heathens so that these should not march against them."[3]

Milhemet mitzvah is not a Biblical term or category. It is a legal construct put forth by the Rabbis at the time of the Bar Kokhba Revolt. "The term *milhemet mitzvah* makes its appearance with the disciples of Rabbi Akiba, and is applied to wars of defence. It may be that it was in this connection that the difference of opinion recorded in the Mishnah arose, as a result of the compulsory mobilization decreed by Bar Kokhba."[4]

Some of the members of the Sanhedrin were opposed to the revolt from the beginning. The leading Sages had predicted that the revolt would end in disaster. "In vain did Gamaliel and Eliezer, ...Joshua and Samuel the Little warn leaders and followers of the folly of the enterprise."[5]

Akiba's Messianic proclamation made the revolt a *milhemet mitzvah*, and that made the approval of the entire Sanhedrin unnecessary. "In the case of a religious war [i.e. a *milhemet mitzvah*], the king does not have to obtain the sanction of the Supreme Court. He may at any time set out independently and compel the people to come out with him. But in case of an optional war, he can bring out the people only by a decision of the court of seventy-one."[6]

The traditional belief was that even as Israel had fallen in blood and fire, so also would Israel be redeemed in blood and fire. The coming of Messiah would be heralded by and accompanied by war. "A Master has said, 'In the sixth year will be thunderings, in the seventh wars, at the end of the seventh the son of David will come' — War is also the beginning of redemption."[7]

Wherever an anonymous authority is quoted, we are to understand the view to be that of R. Akiba. According to this anonymous Master, the war led by the Messiah would be "the beginning of redemption." The initial coinage of the Bar Kokhba Revolt carried the legend, "Year 1 of the redemption of Israel."[8]

All would agree that such a war is a *milhemet mitzvah*.

Akiba's Messianic proclamation also helps to explain the "unity" of the people in what many knew from the beginning was a futile, if not suicidal, effort. There was not much choice. Either they fought under Bar Kokhba's leadership, or they were liable before the Sanhedrin for a capital crime.

Simeon ben Kosiba was a brutal man. To prove the loyalty of his troops, he cut off one finger from each man. He confiscated the property and crops of those who did not support him. He put fetters on the feet of those who did not fulfill his commands. He kicked his godly uncle to death. How would he have treated those who refused to fight?[9]

It would have been possible for Akiba to anoint ben Kosiba as king without proclaiming him the Messiah. But, had he done that, the *Talmidei Yeshua* could still have fought in the war. Once Akiba declared ben Kosiba the Messiah, the *Talmidei Yeshua* had to withdraw from the battle. For them, it would have been apostasy to fight under the banner of a false Messiah. Such a war would be doomed to destruction.

Without Akiba's declaration, the Sanhedrin could still have put the *Talmidei Yeshua* to death for not obeying the Rabbis, but the majority of the people, the *am ha'aretz*, were also guilty of not obeying the Rabbis. To put the *Talmidei Yeshua* to death under that charge would have raised popular outcry and resentment. Even those supporting the struggle against Rome would have blamed the Rabbis for weakening the fighting forces.

But if the *Talmidei Yeshua* themselves, from their own convictions, chose not to fight, then the hostility of the people could be directed against them, especially as the situation worsened. Their refusal to fight would make them guilty unto death before the Beth Din, the rabbinic court which was set up at Bethar.

There were four practical consequences of Akiba's Messianic proclamation. 1. It made the war a commanded war (without the approval of the Sanhedrin) in which everyone was required to fight. 2. It made it impossible for the *Talmidei Yeshua* to fight in the commanded war. 3. It made the *Talmidei Yeshua* guilty of a capital crime. 4. It fully empowered the Sanhedrin to put them to death without public opposition.[10]

Could these have been unintended, unexpected, fortuitous results for R. Akiba? No. These were the obvious, foreseeable effects of his decision. R. Akiba was very astute. He knew what he was doing. He had been engaging in such maneuvers for many decades. He consciously sought to eliminate the non-rabbinic option presented by the *Talmidei Yeshua*. There were no other reasons for proclaiming Simeon ben Kosiba the Messiah. Even under the name Bar Kokhba, he did not qualify.

28. THE TRIAL

"For the death of the wicked benefits themselves and the world." Sanh.71b

Ever since Cain, violence has been part of the human experience. Sometimes it is sporadic and random. At other times it is sustained, organized, and purposeful. Sometimes it is against the law. At other times it is authorized by the law.

Those who want power fight to get it. Those who have power fight to keep it. To rephrase Clausewitz: Violence is the servant of policy. It is a dutiful handmaiden. Even more than that, it often serves as the midwife of revolution; bringing a new life into the world through blood.

The Bar Kokhba Revolt ended 300 years after the Maccabean revolt began. There is a critical aspect of that earlier revolt that is sometimes overlooked: "The first steps taken by Judas in his war were against the 'sinners' of his own people, the Hellenists."[1]

Much of the fighting in Israel from that time on was between one group of Jews and another. Josephus records episodes of violence and murder by the Pharisees and against the Pharisees from the time of the Maccabees on. So do the Rabbis.[2]

The Great Revolt was characterized by warring factions who slaughtered those other Jews they considered their enemies. Ideology, whether it is called "political" or "religious," often relies on violence to achieve its ends.

The Rabbis were not different in this respect. Akiba experienced that himself. He was publicly flogged by Gamaliel at least five times.[3]

The Rabbis believed that their laws brought both temporal and eternal life to themselves, their followers, and all Israel. Consequently, they were not reluctant to prescribe death for a rebellious elder, a deceiver, or anyone who might draw others away from rabbinic teaching and authority.

At the same time that the Rabbis were establishing themselves, increasing numbers of Jews were believing the message of the *Talmidei Yeshua*. The confrontation, as described in both rabbinic and early Christian sources, was a bitter one.

The Rabbis decreed that the *Talmidei Yeshua* should be ostracized from public life. Their legal rights were taken away. Their books were burned. They were turned over to the Roman authorities to be put to death. It was lawful to cast them into a pit to die. As Rabbi Akiba emphasized, "one is deserving of death for disobeying the rulings of the Sages."[4]

Akiba's hatred for the *Talmidei Yeshua* played a part in his commissioning a new Targum and a new Greek translation. It played a part in the novel doctrinal positions which he espoused. It played a part in the conflict with R. Eliezer.

What would have happened when the Rabbis held power under Bar Kokhba? What would have happened when Bar Kokhba, having been proclaimed the Messiah by Akiba, was rejected by a group of Jews who followed another Messiah?

As the revolt faltered, Bar Kokhba kicked his own uncle to death on suspicion of treason. We do not know how many other suspected internal enemies he killed. We do know that the *Talmidei Yeshua* were singled out for death under his rule. Both the rabbinic and Christian sources tell us that.

Justin, a Gentile Christian contemporary of Bar Kokhba and Akiba, said, "For in the present Jewish war it was only Christians whom Bar Chocheba, the leader of the rebellion of the Jews, commanded to be punished severely, if they did not deny Jesus as the Messiah and blaspheme him."[5]

"And again in his Apology to Antoninus Pius, he [Justin] says that 'the Jews count us foes and enemies, and like yourselves they kill and punish us whenever they have the power, as you may well believe. For in the Jewish war which lately raged, Barcochebas, the leader of the revolt, gave orders that Christians alone should be led to cruel punishments.'"[6]

Justin's references to "Bar Kokhba" show that this was the name by which the leader of the revolt was known. It was Akiba who had named ben Kosiba "bar Kokhba." Akiba's declaration was the banner under which the revolt was fought.

Eusebius speaks of "the Jews who took up arms" in the 16th year of Hadrian (132). He does not mention Bar Kokhba in describing that year. That may indicate that Bar Kokhba had not yet been proclaimed Messiah. Eusebius then writes, "Hadrian's Year 17 (133), Cochebas, duke of the Jewish sect, killed the Christians with all kinds of persecutions, (when) they refused to help him against the Roman troops."[7]

Would Bar Kokhba have commanded the *Talmidei Yeshua* to deny Yeshua as the Messiah? Of course. Would Akiba have commanded them to do so? No question. Would Akiba and Bar Kokhba have put them to death if they refused? There is no basis for any doubt.

The Rabbis, led by Akiba, sought to destroy the *Talmidei Yeshua* from the midst of Israel. So they found a justification: "Whence do we derive that we pronounce a curse? — From the text: *Curse ye Meroz* ... Whence do we derive that we quarrel, curse him, smite him, pluck his hair and put on him an oath? — From the text: *And I contended with them...* Whence do we derive that we may fetter, arrest and prosecute them? — From the text: [Let judgment be executed upon him with all diligence], *whether it be unto death, or to uprooting, or to confiscation of goods or to imprisonment.* ...Whence do we derive that [the curse/*herem* falls on one who] eats and drinks with the offender or stands within four cubits of him? ..."[8] Under Bar Kokhba, the Rabbis functioned as the provisional revolutionary government.

Bethar

Bethar was Bar Kokhba's headquarters, the center of his government. The Talmud says that there was an authoritative rabbinic court there. The only purpose of such a Bet Din was to enforce rabbinic law.[9] Abramsky says, "The basically authentic statement about a Sanhedrin at Bethar (Sanh. 17b) suggests that at a certain time a bet din participated in Bar Kokhba's rule."[10]

Gedalia Alon concluded, "On the balance, the probability is that the Sanhedrin did play a real role in the provisional administration established by the rebels...Consequently, it makes sense to suppose that the Sanhedrin, too, was reconstituted in its old form. Of course, it was only to be expected that the Sages would now be the dominant element."[11]

"The court may inflict flagellation and other punishments, even in cases where such penalties are not warranted by the law if, in its opinion, *religion will thereby be strengthened and safeguarded and the people will be restrained from disregarding the words of the Torah....*

"So too if, *in order to bring back the multitudes to religion and save them from general religious laxity*, the court deems it necessary to set aside temporarily a positive or a negative command, it may do so, taking into account the need of the hour. Even as a physician will amputate the hand or the foot of a patient in order to save his life, so the court may advocate, when an emergency arises, the temporary disregard of some of the commandments, that the commandments as a whole be preserved."[12]

The *Talmidei Yeshua* were the only group in Judea who refused to fight in Bar Kokhba's and Akiba's Messianic war of redemption. That was rebellion. As Maimonides affirmed, "The king has a right to execute anyone who rebels against him."[13]

"Our Rabbis taught: Yeshu had five disciples, Matthai, Nakai, Nezer, Buni and Todah. When Matthai was brought [before the court] he said to them [the judges], Shall Matthai be executed? Is it not written, *Matthai* [when] *shall I come and appear before God?* Thereupon they retorted; Yes, Matthai shall be executed, since it is written, *Matthai* [when] *shall* [he] *die and his name perish*. When Nakai was brought in he said to them; Shall Nakai be executed? Is it not written, *Naki* [the innocent] *and the righteous slay thou not?* Yes, was the answer, Nakai shall be executed, since it is written, *in secret places does Naki* [the innocent] *slay*. When Nezer was brought in, he said; Shall Nezer be executed? Is it not written, *And Nezer* [a twig] *shall grow forth out of his roots*. Yes, they said, Nezer shall be executed, since it is written, *But thou art cast forth away from thy grave like Nezer* [an abhorred offshoot]. When Buni was brought in, he said: Shall Buni be executed? Is it not written, *Beni* [my son], *my first born?* Yes, they said, Buni shall be executed, since it is written, *Behold I will slay Bine-ka* [thy son] *thy first born*. And when Todah was brought in, he said to them; Shall Todah be executed? Is it not written, *A psalm for Todah* [thanksgiving]? Yes, they answered, Todah shall be executed, since it is written, *Whoso offereth the sacrifice of Todah* [thanksgiving] *honoured me*."[14]

Herford concluded, "The fact that the prisoners quoted texts of Scripture, and were met with other texts, suggests that the trial took place before a Jewish and not a Roman tribunal. Not, of course, that such a thrust and parry of texts really took place anywhere, but that it would be impossible in a Roman court and only a witty travesty of what would be possible in a Jewish one. Laible (J. C. im Talm., p. 68 fol.) makes the very probable suggestion that the story refers to the persecution of Christians under Bar Cocheba, already mentioned. It is a fantastic account of some incident of that persecution. The reasons for taking this view are, that the story occurs in the same passage as that which describes the death of Jesus, and that we have found the key to the understanding of the statements there made about Jesus in the anti-Christian hatred of Bar Cocheba, and more especially of Aqiba, his chief supporter."[15]

In commenting on this same portion, Dalman said, "Although this narrative in the form presented here is absurd, yet it is not devoid of an historical background...when investigating the time and the immediate circumstances of our story...we shall be obliged to take up our position in the age of Rabbi Akiba... An execution of Christians is here notified to us. What execution then, what slaying of Christians could more easily be preserved in the memory than those which took place under Bar Koch'ba? For although we must note the alleged citation of proof-texts (in Sanh. 43a) as unhistorical, thus much in any case is shown by the narrative, that it was no heathen court of justice, but a Jewish one. This fits in with the period of Bar Koch'ba, the last period of Jewish independence."[16]

The last period of Jewish independence was the only period of Jewish independence after the crucifixion of Yeshua. Yeshua was crucified about 30 A.D. The Bar Kokhba Rebellion took place in 132-135 A.D. The ONLY time when such a trial and execution by the Sanhedrin could have taken place was during the reign of King Simeon ben Kosiba, Rabbi Akiba's Messiah. It took place before four judges, one of whom was R. Akiba, all of whom could prove from the Scriptures that reptiles are clean.

Because they did not accept rabbinic authority, the *Talmidei Yeshua* would have had no legal rights before the Sanhedrin. "We do not accept testimony from them." Their faith in Yeshua was heresy and blasphemy to the Rabbis, punishable by death.[17]

The word games with the Scripture texts that appear in the Sanhedrin passage are similar to what appears in the account of R. Eliezer ben Hyrcanus' trial for *minuth*. They are formed in the same way the Rabbis formed *"Yeshu," "minim,"* and *"avon gilyon."*

Akiba was the acknowledged master of such word play. It was, after all, the way in which he had proclaimed ben Kosiba the Messiah.

In the reign of the Messiah, it was the duty of the sages to execute those who rebelled against the theocratic state. Not to do so would have contradicted their very reason for being.

Ginzberg has noted, "Consistent as Akiba always was, his ethics and his views of justice were only the strict consequences of his philosophical system. Justice as an attribute of God must also be exemplary for man. 'No mercy in (civil) justice!' is his basic principle in the doctrine concerning law. (Ket. ix. 3)...In opposition to the Christian insistence on God's love, Akiba upholds God's retributive justice elevated above all chance or arbitrariness."[18]

"God's retributive justice" was, in Akiba's view, carried out by the Sages. The messianic kingdom of Bar Kokhba required that Akiba's principle - "No mercy in judgment!" - be put into practice. That was the responsibility of the Rabbis, because "the sword comes to the world...on account of those who interpret the Torah not in accordance with the accepted law."[19]

In the tractate Sanhedrin, there is extensive discussion of whom a Sanhedrin should put to death and how. "Four deaths have been entrusted to Beth Din: stoning, burning, slaying (by the sword) and strangulation."[20] Akiba pointed out one limitation for the judges in such executions: "R. Akiba said: Whence do we know that a Sanhedrin which executed a person must not eat anything on the day of the execution? From the verse, *Ye shall not eat anything with the blood.*"[21]

To overthrow Gamaliel, Akiba championed a merciful

Sanhedrin. That battle was long over. So was Akiba's need for a merciful Sanhedrin.

THE CONSEQUENCES OF THE REBELLION

29. THE END OF THE REVOLT

There were four immediate consequences of the Bar Kokhba Revolt:
1. A tremendous loss of life.
2. Multitudes sold into slavery and exile.
3. The name of the land changed from "Judea" to "Palestine".
4. The final split between the Church and the Synagogue.

The Loss of Life

The Midrash Lamentation puts the number of those who died at 80,000 myriads.[1] A myriad is 10,000, making the number 800,000,000. That is obviously exaggerated, but the purpose of the Midrash is not to provide exact historical information, but to convey the sense of the immensity of the tragedy. The Rabbis say that the Romans, "slew the inhabitants until the horses waded in blood up to their nostrils, and the blood rolled along stones of the size of forty se'ah [15 bushels] and flowed into the sea (staining it for) a distance of four miles."[2]

Dio Cassius wrote that, "Five hundred and eighty thousand men were slain in the various raids and battles, and the number of those who perished by famine, disease and fire was past finding out. Thus nearly the whole of Judaea was made desolate..."[3]

The suffering and destruction seemed to be without end. "R. [Simeon b.] Gamaliel said: There were five hundred schools in Bethar, and the smallest of them had not less than three hundred children. They used to say, 'If the enemy comes against us, with these styluses we will go out and stab them!' When, however, (the people's) sins did cause the enemy to come, they enwrapped each pupil in his book and burnt him, so that I alone was left."[4]

According to the Midrash, after three and a half years, only the stronghold of Bethar remained. It was then that Bar Kokhba killed Eleazar of Modim. "A Bath Kol issued forth and proclaimed, 'Woe to the worthless shepherd that leaveth the flock! The sword shall be upon his arm, and upon his right eye' (Zech. 11:17)...Forthwith the sins (of the people) caused Bethar to be captured. Bar Koziba was slain and his head taken to Hadrian."[5] The *Bath Kol* was authoritative. The end, at least, was in heaven.

A few managed to escape to the desert. There, over the edge of a precipice, down a nearly vertical cliff, they found caves and hid in them. At some point, the Romans discovered them, and set camp on the level ground commanding the cliff. We do not know the exact details of what happened next. More than eighteen hundred years later, Yadin and others found the caves, their glass dishes, bronze artifacts, and the bundle of letters from Simeon ben Kosiba.

"Talmudic literature contains a graphic description of the bitter fate of the refugees who hid in caves in the Judaean desert. The midrash tells of people who concealed themselves in caves and consumed the bodies of their friends until one of them found out that he had been eating the flesh of his father's corpse (Lamentations Rabbah i 45). This picture has been corroborated by archaeological evidence in the 'Cave of Horrors' where at least forty men took refuge, finally burning their possessions and dying while under siege."[6]

As an additional judgment and warning, Hadrian forbid the burial of the dead. According to the Talmud, the fifteenth day of the month of Ab is a great day of rejoicing because of the different kindnesses of the Lord on that day. One of those kindnesses: "It is the day when permission was granted for those killed at Bethar to be buried. R. Mattenah further said: On the day when permission was granted for those killed at Bethar to be buried (the Rabbis) at Jabneh instituted (the recitation of) the benediction, 'Who art kind and dealest kindly etc.'; 'Who art kind': Because their dead bodies did not become putrid; 'And dealest kindly': Because permission was granted for their burial."[7]

The Exile and Slavery

"Literary sources, both Jewish and non-Jewish, stress the large number of captives taken among the rebels and sold into slavery. They were so numerous that the price of slaves declined all over the Roman Empire, and in eretz Israel itself, according to one source, fell so low that it was no more than the cost of one portion of fodder for a horse."[8]

Considering the innumerable slaves that there were throughout the Roman Empire, it would have taken a very sizable influx to cause the market price to fall. The defeated Judeans, the booty of war, were sold into prostitution, misery, and chains.

Before the rebellion, most Jews had been living outside Judea, but by their own choice. After the rebellion, "Hadrian then commanded that by a legal decree and ordinances the whole nation should be absolutely prevented from entering from thenceforth even the district round Jerusalem, so that not even from a distance could it see its ancestral home."[9]

The forced exile begun by the Romans lasted from the first part of the second century to the middle of the twentieth when the British withdrew from the Palestinean Mandate. Though Israel had not enjoyed complete national sovereignty for two centuries before the revolt, the end of the rebellion marked THE end of the Jewish state, and the beginning of more than 1800 years of statelessness.[10]

It is impossible to calculate the impact of that in either Jewish history or in the history of Western civilization. A past without the Jewish Diaspora - its suffering and its contributions among the nations - cannot be successfully imagined; at least not in the Western world.

"Judea" becomes "Palestine"

"The suppression of the rebellion was even given verbal symbolism: the name of the country was changed from 'Judea' to 'The Syrian province of Palestine' (derived from the earlier inhabitation of portions of it by the Philistines), a move intended to obliterate the last traces of the Jewish settlement from memory."[11]

Judea had never been called "Palestine" before. It had never been "Palestine" before. It had simply been Judea, the land of the Jews. "Palestine" was the land of the Philistines, which had been a small coastal strip many centuries earlier. The Romans meant the new name to be a sentence of death for the rebellious Jewish nation, a warning to others.

Historians usually seek to understand the past on its own terms, but in this case they bow in obedience to the Roman decree. Seemingly without exception, they speak of "first-century Palestine," though they know that there was no such entity. Theologians do the same. They testify of something that never was, affecting what is and what will be.

Diplomats strive to undo a history of hostility in the Middle East, but dare not move the Roman barrier. The language and intent of the Roman decree continues to exert a powerful impact. It frames the most important question concerning the modern state of Israel: "Is it 'Palestine,' or is it 'Israel'?"

30. THE FINAL SPLIT

Perhaps the most devastating long-term consequence of the revolt was the final split between the Church and the Synagogue. After eighteen and a half centuries, this split seems obvious, natural, and inevitable. At the time of the revolt it was not.

Hugh Trevor-Roper reminds us that, "History is not what happened, but what happened in the context of what might have happened. Therefore history must incorporate the might have beens."[1]

For centuries, partisans on both sides have distorted the original conflict by imposing later issues and terminology upon it. Before the Revolt, although the conflict was quite evident, the division was not.[2] The *Talmidei Yeshua*, like the Pharisees and Rabbis, were Jews distinguished by a particular faith system. The conflict was an internal one between two groups of Jews who functioned under different authorities.

Rabbi Akiba's proclamation of Bar Kokhba as the Messiah precipitated the final split. That was his intention. He wanted the *Talmidei Yeshua* removed from the community of Israel. Unfortunately, this final split has brought with it more destruction than the revolt itself.

The *Talmidei Yeshua* could not fight under Bar Kokhba's Messianic banner. Because they would not fight, they were brought before the Sanhedrin as traitors and deserters, and put to death.

The Gentile Church saw this action as evidence that the Jews as a whole were irreconcilable enemies of the gospel and of those who believed it. The legal execution of the *Talmidei Yeshua* under Akiba and Bar Kokhba was different from all previous persecutions in that it was carried out as official Sanhedrin-State policy.

Justin Martyr saw this as grounds for divine punishment. "And therefore all this has happened to you rightly and well. For ye slew the Just One and His prophets before Him, and now ye reject, and, as far as in you lies, dishonour those that set their hope on Him, and God Almighty and Maker of the universe who sent Him, cursing in your synagogues them that believe on Christ. For you have not authority to raise your own hands against us, because of them who are now supreme. But as often as you could, this also ye did."[3]

Up until that time, there had been a large number of *Talmidei Yeshua* in Jerusalem, with a Jewish bishop, apparently exercising significant authority over the churches among the Gentiles.[4] With the end of the revolt, any surviving *Talmidei Yeshua*, along with their fellow Jews, were exiled from the land. Eusebius records that, following the revolt, "In Jerusalem, the first bishop was appointed from among the gentiles, since bishops ceased to be appointed from among the Jews."[5] The destruction of the *Talmidei Yeshua* in Judea put an end to Jewish authority in the Church.

The *Talmidei Yeshua* had been persecuted by the Rabbis because they did not accept rabbinic authority, and were therefore a threat to it. They were later reviled by others for refusing to fight. Though it had been primarily a case of one sect of Jews persecuting another sect of Jews, later Gentile Christians did not draw such fine distinctions. They saw it simply as Jews persecuting Christians.

The nature of the Church began to change radically after it was cut off from its Jewish roots. Jewish input became unwelcome. Church decrees were issued against the Jewish practices which Yeshua and his disciples had followed. The Jewish believers were compelled to assimilate to the practices and theology of the Church of the Empire. At first, these decrees were enforced by excommunication. Eventually they were enforced by execution.

A new theology taught that the Church had become "Israel." That put a sword in the hand of the Church. It taught that the Jews were forever cursed and rejected. That designated an enemy, an object for the sword.

The persecutions of the Bar Kokhba Revolt became a rationale and justification for all later "Christian" retribution. A Jewish movement, to be a light to the Gentiles, was transformed into an anti-Jewish one.

A Church-State alliance, fueled by a theology which taught that the Church had replaced Israel as the Chosen of God, left a trail of blood across continents and centuries. The statelessness of the Jews was seen as indisputable proof of God's curse and rejection of a people who had cursed and rejected Jesus. The line of polemical reasoning developed through the ages.

John Chrysostom preached: "The Jews say that they hope to see their city restored! No, they are mistaken. The Temple will never rise again, nor the Jews return to their former polity, Jesus Himself says this in Luke xxi.24. The Jew, no doubt, rejects this saying, for, says he, 'He who speaks thus is mine enemy. I crucified Him, and how shall I receive His testimony?' 'Yet, O Jew,' replies Chrysostom, 'herein lies the wonder, that He whom you crucified did afterwards pull down your city, scatter your people, and disperse your nation throughout the whole world' - and not even so do you recognise Him as God and Master!

"...Again, consider the difference of this captivity from those in Egypt and in Babylon. A limit of years was promised to those, but none has been foretold of this. Your three attempts to restore your state have all been failures, under Hadrian, under Constantine ('as is known to your old men'), and, as even your young people know, twenty years since, under that wicked Emperor Julian."[6]

In "your three attempts to restore your state," Chrysostom included the Bar Kokhba Rebellion, but did not mention the Great Revolt. For his polemical purposes, the Bar Kokhba Revolt carried greater importance. It had led to the removal of the Jews from the land of Judea.

Others treated the results of the two revolts as though there had been only one, but it was the enforced wandering among the nations that was pointed to again and again. It was "proof" throughout the Middle Ages that God had cast off the Jews. It was justification for the theology of contempt.

For Martin Luther, the enforced Diaspora proved the hopelessness of the Jews. "In brief: Because you see that after fifteen hundred years of misery (when no end is certain or will ever be so) the Jews are not disheartened nor are they even cognizant of their plight, you might with a good conscience despair of them. For it is impossible that God should let his people (if they were that) wait so long without consolation and prophecy."[7]

Luther took his followers beyond writing off the Jews to eliminating them completely. "A Christian has, next to the devil, no more venomous, bitter enemy than the Jew...(The Jews ought to convert) but if they refuse, we should neither tolerate nor suffer their presence in our midst!"[8]

It has often been said that the final split was inevitable, but Rabbi Akiba would not have agreed. He worked hard to bring it about. One of the most well-known dictums of Rabbi Akiba is, "All is foreseen, but free will is given."[9]

God knows what is, what will be, and what might have been. Man does not. God has given to every man a free will, the ability to make choices. Choices have consequences. That is why God brings all men to judgment for the choices they make.

The split has been set in the sun-hardened, blood-reddened brick of eighteen and a half centuries. What would have been, or what could have been, has long since vanished.

31. RABBI AKIBA'S MARTYRDOM

Gamaliel, Eliezer, Joshua, and Samuel the Little had all warned the people against the folly of provoking the Roman Empire to battle. They knew the might and method of the Roman army. They knew what to expect as the bitter consequences of rebellion. Taking the deaths of Rabbis Ishmael and Simeon as a sign from God, Akiba himself had warned of "what distress is in store for us." How much he foresaw of what that would be, we do not know, but he knew it would be very great.

Even Akiba's own suffering had been prophetically forewarned on different occasions. "During an argument concerning the preparation of sacrifices for slaughter on the Sabbath, Rabbi Eliezer became annoyed at Rabbi Akiba's numerous questions and he said angrily: 'You have contradicted me in matters of slaughter and you will meet your death in slaughter.'"[1]

"When R. Eliezer fell sick, R. Akiba and his companions went to visit him....He then said, 'I will be surprised if these die a natural death'. R. Akiba asked him, 'And what will my death be?' and he answered, 'Yours will be more cruel than theirs'."[2]

Rabbi Akiba was not immediately put to death at the end of the revolt. Initially, perhaps because of his age, he was not even imprisoned. But the Romans, to further eradicate the causes of the rebellion, imposed laws forbidding rabbinic teaching and practice.[3]

Rabbi Akiba did not obey Hadrian's decrees. He was then arrested, but his disciples still came to the outer walls of his prison cell, asking, "What is the halakhah concerning...?" When Akiba was brought to trial, a supernatural sign indicated that it was the end.[4]

After being sentenced to death, Akiba was tortured by having the flesh torn from his body with an iron comb. As the day was beginning to dawn, Akiba began to recite the Shema - "Hear O Israel, the Lord our God the Lord is One. And you shall love the Lord your God with all your heart, with all your soul, and with all your might..."[5]

Even in his death, Akiba laid out the pattern for rabbinic Judaism; the pattern of *"Kiddush ha-Shem,"* sanctification of the Divine Name. His suffering and death, with the Shema on his lips, became the model for all later Jewish suffering. "Akiba was not killed, except to be a model."[6]

Ever since Akiba, the Shema has been the answer of Jewish martyrs to their tormentors. "We may judge the important part it played in the rabbinic consciousness from the fact that the whole

Mishnah opens with the question, 'From what hour is the evening Shema to be read?'... During every persecution and massacre, from the times of the Crusades to the wholesale slaughter of the Jewish population in the Ukraine in the years 1919 to 1921, [through the horrors of the Holocaust], Shema Yisroel has been the last sound on the lips of the victims. All the Jewish martyrologies are written around the Shema."[7]

When Rabbi Akiba died, "The arms of the Law ceased, and the fountains of wisdom were stopped up."[8] He was the primary stength and source of rabbinic law.

His death, like his life and his teaching, shaped the religion and the future of his people. He left a very complete legacy. The more than eighteen hundred and fifty years of Jewish history since his death have followed the pattern of Akiba's life, a pattern of conflict and martyrdom.

A Theology of Suffering

Rabbi Akiba had every reason to expect both the tremendous loss of life and the slavery and exile which came with the failure of the rebellion. He had reasons to expect it, but he had his own way of understanding and utilizing it. "Two points seem indisputable (assuming the reliability of the traditions): that Rabbi Akiba saw the sufferings and death which accompanied the second revolt as not being caused by transgression and that he saw his own death as an expression of his love of God."[9]

R. Simeon b. Gamliel saw the failure of the revolt as caused by the sins of Israel.[10] So did other rabbis. "R. Isaac b. Samuel says in the name of Rab: The night has three watches, and at each watch the Holy One, blessed be He, sits and roars like a lion and says: Woe to the children, on account of whose sins I destroyed My house and burnt My temple and exiled them among the nations of the world."[11]

"As the traditional prayer book states, 'Because of our sins we went into exile from our land.'"[12] The prayer book and the other rabbis applied the connection between sin and judgment laid out in Tanakh. The *Tokhakhah* [Warning] in Leviticus 26 and Deuteronomy 28 presented this connection. So did the prophets.

In Ezekiel the Lord said, "And the nations will know that the people of Israel went into exile for their iniquity, because they broke faith with Me. So I hid My face from them and handed them over to their enemies, and they all fell by the sword."[13] Chapter 9 of Daniel is an eloquent expression of the same.

Akiba did not attribute the failure, suffering, and exile to sin, but he did believe that, "Exile makes atonement for iniquity."[14]

He believed there was no sin involved, not even his own Messianic proclamation. Even if there had been, exile would atone for it.

The positions Akiba took were often chosen for the greater purpose of advancing his struggle. One aspect of his theology of suffering is its presentation of many different ways of atonement other than the prescribed sacrifices. This made the Temple and the priests all but unnecessary.

For Akiba, one's own death also brings atonement. Even the one who has been sentenced by the Sanhedrin to death by stoning may offer his own death as atonement for his sins.[15] Since atonement brings forgiveness and entry into the world to come, there is reason to rejoice in suffering, exile, and one's own death.

Akiba's many ways of atonement also stood in direct opposition to the message of the gospel. The crux of the gospels is that there is only one means of atonement, the death of Yeshua. Akiba made that unnecessary.

Akiba's view of suffering put the revolt and the exile almost outside the realm of sin and guilt. He saw his personal suffering and that of Israel as a means of showing love for God. Also, it was acceptable as payment for "the few wrongs" which he, and Israel, had committed.[16]

Akiba believed that if one sees a righteous man, or a righteous people, suffering, he must be sure that his, or their, (eternal) end will be good. If you know that the man is righteous, then you know that his suffering will only bring a greater reward in the world to come.[17] By definition, those who follow the Rabbis are righteous.

"R. Akiba observed, 'Suffering is precious,'"[18] because it makes atonement for the sufferer.[19] "R. Akiba said: Moreover man should rejoice at chastisements more than at prosperity, for chastisements bring forgiveness for his transgressions."[20]

R. Eliezer dealt with this issue differently. He said, "Israel does not turn in repentance except throught pain and suffering."[21] In his view, the suffering and pain are a means of bringing the guilty to repentance.

Akiba's martyrdom came as a result of the failed Bar Kokhba Revolt which he had supported. Later rabbis did not condemn him for the failure of the revolt. They exalted him for his martyrdom. They were, after all, his disciples.

The doctrine of "*Zacuth Aboth*," the merits of the Fathers, teaches that the good deeds of Abraham, Isaac, and Jacob help persuade God to forgive Israel. The doctrine was extended to include Akiba.[22] "It is remarkable, for instance, that later generations of Rabbis found in Akiba's death the fulfilment of Is.

liii. 12."[23] The books of the *minim* speak of Isaiah 53 as pointing to the atoning death of Yeshua.

The Torah, the prophets, and other rabbis made the connection that "this destruction came about because of our sins." Akiba presented an alternative view: judgment and destruction came through no sin of Israel's, but rather to bring atonement for Israel's sins. There is an obvious internal contradiction. If it is not Israel's sins that bring the judgment, then what need is there for atonement through exile? Akiba's view also leads to significantly different theological and psychological conclusions.[24]

There is much rabbinic discussion of the sins that led to the destruction of the First Temple. Likewise, there are similar discussions concerning the failure of the Great Revolt. One would guess that the purpose of such discussions was to discourage future generations from committing the same sins.

There seems to be, however, a profound silence concerning what manner of sin might have led to the failure of the Bar Kokhba Revolt. Perhaps that is because of the prominent role played by Rabbi Akiba and the Sages in the revolt.

In any case, the emphasis remains on the suffering, rather than on the sin. It is a suffering that goes on and on, without an answer from God. It is like stopping after the 37th chapter of the book of Job. It is like the Jewish experience since the end of the revolt.

32. SOME CONCLUDING REMARKS

It is not easy to overestimate the significance of the Bar Kokhba Revolt. Because of its long-term consequences, it may well be considered the greatest tragedy in Jewish history. It is the most defining.

To the end of his life, Akiba ben Joseph never acknowledged that he had made a mistake in declaring Bar Kokhba the Messiah. Had his declaration been a momentary aberration, he would, no doubt, have confessed his sin and turned from it; and the Talmud would have highlighted his repentance. He never did that. He never spoke of his declaration as an error.

From the beginning, R. Akiba knew that Simeon ben Kosiba would not deliver Israel from the Romans. Yet he did not waver in his decision, but steadfastly pursued the goal he had actively sought since the day he first challenged Rabbi Eliezer.[1]

His disciples continued to seek his counsel and instruction. Even today, he is considered the greatest of Jewish spiritual heroes. Why didn't a mistake of such major significance cast doubt on the direction Akiba had chosen?

Judea was decimated. Multitudes were dead from the sword, from famine, and from the Sanhedrin. Israel was destroyed as a nation.

Akiba had supported, if not initiated, a rebellion against Rome. He had declared that the leader of that rebellion was God's Anointed. R. Akiba commanded all Israel to fight under a false Messiah in a war that he knew would end in disaster. But no blame was cast at him, or at the Sages who counselled Bar Kokhba and governed under him. There are four major reasons why this has been so.

1) Akiba had laid out the principle that an error by an expert carried no personal consequences. This is seen in "M. Bekhorot (iv, 4), where Rabbi Akiba said to Rabbi Tarfon, who had erroneously declared a firstborn permissible: 'You are absolved, since you are an expert (*Mumche*), and whoever is an expert for the Bet Din is absolved from reparation.'"[2]

The reasoning is that if someone who is not an expert makes a mistake, he does so because he does not have enough training. Therefore, he is culpable and liable for his mistake.

An expert has enough training. If he makes a mistake, it is because there was no contrary indication. Therefore, he is absolved of any guilt.

Akiba was "an expert for the Bet Din." If he declared Bar Kokhba the Messiah, then that was what the evidence indicated, or what the need of the hour required. If he was in error, there is no guilt, because he made an expert decision.

2) Akiba taught that the Law was not in heaven, but entrusted to the Rabbis. Even if God contradicted from heaven, Akiba maintained that God was in error. The Rabbis had the authority to decide what was right and what was wrong, what was true and what was false. In the calendrical dispute between Gamaliel and Joshua, Akiba said, "Whether they are announced properly or otherwise, the proclamation makes them holy."[3]

By the same reasoning, if the Rabbis declare someone to be the Messiah, then he IS the Messiah. Even if their declaration is factually wrong, it is still right. As with the calendar, the decision of the Rabbis overrules physical reality. No external criterion or correction is acceptable; not even God Himself speaking from heaven. Nothing and no one can contradict them.

3) The Theology of Suffering provided a no-fault explanation of the failure. The Law and the Prophets spoke of exile as a terrible judgment. Akiba spoke of it as a means of atonement.

4) Akiba's teaching was still sought because there was no other Judaism left in Israel.[4] He had defeated them all. By various means, he had overcome the Priesthood, the Traditional Rabbis, the Scriptures, Divine Revelation, and the *Talmidei Yeshua*. Rabbinic literature was all written by his disciples, and the Rabbis exerted control over the synagogues.

"The indestructable monument of the Pharisees, the molding of letters into legal bricks, when joined to the natural religious tendencies of worship and human charity made Judaism as viable as a religion could be. Whatever evolution would henceforth occur would be only that of legal evolution."[5]

Akiba made a fence of legal bricks around the Torah, and around Israel, making the laws of the Rabbis the highest authority. He established a system that required national conformity to rabbinic law. Whether that law was right or wrong, no one was to depart from it to the left or to the right.

Why did Akiba ben Joseph, the father of rabbinic Judaism, champion Bar Kokhba's cause? I believe we have found the answer in the rabbinic record of the words and deeds of Rabbi Akiba, and in the ideological system which he fathered.

There is a common denominator to Akiba's Judaism and Bar Kokhba's battle plan. Bar Kokhba and his men told God, "Neither help us nor discourage us." Akiba and the Rabbis told God, "It is not in heaven." Their declarations are one and the same: "We will do this without You."

Simeon ben Kosiba was very instrumental in the establishment of rabbinic authority. He was also very instrumental in leading Israel into one of the greatest, if not THE greatest disaster of all Jewish history.

Rabbi Akiba's declaration of Bar Kokhba as the Messianic King was consistent with the one consuming goal of his life: to bring Israel under the authority of the Rabbis. To that end, his choice of Bar Kokhba was not a mistake. More than symbolically, it was the crowning touch.

Bar Kokhba was Rabbi Akiba's Messiah.

APPENDIX A:
THE RABBIS, THE MAJORITY, AND THE MESSIAH

The Rabbis

"From a polemical point of view, not the least of early rabbinic accomplishments was to re-interpret that concept [government through king, priest, and prophet] in a manner suited to the rabbis' own purposes. In pursuit of their corporate communal purposes, 'the sages' progressively modified what appear to have been the normative premises of the paradigm, transforming it from a model of quasi-federal government into a symbol which projected the notion of unitary rabbinic rule. It was partly by so doing that they generated and monitored a revolution in the structure of Jewish organisational life."[1]

"Babylonian academicians apparently found it debatable whether or not the talmudic texts were themselves to be classified as torah, whose study necessitated the recital of a prior blessing (TB Berakhot 11b). What none questioned, however, was the proposition that the students of the law were best fitted to act as Israel's administrative and moral prefects. Mastery of the sacred canon deserved to be transmuted into mastery within and over the community; the greater the scholarship of the sage, the more pronounced his communal authority had to be."[2]

The priests were no longer necessary. "Avot de Rabbi Natan (4:18) speaks of 'the study of torah' being: More beloved of God than burnt offerings. For if a man studies torah he comes to know the will of God (Proverbs 2:5) ...Hence when a sage sits and expounds to the congregation, Scripture accords it to him as though he had offered up fat and blood on the altar."[3]

"R. Eli'ezer ben Jacob (a second-century tana' in 'Eres Yisra'el) was reported to have proclaimed that: "Whoever provides hospitality to a talmid hakham and shares with his wealth is considered as though he had offered up the daily offering."[4]

"Particularly forthright was the consequent rabbinical claim rightfully to enjoy whatever financial concessions local gentile authorities were prepared to make to 'priests of a recognised religion' (or in Bavel, 'servants of the fire'; see TB Nedarim 62b). Enlisting the full scope of their exegetical skills, rabbis and their disciples regularly claimed exemption from several of the taxes imposed upon those of their brethren who were not members of their own scholarly estate. Popular opposition to such concessions, it must be admitted, was often strong.

"'As Neusner has pointed out, the programmatic corollary of all such teachings was that the *keter torah* of the sages had replaced the *keter kehunah* of the priests as the principal arbiter of Israel's collective destiny. From being an act of personal piety, scholarship had been transformed into a determinate of national fortune, one which replicated the influence of the cultic ritual.

"The study of the Torah substitutes for the ancient cult and does for Israel what sacrifice did then: reconcile Israel to its father in heaven, wipe away sin, secure atonement, so save Israel. These deeply mythic convictions gave concrete expression to the view that the Torah not only sanctifies, but saves.

"...One possible lesson to be learnt was retrospective: learning had always been more important than the cult (thus, according to the 'additional opinion' appended to the long catalogue of Second Commonwealth deficiencies attributed to Yohanan ben Zak'ai in Mekhilta' (de-Ba-Hodesh; ed. Lauterbach, II, pp.194-5), the Temple had itself been destroyed because Israel had neglected torah study). Still more powerful, however, was the subsequent projection of those priorities into the future. Scholarly examination of the sacred texts could in effect now be predicated as a route to national regeneration. It was the hum of children's voices in the schoolhouse which ensured Israel's salvation. What is more, through torah study the sage and his students took their place at the very forefront of the messianic process."[5]

In the Talmud, it appears that what displeases God most is disobedience to the Rabbis. Consider "Rav Eliyahu Dessler's famous and oft-cited response to a correspondent who raised the argument that many Jews might have been spared the ravages of the Holocaust had the rabbinic authorities in Eastern Europe encouraged the masses of the Jews to emigrate to the land of Israel. Rav. Dessler writes: 'Whoever was present at their meetings [the Hafetz Hayyim, Rav Hayyim Brisker, and Rav Hayyim Ozer]...could have no doubt that he could see the Shekhinah resting on the work of their hands and that the holy spirit was present in their assemblies....Our rabbis have told us to listen to the words of the Sages, even if they tell us that right is left, and not to say, heaven forbid, that they certainly erred because little I can see their error with my own eyes. Rather, my seeing is null and void compared with the clarity of intellect and the divine aid they receive....This is the Torah view [Daas Torah] concerning faith in the Sages [Emunat Hakhamim]. **The absence of self-negation toward our rabbis is the root of all sin and the beginning of all destruction, while all merits are as naught compared with the root of all - faith in the Sages."**[6]

The Rabbis, on the other hand, cannot displease God no matter what they do. There is no place for the prophet, because there is no place for rebuking the Rabbis. Neither God nor man is authorized to do that.

Messiah?

The rabbinic references to R. Akiba and the Messiah teach four important lessons. This is the only topic on which R. Akiba is successfully rebuked, and he is rebuked in two different ways.

1. Since Akiba is rebuked for placing Messiah's throne next to God's [Dan.7],[7] you should not think of Messiah as a supernatural being. Sometime before Bar Kokhba and the revolt, Akiba held to the prevailing view that Messiah was the supernatural Son of Man, worthy to have his throne next to the throne of God.

2. Since Akiba is rebuked for proclaiming the Messiah,[8] you should not expect to see the Messiah in your own lifetime.

3. Since Akiba's proclamation was in error, do not expect to recognize the Messiah yourself. Trust the judgment of the rabbinic majority.

4. Do not examine the prophecies about Messiah. You are cursed if you calculate from the prophecies the time when Messiah should have come, because you "would say, since the predetermined time has arrived, and yet he has not come, he will never come."[9]

The lessons are intended to limit the thinking of Israel about the Messiah. The failure of the revolt, despite Akiba's proclamation, left a skeptical, if not bitter, taste in Jewish mouths at the thought of "Messiah."

"W.D. Davies has aptly said: '...it is rightly, if humorously, asserted that where there are three Jews, there can be four opinions. For example, there is no one doctrine of the Messiah. It is easily possible for a Jew to claim to be the Messiah without incurring censure, provided he observes the Miswot. Herbert Danby is reported to have once said, playfully no doubt, that he once lectured in Jerusalem when there were six Messiahs in his audience. To observe the Law confers freedom for almost anything else and, to parody Augustine, a Jew might urge: 'Observe the Law and believe what you like'"[10]

The lesson is that the coming of Messiah is not important compared to the observance of rabbinic law. In fact, Messiah's coming is said to be preceded by such terrible times that you might not want him to come in your lifetime. "Ulla said; 'Let him come but let me not see him.'"[11]

The Majority

There are three major aspects of "the majority principle" of the

Rabbis. Each is important in dictating the life of the community. Akiba was involved in establishing them all

1. The law and will of God is determined by whatever the majority of the leading rabbis decide.

2. The world and individuals are judged by the majority of their deeds, whether they are righteous or wicked.

"R. Akiba's saying in Koh. R. to X, 1, 'Man is adjudged in accordance with the preponderance of his deeds; he should always consider himself half guilty and half innocent; one more good deed and it is well with him, one more evil deed, woe to him.'"[12]

"R. Eleazar son of R. Simeon said: Because the world is judged by its majority, and an individual [too] is judged by his majority [of deeds, good or bad], if he performs one good deed, happy is he for turning the scale both for himself and for the whole world on the side of merit; if he commits one transgression, woe to him for weighting himself and the whole world in the scale of guilt, for it is said: 'but one sinner, etc.' — on account of the single sin which this man commits he and the whole world lose much good."[13]

Tanakh presents a different view, perhaps most clearly in Ezekiel. It is not the preponderance of one's deeds that determines one's fate. Rather it is their final direction.

"But if a wicked man turns away from all the sins he has committed and keeps all my decrees and does what is just and right, he will surely live; he will not die. None of the offenses he has committed will be remembered against him. Because of the righteous things he has done, he will live. Do I take any pleasure in the death of the wicked? declares the Sovereign LORD. Rather, am I not pleased when they turn from their ways and live?

"But if a righteous man turns from his righteousness and commits sin and does the same detestable things the wicked man does, will he live? None of the righteous things he has done will be remembered. Because of the unfaithfulness he is guilty of and because of the sins he has committed, he will die.

"Yet you say, 'The way of the Lord is not just.' Hear, O house of Israel: Is my way unjust? Is it not your ways that are unjust? If a righteous man turns from his righteousness and commits sin, he will die for it; because of the sin he has committed he will die."[14]

"Therefore, son of man, say to your countrymen, 'The righteousness of the righteous man will not save him when he disobeys, and the wickedness of the wicked man will not cause him to fall when he turns from it. The righteous man, if he sins, will not be allowed to live because of his former righteousness.' If I tell the righteous man that he will surely live, but then he trusts in his righteousness and does evil, none of the righteous things he has done will be remembered; he will die for the evil he has done.

"And if I say to the wicked man, 'You will surely die,' but he then turns away from his sin and does what is just and right — if he gives back what he took in pledge for a loan, returns what he has stolen, follows the decrees that give life, and does no evil, he will surely live; he will not die. None of the sins he has committed will be remembered against him. He has done what is just and right; he will surely live."[15]

3. Community standards and status are determined by the practice of the majority. What do the majority of Israelites, or the majority of Gentiles, do? What is the case with most men, most women, most boys, most girls? What is the habitual way of most butcher shops, thieves, oxen, birds, seeds or fish? What is the measure of the majority of cubits or the majority of opinions?

It would seem that in some cases, perhaps even in the majority of cases, such a rule would be equitable. On the other hand, it is not a teaching of Tanakh, and legislates conformity as a principle.

Footnotes
1. SA Cohen, Pp.3-4
2. Ibid., P.167
3. Ibid., P.166
4. Ber.10b in ibid., P.168
5. SA Cohen, P.19
6. Eliyahu Dessler, Mikhtav Me-Eliyahu 1:75-77, cited in Lawrence Kaplan, "Daas Torah: A Modern Conception of Rabbinic Authority," Rabbinic Authority and Personal Autonomy, Pp.16-17
7. Hag.14a
8. Mid. Lam. II.2, sec.4
9. Sanh.97b
10. "Torah and Dogma: A Comment", HTR, LXI [1968], pp.88-90)" in Longenecker, P.7n14
11. Sanh. 98b
12. Avoth Ch.3 MISHNAH 13n.102
13. Kid.40b
14. Ezek. 18:21-26
15. Ezek. 33:12-16

APPENDIX B:
MAIMONIDES' CONCEPT OF MESSIAH

The most concise expression of Maimonides' concept of the Messiah is found in his <u>Mishneh Torah</u>, which is authoritative for orthodox Jews.

"Do not suppose that King Messiah will have to perform signs and wonders, create new things in the world, revive the dead, or similar acts. It is not so. Rabbi Akiva was a great sage, one of the authors of the Mishnah, yet he was the right-hand man of Ben Koziva, the ruler, whom he thought to be King Messiah. He and all the sages of his generation imagined Bar Kohkba to be King Messiah until he was slain unfortunately. Once he was slain, it dawned on them that he was not [Messiah]. Yet the sages had not asked him for an omen or a wonder.

"If a king will arise from the house of David, a student of Torah, performing good deeds like his ancestor David, in the spirit of both the Written and the Oral Torah, and prevail upon all Israel to reinstate the Torah and to follow its direction, and will fight the battles of the Lord, he will presumably be the Messiah. If he has done these things and succeeded, having overcome the surrounding enemy nations and rebuilt the sanctuary on its site and gathered the dispersed of Israel, he will certainly be the Messiah. If he has not succeeded to such an extent, or has been slain, it is certain that he is not the one concerning whom the Torah has assured us...."

"It must not be supposed that in the messianic days any of the laws of nature will cease to exist, or that some new creation will then come into being within the created universe. Indeed, the world will continue in its normal course [without change]. What is written in Isaiah; 'The wolf shall dwell with the lamb, and the leopard shall lie down with the kid' (11:6) should be understood figuratively. It signifies that the Israelite people will dwell securely among the world's evil men who are likened to wolves and leopards, as it is written: 'Wolves of the desert ravage them, leopards keep watch round their cities' (Jeremiah 5:6). They will all turn to the true religion, and will neither plunder nor destroy; they will indeed eat what is permissible, gently, along with Israel, as it is written: 'The lion shall eat straw like any ox' (7). So too, all similar biblical passages referring to the Messiah are metaphorical. During the messianic era, their precise metaphorical significance will become known to all.

"The sages have declared: 'The only difference between the present world and the messianic era is our present subjection to foreign powers' (Berakhoth 34b)."[1]

"In that era there will be no famine, no war, no envy, no strife. Prosperity will be plentiful, and all kinds of luxuries will be available like dust. The universal preoccupation will be primarily to know the Lord. Consequently, the people of Israel will be very wise; the things that are now vague and deeply hidden will be revealed to all; they will attain a knowledge of their Creator to the utmost human capacity, as it is written: 'The land shall be full of the knowledge of the Lord as the waters cover the sea' (Isaiah 11:9)."[2]

In Mishneh Torah, Maimonides generally followed Akiba's de-supernaturalized view, though he envisioned great supernatural change in the nature of man and the world in the Messianic age. He pictured Messiah as a halakhically observant Son of David who succeeds in fighting the battles of the Lord, rebuilding the Temple, and regathering all Israel from the Diaspora.

In his "Epistle to Yemen," however, he presents a different view. Then he refers to Messiah's "mysterious lineage," citing Zech.6:12 and Is. 53:2,[3] and concludes by saying that a man will be proved to be the Messiah by the miracles he performs. "The messiah is not a person concerning whom it may be predicted that he will be the son of so-and-so, or of the family of so-and-so. On the contrary, he will be unknown before his coming, but he will prove by means of miracles and wonders that he is the true Messiah."[4]

His statement in Mishneh Torah that "the sages had not asked him [Bar Kokhba] for an omen or a wonder" indicates that Maimonides rejected the account in Sanhedrin 93b where the Rabbis are said to ask Bar Koziba to judge by smell in order to fulfill Isaiah 11. Maimonides himself also saw Isaiah 11 as presenting a Messiah with supernatural powers.

"The Messiah indeed ranks above all prophets after Moses in eminence and distinction, and God has bestowed some gifts upon him that He did not bestow upon Moses, as may be gathered from the following verses: *He shall sense the Torah by his reverence for the Lord* [Isa.11:3]; *the spirit of the Lord shall alight upon him* [Isa.11:12]; *Justice shall be the girdle of his loins* [Isa.11:5]."[5]

He also applies Isaiah 9:5, with its supernatural titles, to Messiah, and concludes that, "God has conferred upon him six appelations in the verse: *For a child has been born to us, a son has been given to us. And authority has settled on his shoulders. He has been named 'the Mighty God is planning grace; the Eternal Father, a peaceble ruler'* (Pele, Yoetz, El, Gibbor, Aviad, Sar-shalom). [Isa.9:5] He continues to magnify him, and declares: *You are My son; I have fathered you this day* [Ps.2:7]. All these statements demonstrate the superiority of the Messiah to all the descendants of Adam."[6]

"What the great powers are that all the prophets from Moses to Malachi ascribe to the messiah may be inferred from various statements in the twenty-four books of Scripture. The most significant of them is that the report of his advent will strike terror into the hearts of all the kings of the earth and their kingdoms will fall; neither will they be able to war or revolt against him...Isaiah refers to the submission of the kings to him in the verse: *kings shall be silenced because of him* [Isa.52:15]. He will slay whom he will by the word of his mouth, none will escape or be saved, as is written: *He shall strike down a land with the rod of his mouth* [Isa.11:4]."[7]

In Mishneh Torah, Maimonides is emphatic in stating that Messiah cannot be slain. That may have been a reaction to the failure of false messiahs in his own day, or to the failure of Bar Kokhba, or it might have been directed against belief in Jesus. In his "Epistle to Yemen," as noted above concerning Isaiah 52:15 and 53:2, he views Isaiah 52:14-53:12 as Messianic. This section speaks of the death of Messiah.

In Sanhedrin, the Rabbis apply Isaiah 53 to the Messiah. "The Rabbis said: His [Messiah's] name is 'the leper scholar,' as it is written, Surely he hath borne our griefs, and carried our sorrows: yet we did esteem him a leper, smitten of God, and afflicted.'"[8]

The text in Isaiah continues [the phrases in **bold** refer specifically to Messiah's death or atonement]: "But he was pierced for our transgressions, **he was crushed for our iniquities**; the punishment that brought us peace was upon him, and by his wounds we are healed.

"We all, like sheep, have gone astray, each of us has turned to his own way; and **the LORD has laid on him the iniquity of us all**.

"He was oppressed and afflicted, yet he did not open his mouth; he was led **like a lamb to the slaughter**, and as a sheep before its shearers is silent, so he did not open his mouth.

"By oppression and judgment he was taken away. And who can speak of his descendants? For **he was cut off from the land of the living; for the transgression of My people he was stricken**.

"**He was assigned a grave with the wicked**, and **with the rich in his death**, though he had done no violence, nor was any deceit in his mouth.

"Yet it was the LORD's will to crush him and cause him to suffer, and though **the LORD makes his soul a guilt offering**, he will see his offspring and prolong his days, and the will of the LORD will prosper in his hand.

"After the suffering of his soul, he will see the light of life and be satisfied; by his knowledge My righteous servant will justify many, and **he will bear their iniquities.**

"Therefore I will give him a portion among the great, and he will divide the spoils with the strong, because **he poured out his life unto death**, and was numbered with the transgressors. For **he bore the sin of many**, and made intercession for the transgressors."[9]

Other rabbinic writings and statements in the Pseudepigrapha speak of Messiah's death. The Targum refers Isaiah 53:13-53:12 to "My servant the Messiah." In 4 Ezra, God says, "For my son the Messiah shall be revealed with those who are with him, and those who remain shall rejoice 400 years. And after these years my son the Messiah shall die, and all who draw human breath."[10] According to some scholars, one parchment fragment of the Dead Sea Scrolls speaks of Messiah being pierced and put to death.[11]

The Talmud refers to Zech.12:9-14 as speaking of the death of Messiah: "It is well according to him who explains that the cause [of the mourning] is the slaying of Messiah the son of Joseph, since that well agrees with the Scriptural verse, 'And they shall look upon me because they have thrust him through, and they shall mourn for him as one mourns for his only son.'"[12]

It is not clear why the Rabbis spoke of Messiah as "the Son of Joseph," perhaps because Joseph saved Israel through his own death. That is, Israel believed that Joseph had died, but he actually had been brought up from the pit and was very much alive. Exiled from the land and people of Israel, Joseph was exalted and became the savior of Israel. He also became the savior of the nations.

The eighteenth of the Psalms of Solomon, written around the middle of the first century B.C., contains the following prayer: "May God cleanse Israel in the day of mercy and blessing, in the day of election when he brings back His Messiah."[13] That would mean that Messiah comes once, departs this earth through death or some supernatural means, and will come again. His coming back brings cleansing, mercy, and blessing to Israel.

2 Baruch, written during the second half of the first century A.D., is believed to have Pharisaic-Rabbinic roots. It says, "And it shall come to pass after these things, when the time of the advent of the Messiah is fulfilled, that He shall return in glory. Then all who have fallen asleep in hope of Him shall rise again."[14] This teaches that Messiah has come and gone. His return will bring the resurrection of the dead.

Maimonides speaks of other verses as being Messianic, such as Num.24:17-18, which R. Akiba applied to Bar Kokhba.[15] He also applied Zech.9:9 to the Messiah: "Rejoice greatly, O daughter of Zion, Shout, O daughter of Jerusalem; Behold, your king comes to you. He is triumphant and victorious, lowly and riding upon an ass, even upon a colt the foal of an ass."[16]

He believed that "The hour of his arrival will be at a time of great catastrophe for Israel....A later prophet too was alluding to the messianic tribulations when he declared: *But who can endure the day of his coming?* [Mal.3:2]"[17]

Messiah's coming would be in a time of great trouble, but also a time of the outpouring of the Holy Spirit and the restoration of prophecy to all Israel. "It is doubtless true that the reappearance of prophecy in Israel is one of the signs betokening the approach of the messianic era, as is stated: After that I will pour out My spirit upon all flesh; your sons and daughters shall prophesy ... [Joel 3:1]."[18]

FOOTNOTES

1. Maimonides' Mishneh Torah, (Yad Hazakah), Ed. by Philip Birnbaum, Hebrew Publishing Co., NY, 1985, P.327 [11:3-4 and 12:1-2]

2. Ibid., P.329 5.

3. "In allusion to his mysterious lineage, God says: *Behold a man whose name is the Shoot, and who shall shoot up* [Zech.6:12]. Similarly Isaiah referring to his arrival, implies that neither his father nor mother, nor his kith and kin will be known, for *he will grow, by his favor, like a sapling, like a root out of arid ground* [Isa.53:2]." Maimonides, Moses, "The Epistle to Yemen [to Jacob al-Fayyumi]," Crisis and Leadership: Epistles of Maimonidies, trans. by Abraham Halkin, JPS, Philadelphia, 1985, P.125

4. Ibid., P.125 He already explained that, "It is, my coreligionists, one of the fundamental articles of the Jewish faith that most surely the future redeemer of Israel will spring only from the stock of Solomon son of David." P.121

5. Ibid., P.124

6. Ibid.

7. Ibid., Pp.125-126

8. Sanhedrin 98b

9. Is. 53:5-12

10. 4 Ezra 7:28-29, cited in Charlesworth, "The Concept of the Messiah in the Pseudepigrapha," ANRW, de Gruyter, Berlin, 1979, P.202

11. 4Q285

12. Sukkah 52a

13. Psalms of Solomon, Charlesworth, P.199

14. 2 Baruch 30:1-2, ibid, P.200

15. Crisis and Leadership: Epistles of Maimonidies, P.121

16. Ibid.

17. Ibid.

18. Ibid., P.122

CHAPTER NOTES

The Jewish numbering of Biblical verses is used throughout, except where they appear otherwise in source quotations.

INTRODUCTION

1. Samuel Abramsky, "Bar Kochba," Encyclopedia Judaica, Vol. 2, Keter Publishing House Ltd., Jerusalem, 1971, P. 236
2. Judaism Despite Christianity, Edited by Eugen Rosenstock-Huessy, U. of Alabama Press, University, Alabama, 1969, P.159
3. Some guidelines from American jurisprudence on the use of evidence will be helpful: "Rule 401. Definition of 'Relevant Evidence' 'Relevant evidence' means evidence having any tendency to make the existence of any fact that is of consequence to the determination of the action more probable or less probable than it would be without the evidence....

"Rule 405. Methods of Proving Character (a) Reputation or opinion. In all cases in which evidence of character or a trait of character of a person is admissible, proof may be made by testimony as to reputation or by testimony in the form of an opinion....(b) Specific instances of conduct. In cases in which character or a trait of character of a person is an essential element of a charge, claim, or defense, proof may also be made of specific instances of that person's conduct."

Federal Civil Judicial Procedure and Rules, 1994 Edition, West Publishing Co., St. Paul, 1994, Pp.327, 331

4. Col. Mark M. Boatner, "The American Revolution: Some Myths, Moot Points & Misconceptions," American History Illustrated, Vol. III, #4, July 1968, P.20

THE REVOLT
1.HISTORICAL SETTING

1. Gertrude Himmelfarb, The New History and the Old, Belknap, Cambridge, 1987, P.30
2. Randall Collins concluded, "If it is too much to say that politics is 'really' religion, it is scarcely going too far to say that at the dynamic level they are virtually identical." J.J. Collins, The Apocalyptic Imagination: An Introduction to the Jewish Matrix of Christianity, Crossroad, New York, 1984, P. 13 That was certainly the case in the time and place we are examining.

Much is often made of the "fact" that politics is concerned with the here and now, while religion is concerned with the hereafter. But decisions made for the here and now are often made with a future beyond the life of the decision maker in view; and concern with what will be hereafter often shapes the decisions that are made in the here and now.

From the Maccabees to Roman Dominance

3. Doron Mendels, The Rise and Fall of Jewish Nationalism: Jewish and Christian Ethnicity in Ancient Palestine, Doubleday, New York, 1992, P. 123
4. משיחו Is.45:1
5. Flavius Josephus, Ant. Bk. XI, Ch. 8, § 5,6
6. Mendels, P.24

7. "And wherever they found the book of the Law, they tore them up and burned them, and if anyone was found to possess a book of the covenant or respected the Law, the king's decree condemned him to death.

"...The women who had circumcised their children they put to death under the decree, hanging the babies around their necks, and destroying their families and the men who had circumcised them." 1Mac.1:54-61

8. "When the time drew near for Mattathias to die, he said to his sons, '...you must be zealous for the Law, and give your lives for the covenant of our forefathers. Remember the deeds of our forefathers which they did in their generations, and you will win great glory and everlasting renown. Was not Abraham found faithful when he was tried, and it was credited to him as uprightness? Joseph in his time of distress observed the commandment and became master of Egypt. Phineas our forefather for his intense zeal obtained the promise of an everlasting priesthood. Joshua for carrying out his orders became a judge in Israel. Caleb for bearing witness before the congregation obtained an inheritance in the land. David for being merciful inherited a royal throne forever. Elijah for his intense zeal for the Law was caught up into heaven. Hananiah, Azariah, and Mishael had faith in God and were saved from the fire. Daniel for his innocence was delivered from the mouths of the lions...." 1Mac.2:49-60

9. H. D. Mantel, <u>Studies in the History of the Sanhedrin</u>, Harvard U. Press, Cambridge, 1961, P. 98.

10. "When he reached the Romans he said, 'Peace to you, O king, peace to you, O king.' He [Vespasian] said: 'Your life is forfeit on two counts, one because I am not a king and you call me king, and again, if I am a king, why did you not come to me before now?' He replied: 'As for your saying that you are not a king, in truth you are a king, since if you were not a king Jerusalem would not be delivered into your hand, as it is written, *And Lebanon shall fall by a mighty one.* 'Mighty one' [is an epithet] applied only to a king...'

"At this point a messenger came to him from Rome saying, 'Up, for the Emperor is dead, and the notables of Rome have decided to make you head [of the State]....'

"He [Vespasian] said [to Johanan ben Zakkai]; 'I am now going, and will send someone to take my place. You can, however, make a request of me and I will grant it.' He said to him: 'Give me Jabneh and its Wise Men, and the family chain of Rabban Gamaliel, and physicians to heal R. Zadok.' " Ibid., P.99

11. Josephus says that, "the nation was against them both and asked not to be ruled by a king, saying that it was the custom of their country to obey the priests of the God who was venerated by them, but that these two, who were descended from the priests, were seeking to change their form of government in order that they might become a nation of slaves." Ant. 14.40-47 in Mendels, P.210

12. As Dio Cassius records, "Thence he proceeded against Palestine, in Syria, because its inhabitants were harming Phoenicia. Their rulers were two brothers, Hyrcanus and Aristobulus, who were themselves quarreling, as it chanced, and stirring up the cities concerning the priesthood (for so they called their kingdom) of their God, whoever he is.

"...but in the siege of Jerusalem [Pompey] found trouble. Most of the city he took without exertion, as he was received by the party of Hyrcanus, but the temple itself, which the others had occupied in advance, he did not capture without labor." Dio Cassius, <u>Dio's Rome</u>, trans. Herbert B. Foster, Vol. 5, Pafraets Book Co., Troy, New York, 1906, P.62

13. "A wrong done to Jews in Asia Minor brings out the Jews in Rome in large numbers to attend the trial." [Pro Flacco 66, 59 B.C.] Bilhah Wardy, "Jewish Religion in Pagan Literature during the Late Republic and Early Empire," P.610, in <u>ANRW</u>, Walter de Gruyter, Berlin, 1979 "All are held responsible for one another." Sanh.27b

From Roman Dominance to the Great Revolt

14. Mendels, P.247

15. "The fact that Yahweh was an indigenous nationalistic God who could not tolerate other cults and other gods created most of the friction that occurred in the first century C.E. between the Jews and non-Jews living in the Land, as well as between the Jews and the Roman authorities."Ibid., Pp.197-198

16. Josephus, Ant. XIII, X, 6

17. "So Alexandra, when she had taken the fortress, ...spoke to the Pharisees, and put all things into their power...as to the affairs of the kingdom...

"So she made Hyrcanus [her son] high-priest because he was the elder, but much more because he cared not to meddle with politics, and permitted the Pharisees to do everything; to whom also she ordered the multitude to be obedient. She also restored again those practices which the Pharisees had introduced, according to the traditions of their forefathers, and which her father-in-law, Hyrcanus, had abrogated. So she had indeed the name of Regent; but the Pharisees had the authority...and the country was at peace, excepting the Pharisees; for they disturbed the queen, and desired that she would kill those that persuaded Alexander to slay the eight hundred men; after which they cut the throat of one of them, Diogenes: and after him they did the same to several, one after another..." Ibid.,13,16,1-2

18. Dio observed that by 38 B.C., "The Jews had committed many outrages upon the Romans—for the race is very bitter when aroused to anger—but they suffered far more themselves. The first of them were captured fighting for the precinct of their god, and later the rest on the day even then called the day of Saturn. And so great still were their religious scruples that the men who had been first captured along with the temple obtained leave from Sosius when the day of Saturn came around again, and went up with the remaining population into the building, where they performed all the customary rites. These people Antony entrusted to one Herod to govern, and Antigonus he bound to a cross and flogged—treatment accorded to no other king by the Romans—and subsequently slew him." Dio, P.243

19. Mendels, P.285

20. Josephus, Ant., 17, 2.4

21. "It is worth quoting Smith here: the influence of the Pharisees with the people, which Josephus reports, is not demonstrated by the history he records. John Hyrcanus was not afraid to break with the Pharisees, and none of the succeeding Maccabees except Salome and the puppet Hyrcanus II felt it worthwhile to conciliate them. As to their relations with Herod, Josephus

contradicts himself; but if Herod had the support of the Pharisees it did not suffice to secure him popularity, and if they opposed him they were not strong enough to cause him serious trouble. During the first century of the Common Era, the only ruler who consistently conciliated them was Agrippa I. If, as Josephus says, they were for peace with Rome, their influence failed to maintain it. After the war broke out, they formed only one party in the coalition upperclass government, which held the initial power in Jerusalem for a short time, but was ousted by groups with more popular support. All this accords perfectly with the fact that Josephus in his first history of the war never thought their influence important enough to deserve mention." Smith, "Palestinian Judaism", P.77 in D. Goodblatt, "The Place of the Pharisees in First Century Judaism: The State of the Debate," JSJ, Vol.XX, No.1, 6/89, 26-27

22. "When the disciples of Shammai and Hillel multiplied who had not served (their teachers) sufficiently, dissensions increased in Israel and the Torah became like two Toroth."Sot.47b

23. "[D]uring the lifetime of Jesus the party of Hillel was not yet in control. The significance of this is obvious. It means that an active and rapidly growing party within the ranks of the scholars was at the time in vigorous protest against the currently accepted interpretation of the Torah...." B.H. Branscomb, Jesus and the Law of Moses, P.54, quoted in W.D. Davies, Paul and Rabbinic Judaism: Some Rabbinic Elements in Pauline Theology, London, SPCK, 1948, P.9, n.1

24. Arnold A.T. Ehrhardt, "Birth of the Synagogue and R. Akiba," Studia Theologica: Scandinavian Journal of Theology, v.9, No.2, 1955, P.89

25. "These men agree in all other things with the Pharisaic notions, but they have an inviolable attachment to liberty; and they say that God is to be their only Ruler and Lord. They think little of submitting to death in unusual forms and permitting vengeance to fall on kinsmen and friends if only they may avoid calling any man Lord.'" Josephus, Ant. 18.1.6

" For still it came to pass that many Jews were slain at Alexandria in Egypt; for as many of the Sicarii as were able to fly thither, out of the seditious wars in Judea, were not content to have saved themselves, but must needs be undertaking to make new disturbances, and persuaded many of those that entertained them to assert their liberty, to esteem the Romans to be no better than themselves, and to look upon God as their only Lord and Master." Josephus, Wars, 7.10.1

The Great Revolt

26. "This fortress was called Masada. It was one Eleazar, a potent man, and the commander of these Sicarii, that had seized upon it." Josephus, Wars, 7.8.1

"And at this time [66 A.D.] it was that some of those that principally excited the people to go to war, made an assault upon a certain fortress called Masada. They took it by treachery, and slew the Romans that were there, and put others of their own party to keep it. At the same time Eleazar, the son of Ananias the high priest, a very bold youth, who was at that time governor of the temple, persuaded those that officiated in the divine service to receive no gift or sacrifice for any foreigner. And this was the true beginning of our war with the Romans: for they rejected the sacrifice of Caesar on this account...

"Hereupon the men of power got together, and conferred with the high priests, as did also the principal of the Pharisees; and thinking all was at stake, and that their calamities were becoming incurable, took counsel what was to be done. Accordingly, they determined to try what they could do with the seditious by words, and assembled the people before the brazen gate...And, in the first place, they shewed the great indignation they had at this attempt for a revolt, and for their bringing so great a war upon their country: after which they confuted their pretence as unjustifiable, and told them, that their forefathers had adorned their temple in great part with donations bestowed on them by foreigners, and had always received what had been presented to them from foreign nations...

"And as they said these things, they produced those priests that were skilful in the customs of their country, who made the report, that all their forefathers had received the sacrifices from foreign nations.—But still not one of the innovators would hearken to what was said..." Josephus, Wars, Bk II, Ch.17, §2,3,4

27. "The *biryonim* [the Zealot gangs] were then in the city. The Rabbis said to them: Let us go out and make peace with them [the Romans]. They would not let them, but on the contrary said, Let us go out and fight them. The Rabbis said: You will not succeed. They then rose up and burnt the stores of wheat and barley so that a famine ensued...."

"Abba Sikra the head of the *biryonim* in Jerusalem was the son of the sister of Rabban Johanan b. Zakkai. [The latter] sent to him saying, Come to visit me privately. When he came he said to him, How long are you going to carry on in this way and kill all the people with starvation? He replied: What can I do? If I say a word to them, they will kill me. He said: Devise some plan for me to escape. Perhaps I shall be able to save a little...." Git. 56a

28. Git. 56a-56b

Johanan ben Zakkai is not mentioned by Josephus or by any other non-rabbinic sources. Consequently, there are those who view the account as a fabrication. Arnold Ehrhardt says, "For the alleged smuggling out of Jochanan ben Zakkai and his subsequent meeting with Vespasian (!) at which he obtained the permission for Gamaliel to follow him in order to found the Jewish Synagogue, cannot be accepted, especially if we believe that Simeon, the father of Gamaliel, had fallen in battle against the Romans as one of the leaders of the insurgents, as the legend asserts. This story, we feel, can only be regarded as a plainly apologetic version, produced by the Jewish leaders in order to justify the position which Gamaliel ii had taken at the head of reconstituted Jewry. It obviously comes from a time when the actual events of his and Jochanan's escape had been forgotten." Ehrhardt, Pp.93-94

Daniel Schwartz says that, "Moreover, we should note that there seems to be no evidence that Josephus knew of the academy in Jabneh..." Daniel R. Schwartz, "Josephus and Nicolaus on the Pharisees," JSJ, Vol.XIV, No.2, 12/83, P.168

29. Josephus says that the people "...did not attend, nor give credit, to the signs that were so evident, and did so plainly foretell their future desolation; but, like men infatuated, without either eyes to see or minds to consider, did not regard the denunciations that God made to them. Thus there was a star resembling a sword, which stood over the city, and a comet, that continued a

whole year.

"Thus also, before the Jews' rebellion, and before those commotions which preceded the war, when the people were come in great crowds to the feast of unleavened bread,...so great a light shone round the altar and the holy house [at nine at night], that it appeared to be bright day-time...At the same festival also, a heifer, as she was led by the high priest to be sacrificed, brought forth a lamb in the midst of the temple. Moreover, the eastern gate of the inner [court of the temple], which was of brass, and vastly heavy, and had been with difficulty shut by twenty men, and rested upon a basis armed with iron, and had bolts fastened very deep into the firm floor, which was there made of one entire stone, was seen to be opened of its own accord about the sixth hour of the night....So these publicly declared, that this signal foreshewed the desolation that was coming upon them.

"...before sun-setting, chariots and troops of soldiers in their armour were seen running about among the clouds, and surrounding of cities. Moreover, at that feast which we call Pentecost, as the priests were going by night into the inner [court of the temple]...they felt a quaking, and heard a great noise, and after that they heard a sound as of a great multitude, saying, 'Let us remove from hence.'" Josephus, Wars, Book 6, Ch.5 §3

30. The range seems to depend on the religious/political commitment of the one giving the opinion. Ehrhardt says, "Nevertheless, A.D. 70 had seen an almost unparalleled disaster, insofar as the one and only bond which had held all Jews together had been broken; and the contemporaries knew of no other, but believed fervently that the end of the world was approaching. All the various Jewish sects and fellowships were torn apart by the disruption of the bond formed by the Jerusalem temple; and nobody could foretell how they might ever be joined together again." Ehrhardt, P.93 "This appears quite clearly in the fourth vision of iv. Esra (9.26f.) as well as in the vision of the waters in Baruch (syr.) liii." Ehrhardt, P.93 n1

Doron Mendels disagrees. "...the concept of the Land did not undergo any drastic changes in 70 C.E.; Palestine had already been under direct Roman rule since 63 B.C.E., when massive changes in attitude really did take place. After 70 C.E. the Land remained as it had been, under Roman rule."

"...Thus, it would not be too much to say that, in spite of the fact that the destruction of the Temple was a traumatic experience for Jews all over the world, the year 70 C.E. should not be regarded as a crucial date in terms of the *continuity* of the concepts of political nationalism." Mendels, Pp.260-261,201

From the Great Revolt to the Bar Kokhba Rebellion

31. Mendels, P.253 Josephus says that Vespasian "...laid a tribute upon the Jews wheresoever they were, and enjoined every one of them to bring two drachmae every year into the Capitol, as they used to pay the same to the temple at Jerusalem. And this was the state of the Jewish affairs at this time." Josephus, Bell. Jud. vii.6,6

32. "A critical and balanced scrutiny of Jewish history in the period of the Mishnah has made it clear that after the destruction of the Second Temple the Jews in Judaea still showed many of the characteristics of an independent people. This follows in particular from the study of the independent Jewish authorities

and their relationship with the Roman government and with the Jewish people in the country and in the diaspora. The Jewish leadership was actively involved in the rehabilitation of the people after the suppression of the First Revolt and the destruction of the Temple. The Jewish authorities created in this period the basic conditions for a continued religious and national life without Jerusalem and the Temple." Benjamin Isaac and Aharon Oppenheimer, "The Revolt of Bar Kokhba: Ideology and Modern Scholarship," JJS, Vol.XXXV, No.1, Spring 1985, P.34

Dio Cassius says, "Thus was Jerusalem destroyed on the very day of Saturn, which even now the Jews reverence most. To commemorate the event it was ordered that the conquered, while still preserving their own ancestral customs, should annually pay a tribute of two denarii to Capitole Jupiter." Dio, P.129

"In times past the God of the Jews had been recognised as a God by Rome, and this decision could not be reversed, for the gods are eternal. Rome maintained the fiction that she had made Jehovah captive, like the gods of other subjected nations, whose images had been brought in triumph to the Roman Capitolium. Since, however, there was no statue of its God in the Jerusalem temple, as Pompey had established in 63 B.C., the Roman government collected the *fiscus Judaicus*, the former temple tithe, which rendered Jehovah a tributary to the victorious Jupiter Capitolinus.

"The reason for this taxation was, therefore, not only fiscal and financial, but still more political and religious. That appears clearly from the fact that no special purpose is indicated to which this revenue was devoted." Ehrhardt, Pp.97-98

33. "The High Priest himself too who, during the first stages of the war, had for a time taken command of the Jewish forces, had not distinguished himself in so doing. The gap between the ideal of the Jewish High Priesthood and the facts about it had turned into a chasm which devoured this sacred office.

"With the High Priest and his supporters, the Sadducees, discredited, their late opponents, the Pharisees, became the leaders of the Jewish nation, and in particular the group surrounding Jochanan and Gamaliel..." Ehrhardt, P.95

34. According to Oppenheimer, it was evident to them that "...the institutions of leadership maintained by the sages... directed the life of the nation not only on the religious plane, but also in the areas of economics and culture, and consequently constituted a national leadership of high quality with a degree of hegemony over the Jews of the Diaspora as well." Aharon Oppenheimer, "The Bar Kokhba Revolt," Immanuel: A Bulletin of Religious Thoughts and Research in Israel, Vol.14, 1982, P.59

35. Ehrhardt asks, "How was it possible that the centre of Judaism was shifted from the Holy City of David to an insignificant, little village in Southern Palestine, Jamnia, of which no ancient writer, before Strabo xvi. 28, had ever made mention?" Ehrhardt, P.96

He also answers the question. For the Pharisees, the answer is to be found in the leader of the group that established itself at Yavneh. "Their head, Jochanan ben Zakkai, was one of the few survivors—allegedly the only one—of the late Jerusalem Sanhedrin, famous as a scribe long before A.D. 70. Although he was already an old man of limited strength, and seems to have died within the first decade of the Academy's existence, his high ranking scholarship gave to it that distinction which was lacking at the other comparable establishments. The Academy at Jamnia could claim an unbroken succession after the Jewish Sanhedrin from the time before the fall of Jerusalem; and through this claim it gained the attention of the Jews throughout the Roman Empire." Ehrhardt, P.97

36. Ehrhardt, Pp.99-100
37. cf. Maimonides, P.3 "...until this date, which is the eighth year of the eleventh century after the destruction of the Temple, corresponding to the year four thousand nine hundred thirty-seven since the creation of the world (1177 common era)."
38. For example, "In Cyrene [117 A.D.], while attacking the Greeks there, the Jews even crowned their ringleader king (the 'king of the Jews'), and according to one source performed terrible atrocities against their non-Jewish neighbors."Mendels, P.386

"Judaisms"

39. Anthony J. Saldarini, "Reconstructions of Rabbinic Judaism," in Early Judaism and Its Modern Interpreters, ed. Robert A. Kraft & George W. E. Nickelsburg, Fortress, Philadelphia, 1986, P.437

"For this period no such thing as 'normative Judaism' existed from which one or another 'heretical' goup might diverge." Jacob Neusner, A Life of Yohanan ben Zakkai, Ca. 1-80 C.E., Studia Post-Biblica, Leiden, 1970, p.25 quoted in David E. Aune, "Orthodoxy in First Century Judaism? A Response to N. J. McEleney," JSJ, Vol VII, No.1, June 1976, P.3

G.F. Moore's assumption of a normative first-century Judaism greatly hindered and skewed efforts to understand that time. According to Neusner, "It is difficult to realize that for fifty years that conception formed a major obstacle on the study of archaeological data, because the literary evidence produced by 'Normative,' that is, Rabbinic, Judaism seemed to make no room for what archaeologists had revealed. Today I cannot think of a single important scholar of the history of Judaism who conceives Rabbinic Judaism to have been 'normative' in a descriptive, historical sense. To be sure, relics of discredited conceptions persist. But they do not stand in the path of or impede the flow of scholarship." Neusner, Early Rabbinic Judaism, Pp. x-xi

40. S.A. Cohen, The Three Crowns: Structure of Communal Politics in Early Rabbinic Jewry, Cambridge, 1990, P.2

Jacob Neusner found that, "The political institutions and social expressions of rabbinism make no appearance in the earliest years of the Yavnean period. They emerge, for the first time, in the development of the government under the patriarchate and its associated rabbinical functionaries, beginning with Gamaliel II—circa A.D. 90—and fully articulated, in the aftermath of the Bar Kokhba debacle, by Simeon b. Gamaliel II, circa A.D. 150. At that point, the rabbinical ideal produced serious effects for the political and social realities of Judaism." Jacob Neusner, Early Rabbinic Judaism: Historical Studies in Religion, Literature, and Art, E.J. Brill, Leiden, 1975, P.70

41. Davies, Paul, Pp.3-4
42. Shaye Cohen reminds us that, "at no point in antiquity did the rabbis

clearly see themselves either as Pharisees or as the descendants of Pharisees....The identification with the Pharisees is secure and central for the first time only in an early medieval text, the scholia to the Scroll of Fasting.

"How can we explain the hesitation of the rabbis to identify themselves with the Pharisees?..."

"Part of the answer is the tendency of all sects to refuse to see themselves as sects. They are the orthodox; the wicked multitudes are the heretics. Jewish sects (e.g. Samaritans, Christians, Qumran Essenes) call themselves 'Israel;' 'Pharisees,' which literally means 'separatists,' was the opprobrious epithet hurled by opponents. Hence it is not surprising that the rabbis refer to themselves as 'sages,' 'sages of Israel,' 'rabbis,' etc., rather than 'Pharisees' and do not acknowledge their sectarian origins." Shaye J.D. Cohen, "The Significance of Yavneh: Pharisees, Rabbis, and the End of Jewish Sectarianism," Hebrew Union College Annual 55, 1984, P.40

Another part of the answer is that the Rabbis [Beth Hillel] were opponents of the Pharisaic group dominant before the destruction of the Temple [Beth Shammai]. When Beth Hillel gained control, the views of Shammai and his disciples were given verbal honor, but overturned and rendered irrelevant.

2. THE SOURCES

1. The study of the American Revolution intermingles history, ideology, and myth in a way that is somewhat parallel to the study of the Bar Kokhba Rebellion.

Sydney G. Fisher reviewed the formation of popular history in a classic article, 'The Legendary and Myth-Making Process in Histories of the American Revolution:" 'Having taken the trouble some years ago to examine the great mass of original evidence relating to the American Revolution, the contemporary documents, pamphlets, letters, memoirs, diaries, the debates in Parliament and the evidence obtained by its committees, I found that very little use of it had been made in writing our standard histories...which have been the general guides and from which school books and other compilations, as well as public orations, are prepared.'" Boatner, P.19

Fisher found four reasons why most of the evidence of the Revolution' was never presented: (1) The outcast American Loyalists never properly presented their side of the story. (2) The intensity of the struggle for existence that followed the war. (3) The principal source used was meticulously written to support the point of view of the victors. (4) A large body of vitally important source material was not discovered until many years later.

In the study of the Bar Kokhba Rebellion, the exact same problems exist, only greatly compounded.

Rabbinic Sources

2. Isaac & Oppenheimer, P.37

3. S.A. Cohen, P.3 Cohen continues, "Thus to acknowledge that the information contained in early rabbinic literature is typically a-historical is not altogether to deny its historiographical utility. On the contrary, and precisely because of their prejudices, the texts do articulate identifiable perspectives on what rabbinic tradents considered to be the vectorial trajectory of Israel's past.

Still more emphaticaly do they mirror their authors' views on the procedures which had confirmed their own God-given right to play a significant role in Jewry's present government."

4. Anthony J. Saldarini, "Reconstructions of Rabbinic Judaism," in Early Judaism and Its Modern Interpreters, ed. Robert A. Kraft & George W. E. Nickelsburg, Fortress, Philadelphia, 1986, P.438

W.D. Davies states an important warning concerning use of the Talmud: "Thus the Mishnah was not compiled till the end of the second century, and most of the other Rabbinic sources are later than the third century. While it is clear that the Rabbinic sources do preserve traditions of an earlier date than the second century, and that it is legitimate to define the Mishnah as a 'deposit of four centuries of Jewish religious and cultural activity in Palestine beginning at some uncertain date possibly during the earlier half of the second century B.C. and ending with the close of the second century A.D.', [Danby, p.xiii] it must never be overlooked that Judaism had made much history in that period. It follows that we cannot, without extreme caution, use the Rabbinic sources as evidence for first-century Judaism." Davies, Paul, P.3

Non-rabbinic Sources

5. Isaac & Oppenheimer, P.33

6. Ibid., P.39 n.24 They continue, "It may be argued that Pausanias rather than Fronto gives us the Roman perspective, for Fronto listed as many disasters as he could. E. Champlin...points out that 'an astonishing note of bitterness pervades Fronto's attitude to Hadrian'." citing E. Champlin, Fronto and Antonine Rome, 1980, P. 95

7. Yehoshaphat Harkabi, The Bar Kochba Syndrome—Risk and Realism in International Politics, Rossel, Chappaqua, New York, 1983, P.52

8. Isaac & Oppenheimer, Pp. 38-39

Modern Sources

9. Isaac & Oppenheimer, P.33

10. ibid., P.35 As with many human groups, scholars have their own coteries, circles, and camps, as well as fashions and fads. The ruminations of some scholars are such that it seems they are merely chewing one another's cud. They simply repeat and reaffirm one another's assumptions and conclusions until "a scholarly consensus" is reached. A scholarly consensus is no guarantee that the truth has been found. Sometimes scholars project their own time, place, culture, or conflicts onto the events they study. G.F. Moore's "orthodoxy" is a very significant case in point.

11. In a review of Peter Schafer's Der Bar Kokhba-Aufstand, P.S. Alexander points out that, "Historians have long bewailed the paucity of information about the Bar Kokhba revolt. That tragic episode in Palestinian Jewish history may have caused almost as much physical devastation and spiritual trauma as the first great war against Rome (A.D. 66-74), but it is hard to assess its significance, or even to be sure of the main events. There was no Josephus for the second revolt. Scholars have been sorely tempted to offset this lack by making the most of every scrap of information that can be gleaned from ancient sources. Some, with great ingenuity, have managed to write sizeable essays or

monographs on Bar Kokhba. Schafer demonstrates that much of this historical writing lacks any solid foundation..." P.S. Alexander, review of Peter Schafer, Der Bar Kokhba-Aufstand: Studien zum zweiten judischen Krieg gegen Rom, JJS, Vol.XXXV, No.1, Spr. '84, P.103
12. Mendels, P. 4

3. THE COURSE OF THE REBELLION
The Cause and Sequence of Events

1.The *Scriptores Historiae Augustae* state: "In the course of these travels, he [Hadrian] conceived such a hatred for the people of Antioch that he wished to separate Syria from Phoenicia, in order that Antioch might not be called the chief city of so many communities. At this time also the Jews began war, because they were forbidden to practice circumcision." Menahem Stern, ed., Greek and Latin Authors on Jews and Judaism, The Israel Academy of Science and Humanities, Jerusalem, 1980, Vol.2, P.511

Many scholars have accepted the statement as true. As expressed by Emil Schurer: "Hadrian first of all intensified the ban on castration already decreed by Domitian; it was to be punished in accordance with the lex Cornelia, i.e. as murder. But circumcision was placed on a par with castration, as may be seen from a later decree of Antoninus Pius permitting Jews to practice circumcision once again." Emil Schurer, The History of the Jewish People in the Age of Jesus Christ, revised and edited by Geza Vermes and Fergus Millar, T & T Clark Ltd., Edinburgh, 1973, Vol. I, Pp.538-9, 541, 542

2. Isaac & Oppenheimer, P.38 They continue, "We may add that the statement there gives the impression of being a hostile pronouncement, disparaging circumcision and providing the reputed reason for the revolt. This does not mean that it is untrue; but Dio, even in Xiphilinus' version, is not hostile."

3. Ber. 61b: "Our Rabbis taught: Once the wicked Government issued a decree forbidding the Jews to study and practise the Torah....soon afterwards R. Akiba was arrested and thrown into prison...When R. Akiba was taken out for execution..." Rabbi Akiba was arrested, thrown into prison, and executed after the revolt.

Rosh HaSh. 19a also places the ban on circumcision after the revolt: "For the Government [of Rome] had issued a decree that they should not study the Torah and that they should not circumcise their sons and that they should profane the Sabbath. What did Judah b. Shammu'a and his colleagues do?...

"Judah b. Shammu'a was the disciple of R. Meir..." R. Meir was a contemporary and disciple of R. Akiba.

Judah b. Shammu'a and his colleagues were the rabbinic generation which followed Akiba and the revolt. They were the ones who had to face the ban on circumcision and the other Roman anti-Torah decrees. The decrees were overturned in their time as well.

4. Dio Cassius, a Roman historian who lived in the second and third centuries, does not mention circumcision, but gives the cause of the rebellion as the building of a Roman temple on the site of the Jewish Temple. "At Jerusalem he [Hadrian] founded a city in place of the one which had been razed to the ground [at the conclusion of the Great Revolt], naming it Aelia Capitolina,

and on the site of the temple of the god he raised a new temple to Jupiter. This brought on a war of no slight importance nor of brief duration, for the Jews deemed it intolerable that foreign races should be settled in their city and foreign religious rites planted there." Roman History, LXIX, 12-14, translated by E. Cary, The Loeb Classical Library, Heinemann Ltd., London and Harvard University Press, 1925, Vol.VIII, Pp.447-451, cited in Yigael Yadin, Bar Kokhba: The Rediscovery of the Legendary Hero of the Last Jewish Revolt Against Imperial Rome, Random House, NY, 1971, P.257

However, Epiphanius, a fourth century bishop in Cyprus, says that Hadrian's temple was not built then, but rather that, "Hadrian made up his mind to [re]build the city, but not the temple....And he gave to the city that was being built his own name and the appellation of the royal title. For as he was named Aelius Hadrian, so he also named the city Aelia." Epiphanius, 'Treatise on Weights and Measures', edited and translated by J.E. Dean, Chicago Press, Chicago, 1935, Pp.30-1, cited in Yadin, P.259

To confuse the matter more, Eusebius, a church historian who lived in the third and fourth centuries, says that Hadrian built the city after the rebellion, rather than before. He says that it was in "Hadrian's Year 20 (AD 136) [that] Aelia was founded by Aelius Hadrianus; and before its gate, that of the road by which we go to Bethlehem, he set up an idol of a pig in marble, signifying the subjugation of the Jews to Roman authority." Eusebius, Chronicon Pascale, cited in Yadin, P.258

5. "The earlier date is now confirmed beyond doubt by the presence of a coin of Aelia Capitolina in a hoard of Bar Kochba denaii from the Judean desert. The honor to Jerusalem, as it was from the Roman point of view, would naturally belong to the year A.D. 130." G.W. Bowersock, "A Roman Perspective on the Bar Kokhba War," in Approaches to Ancient Judaism, edited by William Scott Green, Scholars Press, Chico, CA., 1980, Vol.II, P.135

"Meshorer...reports on a coin-hoard which contained foundation coins along with coins of the revolt. Mildenberg...observes that coins of Aelia bear the legend 'Imp. Caes. Traiano Hadriano', a legend impossible after the Bar Kokhba war. Other coins bear the early legend 'Imp. Caesar Had. Aug.' with a head of Sabina and the inscription 'Sabiona Augusta' (not: Diva Sabina) on the reverse. Sabina died in 136." Isaac & Oppenheimer, P.65n The coin must have been issued before her death and subsequent exaltation to divinity.

G.W. Bowersock concluded that there actually was no Roman temple built on the Jewish Temple mount either before or after. "There was no temple. The temple of Zeus was in fact built farther west, as Wilkinson now shows." Bowersock, P.137 He also concludes that it was Hadrian's ban on circumcision which was the probable cause of the rebellion.

Yigael Yadin, who was in charge of the archaeological expedition that discovered the Bar Kokhba caves, remarks, "How little is actually agreed upon about the real causes of the revolt may be learned from the fact that quite recently one scholar (Hugo Mantel) came to the conclusion that 'not the decrees of Hadrian...caused the Bar Kochba revolt, but the reverse is true. Hadrian's decrees constituted a reaction of the Romans to the Jewish Revolt.'" Yadin, P.22

6. It seems logical, but the Talmud does not mention it. The Talmud, however, may be silent on the issue to avoid naming the Rabbis - who would

have called for resistance in such a scenario - as the authors of a revolt which ended in such disaster.

7. "Underlying the Bar Kokhba revolt was the refusal to become reconciled to Roman rule. Throughout the Second Temple and mishnaic periods, the Jewish people and its leaders never acceded to the legitimacy of foreign control of Eretz Israel.

"...Regardless of what the direct causes of the Bar Kokhba revolt may be, the basic motivation was the refusal of the Jewish people to merge into the Hellenistic Roman regime, and their desire to retain their individualism and yearning for independence." Oppenheimer, Pp.59-60

8. "During the decades following the destruction of the Second Temple, life in the shadow of Roman rule, with its frequent arbitrary changes of policy toward the Jews and their religion—and with the severe edicts of the local governors—evoked unrest within Israel."Harkabi, P.27 That, at least, was the prevailing perspective of the Jews, albeit not of the Romans.

9. Hugo Mantel, "The Causes of the Bar Kochba Revolt," JQR, #3-4, Philadelphia, 1968, P.278

10. There is some indication that there were reasons for expecting a favorable political settlement of Jewish complaints. Dio writes that in A.D. 116, "Trajan, in fear that the Parthians, too, might begin some revolt, decided to give them a king of their own. And when he came to Ctesiphon he called together in a great plain all the Romans and likewise all the Parthians that were there at the time. He mounted a lofty platform, and, after describing in lofty language what he had accomplished, he appointed Parthaspates king of the Parthians and set the diadem upon his head.

"When Bolgaesus, the son of Sanatruces, confronted in battle array the followers of Severus and before coming to an actual test of strength asked and secured an armistice, Trajan sent envoys to him and granted him a portion of Armenia in return for peace." Dio, P.208

Trajan demonstrated a willingness, whatever his motivation, to appoint a king over a rebellious or potentially rebellious people. Hadrian also seemed to favor a policy of accomodation.

11. Isaac & Oppenheimer, Pp.50-51

Hadrian

12. "In talmudic literature Hadrian is on the one hand depicted as an emperor avid for knowledge holding discussions with Rabbi Joshua b. Hananiah and seeking to understand the essence of Judaism..., and on the other cursed: 'may his bones be pulverized.'" Oppenheimer, Pp.60-61 [Gen.R.X.3;Shab.119a; Pesikta Rabbati 21. 99a]

The rabbinic story is told that, "One day on Hadrian's journey in the East, a Jew passed the Imperial train and saluted the Emperor. Hadrian was beside himself with rage. 'You, a Jew, dare to greet the Emperor! You shall pay for this with your life.' In the course of the same day, another Jew passed him, and, warned by example, he did not greet Hadrian. 'You, a Jew, dare to pass the Emperor without a greeting,' he angrily exclaimed. 'You have forfeited your life.' To his astonished courtiers he replied: 'I hate the Jews. Whatever they do, I find intolerable. I, therefore, make use of any pretext to destroy them.'" J.H.

Hertz, ed. The Pentateuch and Haftorahs, Soncino Press, London, 1958, P.501
13. Mantel, "Causes," P.228
14. Ibid., P.275 citing Makkot 24b and Sanhedrin 97b

The Extent of the Revolt

15. "While Hadrian was close by in Egypt and again in Syria, they remained quiet, save in so far as they purposely made the weapons they were called upon to furnish of poorer quality, to the end that the Romans might reject them and they have the use of them. But when he went farther away, they openly revolted.

"To be sure, they did not dare try conclusions with the Romans in the open field, but they occupied advantageous positions in the country and strengthened them with mines and walls, in order that they might have places of refuge whenever they should be hard pressed, and meet together unobserved under ground; and in these subterranean passages they sunk shafts from above to let in air and light.

"At first the Romans made no account of them. Soon, however, all Judaea had been upheaved, and the Jews all over the world were showing signs of disturbance, were gathering together, and giving evidence of great hostility to the Romans, partly by secret and partly by open acts; many other outside nations, too, were joining them through eagerness for gain, and the whole earth, almost, was becoming convulsed over the matter.

"Then, indeed, did Hadrian send against them his best generals, of whom Julius Severus was the first to be despatched, from Britain, of which he was governor, against the Jews. He did not venture to attack his opponents at any one point, seeing their numbers and their desperation, but by taking them in separate groups by means of the number of his soldiers and his under-officers and by depriving them of food and shutting them up he was able, rather slowly, to be sure, but with comparatively little danger, to crush and exhaust and exterminate them.

"Very few of them survived. Fifty of their most important garrisons and nine hundred and eighty-five of their most renowned towns were blotted out. Fifty-eight myriads of men were slaughtered in the course of the invasions and battles, and the number of those that perished by famine and disease and fire was past all investigating.

"Thus nearly the whole of Judaea was made desolate, an event of which the people had had indications even before the war. The tomb of Solomon, which these men regarded as one of their sacred objects, fell to pieces of itself and collapsed and many wolves and hyenas rushed howling into their cities.

"Many Romans, moreover, perished in the war. Wherefore Hadrian in writing to the senate did not employ the opening phrase commonly affected by the emperors: 'If you and your children are in health, it shall be well: I and the armies are in health.'" Dio, Pp.226-227

16. In a letter to Marcus Aurelius, Fronto, his tutor and close friend, wrote, "Again under the rule of your grandfather Hadrian what a number of soldiers were killed by the Jews, what a number by the Britons!" Stern, P.177 Fronto was about forty years old when the rebellion began.

17. "For the Romans, manipulation of apprehension through the considered

use of force was an art." Harkabi, P.61

18. They understood the simple military axiom that, "In war, the main thing is to win the last battle, not the first." Ibid, P.36

19. "At Herodium, which was evidently the rebel administrative center, and at hirbat al-Arrub near the Bethlehem-Hebron road which can reasonably be identified with Kiryat Arabaya in the Bar Kokhba letter, archaeologists found underground caves containing finds from the time of the Bar Kokhba revolt. Networks of such caves have been found at Hirbat Naqiq, Hirbat Etun, Hirbat Kishor and other places several kilometers south of Amatzia (some with apertures for ventilation), which have granaries, rooms, water holes and shafts, all underground. The dating of these systems to the Bar Kokhba revolt seems reasonable. These underground networks, which were attached to the village houses, made clandestine activity possible when necessary. It does not seem likely that such ambitious networks could have been prepared in the throes of the revolt itself, and Cassius Dio's report that they were dug within the framework of preparations for it appears to be confirmed.

"Betar is also connected with preparations for the Bar Kokhba revolt. It is identified with the Arab village of Batir, ten kilometers southwest of Jerusalem. Northwest of that village is a steep hill on which there is a field of ruins which the Arabs call Hirbat al-Yahud (=the ruin of the Jews)." Oppenheimer, P.63

"Tineius Rufus is known as governor of Judaea at the outbreak of the war from Jewish and Christian sources only, but he is attested as suffect consul in 127. Julius Severus is not mentioned in Jewish and Christian sources. Dio mentions his transfer from Britain to Judaea for the suppression of the revolt. This is confirmed by an inscription which lists his career." Isaac & Oppenheimer, Pp.56-57

20. "In the Upper Galilee Avi-Yonah has noted a remarkable continuity in the population which gives no indication of having participated in the Bar Kochba war of 132-35 CE." Eric M. Meyers, "The Cultural Setting of Galilee: The Case of Regionalism and Early Judaism," in <u>ANRW</u>, P.700

"In two recent papers it has been suggested that Roman military and administrative re-organization in Galilee and the Valley of Jezreel successfully prevented the outbreak of large-scale hostilities there..." Isaac and Oppenheimer, P.53 n88

"All hoards containing coins of the second Jewish revolt were discovered in Judaea, notably in the Hebron mountains, west of Jerusalem, and in the Judaean desert. The same is true of the underground hiding-places recently explored, although admittedly not many of those are firmly dated and some have now been found in Lower Galilee as well." Ibid., Pp.53-54 That might indicate that there was preparation for the Revolt in Galilee, but no participation.

Jerusalem

21. Oppenheimer reconstructs it this way: "At the start of the revolt the rebels apparently defeated the Tenth Legion (*Fretensis*) stationed in Jerusalem. The survivors fled the city, and Jerusalem itself fell to the rebels. The legions or parts of legions rushed to Jerusalem from adjacent provinces were likewise repulsed. Especially disastrous was the fate of the Twenty-Second legion (*Deiotariana*) from Egypt. No mention of it appears anywhere after the Bar Kokhba revolt, so that it was either totally annihilated by the rebels, or dissolved

because of its failure and erased from the register of Roman legions."Oppenheimer, P.68

22. Isaac and Oppenheimer, P.54 Appian of Alexandria, a contemporary of the revolt, briefly reviewed the history of Jerusalem from its first destruction. He said, "It was afterward rebuilt and Vespasian destroyed it again, and Hadrian did the same in our time. On account of those rebellions the poll tax imposed upon all Jews is heavier than that imposed upon the surrounding peoples." Harkabi, P.179

"The evidence from Appian and Christian sources would seem decisive. However, as pointed out by Applebaum, the archaeological evidence, as it stands, raises grave doubts, for in the excavations carried out since 1967 in the Old City of Jerusalem almost no coins of the Second Revolt came to light." Isaac and Oppenheimer, P.55 "Applebaum, in his more recent study, follows Milik...in asserting that Jerusalem was indeed captured by the rebels and held at least until September/October of 134." Ibid., P.55 n.98

23. "The coin legends, 'Jerusalem' and 'For the Freedom of Jerusalem', and the design of the Temple on the coinage, are not mint indications but programmatic declarations. Accordingly, they cannot decide whether Jerusalem was taken by the insurgents. They provide, however, the only extant contemporary pronouncements in regard to the values and objectives, both of the leadership of the revolt and of the recipients of the coins. Jerusalem clearly was of central importance to the rebels, whether they temporarily captured the city or not." Isaac and Oppenheimer, Pp.46-47

24. Yaakov Meshorer, "Jewish Numismatics," in Kraft & Nickelsburg, P.214 Another coin "...bears a crude chalice resembling the vessels on the shekels of the first year. The inscription (in paleo-Hebrew) reads: 'For the Redemption of Holy Jerusalem' (Meshorer: 2: 129-31). This type was struck at Gamla [in the Golan Heights], probably during the siege of the Romans at the beginning of the revolt. Such coins were not found at the excavations of Jerusalem or Masada; consequently, it can be concluded that this coin type was Galilean."

25. "The [Bar Kokhba] coins are all overstruck on contemporary Roman coins which had been struck in Rome or the provinces. Overstriking these Roman coins, which bore the portraits of the Roman emperors, with new designs not only saved the stage of preparing flans but also enabled Bar Kokhba to demolish the pagan symbols and designs of the foreign rulers and to replace them with his own symbols and slogans. The silver and bronze coins bear designs related to the Temple in Jerusalem, the one destroyed by Titus in 70 C.E., which Bar Kokhba planned to rebuild after his victory." Meshorer, P.215

26. Ibid.

27. "What the Rabbis aimed at doing was to store away every Hadrianic and Trajanic denarius which had become worn by use because it was coined from [metal captured from] Jerusalem." A.Z. 52b

28. "It is intrinsically likely that a connection existed between the activities of the Jewish authorities at Yavneh and the revolt of Bar Kokhba.

"...Thus they repeatedly emphasized that the Temple would soon be rebuilt. This was not an abstract phrase, but a firm expectation which formed the basis of the development of halakhot and the routine of daily life." Isaac & Oppenheimer, P.49

The Temple

29. In <u>The Holy Temple Revisited</u>, Rabbi Leibel Reznick presents an interesting case for the Temple having been rebuilt. His presentation raises a number of issues that are worth looking at.

"After the destruction of the Holy Temple in 70 C.E., sacrifices were no longer offered. The sacrificial rites could only be performed on the Altar, and the Altar had been destroyed.

"One of the sacrifices brought during the years of the Temple was the Pascal sacrifice....

"One of the unique characteristics of this sacrifice was the fact that it had to be roasted directly over a fire. It could not be cooked or fried like other sacrificial meat. There arose a rabbinic dispute as to whether the Pascal lamb could be roasted over a metal grill. Some rabbis permitted the practice; others said that the portion of the meat that came in contact with the metal grill would be fried by the heat of the metal, not roasted directly over the fire.

"The Talmud records this dispute. One of the talmudic rabbis sought to resolve the matter concerning the use of a metal grill from the fact that Rabban Gamaliel, the illustrious sage, ordered his own servant to roast the Pascal sacrifice on a metal grill (Pesachim 74a). It is quite evident from the Talmud that Rabban Gamaliel lived during the Temple Era when the service of the Pascal sacrifice was still being performed.

"However, Rabban Gamaliel was the grandfather of Judah the Prince, who compiled his magnum opus, the Mishna, in 220 C.E. How is it possible, then, that his grandfather offered a Pascal sacrifice 150 years earlier? Rabban Gamaliel was no youngster when he offered his sacrifice. He was already a renowned scholar with attending servants. How could he have offered a sacrifice?" Liebel Reznick, <u>The Holy Temple Revisited</u>, Jason Aronson, Northvale, NJ, 1993, Pp.153-154

"Bar Kokhba issued coins on which he had inscribed, "Freedom for Israel." Many of these coins depict a temple facade. This type of depiction was very common on Roman coins of that era. But the Roman coins always showed a temple facade that was standing—a facade that was recognizable to anyone who had seen both the particular temple and the coin. Why would Bar Kokhba issue coins of a Jewish temple that had been destroyed sixty years earlier, a temple that was no longer standing, a temple whose facade would not be recognized?

"Bar Kokhba appointed a High Priest and some of the coins include his name, Eleazar the Priest. The High Priest was the highest Temple official. He presided over the Temple service. If there was no Temple, there was no service. Why then did Bar Kokhba appoint a High Priest?

"A primary function of the Jewish Messiah is to rebuild the Holy Temple as described in the Book of Ezekiel (Ezekiel 40-47). Since Bar Kokhba believed himself to be the Messiah, why didn't he at least begin rebuilding the Temple of the Jews during his two-and-a-half-year reign?

"These questions almost suggest their own obvious solution. Bar Kokhba did in fact rebuild the Temple during the years he ruled in Jerusalem. The Temple required a High Priest, a position that was filled by the appointment of Eleazer. The Temple facade that Bar Kokhba built was represented on the Bar Kokhba coins. Bar Kokhba was so convinced that his conquest of Jerusalem heralded the beginning of the Messianic era that he began a new calendar system of counting the years from the date of his conquest. The coins are stamped 'year one,' 'year two,' and 'year three.' Rabban Gamaliel, who lived during the Bar Kokhba revolution, offered his Pascal sacrifice in the Bar Kokhba Temple." Reznick, Pp.155-156

"...In Ezekiel's Third Temple [which is understood to be the Temple that Messiah builds] the Women's Courtyard was a much larger area, almost square.....It was 346 cubits north to south by 340 cubits east to west, or about 519 feet by 510 feet (Tzuras HaBayis, Ezekiel)....

"We have been assuming that a cubit is about 18 inches. That is only an approximation based on an educated guess. What if a cubit is 19 inches, or, more precisely, 19.07 inches? Then the dimensions of the Messianic Temple would be 550 feet by 540 feet. Those are exactly the same dimensions of the Dome of the Rock platform!" Reznick, P.157

"...[S]ubsequent to writing this, I have seen in the writings of the nineteenth-century Lithuanian talmudic commentary of Rabbi Samuel Shtrashun, known as R'shash, in his work on Pesachim 74a, the suggestion that Rabban Gamaliel offered his Pascal sacrifice on the altar of a Messianic Bar Kokhba Temple. He bases his assumption on the words of a noted Roman historian of the period, probably Dio Cassius." Reznick, P.159

There are some problems with the case Reznick presents. First, the Talmud often places certain rabbis, especially those with the same or similar names, in historical periods before or after they actually lived. This is noticeably true concerning Gamaliel I, Gamaliel II, and Simeon ben Gamaliel. So, if the incident actually happened, we cannot be sure which Gamaliel was involved.

Second, the Temple facade that appears on some of the coins, without great detail, could be, as Meshorer claims, that of the Second Temple. It could have represented an objective, rather than an accomplishment.

Third, following the return from Babylon, it took at least 4 years to build the Second Temple (without Herod's later additions). (Ez.3:8-12;6:7-13; Haggai 2:3) [Solomon's Temple took 7 years.] Those were years of peace, and Darius had decreed that the full cost be paid from the royal treasury.

Could the Bar Kokhba rebels have cleared the rubble, laid a foundation, and completely built a new temple, while fighting the Romans, during the two years that they might have held Jerusalem? It does not seem likely.

Fourth, the Dome of the Rock platform may well match the dimensions of Ezekiel's Temple, but that would not establish that it had been built by Bar Kokhba. In one of his "Homilies Against the Jews," John Chrysostom declares, "Your three attempts to restore your state have all been failures, under Hadrian, under Constantine ('as is known to your old men'), and, as even your young people know, twenty years since, under that wicked Emperor Julian. For you then tried even to rebuild the Temple, and so offer sacrifices on the altar. But fire prevented your work. You can still see the foundations lying bare." <u>Adversus Judaeos: A Bird's Eye View of Christian Apologiae until the Renaissance</u>, A. Lukyn Williams, Cambridge U. Press, London, 1935, P.134, John Crysostom, <u>Homilies Against the Jews</u>, c.347-407

The Emperor Julian, "the Apostate," had given the Jews permission to rebuild the Temple. Chrysostom's language—"you then tried **even** to rebuild the Temple"—would indicate that no similar effort had been made in the time of Constantine or Hadrian; or at least that Chrysostom did not know of such. "You can still see the foundations lying bare" indicates that the foundation was part of the work done in the time of Julian, some 20 years before Chrysostom's homily, which was about 250 years after the revolt.

Fifth, although Eleazar seems to have been appointed High Priest, this may again have represented an objective, rather than an accomplishment. It is worth noting that during the time of the return from Babylon, the High Priest had the altar rebuilt and offered sacrifices on it before the foundation of the Temple was laid. Ez.3:2-6 Eleazar could have functioned as High Priest, and Rabban Gamaliel could even have made his Passover sacrifice, without the Temple having been rebuilt.

30. Ta'anit 29a

31. "It may be added that a number of Midrashim speak of Hadrian as 'the destroyer of the Temple'. This is a peculiar statement, and the late date seems to disqualify them as trustworthy sources for the problem here discussed." n.95 Dt.R. eqev iii 13, Tanhuma bereshit vii; Ex. R. li 5; Tanhuma pequde iv; Tanhuma, ed. Buber, p. 128 in Isaac and Oppenheimer, P. 55

32. Mantel, P.278 Jer. Ber.5a "It happened once to a certain Jew, who was standing ploughing, that his cow lowed before him. A certain Arab was passing and heard its voice; he said, O Jew, O Jew! unyoke thine ox, and loose thy plough-share, for the temple has been laid waste. It lowed a second time, and he said, O Jew, O Jew! yoke thine oxen, and bind on thy plough-shares, for King Messiah is born."

4. SIMEON BEN KOSIBA

1. Abramsky, P.230
2. Yadin, P.137-8
3. Yadin, P.125-6
4. Yigael Yadin remarks, Pp.8-9, "It is also a testimony to Bar Kochba's strict religious piety."[4] That is a rather charitable conclusion. G. W. Bowersock puts it more strongly, but, it would seem, more accurately: "We now possess letters of Bar Kochba, if not in his own hand yet almost certainly in his own words. He sounds rather like a pious thug, keeping his sacred observances and threatening his men."[5] Bowersock, P.131
5. Mid. Lam., II.4, 157
6. Harkabi, P.13
7. This stands in marked contrast to the Biblical exhortation: "When you are about to go into battle, the priest shall come forward and address the army. He shall say: 'Hear, O Israel, today you are going into battle against your enemies. Do not be fainthearted or afraid; do not be terrified or give way to panic before them. For the LORD your God is the one who goes with you to fight for you against your enemies to give you victory.'" Dt.20:2-4
8. During the time that Hadrian surrounded Bethar, Bar Kokhba's headquarters and base, "R. Eleazar of Modim...continually wore sackcloth and fasted, and he used to pray daily, 'Lord of the Universe, sit not in judgment today!'" Mid. Lam. II.4, 157 A Samaritan, siding with the Romans, wanted to

put an end to R. Eleazar's prayers, which he saw as preventing Roman victory. So he schemed to falsely accuse him to Bar Kokhba of having plotted to surrender the city to Hadrian. The pious R. Eleazar denied any such involvement or intent. "Bar Koziba flew into a rage, kicked him with his foot and killed him." ibid., 158

National Unity

9. "In contrast to the situation during the Jewish War (66-70/71 C.E.), the nation was now united under the leadership of a single commander in chief. This is evident from documents indicating that even in the final stages of the revolt he still exercised unlimited authority over his men." Abramsky, P.231

10. "...[T]he leaders at Yavneh did much to intensify the unity of the nation. In this period many of the parties and sects disappeared which had typified the life of the people before the destruction of the Temple. At the same time, many groups, including the Jewish Christian sects, were expelled from the Jewish community. It is likely that there was a connection between this policy, which actively sought to unite the people, and the undivided resistance to Rome under the leadership of Bar Kokhba. This unity certainly contributed to the impact of the rebellion, as did the fact that there was no Jewish party at that time opposed to the revolt." Isaac and Oppenheimer, P.49

11. Mid. Lam.II.4, 156-157

12. Gaalyahu Cornfeld, ed., Daniel to Paul, MacMillan, NY, 1962, Pp.349-50

13. Moses Maimonides, Mishneh Torah, (Yad Hazakah), Ed. Philip Birnbaum, Hebrew, New York, 1985, P.327 [11] 3. [See Appendix B for Maimonides' concept of the Messiah.]

14. Abramsky, P.239

THE REVOLUTION
5. AKIBA BEN JOSEPH

1. Louis Ginzberg, "Akiba ben Joseph," in The Jewish Encyclopedia, Edited by Isidore Singer, Funk and Wagnalls, NY & London, 1906, Vol.1, P.304, citing Yer. Shek.iii,47b; R.H. i,56d

2. Gershom Bader, The Jewish Spiritual Heroes, Vol. I, translated by Solomon Katz, Pardes Publishing House, NY, P.282

3. Zebahim 13a

4. Hag.14b

5. Yeb.62b

6. Sotah 49a

7. Sotah 49b

8. The Jewish Encyclopedia, Vol. I, Pp.305-306, citing Jer. Shek. 5:1, 48c

9. Sanh.86a

10. Pesachim 13b n.2

11. The Jewish Encyclopedia, Vol. I, Pp.305-306, citing Jer. Shek. 5:1, 48c

12. Encyc. Jud., Vol.2, Pp.489-490, citing Rosenthal, Beit Talmud, 2, 1881,280

13. Louis Finkelstein, Akiba: Scholar, Saint and Martyr, Atheneum, NY, 1978, P.156

14. Louis Finkelstein, "Akiba," in Great Jewish Personalities in Ancient and

<u>Medieval Times</u>, Bnai Brith Great Books Series: Vol.1, edited by Simon Noveck, 1973, P.125

Akiba's Life

15. Pesahim 49b

16. "As it happened, while Akiba was still in his infancy, Agrippa's peaceful reign had come to an end, giving way to tumult and rebellion, denunciation and bitter strife. The ancient struggles between the Pharisees and the Sadducees, and among the various Pharisaic factions, had broken out anew, and with redoubled vigor." Finkelstein, "Akiba," P.130

17. ibid, P.126

18. "Akiba received a warm welcome from the poor Joshua ben Hananya; the latter sent him to Tarfon, Akiba's contemporary, who later became his closest friend." ibid, P.132

19. Ketuboth 62b-63a, "R. Akiba was a shepherd of Ben Kalba Sabua. The latter's daughter, seeing how modest and noble [the shepherd] was, said to him, 'Were I to be betrothed to you, would you go away to [study at] an academy?' 'Yes', he replied. She was then secretly betrothed to him and sent him away. When her father heard [what she had done] he drove her from his house and forbade her by a vow to have any benefit from his estate. [R. Akiba] departed, and spent twelve years at the academy.

"When he returned home he brought with him twelve thousand disciples. [While in his home town] he heard an old man saying to her, 'How long will you lead the life of a living widowhood?' 'If he would listen to me,' she replied. 'he would spend [in study] another twelve years'. Said [R. Akiba]: 'It is then with her consent that I am acting'. and he departed again and spent another twelve years at the academy.

"When he finally returned he brought with him twenty-four thousand disciples. His wife heard [of his arrival] and went out to meet him, when her neighbours said to her, 'Borrow some respectable clothes and put them on', but she replied: A righteous man regardeth the life of his beast. On approaching him she fell upon her face and kissed his feet. His attendants were about to thrust her aside, when [R. Akiba] cried to them, 'Leave her alone, mine and yours are hers'.

"Her father, on hearing that a great man had come to the town, said, 'I shall go to him; perchance he will invalidate my vow', When he came to him [R. Akiba] asked, 'Would you have made your vow if you had known that he was a great man?' '[Had he known]' the other replied. 'even one chapter or even one Single halachah [I would not have made the vow]'. He then said to him, 'I am the man'. The other fell upon his face and kissed his feet and also gave him half of his wealth."

20. B. Gittin 67a, Abot of R. Nathan 18, 34a

6. WHAT IS A RABBI?

1. Shab.14b, Note 13
2. Ez.7:5-6,11,12,21
3. 2 Kings 25:8; Dan.2:48; Jon.1:6
4. E.g. Ex.7:11 & 36:4; Dan.2:14, Esth.1:13

5. Job 32:9 Note also the Lord's rebuke to the generation which saw the destruction of the First Temple: "How can you say, 'We are wise [חכמים], for we have the law of the LORD,' when actually the lying pen of the scribes [סֹפְרִים] has handled it falsely? The wise will be put to shame; they will be dismayed and trapped. Since they have rejected the word of the LORD, what kind of wisdom [חכמה] do they have?" Jer. 8:8-9

6. S.A. Cohen, P.151

In the Talmud

7. Horayoth 13a Only in the apostate northern kingdom of Israel could it be said that, "all Israel is eligible for kingship". From God's choice of David on, all the rightful kings were from the tribe of Judah, from the house of David.

8. Ket. 111b

9. Sanh.99a quoting Is.64:4, which continues, "who acts on behalf of those who wait for him."

10. "R. Eliezer the son of R. Jose the Galilean began to speak in praise of hospitality, expounding the verse, *And the Lord blessed Obed-Edom and all his house....because of the Ark of God.* Have we not here an argument *a fortiori*? If such was the reward for attending to the ark which did not eat or drink, but before which he merely swept and laid the dust, how much more will it be for one who entertains a scholar in his house and gives him to eat and drink and allows him the use of his possessions!" Ber.63b

11. Pes.53b quoting Eccl. 7:12, which continues, "but the advantage of knowledge is this: that wisdom preserves the life of its possessor." The rabbinic interpretation is that those who give money to the wise, i.e. the Rabbis, have their lives preserved by the wisdom of the Rabbis.

12. Ber.47b
13. Ned. 62a
14. Ned. 62b
15. Shevu'oth 41a and note.
16. Git.36b
17. Naz. 66a
18. Hag.14a, n.31
19. Meg.28b
20. Ta'anith 29b
21. Ber.19a
22. Ber.19a
23. Men. 68b
24. Eruvin 63a
25. B.M. 88a
26. Ab. 3.9, cf.Men.99b & Gerhardson, Memory and Manuscript, P.168
27. Shab.119b
28. Avoth 5. 8

The Battle for Torah
7. TANAKH AND THE ORAL LAW
The First Talmudic Claim

1. Eruvin 54b

The Record of the Torah
2. Ex. 17:14
3. Exod. 24:4-8
4. Exod. 24:12
5. Lev. 26:46
6. Num. 36:13
7. Deut. 17:18-20
8. Lev. 10:11
9. Deut. 27:2-3,8
10. Deut. 27:26
11. Deut. 28:58-62
12. Deut. 28:69
13. Deut. 29:8
14. Deut. 29:19-20
15. Deut. 29:23-26
16. Deut. 30:8-10
17. Deut. 31:9-13
18. Deut. 31:19
19. Deut. 31:24-26

The Record from Moses to the Exile
20. Josh. 1:7-8
21. Josh. 8:31-2,34-35
22. Josh. 23:2,6
23. Josh. 24:25-26
24. 1Chr. 16:39-40
25. 1Kgs. 2:1-4
26. 2Kgs. 14:5-6
27. 2Chr. 23:18
28. 2Chr. 30:5,18
29. 2Chr.30:16
30. 2Chr. 31:3
31. 2Kgs. 22:13
32. 2Kgs. 22:16
33. 2Kgs. 23:2-3
34. 2Kgs. 23:21
35. 2Chr. 35:12
36. 2Kgs. 23:24-25

The Record in the Exile and in the Return
37. Dan.9:2, referring to Jer.25:11-12
38. Dan.9:3
39. Dan. 9:11,13
40. Ezra 7:10
41. Ezra 3:2,4
42. Ezra 6:14,18
43. Neh. 8:1-3,5-8
44. Neh. 8:13-15
45. Neh. 8:18

46. Neh. 9:3
47. Ezra 9:10-12
48. Neh. 10:29-30
49. Neh. 10:31-38
50. Neh. 13:1, citing Dt.23:3
Additional Testimony
51. Exod. 32:30
52. Exod. 32:32
53. 1Sam. 8:7,10:19
54. 1Sam. 10:25
55. Neh. 7:5
56. Neh. 10:1
57. Neh. 10:2-30
58. 1Kgs. 14:29
59. Jer. 25:13
60. Dan. 10:21
61. Mal. 3:16
62. Yaakov Elman, "R. Zadok HaKohen on the History of Halakha," Tradition: A Journal of Orthodox Jewish Thoughts, Vol.21, No.4, P.4

8. THE ORAL LAW AS INTERPRETATION
The Second Talmudic Claim
1. Menahoth 29b, P.190, P.190n.
2. cf.Sanh.37a Ehrhardt comments: "A second Moses, and greater than he, as predicted in Deut. xviii. 15, such is the verdict of this talmudic appreciation of Akiba. But a second Moses meant a new foundation of Judaism, for it had been Moses who had first established Israel as a nation."

"n1. This follows from the eighth row to which Moses is removed—after the period of one Aeon, seven 'days'." (cf. Harv. Theol. Rev., 1945, 177f, Ehrhardt P.110

The Talmud to the Contrary
3. Neusner, Early Rabbinic Judaism, P. 27
4. Ibid., P.26
5. Ibid., P.28
6. Ibid.
7. A.Z. 38a
8. Pesachim 10a
9. Pesachim 14a
10. Mayer I. Gruber, "The Mishnah as Oral Torah: A Reconsideration," JSJ, Vol. XV, 1984, P. 117
11. M. Gruber, P.119
12. M. Gruber, P.121
13. Shevi'ith 10:3 Soncino n.14
14. Shevi'ith 10:3
15. M. Gruber, P.121

9. TORAH SHE'B'AL PEH
1. Shab.31a
2. M. Gruber, P. 115 n.13
3. cf. Gen. 26:5
4. Gittin 60b
5. Ex.34:27-28
6. Baumgarten, Pp.7-29, P.19, n.5
7. Ibid., P.16
8. Deut. 17:8-12
9. Dt.12:5,11,14,18,26; 14:23,24,25; 15:20; 16:2,6,7,11,15,16; 18:6; 26:2; 31:11
המקם µ אשר יבחר יהוה אלהיך

10. cf. Ber. 5a which divides the verse even more: "'Tables of stone': these are the ten commandments; 'the law': this is the Pentateuch; 'the commandment': this is the Mishnah; 'which I have written': these are the Prophets and the Hagiographa; 'that thou mayest teach them': this is the Gemara."

Al Pe and *B'Yad Moshe*

11. Jer.36:4, df. vv. 17,27,32
12. Exod. 9:35
13. Lev. 10:11
14. Num. 17:5

History to the Contrary

15. All peoples and cultures (and probably every person as well) accumulate traditions. Traditions are an almost indispensable part of life.

Given that, it was inevitable that traditions would develop concerning the fulfillment of Torah. As Hayim Donin noted, "The Written Torah commands us to 'bind them as a sign upon your hands and as frontlets between your eyes.' This reference to *tefillin* leaves us in the dark as to how they were to be made up, what they were to consist of, how they were to be donned...The Written Torah prescribes capital punishment for various crimes. What legal rules and procedures had to be followed before such a verdict could be handed down? What were the limitations? The Written Torah does not say." Hayim Halevy Donin, To Be a Jew, Basic Books, 1991, P.26

In terms of *tefillin*, it could be argued that the lack of specificity indicated God's indifference to the particulars; and in terms of judicial procedure, that God had clearly laid out the principles for making judgments. While that may be so, the *tefillin* and the judicial inquiry still had to be made in some particular way. That would inevitable lead to the development of tradition or sets of different traditions. The issue that concerns us here is the claim that the source of the Pharisaic and rabbinic tradition is God, not man.

16. Baumgarten, P. 15
17. C. Apion, II., xv, §152, in A. Lukyn Williams, Talmudic Judaism and Christianity, S.P.C.K., London,1933, P.46
18. Josephus, Ant.13,16,2
19. Josephus, Ant.XIII,X,6
20. Baumgarten, p13
21. Mk.7,3.5 (Mt. 15,2); cf. Galatians 1,14 and Eusebius, Ecclesiastical History,

IV, 22,8, Baumgarten, P.14
    22. Baumgarten, P.12
    23. M. Gruber, Pp.113-114
    24. "'The most necessary business of our whole life,' writes Josephus, 'is to observe the laws which have been given us, and to keep those rules of piety that have been delivered down to us.'" Williams, Pp.43-44

The Development of the Doctrine of the Oral Law

25. J.M. Baumgarten, "The Unwritten Law in the Pre-Rabbinic Period," JSJ, Vol.III, Oct. 1972, P.23
    26. Neusner, Early Rabbinic Judaism, P. 85
    27. Ibid., P. 86 The Oral Torah became the distinctive of Israel. "...said R. Avin, [God said] 'Had I written for you the bulk of my Torah, you would be considered like a foreigner.' [For] what [is the difference] between us and the Gentiles? They bring forth their books, and we bring forth our books; they bring forth their national records, and we bring forth our national records.' [The only difference between Israel and the Gentile nations is that a portion of the Torah remains oral, and has a special claim upon the nation of Israel.]" The Talmud of the Land of Israel, Vol. 2, Peah, Trans. by Roger Brooks, U. of Chicago Press, Chicago, 1990, P.127
    28. Baumgarten, P.18
    29. Williams, P.41
    Edersheim, following Herxfeld and Peiser, says there are 55. Alfred Edersheim, The Life and Times of Jesus the Messiah, Vol.2, Longmans, Green, and Co., London, 1903, P.683
    30. QM 80b; Elman, P. 15
    31. "All that is inherent in Written Torah, was revealed to Moses in potential form, and to R. Aqiva *in actu*." Elman, P. 9
    32. Lev. R. 22,1; j.Peah II, 6,17a; j. Megillah IV, 1, 74a

10. CONFRONTING THE SCRIPTURES

1. Finkelstein, "Akiba," P.139
    2. Ginzberg, "Akiba," The Jewish Encyclopedia, P.307
    3. Alexander Guttman, Rabbinic Judaism in the Making, Wayne State U. Press, Detroit, 1970, P.229
    4. Finkelstein, Akiba, Pp.173-174
    5. David Daube, "Rabbinic Methods of Interpretation and Hellenistic Rhetoric," HUCA, XXII, 1949, P.23
    6. Finkelstein, Akiba, P.158; Sifra Zav perek 11.6 B. Menahot 89a; Niddah 72b; Zebahim 82a; Sifra Emor par 7.2,98a
    7. Sifra ad 13.49, ed. Weiss 68b; Birger Gerhardson, Memory and Manuscript, trans. E. J. Sharpe, Lund, Gleerup, 1961, P.172 n1
    8. Finkelstein, Akiba, P.89; B.Sanh. 51b
    9. Sifre Num §112, H.121, in Daube, P.23
    10. Ginzberg, "Akiba," P.306
    11. John Bowman, The Fourth Gospel and the Jews, Pickwick, Pittsburgh, 1975, P.6
    12. "M. Sotah IX, 15 informs us, 'When Rabbi Akiba died the glory of the

Torah ceased.' The corresponding Mishnah in the Palestinean Talmud, 'When Rabbi Akiba died the interpreters ceased' probably indicates what the 'glory of the Torah' here means: its elaborate interpretation as undertaken by Rabbi Akiba." Guttmann, P.230

13. Bowman, P.374, citing Aboth de Rabbi Nathan IV
14. Rosh HaSh. II.7
15. Lev.23:29-30
16. R. H. Charles, trans., The Book of Jubilees or the Little Genesis, 6,37 in J.C. Vanderkam, "2 Maccabees 6, 7A and Calendrical Change in Jerusalem," JSJ, Vol.XII, No.1, 7/81, P.53 n4
17. Rosh HaSh. 25a
18. Rosh HaSh., P.111, n.2
19. Men. 34b
20. Men.34b, P.215, n.4
21. "Rabbi Akiba" - "Rabi[Russian] A[Greek]ki[Japanese]ba[Hebrew]" - can be transformed into a sober warning against following Akiba: "Slaves! He comes without the spirit."
22. Yeb.68b
23. Men. 87b
24. Yeb.11b
25. Not in Heaven: the Nature and Function of Halakha, Eliezer Berkovits, Ktav Publishing Co., NY, 1983, P.5
26. Ibid., P.7; cf.Berakot 37a; Yeb.108a; Git.15a; Ket.48b; Kid.59b

Additional Impact on the Scriptures

27. The Jewish Encyclopedia, Vol. I, Pp.305-306, citing Jer. Shek. 5:1, 48c
28. Baumgarten, Pp. 21-22
29. There are two alternative views that need to be expressed. 1. Josephus indicates that the text had been fixed for some time. "...how firmly we have given credit to those books of our own nation is evident by what we do; for during so many ages as have already passed, no one has been so bold as either to add anything to them or take anything from them, or to make any change in them..." Against Apion I 8 2. Modern scholarship holds that the Masoretic text was not finally fixed until the 12th century. Cf., The Canon and Masorah of the Hebrew Bible, ed. Sid Z. Leiman, Ktav Publishing House, NY, 1974, especially the last chapter by Harry Orlinsky, "The Masoretic Text: A Critical Evaluation," Pp. 833-877

The truth is probably to be found in the combination of these three seemingly incompatible views - each being partly true, but not the whole story. As Orlinsky notes, "There never was, and there never can be, a single masoretic text of the Bible! It is utter futility and pursuit of a mirage to go seeking what never was." Orlinsky, P.850

30. Richard N. Longenecker, Biblical Exegesis in the Apostolic Period, Eerdmans, Grand Rapids, 1975, P.143
31. Orlinsky, P.852

"There are in the Mishnah sixteen variations...In the Talmud, 105 such variations occur..." Alfred Edersheim, The Life and Times of Jesus the Messiah, Vol.2, Longmans, Green, and Co., London, 1903, P.691

32. "J.T. Milik points out that the determination of the text at Jamnia was

arrived at in a somewhat mechanical manner by selecting only the majority reading in each case, that after this standardization of the text took place all diverging recensions were eliminated, and that the situation is illustrated by the variety of readings found at Qumran that are prior to Jamnia but the identity of the texts in the fragments from the Murabbaat caves (so far as the evidence goes) with the MT after Jamnia." J.T. Milik, <u>Ten Years of Discovery in the Wilderness of Judaea</u>, Pp.28f, cited in Longenecker, 143n

Milik's point concerning how the standardization of the text took place is an assumption. We know that there were a variety of different readings at the time, but we do not know what the majority of texts read. We do not have any way of knowing. We do not have all those texts, and therefore have no way of determining what a majority of them read. Even if we knew, what would the reason be for following the majority? Nor can we assume that the partisans who fixed the text acted impartially.

33. Men. 34b, P.215, n.4
34. Herbert Basser, "The Development of the Pharisaic Idea of Law as a Sacred Cosmos," <u>JSJ</u>, Vol.XVI, 6/85, no.1, P.110 n.17
35. Davies, <u>Paul</u>, P.5

"M. Schwabe by his epigraphical research also concluded, that not only the Jews in Alexandria or Antiochia, who were so completely hellenized that they did not understand Hebrew any more, but even those in Judea knew Greek well and used it frequently. His conclusions are mostly based on the collection of tomb-stone inscriptions that archeologists have found in different places in Judea. In Beth-Shearim, for instance, among 209 inscriptions found, 175 are in Greek and only 34 in Hebrew or Aramaic. A striking example is the fact that the highest legal and juridical institution in Judea had a Greek name, *Sanhedrin*." Wardy, Pp.640-641

36. Ginzberg, "Akiba," Pp.305-6
37. Orlinsky, P.854
38. <u>Encyc. Jud., Vol.2</u>, Pp.489-490
39. Neh.8:8
40. <u>Encyc. Jud.</u>, Vol.2, Pp.489-490

11. TALMUDIC REVISIONISM

1. George Orwell, <u>1984</u>, Harcourt, Brace & World, Inc., NY, 1949, P.35

The People in the Bible

2. Sanh. 38b, also A.Z. 5a
3. Sanh. 24a
4. A reference to Gen. 26:5
5. Yoma 28a
6. Basser, P.105
7. B.M. 59a
8. Basser, P107
9. Mak.24a Cf. 2 Kings 2:12.
10. Mak.24a n3, Cf. Aboth., VI,3.
11. B.M. 85b
12. Meg. 16b

13. Meg. 13b
14. Basser, P.114 [Sanh.97a]

The Teachings of the Bible

15. Sanh.32b
16. Shab. 119b [1Ch.16:22
17. Shab. 31b [Is.33:6]
18. Sanh. 24a
19. Sanh. 87a
20. Midrash Rabbah, Leviticus, trans. Judah Slotki, Soncino, London, 1939 [mid 7th c.] Pp.276-77 XXII.1
21. A.Z. 17b [2Ch.15:3] Later rabbinic writings increased the emphasis on the Oral Law at the expense of the written Law. "Israel did not accept the Torah until the Holy One, blessed be he, suspended the Mount (over their heads) like a roof, as Scripture states: 'They stood beneath (betahtit, at the bottom, interpreted as 'in the underside of') the mount.' Said R. Dimi b. Hama, 'The Holy One, blessed be He, said to Israel: if you accept the Torah, good; if not, your burial ground will be here.' And if you say, it was on account of (their reluctance to accept) the Written Torah (that) he suspended the mount on them....did they not all answer 'we will do and obey'? (This ready acceptance of Written Torah came) because there is no effort and pain (attendant on its study), and it is (relatively) small (in extent). No, rather, he threatened them on account of (their reluctance to accept) the Oral Torah, which contains details of the commandments, light and severe; it is strong as death and its zeal is strong as She'ol." Elman, 10 Tanhuma Parshat Noah 3, last part based on Song of Songs 8:6

The God of the Bible

22. Bowman, P.373, n. 241
23. Is.6:3

Replacement and Substitution

24. Hag.27a
25. Pesikta 60b
26. Rava in Men. 110a
27. Ta'anith 27b, P.145
28. Ber.26b
29. Dan.6:11 The psalmist prayed seven times a day. "Seven times a day I praise you for your righteous laws." Ps. 119:164
30. A.Z. Idelsohn, Jewish Liturgy and Its Development, Schocken Books, NY, 1967, P.xix
31. Num. 28:3 See vv.1-8 for the complete description.
32. Donin, To Be A Jew, P.160 Ber.26b says that parts of the two sacrifices were not burned until night, equating that with the evening time of prayer.
33. Shab.119b
34. Meg.29a
35. S.A. Cohen, Pp.169-170
36. Avot 6:6, Meg.15a, cited in Elman, P.21

12. UPROOTING THE SCRIPTURES
1. Kid. 26b, P.126, n.12
2. Dt.15:1-2,9
3. Git. 36a, cf. Shevi'ith X,3; Pe'ah III,6; Git.36b
4. Basser, Pp.111-112
5. "Authority, Rabbinical," The Jewish Encyclopedia, Vol.2, ed. Isidore Singer, Funk & Wagnalls Co., NY, 1909, P.337
6. Yeb.89b
7. Yeb.90a
8. Yeb.12a
9. Dt.24:1-4
10. Sot.47a
11. Jonathan Sacks, "Creativity and Innovation in Halakhah," in Rabbinic Authority and Personal Autonomy, ed. Moshe Sokol, Jason Aronson Inc., Northvale, NJ, 1992, P.135 Sacks is Chief Rabbi of the British Commonwealth
12. Tos. to Yev. 89b cited in Basser, P.111, n.23
13. Ibid., cf.Tos. to Babba Mezia 20a *shover*
14."Authority," P.337
15. Sanh.90a
16. Emphasis added, Ket.84a

ורב סבר ירושת הבעל דרבנן וחכמתן עשו חיזוק לדבריהן כשל תורה

17. To a limited degree there are parallels to this in Marbury v. Madison and the issue of judicial liberty v. original intent.
18. Baumgarten, P.22 n5, "on the authority of the sages to nullify biblical laws see Tchernowits, I, Pp. 118-23"
19. "Authority," P.337, (Yer. R. H. i. 57b; compare also Mak.22b)
20. Vanderkam, P.52 Vanderkam continues, "If a group developed new notions about what was the correct cultic calendar, or if they wished to retain a system which other priestly authorities had discarded, they were in effect challenging the establishment's cultic control. The consequent strife often resulted in schism by those who lacked the political power to implement their program. The religious calendar of ancient Judaism had, then, political as well as religious overtones.

"The Qumran texts furnish ample evidence that the sectarians not only followed a cultic calendar which differed from the one then in use in Jerusalem but also accorded their system a divine origin."

Also, P.55, "Consequently, it comes as no surprise when the Damascus Document prescribes that novices who desired to assume full membership in the group '...keep the Sabbath day according to its exact rules and the appointed days and the fast-day according to the finding of the members of the "new covenant" in the land of Damascus....'" (CD 6, 18-19)"

21. Eruv. 77a; Ket. 56a
22. Zeb.100b-101a
23. Sanh.88b, Mishnah X.5
24. Talmud of the Land of Israel, Pp.127-128 This is the portion that contains the saying, "...even that which a learned student someday in the future will recite before his master has the status of a law transmitted to Moses on Sinai." The explanatory comments in brackets are those of the translator.

26. "Authority," P.337
27. Yev. 40a

13. A FENCE AROUND THE TORAH
The Third Talmudic Claim
1. J. Israelstam, Aboth I,1 n.7 Cf. Pes. 2b, Er.100b, and Sanh.46a
2. Pesachim 2b Another example is found in Erub.100b: "For did not Rab once visit Afsatia where he forbade the use of a stripped tree?—Rab found an open field and put up a fence round it." Israel Slotki explains that "The people of that place were lax in their religious observance (morally exposed like an 'open field'), and Rab imposed upon them additional restrictions in order to keep them away thereby from further transgressions." Er.100b, P.695, n.8
3. Sanh.46a
4. Baba Metzia 33a
5. Baba Bathra 42a
6. Baba Bathra 52b
7. B.B. 53a
8. Avoth 3.13
9. Eruv.15b
10. cf. Shab.97a

11. Bilhah Wardy observed that, "After the destructive uprising of Bar-Cochbah and the edicts of Hadrian, Rabbi Akkibah, the spiritual leader of his generation, confirmed the laws intended to strengthen the remnants of the Jewish people during this time of its greatest crisis, and to fence them off (the Hebrew term is s^ejag latorah, סיג לתורה) from the charms of the pagan culture and the dangers of a complete absorption by this world." Wardy, P. 640

R. Akiba did more, however, than seek to fence the people off from pagan influences. He sought to fence them off from any Jewish influences that would hinder obedience to rabbinic authority.

12. Etan Levine, The Aramaic Version of the Bible, de Gruyter, NY, 1988, P.143

Adversaries
14. CONFLICT WITH THE PRIESTS, BACKGROUND
1. Jer. 6:13
2. Jer. 5:31 The priests were among those who beat and sought to kill Jeremiah. (Jer. 20, 26)
3. Ezek. 22:26
4. Lam. 4:13
5. 2 Bar. 10:18 in R. Kirschner, "Apocalyptic and Rabbinic Responses to the Destruction of 70," Harvard Theological Review, 78, 1985, Pp.35-36
6. Ta'anith 29a
7. Neh. 10:30
8. Mal. 1:6,10
9. "Thus, after Alexander the Great, the priesthood was almost the only institution in the various countries recognized by the indigenous populations as the champion of their national interests - as can be seen in Judea in the sixties of the second century B.C.E., when a minor priestly house started a national

upheaval. In fact, we can see that in the Near East during the Hellenistic period, the priesthood in many places dominated much of the daily life and the 'politics' of the indigenous populations who did not mingle with the Greek classes." Mendels, P.108

10. "In both books of Maccabees the priesthood of those days is heavily denigrated, and in fact it is directly blamed for the events leading to the Seleucid intervention." Mendels, P.123

11. Mendels, P.134

12. Mendels, P.279

13. "After 152 B.C.E. the high priests became also the secular leaders of the emerging Jewish state, and from 104/3 B.C.E. they also were the kings of this state. When Herod the Great was crowned king of Judea by the Romans in 40 B.C.E., the whole situation changed. Then, ...the Temple again became 'native' in the sense that all other native temples in the East were under Hellenistic monarchs. The Temple was divested of its dominant political role in the Jewish client state of Herod; the high priesthood became of secondary importance because the king was no longer the high priest." Mendels, P.113

14. "Rome acted in accordance with the imperial policy of not violating the religious autonomy of a native population provided it did not jeopardize Roman rule." Mendels, P.301

15. Mendels, P.317 "When Gratus arrived to become governor of Judea in 15 C.E., he was given the authority to appoint high priests, as were the Roman governors following him. Thus Rome had taken over the responsibility for the appointment of high priests, which was the last nail in the coffin of a significant Jewish nationalistic symbol, at least for the time being." Mendels, P.295, cf. Ant.18.33-35

16. Pes.57a The bracketed comments are in the Soncino footnotes.

17. 1 Sam. 2:12

18. 1 Sam. 2:22

19. Josephus, Ant., XX, 9, 2-4

20. Alfred Edersheim, <u>The Life and Times of Jesus the Messiah</u>, Anson D.F. Randolph and Company, New York, 1883, Vol. I, Pp.371-2, citing Siphre on Dt. sec.105, end, ed. Friedmann, P.95a; Jer. Peah i.6

21. Mendels, P.301, citing Josephus, Ant., 20.165-167 and War, 2.254-257 Immediately prior to this, Mendels comments, "The priestly houses became even more notorious than before for their involvement in public life during the fifties under Felix (52-60 C.E.). It started with the murder of Jonathan (not the high priest, but his brother), by the *lestes* (bandit) Doras, who had been bribed by Governor Felix. Josephus argues that 'as the murder remained unpunished, from that time forth the brigands with perfect impunity used to go to the city during the festivals and, with their weapons similarly concealed, mingle with the crowds.' He adds that these murders were committed not only in certain sections of Jerusalem, but even in some cases inside the Temple itself."

Josephus says that, "A sedition arose between the high priests, with regard to one another; for they got together bodies of the people, and frequently came, from reproaches, to throwing of stones at each other; but Ananias was too hard for the rest, by his riches, - which enabled him to gain those that were the most ready to receive. Costabarus, also, and Saulus, did themselves get together a multitude of wicked wretches...but still they used violence with the people, weaker than themselves. And from that time it principally came to pass, that our city was greatly disordered, and that all things grew worse and worse among us." Josephus, Ant., XX, 9, 2-4

The particular Annas, or Ananias, to whom Josephus refers is not the same as the one depicted in the gospels. He is of the same family, only a generation later. He may well be the same Ananias referred to in the confrontation recorded in Acts 23 between the Apostle Paul and the Sanhedrin.

During Paul's trial, Ananias ordered him to be struck. Paul realized that he would not be given a hearing. "Then Paul, knowing that some of them were Sadducees and the others Pharisees, called out in the Sanhedrin, 'My brothers, I am a Pharisee, the son of a Pharisee. I stand on trial because of my hope in the resurrection of the dead.'

"When he said this, a dispute broke out between the Pharisees and the Sadducees, and the assembly was divided. (The Sadducees say that there is no resurrection, and that there are neither angels nor spirits, but the Pharisees acknowledge them all.)

"There was a great uproar, and some of the teachers of the law who were Pharisees stood up and argued vigorously. The dispute became so violent that the commander was afraid Paul would be torn to pieces by them. He ordered the troops to go down and take him away from them by force and bring him into the barracks." Acts 23:6-10

22. Yoma 2a

23. Yoma 26b

24. Yoma19b The Qumran community, for their own reasons, also rejected the leadership of the Jerusalem priesthood. "The priestly establishment, headed by the Wicked Priest, and the people who accepted their spiritual leadership worshipped according to a differing calendrical system, and on this account the Essenes from Qumran considered them sinners, willing violators of divine instructions." Vanderkam, P.54

The Priests and the Empire

25. Richard A. Horsley, "High Priests and the Politics of Roman Palestine," JSJ, 17, 1986, P.28

26. Ibid., P.24

27. Ibid., P.29

28. "The Roman system also made provision for dealing with unjustified exploitation and brutality by its governors. In many cases of unsatisfactory behavior the governor was simply recalled. But it was also possible for the provincial authorities to bring accusations before the Senate or the Emperor. Of course, it was extremely difficult for the provincials to mount the necessary expedition of accusers to Rome, and the Senate was inclined to treat members of its own order somewhat leniently. Nevertheless, in the large majority of known cases the accused governors were convicted - or committed suicide before the trial." Horsley, P.28

This sheds light on the threat of the High Priests in John 19:12: "From then on, Pilate tried to set Jesus free, but the Jewish leaders kept shouting, "If you let this man go, you are no friend of Caesar. Anyone who claims to be a king opposes

Caesar."

15. THE RABBIS DISPLACE THE PRIESTS
1. Mal. 2:6,7
2. Ezek. 44:23-24
3. Ezek. 22:26
4. Num. 29:1
5. Num. 10:7-8
6. Rosh HaSh. IV.1. A Bet Din, literally "a house of judgment," is a religious court or "sanhedrin."
7. Rosh HaSh. 29b
8. Pes.66a, P.333 n.6
9. Baba Bathra 84b-85a
10. S.A. Cohen, Pp.34-135
11. Ibid., P.138 In comparing the Pharisees to the Sadducees at the beginning of the age, Josephus says that the doctrines and conduct of the Pharisees were such that "they are able greatly to persuade the body of the people; and whatever they do about divine worship, prayers, and sacrifices, they perform them according to their direction..." Ant. Bk XVIII, Ch.1, §3
12. Shaye J.D. Cohen says that, "The Yavnean rabbis were much interested in the laws of the temple and the cult (Neusner even suggests that mishnaic materials from the period of 70-132 'revolve around the altar') and this is not surprising. They expected the temple to be rebuilt shortly (in 'seventy years') and part of their sectarian legacy was interest in this legislation." S.J.D. Cohen, P.45
13. Zera'im Introduction, Pp. xii,xiv
14. Josephus, Wars, Bk II, Ch.17, §2,3,4
15. Finkelstein, Akiba, P.217

Akiba's Role
16. Rosh HaSh. IV,1
17. B.B.28a
18. Jacob Neusner, "The Use of the Mishnah for the History of Judaism Prior to the Time of the Mishnah," JSJ, Vol. XI, Dec. 1980, No.2, Pp.178-179
19. Ginzberg, "Akiba," P.307
20. Cf. Leviticus 19:19: "You are to keep My statutes. You shall not breed together two kinds of your cattle; you shall not sow your field with two kinds of seed, nor wear a garment upon you of two kinds of material mixed together." Similarly, later, in Deuteronomy 22:9-11: "You shall not sow your vineyard with two kinds of seed, lest all the produce of the seed which you have sown, and the increase of the vineyard become defiled. You shall not plow with an ox and a donkey together. You shall not wear a material mixed of wool and linen together."
21. Haggai 2:11-13
22. Finkelstein, Akiba, P.287
23. Ibid, P.291 [Tos. Bekorot 3.15 p.538]
24. Akiba followed the school of Hillel when he agreed with it, or rather when it agreed with him. When he differed, he simply followed his own views, without any qualms or hesitation.

25. Bowman, P.109
26. S.A. Cohen, P.167

16. SILENCING THE TRADITIONAL RABBIS
1. Ehrhardt, Pp.102-103
2. Finkelstein, ASSM, P.115
3. Ibid., P.113 from Sifra, Kedoshim, perek 4.9, Arakin 16b
4. Ibid, P.118 Finkelstein attributed this and other conflicts to Akiba's determination to champion the cause of the "plebeians" against that of the "patricians." He sees this as a consistent theme in Akiba's attacks. Finkelstein focuses on the economic aspect of the struggle between the "plebeians" and the "patricians." There is a suggestion of this in Ber.28a, but the entire struggle can be understood in terms of the contemporary controversy over the relative position of the priests and the rabbis. The priests had always controlled the Sanhedrin or rabbinic academy.

Anthony Saldarini sums up the current scholarly opinion of Finkelstein's analysis: "L. Finkelstein wrote a more elaborate and ambitious biography of Akiba, in which he placed Akiba within his overall interpretation of the development of rabbinic traditions and society. Finkelstein must still give hypothetical order and meaning to many disconnected incidents and sayings of Akiba. Moreover, his controlling thesis that conflict between rural and urban groups was the matrix for the development of rabbinic society and law has been often refuted and generally rejected." Saldarini, P.451

5. Finkelstein, Akiba, P.159, from B.Baba Batra 56b; Tos. Ma'aser Sheni 1.13, P.87
6. Ibid., P.153 citing Tosefta Yom Tov 2.12 p.204
7. Ehrhardt, P.103
8. R.H. 25a
9. Sol Roth, Halakhah and Politics: The Jewish Idea of the State, Ktav Publishing House, NY, 1988, P.140
10. Ber.27b
11. Ber. 28a

The Conflict with Eliezer Ben Hyrcanus
12. Ab.2.8, cf.Betzah 5a-b
13. e.g. Ber.32a, B.M.59b
14. A.Z. 16b-17a
15. Eruvin 13b
16. Ber.11a
17. Yeb. 16a
18. Ber.36b "When R. Akiba conflicts with R. Eliezer, we follow him, and the opinion of Beth Shammai when it conflicts with that of Beth Hillel is no Mishnah."
19. Pes.66a
20. Finkelstein, Akiba, P.94
21. Bowman, P.19 cf. Suk.28a where R.Eliezer b. Hyrcanus says, "nor have I ever in my life said a thing which I did not hear from my teachers.'"

It is not quite accurate to say that "Rabbi Eliezer was the greatest exponent of traditional oral law." There was no traditional oral law in the time of Rabbi Eliezer. The oral law was a later innovation. Rabbi Eliezer was the greatest exponent of traditional Pharisaic Judaism.

22. Neusner, Early Rabbinic Judaism, P.63

The Creation of Tradition

23. Finkelstein, Akiba, P.166
24. Finkelstein, "Akiba," P.138
25. Saul Liberman, "The Publication of the Mishnah," Hellenism in Jewish Palestine. Studies in the Literary Transmission, Beliefs, and Manners of Palestine in the I Century B.C.E. - IV Century C.E., NY, 1950, cited in Neusner, Early Rabbinic Judaism, P.86
26. Baumgarten, P.7 cf. Git.60b, Tem. 14b
27. Ibid., P.7n
28 Erubin 21b in Baumgarten, P.23
29. Finkelstein, Akiba, P.155
30. Guttmann, P.229 e.g. Sanh.27b: "This is R. Akiba's Mishnah, but the first Mishnah..."
31. Sanh. 27b
32. A.Z. 55b
33. Rosh HaShanah 17b
34. Shab. 64b
35. Finkelstein, Akiba, P.187-188
36. Guttman, P.228
37. Liberman, cited in Neusner, Early Rabbinic Judaism, Pp.86-87
38. Sanh. 86a, Pp.566-567
39. Neusner, Early Rabbinic Judaism, P.x
40. Ibid., P.10
41. J Pes. vi.I 33a, cf. bPes.66a in Williams, P.46 "J. Neusner concludes that the traditions about Hillel were shaped after 70 and sometimes after 140, when there 'was interest in recovering usable spiritual heroes from within Pharisaism itself, in place of Bar Kokba and other messianic types.'" "The Figure of Hillel: A Counterpart to the Problem of the Historical Jesus," in Judaism in the Beginning of Christianity, Philadelphia, 1984, Pp.63-88, cited in James H. Charlesworth, Jesus Within Judaism, Doubleday, NY, 1988, P.29 n.9

"Where in my detailed survey of the whole of Mishnah I did find a reason to doubt the validity of attributions, it consistently concerned what I had in the names of the Houses. The reason is that it is not uncommon to find that the House of Shammai and the House of Hillel take up positions on points profoundly rooted in the period after Bar Kokhba, that is, in the names of authorities a century after the Houses.

"...in other instances, it can be shown that ideas in the mouths of the Houses express points at issue in disputes among authorities a hundred years later." Neusner, "Use," P.183

42. Pesachim 13b n.2
43. Shevi'ith 8.9
44. Shebi'ith 8.10
45. Shevi'ith 8.10, n.49

17. IT IS NOT IN HEAVEN
1. Baba Mezia 59b, Pp.352-353
2. Dt. 13:2-4
3. Exod. 4:8-9
4. Num. 17:20-25
5. Lev.14:33-34,37-40

The Bath Kol
6. Yoma 9b; Sot.48b; Sanh.11a
7. Mak. 23b
8. Pesachim 93a
9. Megillah 3a The passage referred to in the Writings which foretells the date of the Messiah is Dan.9:24-25.
10. Eruv. 13b
11. Eruv. 7a
12. Ta'anith 29b
13. Ta'anith 25b
14. Aboth 6, Baraita 2.
15. Ber. 61b
16. Dt. 30:11-14
17. Sanh. 2a
18. Sacks, P.127
19. Derashot ha-Ran, ed. L. Feldman, 7:112 in Sacks, P.128
20. Yeb.40a
21. Num.16:2
22. Rashi, BeMid.16:1, Pp.162-163
23. The Rabbis presented the story differently. "Over the years the Korah story assumed great importance. Rabbis of mishnaic and talmudic times viewed themselves as direct spiritual descendants of Moses, and they interpreted the punishment of Korah as a warning to their own contemporaries who challenged the divine sanctity of rabbinic teaching. However, since a repetition of biblical miracles could not be counted on, the Rabbis threatened their challengers with eternal damnation...It is in this light that we must see the assertion of Rabbi Akiba that Korah not only was punished in the desert but excluded from divine grace for all time to come." The Torah, A Modern Commentary, UAHC, NY, 1981, P.1132

In Tanakh, that is the fate of those who do not obey the voice of the Lord. "But Samuel replied: Does the LORD delight in burnt offerings and sacrifices as much as in obeying the voice of the LORD? To obey is better than sacrifice, and to heed is better than the fat of rams. For rebellion is like the sin of divination, and arrogance like the evil of idolatry. Because you have rejected the word of the LORD, he has rejected you as king." 1Sam. 15:22-23

24. "Behold, like the clay in the potter's hand, so are you in My hand, O house of Israel." Jer.18:6b
25. Ps. 59:8-9
26. Ps. 37:12-13
27. Ps. 2:1-6
28. Prov. 1:20-26

29. Ab.2.8
30. Kid. 57a, P.284
31. Sacks, P.129. "What they decide is what God has commanded" is exactly the same claim that the Emperor Constantine made for the bishops in council, when he set up a similar system. Rabbinic Judaism and Constantinian Christianity share these three major principles: 1. The will of God is established by the majority of Sages/bishops in Sanhedrin/council. 2. A profession of upholding the Scriptures, though the authorized "interpretation" may be unrelated to the text. 3. State sword support of the synagogue/church.

18. THE RABBIS REPLACE THE PROPHETS

1. Amos 7:14-15
2. "It is clear that the author of '1 Enoch' wanted his book to be read in the category of the prophetic writings." Ithamar Gruenwald, "Jewish Apocalyptic Literature," in <u>ANRW</u>, P.111
3. "After the destruction of the Temple, as well as before it, a great number of prophecies can be found. For instance in the Sibylline Oracle 1.385-400 it is said that 'when the Temple of Solomon falls in the illustrious land cast down by men of barbarian speech with bronze breastplates, the Hebrews will be driven from their land,' and in Sibylline Oracle 3.213-217, 'Evil will come upon the pious men who live around the great Temple of Solomon, and who are the offsping of righteous men,' and later, in 265-290, 'and you will surely flee, leaving the very beautiful Temple, since it is your fate to leave the holy plain' (referring to the destruction of the First Temple, which was demolished in 586 B.C.E.). Then 'there will be again a terrible judgment...because you have utterly destroyed the great house of the immortal' (326-328), and in 657-668: 'The Temple of the great God (will be) laden with very beautiful wealth...gold, silver, and purple ornament...but again the kings of the people will launch an attack together against this land, bringing doom upon themselves, for they will want to destroy the Temple of the great God and most excellent men when they enter the Land' (also 688; and 4.115-129)" Mendels, P.319
4. "But what is still more terrible, there was one Jesus, the son of Ananus, a plebeian, and an husbandman, who, four years before the war began, and at a time when the city was in very great peace and prosperity, came to that feast whereon it is our custom for every one to make tabernacles to God in the temple, and began on a sudden to cry aloud, 'A voice from the east, a voice from the west, a voice from the four winds, a voice against Jerusalem and the holy house, a voice against the bridegrooms and the brides, and a voice against this whole people!'

"This was his cry, as he went about by day and by night, in all the lanes of the city. However, certain of the most eminent among the populace had great indignation at this dire cry of his, and took up the man, and gave him a great number of severe stripes; yet did not he either say anything for himself, or anything peculiar to those that chastised him, but still he went on with the same words which he cried before.

"Hereupon our rulers supposing, as the case proved to be, that this was a sort of divine fury in the man, brought him to the Roman procurator — where he was whipped till his bones were laid bare; yet did he not make any supplication for himself, nor shed any tears, but turning his voice to the most lamentable tone possible, at every stroke of the whip his answer was, 'Woe, woe to Jerusalem!'"Josephus, Wars, Book 6, Ch.5 §3

5. Josephus, Wars, Book 6, Ch.5 §2

6. Without the Holy Spirit, there would be no prophecy, for it is the Holy Spirit that moved the prophets of God. A prophet who spoke without the Spirit of the Lord was a false prophet. This can be seen most clearly in an incident that occurred when Jehoshaphat, king of Judah, joined Ahab, king of Israel, in warring against the king of Aram.

Ahab had about 400 false prophets who all prophesied a great victory, especially Zedekiah the son of Kenaanah. "But Jehoshaphat asked, 'Is there not a prophet of the LORD here whom we can inquire of?'" 1Kgs. 22:7

Micaiah was brought and he prophesied disaster. He told Ahab, "'So now the LORD has put a lying spirit in the mouths of all these prophets of yours. The LORD has decreed disaster for you.'

"Then Zedekiah son of Kenaanah went up and slapped Micaiah in the face. 'Which way did the spirit from the LORD go when he went from me to speak to you?' he asked." 1Kgs. 22:23-24

Inasmuch as the prophecy of Micaiah was fulfilled, whereas that of Zedekiah was not, we can clearly judge which one of them spoke by the spirit of the Lord.

On the Holy Spirit, the Rabbis say, "Study leads to precision, precision leads to zeal, zeal leads to cleanliness, cleanliness leads to restraint, restraint leads to purity, purity leads to holiness, holiness leads to meekness, meekness leads to fear of sin, fear of sin leads to saintliness, saintliness leads to [the possession of] the holy spirit, the holy spirit leads to life eternal, and saintliness is greater than any of these." A.Z. 20b

They made similar statements about the Shechinah. For example: "When two scholars pay heed to each other in halachah, the Holy One, blessed be He, listens to their voice, as it it said, 'Thou that dwellest in the gardens, The companions hearken to thy voice: Cause me to hear it.' But if they do not do thus, they cause the Shechinah to depart from Israel, as it is said, 'Flee, my beloved, and be thou like', etc." Shab.63a

Prophecy in the Talmud

7. Ber. 55b

8. Tradition itself also stood in the place of prophecy. "R. Eliezer, furthermore, had a disciple who once gave a legal decision in his presence. 'I wonder', remarked R. Eliezer to his wife, Imma Shalom, 'whether this man will live through the year'; and he actually did not live through the year. 'Are you', she asked him,'a prophet?' 'I', he replied: 'am neither a prophet nor the son of a prophet, but I have this tradition: Whosoever gives a legal decision in the presence of his Master incurs the penalty of death'." Eruvin 63a

In this account, R. Eliezer applies the words of Amos — 'I am neither a prophet nor the son of a prophet' — to himself. The authority of the Sages was maintained by a prophetic rabbinic tradition.

9. Sanh.11a

10. Sanh.11a n.7.

11. "In the footsteps of the Messiah insolence will increase and honour dwindle; the vine will yield its fruit but wine will be dear; the government will turn to heresy [*minuth*] and there will be none [to offer them] reproof; the meeting-place [of scholars] will be used for immorality; Galilee will be destroyed, Gablan desolated, and the dwellers on the frontier will go about [begging] from place to place without anyone to take pity on them; the wisdom of the learned will degenerate, fearers of sin will be despised, and the truth will be lacking; youths will put old men to shame, the old will stand up in the presence of the young, a son will revile his father, a daughter will rise against her mother, a daughter-in-law against her mother-in-law, and a man's enemies will be the members of his household; the face of the generation will be like the face of a dog, a son will not feel ashamed before his father. So upon whom is it for us to rely? Upon our Father who is in heaven." Sot.49b

12. "[In Numbers Rabba, we are told,] 'The Holy One, blessed be He, said: In this world individuals were given prophetic power, but in the world to come all Israel will be made prophets, as it is said, (Joel 2.28): And it shall come to pass afterward, that I will pour out my spirit upon all flesh; and your sons and your daughters shall prophesy, your young men shall see visions; and also upon the servants and the handmaids in those days will I pour my spirit. Thus did R. Tanhuma son of R. Abba expound.'

"We cannot doubt that the Rabbinic Judaism of the first century would have regarded the Messianic Age or the Age to Come as the Era of the Spirit." Davies, Paul, P.216

The Rabbinic Interpretation of Dreams

13. Ber.55b
14. Gen. 40:8
15. Gen. 41:15-16
16. Ber.56a

17. "Subsequently Raba went to him by himself and said to him: I dreamt that the outer door fell. He said to him: Your wife will die. He said to him: I dreamt that my front and back teeth fell out. He said to him: Your sons and your daughters will die. He said I saw two pigeons flying. He replied: You will divorce two wives. He said to him: I saw two turnip-tops. He replied: You will receive two blows with a cudgel. On that day Raba went and sat all day in the Beth ha-Midrash. He found two blind men quarrelling with one another. Raba went to separate them and they gave him two blows. They wanted to give him another blow but he said, Enough! I saw in my dream only two.

"Finally Raba went and gave him [Bar Hedya] a fee. He said to him: I saw a wall fall down. He replied: You will acquire wealth without end. Etc....

"[Sometime after this,] Bar Hedya was once travelling with Raba in a boat. He said to himself: Why should I accompany a man to whom a miracle will happen? As he was disembarking, he let fall a book. Raba found it, and saw written in it: All dreams follow the mouth. He exclaimed: Wretch! It all depended on you and you gave me all this pain! I forgive you everything except (what you said about) the daughter of R. Hisda [Raba's wife]. May it be God's will that this fellow be delivered up to the Government, and that they have no mercy on him! Bar Hedya said to himself: What am I to do? We have been taught that

a curse uttered by a sage, even when undeserved, comes to pass; how much more this of Raba, which was deserved! He said: I will rise up and go into exile. For a Master has said: Exile makes atonement for iniquity. He rose and fled to the Romans." Ber.56a
18. Dan. 2:27,28,30
19. Num. 24:13 See also Num.22:18,38
Authoritative Citation vs. "the Word of the Lord"
20. Ketuboth 57a
21. Ber. 55b
22. Meg.15a
23. Looking at the world as it then was, or as it now is, the question arises, 'What kind of deliverance has been brought by this practice?' To restrict the role of the prophet, the Talmud says, "a prophet may henceforth (i.e. after Moses) make no innovations!" Shab. 104a To justify rabbinic innovation on the other hand, the Talmud says that, "*And Jehoshaphat stood in the congregation of Judah and Jerusalem, in the house of the Lord, before the new court.* What does 'the new court' mean? That they innovated [*khadshu*] a law there and ruled: A tebul yom must not enter the Levitical Camp." Pesachim 92a

Prophets who were not accepted sages could no longer innovate or bring a new revelation from God, but there was no limit to the innovations or revelations of the Rabbis. As R. Zadok HaKohen pointed out, "Oral Torah is what the sages of Israel and Keneset Yisra'el innovated by their own perception of heart and mind of the will of God, and that is the understanding that God apportioned to them according to the limits of their capacity." [QM 80b] Elman, P.15

Or as Maimonides said, "In the same manner they [the Rabbis] have the power temporarily to dispense with some religious act prescribed in the Law, or to allow that which is forbidden, if exceptional circumstances and events require it....By this method the Law will remain perpetually the same and will yet admit at all times and under all circumstances such temporary modifications as are indispensable." Moses Maimonides, Guide for the Perplexed, 3:41, in Sacks, P.124

24. Megillah 3a
25. Sanh.97b That it is the prophecy of Daniel that is specifically put off limits also appears from Daniel's use of the phrase "the time of the end" in 8:17,19; 11:35,40; and 12:4,9,12,13; and the simple phrase "the end" in 9:26,27.

Enforcement
19. THE SANHEDRIN
1. "A king is not to be appointed except by the decision of the Great Council of Seventy-one. The minor councils through the tribes and towns are not to be established except by the Council of Seventy-one. Judgment is not to be passed on a tribe that has been entirely seduced, nor upon a flase prophet, nor upon a high priest in capital cases, except by the Great Council...In like manner an elder is not declared rebellious, nor a city dealt with as seduced, nor the bitter waters administered to the suspected adulteress, except by the Great Council. Neither is an addition made to the city nor to the courts. Neither are armies led forth to the wars of permission; nor the elders led forth to measure in the case of a slain person except by command of the Great Council, for it is said, 'Every

great matter they shall bring to thee.'" Hilchoth Sanhedrin, c.v.1 in Alexander McCaul, <u>The Old Paths</u>, London Society's House, London, 1846 The last quotation, from Ex.18:22, puts the Sanhedrin in the seat of Moses.

2. They often had influence beyond their numbers, depending upon the issue. Josephus indicates that during the time of John Hyrcanus, "These have so great a power over the multitude, that when they say anything against the king or against the high priest, they are presently believed." Josephus, Ant., Book 13, Ch.10, §5

3. Aaron Kirschenbaum, "Subjectivity in Rabbinic Decision-Making," in Sokol, P.70-71

The Nature of the Sanhedrin

4. Sanh.17a ["'R. Tam queried, What is the purpose of such meaningless mental gymnastics?' Ramo, in responsum, explains...that this statement does not refer to the meaningless capacity for intellectual gamesmanship, nor does it seek only to insure the appointment of judges with an impressive grasp of a great deal of knowledge. In fact, it establishes that a measure of additional sophistication regarding the inner workings of the halakhic process, including the ability to assess the implications of nonnormative possibilities and to utilize halakhic debate to shed light on the nuances of a topic which might have some normative impact, is a necessary precondition to judicial appointment where the stakes are so high." Kirschenbaum, Pp.105-106 [Tosafot, Sanh.17a; R. Moses Isserles, <u>Responsa of Ramo</u>, Jerusalem, 1977, no.107]

5. Deut. 18:10-12; cf Git.69a for rabbinic use of magical words, and Shab.61a-61b for rabbinic use of magical amulets. מִכשְׁפִּ בעלי is the wording for "a master of sorcery" in Sanh.17a.

6. B.B. 134a The Apostle Paul's statement in 1Co.13:1. "If I speak in the tongues of men and of angels, but have not love, I am only a resounding gong or a clanging cymbal."

7. Sanh.17b

8. According to the need of the moment, "The Rabbis do not hesitate to pronounce upon and on occasions alter the relation between man and God in the operation of the legal system." Bernard S. Jackson, "The Concept of Religious Law in Judaism," P.47

9. "Authority," P.338 In Tanakh, placing someone or something under the ban means to devote that thing or person wholly to the Lord. Throughout the book of Joshua, the phrase is applied to the enemies of Israel who were to be utterly destroyed — man, woman, and child.

10. Roth, P.141

11. Maimonides tells us that, "The Supreme Court in Jerusalem represents the essence of the Oral Torah. Its members are the pillars of direction; law and order emanate from them to all of Israel. Concerning them the Torah assures us, as it is written: 'You shall act in accordance with the directions they give you' (Deuteronomy 17:11). This is a positive command. Anyone who believes in Moses, our teacher, and in his Torah, must relate religious practices to them and lean upon them." Maimonides, P.314 [Rebels 1] 1.

Saved at the Cost of their Lives

12. "And it has also been taught: Forty years before the destruction of the

Temple, the Sanhedrin were exiled and took up residence in Hanuth. Whereon R. Isaac b. Abudimi said: This is to teach that they did not try cases of *Kenas*. 'Cases of *Kenas*!' Can you really think so! Say rather, They did not try capital charges." Sanh. 41a The gospels also mention that the Sanhedrin was not empowered to try capital cases. John 19:6-7.

The Talmudic claim of authority extends to all Jews, no matter where they live. "A Sanhedrin has jurisdiction within the land and outside it." Mak. 7a

13. Mak. 7a
14. Finkelstein, Akiba, P.89; B.Sanh. 51b
15. Sanh. 81b
16. Bernard S. Jackson, "The Concept of Religious Law in Judaism," in ANRW, P.46
17. Jackson, P.45, referring to Mak.3:15
18. Moed Katan 16a
19. "No man should have any dealings with Minim, nor is it allowed to be healed by them even [in risking] an hour's life. It once happened to Ben Dama the son of R. Ishmael's sister that he was bitten by a serpent and Jacob, a native of Kefar Sekaniah, came to heal him but R. Ishmael did not let him; whereupon Ben Dama said, 'My brother R. Ishmael, let him, so that I may be healed by him: I will even cite a verse from the Torah that he is to be permitted'; but he did not manage to complete his saying, when his soul departed and he died. Whereupon R. Ishmael exclaimed, 'Happy art thou Ben Dama for thou wert pure in body and thy soul likewise left thee in purity; nor hast thou transgressed the words of thy colleagues, who said, *He who breaketh through a fence, a serpent shall bite him*'? — It is different with the teaching of Minim, for it draws, and one [having dealings with them] may be drawn after them." A.Z.27b
20. Sanh.73a
21. "Come and hear: R. Eleazar b. Jacob stated, 'I heard that even without any Pentateuchal [authority for their rulings]. Beth din may administer flogging and [death] penalties; not, however, for the purpose of transgressing the words of the Torah but in order to make a fence for the Torah. And it once happened that a man rode on horseback on the Sabbath in the days of the Greeks, and he was brought before Beth din and was stoned; not because he deserved this penalty, but because the exigencies of the hour demanded it." Yeb.90b, cf. Sanh.46a

20. THE REBELLIOUS ELDER

1. Deut. 17:12-13
2. S.J.D. Cohen, P.50 n.60
3. Sanh.87a
4. M. Gruber, P.117
5. Sanh. 87a n.10
6. Sanh. 86b
7. Sanh.89a
8. Michael Rosensweig, "Eilu ve-Eilu Divrei Elohim Hayyim: Halakhic Pluralism and Theories of Controversy," in Sokol, P.112
9. Shaye J.D. Cohen maintains that, "Those rabbis who could not play by the new rules were too great a danger to be punished with just a curse. They

were expelled....

"Their interest was the future, not the past. There is little evidence for 'witch-hunting' in general and anti-Christian activity in particular. The sages were not a party triumphant which closed the ranks, defined orthodoxy, and expelled the unwanted. Yavneh was a grand coalition of different groups and parties, held together by the belief that sectarian self-identification was a thing of the past and that individuals may disagree with each other in matters of law while remaining friends. Those who refused to join the coalition and insisted on sectarian self-definition were branded minim and cursed. Those rabbis who could not learn the rules of pluralism and mutual tolerance were banned." S.J.D. Cohen, P.50

There are insurmountable problems to his claim. 1. Who was in this "grand coalition of different groups and parties"? Only the Rabbis. And among them, only the heirs of Beit Hillel. 2. The basis for any unity was submission to their platform. I.e., "Now that we have control, unite under us." 3. The ground for unity was accepting the sages as the ultimate authority—above the priests, above the prophets, above the scriptures, and above God. 4. Everyone who would not submit to their authority was cursed and banned. That was the one rule of "pluralism and mutual tolerance". 5. The sages did define orthodoxy, and did expel the unwanted.

The *Mesith* and Others
   10. Deut. 13:7-12
   11. Sanh.33b
   12. Sanh. 29a
   13. Lk.23:2
   14. Lk.23:14
   15. Shab.75a
   16. Mt.2:1-2

   15. On one occasion, R. Shila called the Roman rulers "asses". Another man overheard the remark. "He noticed that the man was about to inform them that he had called them asses. He said: This man is a persecutor, and the Torah has said: If a man comes to kill you, rise early and kill him first. So he struck him with the staff and killed him." Ber. 58a
   17. Mt.2:2
   18. Ta'anith 7b
   19. Pes.113b

21. AM HA'ARETZ
   1. Haggai 2:4
   2. S.A. Cohen, P.148
   3. Sot. 22a
   4. A thousand years later, Maimonides was repulsed by the practices that had developed. "He sharply criticized the way they [the geonim]: 'fixed for themselves monetary demands from individuals and communities and caused people to think, in utter foolishness, that it is obligatory and proper that they should help sages and scholars and people studying Torah.' " "Maimonidean Controversy," Encyclopedia Judaica, Vol.11, P.746
   5. S.A. Cohen, P.151

6. Pes. 49b
7. "Authority," P.337
8. Pes. 49b
9. Ibid.
10. Ket. ix. 3 Maimonides shows the authoritarian nature of this power: "And in like manner the wise man himself may, on account of his honour, excommunicate an unlearned man who has treated him with contumely, and there is no need of witnesses nor admonition. And the excommunicate person is not to be absolved until he appease the wise man. But if the wise man die, three persons come and absolve him. If, however, the wise man wish to pardon, and not excommunicate him, the power is in his own hand." Maimonides, Hilchoth Talumud Torah, c. vi. 12, cited in McCaul, The Old Paths, P.330

11. Peter Schafer review of Martin Goodman, State and Society in Roman Galilee, A.D. 132-212, JJS, Vol.XXXV, No.1, Pp.120-121

12. Meyers, P.693 "One thing, however, surprises us in his treatment of the people of Galilee, and that is his presentation of them as a people deeply devoted to the Law in theory and practice, quite contrary to most popular conceptions of the Galilean that we find in the rabbis or the New Testament." Ibid., P.701

In John 7:52, the chief priests and Pharisees rebuke Nicodemus for speaking up for Jesus: "They replied, 'Are you from Galilee, too? Look into it, and you will find that a prophet does not come out of Galilee.'" In Matt. 4:25, we are told, "Large crowds from Galilee, the Decapolis, Jerusalem, Judea and the region across the Jordan followed him."

13. Etan Levine, The Aramaic Version of the Bible, de Gruyter, NY, 1988, P.148

Revolutionary elites often have mixed feelings toward the common people. In their struggle against the entrenched powers, revolutionaries present themselves as champion of the people. When they attain power and encounter the people's lack of revolutionary zeal, the praise often turns to contempt.

14. Mk.12:37
15. Matt. 21:23-26,45-46
16. John 7:45-49
17. John 12:19,42
18. John 11:47-50

22. THE FIRST CENTURY CONCEPT OF MESSIAH

1. Mendels, P.225
2. James H. Charlesworth, "The Concept of the Messiah in the Pseudepigrapha," in ANRW, Pp.194-5

Government

3. Collins, P.114

The seventeenth Psalm of Solomon "mentions that the son of David shall be ruler over Israel and will 'destroy the unrighteous rulers, to purge Jerusalem from gentiles who trampled her to destruction; in wisdom and in righteousness to drive out the sinners from the inheritance...to destroy the unlawful nations with the word of his mouth.' He will also gather the holy people and 'will distribute them upon the land according to their tribes.' It is not accidental that this son of David is later associated with God himself as the Messiah (17:21-

46)." Mendels, P.227

4. "Important and rich concepts of the Messiah are found in 2 Baruch which was written sometime during the second half of the first century A.D....In chapter 72, it is said that the Messiah shall summon all the nations; he shall spare those who have not oppressed or known Israel; but he shall slay those who have ruled over her." Charlesworth, Pp.200-201

4 Ezra 12:31-34: "And as for the lion whom you saw rousing up out of the forest and roaring and speaking to the eagle and reproving him for his unrighteousness, and as for all his words that you have heard, this is the Messiah whom the Most High has kept until the end of days; who will arise from the posterity of David, and will come and speak to them; he will denounce them for their ungodliness and for their wickedness, and will cast up before them their contemptuous dealings. For first he will set them living before his judgement seat, and when he has reproved them, then he will destroy them. But he will deliver in mercy the remnant of my people, those who have been saved throughout my borders, and he will make them joyful until the end comes, the day of judgment, of which I spoke to you at the beginning." Ibid., P.204

5. 1 Enoch 44,4-5 tells us that, "this Son of Man whom thou hast seen shall raise up the kings and the mighty from their seats and the strong from their thrones. And shall loosen the reins of the strong, and break the teeth of the sinners. And he shall put down the kings from their thrones and kingdoms, because they do not extol and praise Him." Gruenwald, P.114

"And in the days preceding the ministry of Jesus, the idea of the Messiah as God's deliverer in the eschatological consummation was becoming fixed in the expectations of many." Longenecker, Christology, P.64

Righteousness

6. Collins, Pp.146,148. "The Similitudes, then, are exceptional among the Jewish apocalypses in focusing attention on a single figure, who is designated as the 'Chosen One' or 'that Son of Man,' or even 'messiah' (48:10; 52:4)." ibid., P.147

7. "'Salvation' (ישע, ישועה) appears as a messianic title in other portions of Jewish literature as well. Jubilees, in speaking of the expectations associated with the tribe of Judah, says: 'In thee shall be the Help of Jacob, and in thee be found the Salvation of Israel.' [Jub.31.19] The Hymns of the Qumran community tell of waiting 'for Salvation to bloom and for a Shoot to grow up to give shelter with might'. [[1QH 7.18f]] The Damascus Document assures the faithful that a 'book of remembrance' [cf. Mal.3:16] is being written for them 'until Salvation and Righteousness be revealed', [CDC 20.20 (9.43)] and that they 'shall see his Salvation'. [CDC 20.34 (9.54)] In the comment on II Sam. 7.14 in 4Q Florilegium where the Davidic Messiah is identified as the 'son' in question, Amos 9.11 is quoted in substantiation and applied to 'him who will arise to bring salvation to Israel' - thus equating 'sonship', the 'Scion of David', and the One 'who will arise to bring salvation to Israel'. The rabbis, too, seem to have appreciated this equation, for in commenting on Gen. 49.11 and Zech. 9.9 - two passages considered by them to be messianically related - 'Salvation' and 'Messiah' are employed interchangeably in the tractate Berakoth. [Ber.56b,57a] This identification is continued in the Testaments of the Twelve Patriarchs. Testament of Dan 5.10 reads: 'And there shall arise unto you from the tribe of Judah and

of Levi the Salvation of the Lord, and he shall make war against Beliar'; and the Test. Naph. 8.3; Test. Gad 8.1, and Test. Jos. 19.11 exhort the people to 'honour' and 'be united to' Levi and Judah, 'for from them shall arise the Salvation of Israel'." Longenecker, Christology, Pp.100-101

8. "...In their final form the Testaments envisage one messiah, who is associated with both Levi and Judah and is evidently identified as Christ. Since the messiah is associated with both these tribes and they are both singled out for leadership, it is probable that the Testaments adapt an earlier Jewish expectation of two messiahs. The main parallel for such a conception is found in the Qumran scrolls, which speak of messiahs from Aaron and Israel." Collins, P.112

9. cited in Charlesworth, P.199

Torah

10. "2 Baruch goes beyond 4 Ezra in clarifying the composition of the people who will benefit from the messiah. The criterion is not ethnicity but observance of the law. Proselytes are included, apostates are not. 2 Baruch envisages fulfillment of the covenantal promises, but in the process the covenantal people must be redefined. Conversion to Judaism is still a prerequisited for salvation, but the promises do not apply to all Jews." Collins, P.175

11. "The Master (*maskil*) [who] shall instruct and teach all the Sons of Light..." 1QS 3.13 in James H. Charlesworth, "Reinterpreting John: How the Dead Sea Scrolls Have Revolutionized Our Understanding of the Gospel of John," Bible Review, Feb.1993, P.21

"In CD 7:18-20, however, the interpreter is identified with the star of Balaam's oracle, the scepter is the 'prince of the whole congregation,' and the allusion is most probably messianic. In 4QFlor 1:11-12 the Interpreter is clearly messianic: the 'Branch of David' will arise with the Interpreter of the Law in Zion at the end of days. 'Interpreter of the Law,' then can refer to a figure of the past or to a messiah, or even in 1QS 6 to a present figure in the community. This ambiguous usage becomes intelligible if we bear in mind that the scrolls are concerned with functions and institutitons rather than with personalities." Collins, P.126

12. Concerning the defiled altar stones: "So they took down the altar, and deposited the stones in the temple mountain, in a suitable place, until a prophet should come and declare what should be done with them." 1Mac.4:46

13. Yalqut on Is.26 in Davies, P.74

14. "The Lord permits the forbidden (Ps.146:7) [A.V. and R.V. 'looses the prisoner'; the word 'forbidden' is got by a pun]. What does this mean? Some say that in the time to come all the animals which are unclean in this world God will declare to be clean, as they were in days before Noah. And why did God forbid them [i.e., make them unclean]? To see who would accept his bidding and who would not; but in the time to come he will permit all that He has forbidden." Mid. Teh. 146:7 in W.D. Davies, Torah in the Messianic Age and/or the Age to Come, 1952, P.58 cf. ibid.. P.59

15. Eccl.Rab. 11:7

16. Kid.72b in Berkovits, P.29

17. Peri Zadik V, p.39b in Elman, P.23

18. "In the J. Hag. II, 2 we are told: At first there was no controversy in Israel except over the laying on of the hands alone. But Shammai and Hillel arose and made them four... When the disciples of the School of Hillel increased, and they did not study sufficiently under their masters (lit., 'did not sufficiently minister to their masters'), the controversies in Israel increased, and they became divided into two companies, the one declaring unclean, the other declaring clean. And (the Torah) will not again return to its (uncontroversial) place until the son of David (i.e., the Messiah) will come." Hag., P.105 n.1

19. Yeb.90b

The Supernatural

20. Richard N. Longenecker, The Christology of Early Jewish Christianity, Alec R. Allenson Inc., Naperville, IL, Pp.32,33. Also on P.33: "Ideas regarding the exact nature of this prophetic activity, however, were often loose and mixed; and there were differences concerning the identity of the expected figure or figures. I Maccabees 4.46 and 14.41, for instance, speak rather indefinitely of 'a faithful prophet' who should 'come' or 'arise'. Attention in Sir. 48.10f. and Genesis Rabbah 71:9 and 99.11 is centred upon Elijah as the coming prophet who would inaugurate the final age and be God's restorer. In other passages, notably IV Ezra 6.26 and 7.28, all the men taken from the earth without dying - Enoch and Elijah, later Moses, and possibly Ezra, Baruch, and Jeremiah - are expected to accompany the Messiah and to have prophetic functions in the establishment of the eschatological period of salvation.

And on P.35: "For, as Cullmann points out, the acclamation of Jesus as a prophet is not the same as the attribution of the honorific title rabbi; in days when the restoration of prophecy was viewed as signalling the beginning of the last days, such an acclamation was fraught with eschatological significance." O.Cullmann, Christology of the New Testament, Pp. 13-15

21. Dt. 34:10-12
22. Charlesworth in ANRW, Pp.201-202
23. 4Ezra in Collins, P.162
24. 4Q521, Neil Asher Silberman, "Searching for Jesus," Archaelogy, Nov-Dec. 1994, P.31
25. 4Q246 and 4Q521 in Charlesworth, "Reinterpreting John," P.22
26. Charlesworth, Jesus Within Judaism, Pp.149-151
27. 4Q521 in Charlesworth, "Reinterpreting John," P.22
28. Collins,P.149

Common Messianic Expectation Evidenced in the Gospels

29. Collins, P.175 cf. Charlesworth in ANRW, P.200: "[W]e have an intriguing idea in [2 Baruch] 30:1-2: "And it shall come to pass after these things, when the time of the advent of the Messiah is fulfilled, that He shall return in glory. Then all who have fallen asleep in hope of Him shall rise again."

30. John 12:16 On another occasion, "He said to them, 'How foolish you are, and how slow of heart to believe all that the prophets have spoken! Did not the Messiah have to suffer these things and then enter his glory?' And beginning with Moses and all the Prophets, he explained to them what was said in all the Scriptures concerning himself." Luke 24:25-27

31. John 7:27
32. John 7:41-42, cf. Matt. 2:1-6; Mic.5:2
33. Matt. 17:10; cf. Mal.4:5
34. cf.John 1:24-25
35. Matt. 22:42-44; cf. Ps.110
36. cf. Matt. 20:20-21
37. Matt. 21:9
38. cf. Matt. 3:11-12
39. cf. Luke 2:26-32; John 4:42
40. cf. Matt. 9:27-28; 15:22; 20:30-33 John 7:31 Matt. 11:2-5
41. John 4:25,29 cf. John 1:48-49
42. Matt. 26:67-68
43. Matt. 26:64; cf. John 12:34
44. cf. John 6:69
45. cf. Matt. 16:16 Matt. 26:63
46. cf.Matt. 27:39-27:42; Luke 23:35,42
47. cf. John 12:34

23. YESHUA, THE PHARISEES AND THE RABBIS

1. G. Vermes, "The Qumran Interpretation of Scripture in its Historical Setting," ALUOS, VI (1966-68), p.95, cited in Longenecker, Biblical Exegesis, P.15

2. Yeshua took a strict position on divorce. In the Sermon on the Mount, he said, "It has been said, 'Anyone who divorces his wife must give her a certificate of divorce.' But I tell you that anyone who divorces his wife, except for marital unfaithfulness, causes her to become an adulteress, and anyone who marries the divorced woman commits adultery." Matt. 5:31-32

"Had the Rabbinic Judaism of 4 B.C. to A.D. 70 anything to say on the subject of Divorce? Had it not indeed! It was one of the great subjects on which the two Pharisaic parties in the middle of the first century, the School of Shammai and that of Hillel, differed strongly. For while the former with its usual strictness allowed Divorce only for sexual sin, the latter thought other reasons were sufficient. For, after all, meant Hillel, marriage was intended to bring unity in the household, not discord. Therefore anything which promoted discord was sufficient cause for the husband to divorce his wife." Williams, Talmudic Judaism, P.51

3. Note the challenge to Yeshua in Mt.21:23, "Tell us by what authority you are doing this?"

4. In Matthew, the public teaching of Yeshua begins with his declaration "But I say to you...", and his assertion of supreme authority: "Not everyone who says to me, 'Lord, Lord,' will enter the kingdom of heaven, but only he who does the will of my Father who is in heaven. Many will say to me on that day, 'Lord, Lord, did we not prophesy in your name, and in your name drive out demons and perform many miracles?' Then I will tell them plainly, 'I never knew you. Away from me, you evildoers!'...

"When Jesus had finished saying these things, the crowds were amazed at his teaching, because he taught as one who had authority, and not as their teachers of the law." Mt.7:21-3, 28-29

In <u>The Christology of Early Jewish Christianity</u>, Richard Longenecker examined the similarities and diffferences of Yeshua's statements in the Sermon on the Mount with those of the Rabbis. He concluded: "Evidently, there is a Rabbinic form expressing a contrast between the 'hearing', the 'literal understanding', of a rule and what we must 'say' it actually signifies. Here lies the source of Matthew's pattern.

"At this point, however, the real problem for form criticism only begins. There are striking differences between the Rabbinic form and the Matthean. If our method is correct, they must reflect the differences in setting; or in other words, any deviations in Matthew from the Rabbinic model must be explicable by his changed premises and objects. This is indeed the case. Matthew has adapted an academic form to his peculiar legislative purposes.

"In the Rabbinic form, it is the cautious, scholarly, devout interpreter of holy writ who speaks and is spoken to. 'I might understand literally' — 'I', namely, the scholar investigating the text. 'But thou must say' — 'thou', namely, again, a scholar investigating, a fellow-scholar addressed in an imaginary debate...." (P.57)

"In the Matthean form, little remains of this atmosphere of self-contained, orderly exposition. Instead of 'I might understand literally', we find 'Ye have understood literally' or 'Ye might understand literally'. The interpretation to be discarded is not a possibility turned over in his mind by an exact scholar. It is put into the mouth of a public as yet blind or even antagonistic. Then, the reply also is far from academic in tone. 'But I say unto you' replaces the Rabbinic 'But thou must say'. Note not only the first person, 'I say', but also the 'unto you', not present in the Rabbinic form. The tone is not academic but final, prophetic, maybe somewhat defiant. Nor is there any reasoning. The correct attitude is simply stated...

"The point is that, in Matthew, we have before us, not a scholarly working out by some Rabbis of a progressive interpretation as against a conceivable narrow one, but a laying down by Jesus, supreme authority, of the proper demand as against a view, be it held by friends or enemies, which would still take the exact words of the Scriptural precept as a standard of conduct." Longenecker, <u>The Christology of Early Jewish Christianity</u>, Allenson, Naperville, IL, 1970, P.58

5. Matt. 15:1-3, 7-9, 12-14

6. "A certain min said to R. Hanina: Hast thou heard how old Balaam was? — He replied: It is not actually stated, but since it is written, Bloody and deceitful men shall not live out half their days, [it follows that] he was thirty-three or thirty-four years old. He rejoined: Thou hast said correctly; I personally have seen Balaam's Chronicle, in which it is stated, 'Balaam the lame was thirty years old when Phinehas the Robber killed him.' Mar, the son of Rabina, said to his sons: In the case of all [those mentioned as having no portion in the future world] you should not take [the Biblical passages dealing with them] to expound them [to their discredit], excepting in the case of the wicked Balaam: whatever you find [written] about him, lecture upon it [to his disadvantage]." Sanh.106b

7. Sanh. 43a "This passage has been expunged in all censored editions." Sanh. 43a n.

8. Matt. 23:6-8,10,13,15-16,23-25,27-33

9. Dalman, P.7n
10. Sanh. 61a
11. Sanh. 61b and note. S. Funk, Die Juden in Babylonien, P. 94, n.2
12. Bowman, P.158
13. Haman's decree to annihilate the Jews was written on the 13th of Nisan. (Est.3:12) We can presume that it was on the same day that Mordecai wept in sackcloth at the king's gate, and his message was delivered to Esther. It might have been later, but it could not have been earlier, before the decree was written.

Presuming that Esther replied on the 13th, the earliest she dould have gone before the king, after fasting "three days, night and day" (Est.4:16), would have been the 15th. Apparently the phrase "three days, night and day" does not mean 72 hours, because Esther went to the king on the third day. (Est.5:1)

It could mean part of the 13th - the short time remaining after Esther answered Mordecai until sundown - all of the 14th, and part of the 15th - until she goes to the king. The first banquet could still have taken place before the end of the 15th, but the second banquet would then have taken place on the 16th. That is the earliest it could have taken place. After the second banquet, Haman was hung on the tree.

24. THE MINIM

1. Gustaf Dalman, Jesus Christ in the Talmud, Midrash, Zohar and the Liturgy of the Synagogue, Arno Press, NY, 1973 (1893), Pp. 1, 3

2. R. Travers Herford analyzed the various rabbinic passages which speak of Yeshua and the minim. He concluded that "whatever may be the precise significance of that term, it will be shown subsequently that it includes [Jewish] Christians, though it may possibly include others also." R. Travers Herford, Christianity in Talmud and Midrash, Reference Book Publishers, Clifton, NJ, 1966, P.44

Note also passages which present rabbinic apologetics, like Sanh.38b: "R. Johanan said: In all the passages which the Minim have taken for their heresy, their refutation is found near at hand. Thus: 'Let us make man in our image; [Gen. 1:26]; 'And God created [sing.] man in His own image' [Gen. 1:27], 'Come, let us go down and there confound their language' [Gen.11:7]; 'And the Lord came down [sing.] to see the city and the tower; [Gen. 11:5]; 'Because there were revealed [plur.] to him God' [Gen. 35:7]; 'Unto God who answers [sing.] me in the day of my distress' [Gen.35:3]; 'For what great nation is there that hath God so nigh [plural] unto it, as the Lord our God is nigh unto us whensoever we call upon Him' [singular, Deut. 4:7]; 'And what one nation is the earth is like thy people, Israel, whom God went [plur.] to redeem for a people unto Himself' [sing., 2Sam. 7:23]; 'Till thrones were placed and one that was ancient did sit' [Dan. 7:9].

"...One [throne] was for Himself and one for David...This is R. Akiba's view..."

3. Bowman, P.2 The bracketed words, "Talmide Yeshu," are Rashi's. Maimonides said: "Five types of persons are termed minim: 1) he who says that there is no God and the world has no Ruler; 2) he who says that there is not one Ruler but two or more; 3) he who says that there is one Lord, but he has body and form; 4) he who says that God is not the First Cause and Creator of

all things; and so too, 5) he who worships some other god that should function as an intercessor between him and the Lord of the universe. Each of these five is called a min." Mishneh Torah, 38.7-39 The Rabbis would definitely have included the Talmidei Yeshua in the second, third, and fifth types.

4. Herford, Christianity, P.163

The Threat of *Minuth*

5. Ehrhardt, P.104
6. Hag.15b
7. Hag.15a
8. Acts 21:20
9. Marcus Lehman, Akiba: The Story of Rabbia Akiba and His Times, trans. Joseph Leftwich, Feldheim, New York, 1956, Pp.130-1
10. A.Z. 16b
11. Acts 22:3
12. Gal.1:14
13. A.Z.27b cf. 145, Midrash Rabbah on Ecclesiastes, Shab.110a: "Abaye observed to them. 'Perhaps he was bitten by a snake of the Rabbis, for which there is no cure, as it is written, and whoso breaketh through a fence, a serpent shall bite him?'"

R. Akiba vs. the Minim

14. Sanh.67a
15. Dalman, P. 38
16. Herford, Christianity, P.44
17. In this regard, it is important to note that, "It is likely that the Jewish authorities were also established at Lydda for some time in the years between the revolt under Trajan and the Bar Kokhba revolt." Isaac & Oppenheimer, P. 52 n. 83
18. Ginzberg points out what a strong, conscious motive this was for Akiba. "To the same motive underlying his [Akiba's] antagonism to the Apocrypha, namely, the desire to disarm Christians - especially Jewish Christians - who drew their 'proofs' from the Apocrypha, must also be attributed his wish to emancipate the Jews of the Dispersion from the domination of the Septuagint, the errors and inaccuracies in which frequently distorted the true meaning of Scripture, and were even used as arguments against the Jews by the Christians. Aquila was a man after Akiba's own heart; under Akiba's guidance, he gave the Greek-speaking Jews a rabbinical Bible (Jerome on Isa.viii.14, Yer. Kid. i.59a)...thus Judaizing the Bible, as it were, in opposition to the Christians." Ginzberg, "Akiba," Pp.305-306

On the other side, Aquila is described by Epiphanius as a Gentile who became a Christian, but would not let go of his faith in astrology. "Hence, as one who proved useless and could not be saved, he was expelled from the church. But as one who had become embittered in mind over how he had suffered dishonour, he was puffed up with vain jealousy, and having cursed Christianity and renounced his life he became a proselyte and was circumcised as a Jew. And, being painfully ambitious, he dedicated himself to learning the language of the Hebrews and their writings. After he had first been thoroughly trained for it, he made his translation. He was moved not by the right motive, but (by the desire) so to distort certain of the words occurring in the translation of the seventy-two." Epiphanius, "Treatise on Weights and Measures," Pp.30-1 cited in Yadin, P. 259

There has been dispute over whether or not Aquila was also the author of the Targum Onkelos, an early colloquial translation or paraphrase. The prevailing view seems to be that he was. Solomon Zeitlin said that: "...There was in fact no such person as Onkelos. 'Onkelos' is identical with Aquila. The Hebrew spelling of Aquila is 'Ekulos.' Since the first Hebrew vowel, an 'ayin, was given a nasal pronunciation in Judaea, the Judaean pronunciation of the name of Aquila sounded to Babylonian ears like 'Onkelos.' Hence the name 'Onkelos' in the Babylonian Talmud." Solomon Zeitlin, The Rise and Fall of the Judean State, Vol.3, Jewish Publication Society, Philadelphia, 1978, P.200

A.E. Silverstone has noted that, "...when he (Onkelos) included in his version halachic or haggadic elements he followed Rabbi Akiba in preference to any other tanna." A.E. Silverstone, Aquila and Onkelos, Manchester Univ. Press, Manchester, 1931, P.107 Akiba's influence meant that the Targum would be another way by which he could isolate the Talmidei Yeshua and establish rabbinic authority.

19. "It became recognized that these Jewish Christians knew their Bible, which was the common Bible of the Jews. Some may have argued from the Septuagint, a Jewish Greek translation, so this had to be countered by a Jewish Greek translation, that of Aquila. Some may have argued from the Targum, hence R. Akiba's interest in standardizing the Targum, or at least in moving towards an official Targum." Bowman, P.2

20. "If the older Halakah is to be considered as the product of the national struggle between Phariseeism and Sadduceeism, the Halakah of Akiba must be conceived as the result of an external contest between Judaism on the one hand and Hellenism and Hellenistic Christianity on the other." Ginzberg, "Akiba," P.306

21. "Next to the transcendental nature of God, Akiba insists emphatically, as has been mentioned, on the freedom of the will, to which he allows no limitations. This insistance is in opposition to the Christian doctrine of the sinfulness and depravity of man, and apparently controverts his [Akiba's] view of divine predestination. He derides those who find excuse for their sins in this supposed innate depravity (Kid. 81a). But Akiba's opposition to this genetically Jewish doctrine is probably directed mainly against its Christian correlative, the doctrine of the grace of God contingent upon faith in Christ and baptism. Referring to this, Akiba says, 'Happy are ye, O Israelites, that ye purify yourselves through your heavenly Father, as it is said (Jer. xvii.13, Heb.), "Israel's hope is God"' (Mishnah Yoma, end). This is a play on the Hebrew word mikveh ('hope' and 'bath'). In opposition to the Christian insistence on God's love, Akiba upholds God's retributive justice elevated above all chance or arbitrariness." Ibid, P.307, citing Mekilta, Beshallah, 6

22. Sanh. XI.1

23. Michael Avi Yonah, The Jews Under Roman and Byzantine Rule, Schocken Books, NY, 1984, P.143 The scripture to which Rabbi Akiba referred is Exodus 15:26: "And He [the Lord] said, 'If you will give earnest heed to the voice of the Lord your God, and do what is right in His sight, and give ear to His commandments, and keep all His statutes, I will put none of the diseases

on you which I have put on the Egyptians; for I, the Lord, am your healer." Apparently, at that time the Talmidei Yeshua, such as Jacob of Kefar Sekaniah, were using the verse in healing. The verse is still used today by followers of Jesus who believe in divine healing.

24. Lawrence H. Schiffman, Who Was a Jew - Rabbinic and Halakhic Perspectives on the Jewish Christian Schism, Ktav, Hoboken, NJ, 1985, P.73

25. Matthew records that after the resurrection, Yeshua told his disciples, "All authority has been given to Me in heaven and on earth." Mt. 28:18 That did not leave much room for the Rabbis.

26. "But the righteousness based on faith speaks thus, 'Do not say in your heart, *Who will ascend into heaven?* (that is, to bring Messiah down), or *Who will descend into the abyss?* (that is, to bring Messiah up from the dead).' But what does it say? *'The word is near you, in your mouth and in your heart'* - that is, the word of faith which we are preaching, that if you confess with your mouth Yeshua as Lord, and believe in your heart that God raised Him from the dead, you shall be saved; for with the heart man believes, resulting in righteousness, and with the mouth he confesses, resulting in salvation." Romans 10:6-10

27. e.g., Matthew 3:16,17: "And after being baptized, Jesus went up immediately from the water; and behold, the heavens were opened, and he [John] saw the Spirit of God descending as a dove, and coming upon Him, and behold, a voice out of the heavens, saying, 'This is My beloved Son, in whom I am well-pleased.'"

28. Hebrews 12:25, 26

29. Hebrews 3:7-9

30. Saul of Tarsus was on his way to Damascus with letters from the high priest which authorized him to arrest any Jewish followers of Yeshua whom he found there and to "bring them bound to Jerusalem. And it came about that as he journeyed, he was approaching Damascus, and suddenly a light from heaven flashed around him; and he fell to the ground, and heard a voice saying to him, 'Saul, Saul, why are you persecuting Me?' And he said, 'Who art thou Lord?' And He said, 'I am Yeshua whom you are persecuting...'" Acts 9:2-5

31. Guttmann, P.225 [Pal.Sheq.V,1:48c]

32. Gedalyahu Alon, Jews, Judaism, and the Classical World, trans. Israel Abrahams, Magnes, Jerusalem, 1977, P.122

A Time to Act

33. Charlesworth, "Reinterpreting John," P.24 All the incidents take place in Judea.

John 9:22 "His parents said this because they were afraid of the Iudaioi [Jews], for already the Iudaioi [Jews] had decided that anyone who acknowledged that Jesus was the Christ would be put out of the synagogue." It is clear in the context, 9:13-16, that Iudaioi here means the Pharisaic leaders.

John 12:42 "Yet at the same time many even among the leaders believed in him. But because of the Pharisees they would not confess their faith for fear they would be put out of the synagogue."

John 16:2 "They will put you out of the synagogue; in fact, a time is coming when anyone who kills you will think he is offering a service to God."

34. Sanh. 96b

35. "As he was leaving the temple, one of his disciples said to him, 'Look, Teacher! What massive stones! What magnificent buildings!'
"'Do you see all these great buildings?' replied Yeshua. 'Not one stone here will be left on another; every one will be thrown down.'" Mark 13:1-2

One of the charges made against him before the Sanhedrin was that, "We heard him say, 'I will destroy this man-made temple and in three days will build another, not made by man.'" Mark 14:58

During the Great Revolt, the Talmidei Yeshua had applied two prophecies of Yeshua to their circumstances. The first was, "But when you see Jerusalem encircled by armies, then know that her desolation has drawn near. Then let those in Judea flee to the mountains; and those in her midst let them depart out, and let not those in the countryside enter into her; for these are days of avenging, that all things that have been written may be accomplished." Luke 21:21-22

The second was, "When therefore you shall see the abomination of desolation, which was spoken of by Daniel the prophet, standing in the holy place - let the reader understand - then let those who are in Judea flee to the mountains; let him who is on the housetop not come down to take anything out of his house; and let him who is in the field not retun back to take his cloak...for then there will be a great tribulation, such as has not occurred since the beginning of the world until now, or ever shall." Mt.24:15-18, 21 Accordingly, the Talmidei Yeshua took advantage of a brief break in the Roman siege of Jerusalem under Titus, to flee the city for the mountains.

Though some modern writers have excoriated the Talmidei Yeshua for deserting the city, that does not appear to have been the attitude of the time. There were others in Jerusalem and throughout Israel, including the Sages, who were opposed to the war. cf. Git.56a

"Even Abba Sikra, head of Jerusalem's Zealots and nephew of the moderate sage Rabban Johanan ben Zakkai, became convinced of the hopelessness of the fighting. Secretly, Rabban Johanan invited him to discuss the situation only to find that the Zealot leader agreed, but pleaded, 'What shall I do? If I say anything to them, they will kill me.' Such extremism was prevalent among the Zealots that a radical wing emerged of which the leader himself was afraid, and which he reluctantly followed." Harkabi, P.11

There were those in the city whom the Zealots killed for counselling surrender to the Romans. That is why Johanan ben Zakkai had himself smuggled out of the city in a coffin, with the help of his nephew. Josephus says that the Zealots, after their character became evident, had no popular support in the city, and that they killed every man of reason, character, position, or substance. He gives the impression that almost everyone in Jerusalem would have left if they could have. Perhaps that is an exaggeration on his part, because of his own personal history, but the Midrash presents a similar picture.

Johanan ben Zakkai's prophetic greeting of Vespasian - 'Vive domine Imperator!' - was based on his confidence that Vespasian would destroy the Temple. That greeting is said to have earned him the privilege of starting the rabbinic academy at Yavneh.

That makes it highly unlikely that those at the Academy would have attacked Yeshua for prophesying the destruction of Jerusalem or his disciples for leaving the city. Later opponents certainly may have, but it would have made no sense for the Rabbis to do so. Indeed, they do not mention the issue.

36. "R. Levi said: The benediction relating to the Minim was instituted in Jabneh. ...Our Rabbis taught: Simeon ha-Pakuli arranged the eighteen benedictions in order before Rabban Gamaliel in Jabneh. Said Rabban Gamaliel to the Sages: Can any one among you frame a benediction relating to the Minim? Samuel the Lesser arose and composed it." Ber. 28b

37. Gedalia Alon, The Jews in their Land in the Talmudic Age, Vol. I, Magnes, Jerusalem, 1980, Pp.289, 290n

The Spanish "Ordinances of Soria" proclaimed in 1380 that, "Whereas we have been informed that the Jews are commanded by their books and other writings of the Talmud, daily to say the prayer against heretics, which is said standing [the Aleynu Prayer], wherein they curse Christians and churches, we strictly command and forbid any of them, hereafter, to say it or have it written in their rituals or any other books; and those that have it written in the said books are to erase and cancel it in such manner as not to be legible, which is to be done within two months after the publication hereof; and any one who says or responds to it shall publicly receive one hundred lashes. And if it be found in his breviary or other book, he is to be fined one thousand maravedis; and if he cannot pay the fine, one hundred lashes are to be given to him." Scattered Among the Nations, ed. Alexis Rubin, Jason Aronson Inc., Northvale, NJ, 1995, P.82

38. E.g., B.B. 91a: "R. Hanan b. Raba further stated in the name of Rab: [The name of] the mother of Abraham [was] Amathlai the daughter of Karnebo; [the name of] the mother of Haman was Amathlai, the daughter of 'Orabti; and your mnemonic [may be], 'unclean [to] unclean, clean [to] clean'. The mother of David was named Nizbeth the daughter of Adael. The mother of Samson [was named] Zlelponith, and his sister, Nashyan. In what [respect] do [these names] matter? — In respect of a reply to the heretics."

Soncino note: "Minim (sing. min), applied especially to Jewish-Christians. Should the minim ask why the names of the mothers of these important figures are not given in the Bible narrative, they can be answered that these had been handed down by oral tradition." [v. Herford, Christianity, P. 326]"

39. Shab. 116a Soncino n.15 "Jast. s.v. *gilyon* translates, the gospels, though observing that here it is understood as blanks. V. Herford, R.T., 'Christianity in the Talmud', p. 155 n."

40. Shab. 116a Soncino note...(29) Uncensored text adds: "R. Meir called it (the Gospel) *'Awen Gilyon*, the falsehood of blank Paper; R. Johanan called it *'Awon Gilyon*, the sin of etc. On the whole passage v. Herford, Christianity, Pp. 161-171."

41. Naso, Sec. 16
42. Git. 45b
43. Sanh. XI,1
44. Gen.37:24
45. Jer.38:6
46. A.Z. 26a-26b

47. Hullin 13b The particular first century group of minim that concerned the Rabbis was one that consisted of both Israelites and gentiles. Was there any

other besides the followers of Yeshua?

48. Herford, Christianity, P.389, T. Hull, ii. 20,21 Herford adds, "This is not a halachah, an authoritative legal decision, but it represents a consensus of opinion amounting almost to a law."

49. R.H.17a is more explicit: "But as for the minim...these will go down to Gehinnom and be punished there for all generations."

50. Midrash Eccl., I. 8, sec. 4

25. THE ROMAN TRIALS

1. On the Laws, cited in Eberhard Arnold, The Early Christians after the Death of the Apostles, Plough Publishing House, Rifton, NY, 1972, P.59

2. As Arnold points out, "The Roman Empire, as the clearest and most typical example of a State, shows that a unified State religion, however broad and tolerant the concept, will of necessity appear indispensable to the very existence of such a State. Therefore any religion that excludes or opposes the religious State-concept or the recognized State religions is an extremely dangerous attack on the State at its very core. The Roman emperor-cult was but the sum total, the visible culmination, of the State religion which pervaded all of Roman civilization. Consequently, on this point there could be no tolerance on the part of Rome until later a new religious concept of the State placed the institutional Church at the service of the State." Arnold, P.335 The new State religion, Constantinian Christianity, proved to be equally intolerant, for precisely the same reason — the need for "unity" to preserve political power.

3. Philip Schaff, History of the Christian Church, vol. 2, Scribner, New York, 1883, P.42

4. Legal decree according to the second-century jurist Julius Paulus. Five books of Collected Sentences V.21, cited in Arnold, P.59

5. Exod. 20:5-6

6. From time to time, some emperors were not. According to Suetonius, "Tiberius suppressed foreign cults and Egyptian and Jewish religious rites and forced those who were enslaved by this kind of superstition to burn their religious vestments and all the paraphernalia of their cults. He dispersed Jewish youths to provinces with a more rugged climate, ostensibly to do military service. Others belonging to this people, or persons holding similar beliefs, he removed from the city on pain of slavery for life if they did not want to obey." [Suetonius (died A.D.140) on Tiberius, who ruled A.D. 14-37, ch.36, cited in Arnold, P.61]

7. G.F. Moore, Judaism in the First Centuries of the Christian Era, Harvard U. Press, Cambridge, 1927-40, P.350

8. Tacitus said, "No humane endeavors, no princely generosity, no efforts to placate the gods were able to dispel the scandalous suspicion that the burning of the city was the result of an order. To silence this rumor, Nero pushed the Christians forward as the culprits and punished them with ingenious cruelty, as they were generally hated for their infamous deeds.

"The one from whom this name originated, Christ, had been executed during the reign of Tiberius at the hands of the procurator, Pontius Pilate. For a time this pernicious superstition was suppressed, but it broke out again, not only in Judea where this evil thing began, but even in the city itself where everything atrocious and shameful from all quarters flows together and finds adherents.

"To begin with, those who openly confessed were arrested, and then a vast multitude was convicted on the basis of their disclosures, not so much on the charge of arson as for their hatred of the human race. Their execution was made into a game: they were covered with the skins of wild animals and torn to pieces by dogs. They were hung on crosses. They were burned, wrapped in flammable material and set on fire as darkness fell, to illuminate the night. Nero had opened his gardens for this spectacle and put on circus games. He himself mingled with the crowd dressed as a charioteer or stood up high on a chariot... Although these people were guilty and deserved the severest penalty, all this gave rise to compassion for them, for it was felt that they were being victimized, not for the public good, but to satiate the cruelty of one man." Tacitus, Annals XV.44. cited in Arnold, Pp.61-62

9. John 18:29-31

10. The gospel account indicates that Pilate was reluctant. Later he said, "You take him and crucify him." Jn. 19:6 In effect, he was saying he would look the other way if the Sanhedrin illegally executed Yeshua on its own.

The leaders of the Sanhedrin insisted that Pilate fulfill his customary Roman role. Inasmuch as Yeshua had a significant popular following, perhaps they did not want to bear the public responsibility for his death. They presented Pilate with the implicit threat that they would file charges against him in Rome if he did not: "If you let this man go, you are no friend of Caesar. Anyone who claims to be a king opposes Caesar." John 19:12 We know historically that such charges could have cost Pilate his life. We also know historically that Pilate was not reluctant to shed blood to keep his position secure. e.g. Lk.13:1

11. "Forty years before the destruction of the Temple the Sanhedrin went into exile and ...They did not adjudicate in capital cases." Shab.15a

12. "Josephus says that...Ananus, exploiting the fact that Festus was dead and Albinus was still on his way to Palestine, convened the judges of the Sanhedrin and accused James, the brother of Jesus, of having transgressed the law. James and some of his friends were delivered to be stoned to death. For these acts King Agrippa II removed Ananus from the high priesthood, which he had held for three months, and replaced him with Jesus the son of Damnaeus (20.203)..." Mendels, P.303

13. Acts 26:9-11; 22:19 Paul also testified of his background: "I am a Jew, born in Tarsus of Cilicia, but brought up in this city. Under Gamaliel, I was thoroughly trained in the law of our fathers and was just as zealous for God as any of you are today....According to the strictest sect of our religion, I lived as a Pharisee." Acts 22:3; 26:5

14. Josephus, Wars, Book 6, Ch.5 §3 That "he was whipped til his bones were laid bare" indicates that the Romans did not respect the Jewish limitation of 39 strokes. That is probably the reason why the rulers brought him to the procurator, rather than scourging him themselves.

15. "Yet at the same time many even among the leaders believed in him. But because of the Pharisees they would not confess their faith for fear they would be put out of the synagogue." John 12:42

16. As Festus explained to King Agrippa about the prisoner Paul: "When

his accusers got up to speak, they did not charge him with any of the crimes I had expected. Instead, they had some points of dispute with him about their own religion and about a dead man named Jesus who Paul claimed was alive. I was at a loss how to investigate such matters..." Acts 25:18-20

17. Philip Schaff, vol. 2, Pp.40, 41
18. Avi Yonah, P.148
19. cf. Josephus, Against Apion, 2:40, P.636
20. Moore, Pp.350-351
21. Dio, P.170 Scholars have disagreed on whether Flavius and his wife had become Jews or Christians. From the little information we have, we cannot be sure. "The complaint brought against them both was that of some kind of Jewish atheism", i.e. a rejection of the gods of Rome. If they had converted to Judaism, Dio would probably not have said that they "**drifted** into Jewish ways."

We do know that Domitian zealously collected the special poll-tax on Jews and those who lived like Jews. So if Flavius Clemens and Flavia Domitilla had only 'drifted' to living like Jews, that might have increased their taxes, not cost them their lives.

If they had believed in Jesus, that would have been legally classified as atheism, and it would have brought them into what were perceived as Jewish ways. It seems to be the best fit for their crime. Nevertheless, they could have been deported rather than executed, so there may have been some personal motives involved.

22. Cited by Arnold, Pp.63-65
23. Herford, Christianity, P.388 "During the Roman persecution of Christians in Palestine in the year 109 under Trajan (Herford, loc. cit.) R. Eliezer b. Hyrcanus was arrested on suspicion of following that sect." A.Z. 16b, n.18
24. A.Z. 16b-17a
25. Ta'anith 25b
26. "For R. Joseph said, and similarly taught R. Hiyya: From the day the Temple was destroyed, although the Sanhedrin ceased to function, the four modes of execution did not cease....He who would have been condemned to decapitation is either handed over to the (Gentile) Government or robbers attack him." Sotah 8b This is the only one of the four categories of offenses in which the Sanhedrin is called to act.

What criminals would have been condemned to decapitation by a functioning Sanhedrin? "The following are decapitated: A murderer and the inhabitants of a seduced city." Sanh.52b

27. Sanh.111b
28. James Parkes, The Conflict of the Church and the Synagogue, Atheneum, NY, 1969, P.126 Cf. "The Martyrdom of the Holy Polycarp"
29. Parkes, P.110

When the followers of Yeshua gathered together, they would symbolically commemorate the Last Supper. cf. Matt. 26:26-28 "While they were eating, Jesus took bread, gave thanks and broke it, and gave it to his disciples, saying, 'Take and eat; this is my body.' Then he took the cup, gave thanks and offered it to them, saying, 'Drink from it, all of you. This is my blood of the covenant, which is poured out for many for the forgiveness of sins.'"

The rumor was spread that, in doing this, they ate the flesh and drank the blood of an infant. This was essentially the same accusation as the blood libel of the Middle Ages. According to Tertullian, Origen, and Justin, this accusation was spread by men sent from the religious leaders.

Justin says this in his <u>Dialogue with Trypho the Jew</u>. "You (plural) chose special men and sent them from Jerusalem throughout the world to proclaim that with Christianity a godless sect had arisen and to bring those accusations against us which now are raised by all those who do not know us." Justin, <u>Dialogue with Trypho the Jew</u> 17.1, in Arnold, Pp.86-87

"...I must ask you this: do you also hold the opinion about us that we actually eat men and that, after a carousal, we extinguish the lights and engage in promiscuous intercourse? Or do you simply condemn us because we follow the one or the other teaching but do not follow that belief which you hold to be the true one?'

"Trypho replied, '...concerning the things of which the masses speak, they are not worth believing, for they go right against human nature....'" ibid, P. 87

Trypho did not believe the accusations, but then Trypho was transgressing rabbinic teaching by having discussions with a min.

30. Acts 5:34-39

26. "THIS IS KING MESSIAH"

1. "That the very appellation expresses a messianic belief in the 'star out of Jacob' as an ideal ruler can be seen from apocryphal literature (Test. Patr., Levi 18:3; and Judah 24:1; and cf. Rev. 22:16; the Damascus Document, 7:19-20; and War of the Sons of Light with the Sons of Darkness, 7:5,1)." Abramsky, "Bar Kochba," P.230

2. <u>Mid. Lam.</u> II.2, sec.4

3. "The fact that Akiba's positive attitude is described so explicitly in the rabbinic literature also argues strongly for its historical authenticity. People might have preferred to keep quiet about such a misconception on the part of one of the most important rabbis in later times." Henk Jagersma, <u>A History of Israel from Alexander the Great to Bar Kokhba</u>, Fortress Press, Philadelphia, 1986, P.158

4. "Bar Koziba reigned two and a half years, and then said to the Rabbis, 'I am the Messiah.' They answered, 'Of Messiah it is written that he smells and judges: let us see whether he [Bar Koziba] can do so.' When they saw that he was unable to judge by the scent, they slew him." Sanh.93b

The reference is to Is. 11: "A shoot will come up from the stump of Jesse; from his roots a Branch will bear fruit. The Spirit of the LORD will rest on him — the Spirit of wisdom and of understanding, the Spirit of counsel and of power, the Spirit of knowledge and of the fear of the LORD — and he will delight in the fear of the LORD.   He will not judge by what he sees with his eyes, or decide by what he hears with his ears; but with righteousness he will judge the needy, with justice he will give decisions for the poor of the earth. He will strike the earth with the rod of his mouth; with the breath of his lips he will slay the wicked." Isa. 11:1-4

We do not know whether ben Kosiba was descended from Jesse, David's father. We are not told that he was. We do not know what tribe he was from. The Messiah was usually understood to be from the tribe of Judah, descended from King David. Eleazar of Modim, a priest, appears to have been Bar Kokhba's uncle. That would mean that all we know about ben Kosiba's genealogy is that he was related to the tribe of Levi.

The account of the Rabbis slaying Bar Kokhba, which appears only in the Babylonian Talmud, indicates that the Rabbis expected Messiah to have supernatural powers of discernment. Bar Kokhba did not fulfill these expectations. Because he falsely presented himself as the Messiah, the Rabbis immediately put him to death, so that he never ruled as Messiah.

For several reasons, this appears to be a later attempt to disassociate the Rabbis from the false Messiah who led Israel into such an horrendous disaster. First, there is no mention of Akiba's declaration, which would have been the equivalent of false prophecy, a capital crime. If the Rabbis put ben Kosiba to death for claiming to be the Messiah, then they would have had to put R. Akiba to death for proclaiming him the Messiah.

Second, the letters of Bar Kokhba indicate that he was still giving orders towards the end of the revolt. "[T]he written documents of Bar Kokhba found in the Judean Desert caves do bear the dates 'Year 3' and 'Year 4'..." Kraft & Nickelsburg, citing Yaakov Meshorer, "Jewish Numismatics," P.215 So, regardless of what point in the revolt Bar Kokhba began to rule, 2 1/2 years later there was no need to question his discernment or Messiahship. The situation then was utterly hopeless.

Only if he were expecting divine intervention would that have been the time to present himself, or for Rabbi Akiba to present him, as the Messiah. Neither Akiba nor Bar Kokhba expected or requested such intervention.

Third, the slogan of the earliest Bar Kokhba coinage is the most Messianic. "Year 1 of the Redemption of Israel" changed to Year 2 of the Freedom of Israel." This was followed by the slogan "For the freedom of Jerusalem" on the undated coinage of the third and fourth years.

Fourth, the Rabbis appear to have supported Bar Kokhba, rather than opposed him. As Maimonides concluded: "Rabbi Akiva... and all the sages of his generation imagined Bar Kohkba to be King Messiah until he was slain unfortunately."

Fifth, the Midrash says that Bar Kokhba was killed in battle.

5. Dan. 7:9-10, 13-14

6. "If they [the people of Messiah's generation] are meritorious, (he will come) *with the clouds of heaven*; if not, *lowly and riding upon an ass*. [Zech.9:9]" Sanh.98a

7. Hag.14a

8. "Again the high priest asked him, 'Are you the Messiah, the Son of the Blessed One?'

"'I am,' said Yeshua. 'And you will see the Son of Man sitting at the right hand of the Mighty One and coming on the clouds of heaven.'

"The high priest tore his clothes. 'Why do we need any more witnesses?' he asked. 'You have heard the blasphemy. What do you think?' They all condemned him as worthy of death." Mark 14:61b-64

9. There is extensive discussion in the tractate Sanhedrin of different aspects of the reign of Messiah, including the regathering of the 10 tribes. Peter Schafer comments, "J. Heinemann has understood this text, I think rightly, as proof of

the concrete national and earthly nature of Akiba's messianic expectations, in which no utopian features can be identified. 'There is no doubt, therefore, that Akiba's determination that the ten tribes are not destined to return had practical implications for the messianic aspirations and activists of his time. He who saw in Bar Kokhba the King Messiah... and held that the process of redemption had certainly begun, was forced to utterly disavow all utopian and unrealistic elements of the messianic redemption and to remove them from the first stages.'" Peter Schafer, "Rabbi Akiba and Bar Kokhba," in Approaches to Ancient Judaism, ed. Green, Vol. II, P.120

The traditional belief was that all the tribes would be regathered in the reign of Messiah. Since that would have required a miracle of major proportions, Akiba did not count on that happening under Bar Kokhba. He, therefore, disavowed such a belief and proclaimed the oposite. (R. Eliezer opposed him in this.) Akiba's King Messiah did not need to be confirmed by God through the miraculous.

Ginzberg wrote in support of Akiba's position: "For, in spite of his philosophy, Akiba was an extremely strict and national Jew. His doctrine concerning the Messiah was the realistic and thoroughly Jewish one, as his declaration that Bar Kokhba was the Messiah shows. He accordingly limited the Messianic age to forty years, as being within the scope of a man's life - similar to the reigns of David and Solomon - against the usual conception of a millennium." Ginzberg, "Akiba," P.308, citing Midr. Teh. XC.15

What Ginzberg and other modern writers seem to mean by a "realistic" Messiah is one removed from anything supernatural. That may be "realistic" to the modern mind, but it was not so to first century Jews. Additionally, what was realistic about proclaiming Bar Kokhba the Messiah?

10. John 5:36
11. Finkelstein, Akiba, P.269
12. Mid. Lam. II.4, 157
13. Finkelstein, Akiba, P.229
14. Sot.48b
15. Finkelstein, "Akiba," P.144
16. Dio, P.227
17. There had been supernatural warnings before the Great Revolt also. "Our Rabbis taught: During the last forty years before the destruction of the Temple the lot ['for the Lord'] did not come up in the right hand; nor did the crimson-coloured strap become white; nor did the westernmost light shine; and the doors of the Temple would open by themselves, until R. Johanan b. Zakkai rebuked them, saying: Temple, Temple, why wilt thou be the alarmer thyself? I know about thee that thou wilt be destroyed, for Zechariah ben Ido has already prophesied concerning thee: Open thy doors, O Lebanon, that the fire may devour thy cedars." Yoma 39b

18. "However, there is hardly any room for doubt that the majority of the Pharisees were in agreement with Rabbi Akiba and Bar Kochba, for otherwise this war, which lasted three and one-half years, and in which myriads upon myriads of Jews took part, could not have started at all..." Alon, Jews, P.45

Alon's statement continues, "and at that time, there were only Pharisees in Jewry." That, however, is not so. Most Jews were not Pharisees then. The Am

HaAretz were not. The powerless priests were not. The Talmidei Yeshua were not. The Sadducees, Essenes, and most other groups may have faded from the scene, but most of the people had never belonged to any of these groups.

How many Pharisees were there at the time? Josephus says that there were more than 6000 of them in the early part of the 1st century. That figure would count only adult males. Of the Essenes, he said, "There are about 4000 men that live in this way..." Ant.18.1.5 The Talmudic attacks on the am haAretz are evidence of a very significant non-Pharisaic population.

19. Isaac & Oppenheimer, P.56

20. As Yadin writes, "Now apparently some of the Tekoans were disregarding the mobilisation orders of Bar-Kokhba, and were seeking refuge in the somewhat remote En-gedi." P.125

"From Shimeon bar Kosiba to the men of En-gedi....In comfort you sit, eat and drink from the property of the House of Israel, and care nothing for your brothers." P.132

"...Yehonathan and Masabala were not the only insubordinate commanders in Bar-Kokhba's army - at least not towards the end of the revolt. Nothing fails like failure!" Bar Kokhba, Yadin, P.134

21. "The judgments of those historians who contend that the Galilean Jews did not take part in the rebellion are summarized by Avi-Yonah. 'Since the fact is that in the Bar Kokhba Rebellion the Romans demolished every settlement associated with the war, thus actually leaving no Jewish settlement in the areas in which they had fought, and futher, inasmuch as we know that the Galilee, in contrast with Judea, remained Jewish even after the war, it then is possible to say that the Galilee did not at all participate in this insurrection or to assert that its participation was temporary and suppressed at the very beginning of the rebellion without leaving many traces behind.'" Harkabi, P. 37 citing Raffel, P.319, History of the Land of Israel [in Hebrew], Tel Aviv, Publications Dept. Ministry of Defense, 1980

22. J. Hag. II, 2, cited in Hag. 16a n.42

23. BKR, Oppenheimer, 65 Rabbi Akiba had his own definition for what the rule of Messiah should be. "Rabbi Akiba and many of his colleagues were 'messianists.' The messiah's reign was to be a reign of Law and his state a Torah state. For the implementation of the Torah, the Temple was necessary...This gave much impetus to Rabbi Akiba's drive to discover more and more halakoth from even the tittles and crowns of the individual letters in the words of the Law. It was the revelation of the blueprint for the constitution of the Messianic Age." Bowersock, P.22 In Akiba's Torah state, it was not the Messiah who revealed and restored the Torah; it was the Rabbis.

Akiba's Role in the Revolt

24. 1 Kings 15:27-28; 2 Kings 23:34; 1 Kings 1:23-40; 2 Kings 14:21; 1 Samuel 16:1-13; 2 Kings 11

25. 1 Kings 1:34

26. Alon (Jews, Judaism and the Classical World) mentions Sacher, Margolis, Marx, Roth, and Grayzel in this regard.

27. Harkabi, Pp. 42-43 citing Maimonides, Mishneh Torah, Hilkhot Melakhim, 11

28. The remarks of a modern rabbinic sage are suggestive. "In one striking

passage Rav Soloveitchik states: 'The very same priest, whose mind was suffused with the holiness of the Torah of R. Akiva and R. Eliezer, of Abbaye and Raba, of the Rambam and Rabad, of the Beth Yosef and the Rema, could also discern with the holy spirit [roeh be-ruah ha-kodesh] the solution to all current political questions, to all worldly matters, to all ongoing current demands.'" Divrei Hagut ve-Haarakhah, 192 "in Lawrence Kaplan, "Daas Torah: A Modern Conception of Rabbinic Authority," Pp.8-9 <u>Rabbinic Authority and Personal Autonomy</u>, ed. Moshe Sokol, Jason Aronson Inc., Northvale, NH, 1992

It may be doubted, however, that R. Akiba was able to discern the solution to the problems of his own times.

29. Bader, Pp. 291-2 The Hagada relates the story of the Exodus of the children of Israel from Egyptian slavery. That emancipation came about through the ten plagues and the Divine destruction of Pharaoh's army in the waters of the Red Sea.

30. In a passage that comes just before the Talmud's extended discussion of Messiah, we are told that it was in Bnei Brak that "the descendants of Haman studied Torah," and that it was there that the decision to give them over to destruction was made. Sanh.96b Given the Talmudic equation of Haman and Yeshua, it seems clear that the Talmidei Yeshua are the ones referred to as "the discendants of Haman."

31. Bowersock, P.141

27. MILHEMET MITZVAH

1. Dt. 20:2-8
2. Alon, <u>The Jews in Their Land</u>, Vol. 2, P.629 Sot. 44b: "R. Judah says, 'To what does all the foregoing apply? To voluntary wars, but in the wars commanded by the Torah all go forth even a bridegroom from his chamber and a bride from her canopy.'"
3. Sot. 44b
4. Alon, <u>The Jews in their Land</u>, Vol. II, P.630
5. Finkelstein, <u>Akiba</u>, P.229
6. Maimonides, P.324, 5:2
7. Meg. 17b
8. Meshorer, "Jewish Numismatics," P.215
9. As Bar Kokhba wrote in one of his letters, "Concerning every man of Tekoa who will be found at your place - the houses in which they dwell will be burned and you [too] will be punished." In another, "I take heaven to witness against me that unless you 'mobilize' [or possibly, 'destroy'] the Galileans who are with you, every man I will put fetters on your feet as I did to Ben Aphlul." Yadin, Pp. 137-138

Some have maintained that the "Galileans" referred to are the Talmidei Yeshua, since many of the original disciples were from Galilee, as was Yeshua. Yadin, however, does not agree. He maintains that the term was often used in its normal geographical sense to describe others, like Rabbi Jose the Galilean.

For two additional reasons, it would appear that Yadin is correct. 1) The Rabbis sometimes called the Talmidei Yeshua "Talmidei Yeshu," or "minim," or "Nazarenes," but we have no record of their calling them "Galileans." Even today, the Hebrew word for "Christians" is "Nazarenes" (Notzrim, נוצרין). 2)

The evidence shows that the inhabitants of the Galilee did not participate in the revolt - at least not to its conclusion. That would have brought forth Bar Kokhba's threat.

In Bar Kokhba's eyes, of course, the Talmidei Yeshua were guilty of the same crime.

10. In one discussion on the proper means of execution for a particular offender, "R. Joseph queried: (Do we need) to fix a halacha for (the day of) the Messiah?" The footnote adds, "Since the Sanhedrin no longer had jurisdiction in capital offences, there is no practical utility in this ruling, which can become effective only in the days of the Messiah." Sanh. 51b

Rabbi Joseph's question demonstrates the traditional understanding that when Messiah is enthroned, the Sanhedrin would again have the authority to put to death those guilty of capital offenses. Another rabbi challenges R. Joseph's conclusion - that the halachah did not need to be fixed - but, in so doing, confirms the tradition that in the days of Messiah, the Sanhedrin will have such authority.

28. THE TRIAL

1. Mendels, P.166
2. The life of Simeon b. Shetah illustrates both aspects. "Straightway, the evil burst forth through Eleazar son of Po'irah, all the Sages of Israel were massacred, and the world was desolate until Simeon b. Shetah came and restored the Torah to its pristine [glory]." Kid.66a What did Simeon b. Shetah do that "restored the Torah to its pristine [glory]"?

"The sages say: 'A man is hanged, but not a woman. Whereupon R. Eliezer said to them: but did not Simeon b. Shetah hang women at Ashkelon? They retorted: [On that occasion] he hanged eighty women, notwithstanding that two [malefactors] must not be tried on the same day.'" [Sanh. VI,6] Sanh.45b To 'restore the Torah to its pristine glory,' Simeon b. Shetah killed those who stood in the way. In the urgency of the moment, he violated regular halakha.

3. Sifra, Kedoshim, perek 4.9, Arakin 16b in Finkelstein, <u>Akiba</u>, P.113
4. Alon, <u>Jews</u>, Pp.220-221 citing Baraita Eruvin 21b
5. Quoted by Eusebius in <u>Ecclesiastical History</u>, cited in Yadin, P.258
6. Quoted in Parkes, <u>The Conflict of the Church and the Synagogue</u>, P.126 Justin speaks of "Christians", but it was specifically the Talmidei Yeshua who were so treated. Justin, later Church writers, and many historians did not make the distinction.
7. Eusebius, Chronicle, cited in Bar Kokhba, Yadin, P.258
8. Moed Katan 16a

Bethar

9. "Rab Judah said in Rab's name: A Sanhedrin must not be established in a city which does not contain (at least) two who can speak (the seventy languages) and one who understands them. In the city of Bethar there were three and in Jabneh four (who knew how to speak them): R. Eliezer, R. Joshua, R. Akiba, and Simeon the Temanite..." Sanh.17b
10. Abramsky, P.230
11. Alon, <u>The Jews in their Land</u>, Vol. II, P.626
12. Mishneh Torah, Mamrim 2:4 in Sacks in <u>Rabbinic Authority</u>, P.138
13. Maimonides, P.323 [Kings 3]

14. Sanh. 43a

15. Herford, Christianity, P. 94 Earlier, Herford explains, "I suggest that the case stand thus: - five disciples of Jesus, i.e. five Christians, were on some occasion condemned to death, that their real names, if known, were not mentioned, that one of them was designated Matthai with reference to the name attached to the first Gospel, that the play upon his name suggested a similar device in the case of the others, and that for them other names were invented, each of which had some reference to Jesus, as regarded of course by Christians. Thus Naqi, the innocent, is obviously applicable to Jesus from the Christian point of view, and is as obviously satirical from that of the Rabbis, as already shown....

"These are said to have been condemned to death; and when they quoted Scripture texts as a plea for their lives, they were met with other texts demolishing their plea. That any tribunal of justice, or of arbitrary violence, ever conducted its business in such a manner, it is hard to believe; and we can only regard this fencing with texts as a jeu d'esprit, occasioned no doubt by some actual event. That event would naturally be an execution of Christian disciples, if such took place. The dialogue as given in the Talmud can certainly not be taken as historical; but it may yet give some indication of the historical circumstances under which it was composed..." Herford, Pp. 93, 92

"Netzer", branch, was a recognized Messianic title, appearing in Is.11:1 and Zech.6:12. "Beni", My Son, is what God calls Messiah in Ps.2:6. It is what the gospels say that God said to Yeshua at his baptism - Mt.3:17 - and on the Mt. of Transfiguration - Mt.17:5.

16. Dalman, Pp. 74-75 Dalman's analysis seems accurate, but his phrasing is not. In speaking of "the hatred of Judaism towards Christianity", he is distorting the issue. It is the same error we have seen before, only on the other side. It would be accurate to replace it with "the hatred of the Rabbis toward the Talmidei Yeshua." Though the Rabbis had no love for the Gentile minim, this was still essentially a conflict between two different groups of Jews.

17. In the trial of a blasphemer, "The blasphemer is punished only if he utters (the Divine) Name. R. Joshua B. Karha said: The whole day (of the trial) the witnesses are examined by means of a substitute for the Divine Name, thus, 'May Jose smite Jose.'" Sanh. 7.7

"According to Levy, ...the first Jose stands for Jesus (huios, son), and the second is an abbreviation of Joseph, the Father, by which, however, God was to be understood. The witnesses were accordingly asked whether the accused in his blasphemy had set Jesus above God." Sanh. 7.7n.

18. Ginzberg, "Akiba," P.308 Earlier in his life, Akiba had championed a lenient position against capital punishment. In the tractate Makkoth, i.e. "beatings," "R. Tarfon and R. Akiba say: Were we members of a Sanhedrin, no person would ever be put to death. (Thereupon) Rabban Simeon b. Gamaliel remarked, (Yea) and they would also multiply shedders of blood in Israel!" Makkoth 1:10

At that time, Akiba was involved in his ongoing struggle against the leadership of the Academy. As we have previously seen, Akiba would readily hold to an occasional position that was not really his own in order to overcome an opponent. His actual position concerning capital punishment was quite different than what he had argued before he was on the Sanhedrin.

When the Rabbis had gained control, Rabbi Akiba made it clear, as already noted, that "He who does not serve the sages is worthy of death."

19. Avoth 5. 8

20. Sanh. 7:1 49b None of them evidenced any mercy. For example, "The manner in which burning is executed is as follows: He who had been thus condemned was lowered into dung up to his armpits; then a hard cloth was placed within a soft one, wound round his neck, and the two loose ends pulled in opposite directions, forcing him to open his mouth. a wick was then lit, and thrown into his mouth, so that it descended into his body and burnt his bowels....R. Eleazar b. Zadok said: It once happened that a priest's daughter committed adultery, whereupon bundles of faggots were placed round about her and she was burnt. The Sages replied, that was because the Beth Din at that time was not well learned in law." M. Sanh. 7:2, P.349 The other means of execution were similar.

21. Sanh. 63a

29. THE END OF THE REVOLT
The Loss of Life

1. A. Cohen, trans., "Lamentations," in Midrash Rabbah, Vol. 4, edited by H. Freedman & Maurice Simon, Soncino Press, London, 1977, II. 2, sec.4, P.157

2. Ibid, P.159 cf. Git. 57a: "R. Zera said in the name of R. Abbahu who quoted R. Johanan: These are the eighty [thousand] battle trumpets which assembled in the city of Bethar when it was taken and men, women and children were slain in it until their blood ran into the great sea. Do you think this was near? It was a whole mile away. It has been taught: R. Eleazar the Great said: There are two streams in the valley of Yadaim, one running in one direction and one in another, and the Sages estimated that [at that time] they ran with two parts water to one of blood. In a Baraitha it has been taught: For seven years the Gentiles fertilised their vineyards with the blood of Israel without using manure."

3. Dio, Roman History, cited in Yadin, P.257

4. Mid. Lam., II. 2, sec.4 Footnote: "Rashash emends: R. Simeon b. Gamaliel." cf. Git.58a: "Rab Judah reported Samuel as saying in the name of Rabban Simeon b. Gamaliel; What is signified by the verse, Mine eye affecteth my soul, because of all the daughters of my city? There were four hundred synagogues in the city of Bethar, and in every one were four hundred teachers of children, and each one had under him four hundred pupils, and when the enemy entered there they pierced them with their staves, and when the enemy prevailed and captured them, they wrapped them in their scrolls and burnt them with fire."

5. Mid. Lam., II. 2, sec.4

6. Isaac & Oppenheimer, n121; yTa'anit iv 69a; Lamentations Rabbah ii 4

7. Ta'anith 31a, P.163

The Exile and Slavery

8. Chronicon Paschale in Oppenheimer, P.74

9. Eusebius, Ecclesiastical History, IV, 6, translated by K. Lake, The Loeb Classical Library, Vol.I, Pp.311-313 cited in Yadin, P.258

10. "After the revolt, the Romans issued a number of decrees of religious persecution against the Jews there, but although they interfered with several aspects of religious life, their purpose was not the suppression of Jewish religion as such. Their tendency was to suppress those elements in the Jewish religion which were of national significance and to abolish the autonomy of the Jewish people." Isaac & Oppenheimer, P.59

"The Bar Kokhba revolt, which took place in 132-135 C.E., was the last serious attempt in antiquity to restore the independence of the Jewish people in its own country.

"...The aftermath of this revolt was also more drastic than that of the preceding ones, not only because of the number of casualties and captives sold into slavery, but also because of the ensuing persecution and martyrdom, and the dire economic crisis as the population of Judaea diminished and the center moved to Galilee, and emigration from Eretz Yisrael to the Diaspora increased." Oppenheimer, P.58

"The focus of Jewish life was transferred to Galilee and the authorities established Ushah in Lower Galilee as their centre. Refugees moved from Judaea to Galilee, as is illustrated by the organization of priestly courses in settlements in Galilee. Most of these courses were in Judaea in the period of the Second Temple." Isaac & Oppenheimer, P.54

"Judea" Becomes "Palestine"
11. Harkabi, P.48

30. THE FINAL SPLIT

1. Hugh Trevor-Roper, The Times (London), Library Supplement, 7/25/80; Harkabi, P.77

2. "In those days, the Jewish-Christians were very near to the Jews. They differed only in faith. Their contacts were all with Jews, and they interpreted the Jewish law in the name of their master; they attended the synagogues and the Apostles preached in the synagogues." Lehman, P.130 The Jewish-Christians were **not** "very near to the Jews," they **were** Jews.

"It is well known that Christianity and Judaism drew further and further apart in the Jabneh period. The Bar Kokhba revolt can be viewed as the culmination of that process and its termination, as even Christian sects that had still wished to maintainsome connection with Judaism were kept at a distance." Oppenheimer, P.73

3. Justin Martyr, The Dialogue with Trypho, trans. A. Lukyn Williams, Pp.32-34 16.2-4 Justin also moderates his tone: P. 224 108.3: "In addition to all this, although your city has been taken, and your land laid waste, you do not repent, but dare even to curse Him and all them that believe on Him. And, as for us, we do not hate you, nor them that because of you accept such suspicions of us, but we pray that even now you may repent and find mercy from God the Father of the universe, who is tender-hearted and full of compassion."

Eusebius does not: "The Jewish War that was conducted in Palestine reached its conclusion, all Jewish problems having been completely suppressed. From that time (on), the permission was denied them even to enter Jerusalem; first and foremost because of the commandment of God, as the prophets had prophesied; and secondly by authority of the interdictions of the Romans." Chronicon Paschale, cited in Yadin, P.258

Like Dio Cassius, Eusebius saw the tragic outcome as the judgment of God. Both the Church and the Empire saw it that way. It was a resolution of "all Jewish problems." That is a haunting phrase.

4. Cf. Acts 15:1-31; 21:15-26
5. Chron. Pasc. cited in Yadin, P.258
6. Williams, Adversus Judaeos, P.134; John Crysostom, Homilies Against the Jews, c.347-407 Chrysostom's statement is evidence that Jews were still in the land in significant numbers through the end of the fourth century.
7. Weimarer Ausgabe 50:336, 1-6, Quoted in Heiko Oberman, The Roots of Anti-Semitism in the Age of Renaissance and Reformation, Fortress Press, Philadelphia, 1983, P.64

"Or if such an event fails to come about, then let them head for Jerusalem, build temples, set up priesthoods, principalities, Moses with his laws, and in other words themselves become Jews again and take the land into their possession. For when this happens, they will see us come quickly on their heels and likewise become Jews. But if not, then it is entirely ludicrous that they should want to persuade us into accepting their degenerate laws, which are surely by now after fifteen hundred years of decay no longer laws at all. And should we believe what they themselves do not and cannot believe, as long as they do not have Jerusalem and the land of Israel?" WA 50:323, 36-324, 8 in ibid., P.64

8. Weimarer Ausgabe 51:196,16f.; cf. ibid. 53:530,25-28; 31f, Quoted in Oberman, P.113
9. Mish. Abot 4:2

31. RABBI AKIBA'S MARTYRDOM

1. Bader, P.307 citing Pesahim 69a
2. Sanh.68a
3. "In the wake of the Bar Kokhba revolt the Romans promulgated a series of anti-Jewish measures known as the 'persecutions.' They prohibited various practices such as wearing phylacteries, fringes, fixing the mezuza to doorposts, eating unleavened bread on Passover, lighting candles on Hanuka, etc. They also banned the ordination of sages, and gathering in study houses and synagogues, and any assembling for the study or teaching of the Torah. The purpose of these prohibitions was to undermine the elements of Judaism that have nationalist implications, destroy the internal leadership of the Jewish people.

"...While the edicts were strictly enforced only during Hadrian's lifetime, that is, till 138 C.E., the Bar Kokhba revolt had longer-lasting results. Among them was the reconstruction of Jerusalem as Aelia Capitolina, which Jews were forbidden to live in or even approach. Another effect was a grave depression, arising partly from the wholesale devastation and partly from the heavy taxes levied by the Romans. Much of the population was unable to cope with the economic crisis, and a considerable emigration ensued. Most of the emigrants left for Babylonia, which already had a Jewish population established since the destruction of the First Temple, and which was outside the Roman Empire.

The evolution of the Babylonian center in competition with the center in Eretz Yisrael began in the period following the Bar Kokhba revolt. The Usha sages made a great effort to stop the emigration and formulated a long series of regulations designed to do so." Oppenheimer, Pp.74-75

4. "Finally Akiba was brought to trial; his judge was to be his former friend Rufus. There was no possible defense against the charges; Akiba had violated the Law by offering instruction to his disciples. Yet Joshua ha-Garsi, standing in the open Court, at a little distance from the prisoner, and in front of the grim Roman general, prayed that somehow the aged scholar might be saved. But even as the half-smothered words came from his mouth, he noticed a cloud covering the sun and the sky. 'I knew then that our prayer was useless,' he said, 'for it is written, 'Thou hast covered Thyself with a cloud, so that no prayer can pass through.'" Finkelstein, Akiba, P.276 citing Lam. R. 3:44 Proof was brought from a cloud.

5. "Rufus, the Roman general who superintended the horrible execution, cried out: 'Are you a wizard or are you utterly insensible to pain?' 'I am neither,' replied the martyr, 'but all my life I have been waiting for the moment when I might truly fulfill this commmandment. I have always loved the Lord with all my might, and with all my heart; now I know that I love him with all my life.' And, repeating the verse again, he died as he reached the words, 'The Lord is One.'" Ibid., P.276 (B. Berakot 61b; Yer. ib. 9.5, 14b; Lam. R. loc. cit.)

6. Harkabi, P.88 citing Sem.2:18

7. J. H. Hertz, The Pentateuch and Haftorahs, P. 922 During the communist and Nazi persecutions which followed R. Hertz's remarks, the response remained the same.

8. Sotah 49b

A Theology of Suffering

9. E.P. Sanders, "Rabbi Akiba's View of Suffering," Jewish Quarterly Review, 63:4, 4/73, P.334 In Men.29b, Moses asks to see Akiba's reward. The Lord told him to turn around, "and Moses turned round and saw them weighing out his flesh at the market-stalls. 'Lord of the Universe', cried Moses, 'such Torah, and such a reward!' He replied, 'Be silent, for such is My decree'."

10. Mid. Lam., II. 2, sec.4

11. Ber. 3a

12. Harkabi, xvi ומפני חטאינו גלינו מארצנו ונתרחקנו מעל אדמתנו High Holiday Prayer Book, compiled by Morris Silverman, Prayer Book Press, Hartford, 1949, e.g. P.127

13. Ezek. 39:23 cf. Isa. 5:13: "Therefore My people are gone into captivity for lack of understanding; their honorable men will die of hunger and their multitudes will be parched with thirst."

14. An "anonymous" Master in Ber. 56a In contrast to this view of exile, a later Midrash attributes redemptive and protective power to the rabbinic teaching. "All who occupy themselves in the study of Torah are saved from oppression by the ruling powers...the disciples of the wise remove the yoke of exile from themselves." Mid Tanh., end, in Harkabi, P.95

15. Sanh.VI, 2

16. Sanh. 101a: "When R. Eliezer fell sick, his disciples entered (his house) to visit him. He said to them, 'There is a fierce wrath in the world.' They broke

into tears, but R. Akiba laughed. 'Why dost thou laugh?' they enquired of him. 'Why do ye weep?' he retorted. They answered, 'Shall the Scroll of the Torah [I.e., R. Eliezer] lie in pain, and we not weep?' - He replied, 'For that very reason I rejoice. As long as I saw that my master's wine did not turn sour, nor was his flax smitten, nor his oil putrefied, nor his honey become rancid, I thought, God forbid, that he may have received all his reward in this world (leaving nothing for the next); but now that I see him lying in pain, I rejoice (knowing that his reward has been treasured up for him in the next)." He (R. Eliezer) said to him, 'Akiba, have I neglected anything of the whole Torah?' - He replied, 'Thou, O master, hast taught us, "For there is not a just man upon earth, that doeth good and sinneth not."' (citing Eccl.7:20)

Akiba reminded Eliezer that every man sins, and has therefore earned Divine punishment. Akiba saw Eliezer's pain as the earthly punishment of God for Eliezer's sins. That meant that in the world to come, Eliezer would not be punished, but would only receive his due reward. That is why Akiba rejoiced.

17. Psalm 36:6 (36:7 in Hebrew), says "Thy righteousness is like the great mountains; Thy judgments are like a great deep. O Lord, Thou preservest man and beast." In commenting on it, Akiba said, "He [God] deals strictly with both, even to the great deep. He deals strictly with the righteous, calling them to account for the few wrongs which they commit in this world, in order to lavish bliss upon and give them a goodly reward in the world to come; he grants ease to the wicked and rewards them for the few good deeds which they have performed in this world in order to punish them in the future world." Sanders, P.337, citing Breshith Rabbah 33:1 Cf. Pesikta of R. Kahana, Shor, 73a; Lev. R. 27:1

18. Sanh. 101

19. Sanh. 101a, P.687n

20. Mekilta Bahodesh 10; Sifre Deut. on 6.5, sec.32., in Davies, Paul, P.263

21. Pirke de R. Eliezer 43a in Harkabi, Pp.160-1 The blessings of obedience, laid out in Dt.28:1-8 and elsewhere, is the complementary aspect of this view.

22. "The willingness to offer one's life has become a means of effecting mediation between God and Israel, a radical means especially necessary in the face of a reduction in traditional prophecy. Henry Fischel has taken special note of the phenomenon found in Jewish and Christian literature whereby the prophet is viewed as a martyr and the martyr as a prophet. The process is linked in turn to the concept of vicarious suffering. Thus the prophet's martyrdom is for the sake of Israel). This notion lies behind the midrash complex associated with the sacrifice of Isaac. One excellent example is found in Mekhilta Pisha 7, an interpretation of 'And when I see the blood':

"I see the blood of the binding of Isaac. For it is said, 'And Abraham called the name of the place "The Lord will see"' etc. (Gen.22,14). And it says elsewhere, 'And as he was about to destroy, the Lord beheld and he repented (of the evil...)' etc. (1Chron.21,15). What did he see? He saw the blood of the binding of Isaac as it is said, 'God will for himself see the lamb' etc (Gen. 22,8) (Pisha 7, 11.78-82; see also 11.92-96).

"The martyr, like the meritorious ancestor hero, can intercede between God and Israel." Susan Niditch, "Merits, Martyrs, and 'Your Life as Booty'," JSJ, Dec. 1982, Pp.166-167

23. cf. W. Bacher, Agada der Tannaiten, 2nd ed., 1903, i. 269. in Ehrhardt, 111

24. Examining all those conclusions and their development would be quite an enterprise in itself, but one example is especially relevant here. Akiba's emphasis led to the view that God goes into exile with His people.

"So far I only know that He shares in the affliction of the community. How about the affliction of the individual? Scripture says: 'He shall call upon Me, and I will answer him; I will be with him in trouble' (Ps.91:15). It also says: 'And Joseph's master took him,' etc. (Gen.39:20). And what does it say then? 'But the Lord was with Joseph' (ibid., 39:21, And thus it says: 'From before Thy people, whom Thou didst redeem to Thyself out of Egypt, the nation and its God' (2 Sam. 7:23)....R. Akiba says: Were it not expressly written in Scripture, it would be impossible to say it. Israel said to God: Thou hadst redeemed Thyself, as though one could conceive such a thing. Likewise you find that whithersoever Israel was exiled, the Shekhinah went into exile with them. When they went into exile to Egypt, the Shekhinah went into exile with them, as it is said; 'I exiled Myself unto the house of thy fathers when they were in Egypt (1 Sam.2:27). When they were exiled to Babylon, the Shekhinah went into exile with them, as it is said: 'For your sake I ordered Myself to go to Babylon' (Is. 43:14)." Mekhilta d'Rabbi Ishmael, Massekhet d'Pisha, parashah 14 in Norman J. Cohen, P.151

This is a beautifully poetic representation of how closely God feels the suffering of His people. What is missing, however, is the sense Jeremiah and all the prophets had that exile is God's long-delayed judgment for turning away from Him.

32. SOME CONCLUDING REMARKS

1. R. Eliezer's response is worth repeating: "Akiba! ...you would erase what is written in Torah!" Pes.66a

2. Alon, Jews, P. 412

3. Finkelstein, Akiba, Pp.119-120 citing Mishna Rosh HaShanah 2.8,9

4. Centuries later, the Karaites rose in rebellion against the Rabbis. For several centuries, they championed a rejection of rabbinic authority and a return to Tanakh. The movement subsided, however, though there are still a few small Karaite communities in existence.

5. Basser, P. 111

BIBLIOGRAPHY

1. Abramsky, Samuel, "Bar Kochba," Encyclopedia Judaica, Keter Publishing House, Ltd., Jerusalem, 1971, Vol.2, Pp.229-239
2. "Akiba," Encyclopedia Judaica, Keter Publishing House Ltd., Jerusalem, 1971, Vol.2, Pp.488-492
3. Alexander, P.S., review of Peter Schafer, Der Bar Kokhba-Aufstand: Studien zum zweiten judischen Krieg gegen Rom, Journal of Jewish Studies [JJS], Vol.XXXV, No.1, Spr. '84, Pp.103-105
4. Alon, Gedalyahu, Jews, Judaism, and the Classical World, translated by Israel Abrahams, The Magnes Press, Jerusalem, 1977
5. Alon, Gedalia, The Jews in Their Land in the Talmudic Age, Magnes Press, Jerusalem, 1980
6. The Apocrypha; An American Translation, translated by Edgar J. Goodspeed, Vintage Books, NY, 1959
7. Arnold, Eberhard, The Early Christians after the Death of the Apostles, Plough Publishing House, Rifton, NY, 1972
8. Aufstieg und Niedergang Der Romischen Welt, II, Religion, Walter de Gruyter, Berlin, 1979
    Bernard S. Jackson, "The Concept of Religious Law in Judaism," Pp.33-52
    Ithamar Gruenwald, "Jewish Apocalyptic Literature," Pp.89-118
    James H. Charlesworth, "The Concept of the Messiah in the Pseudepigrapha," Pp.188-218
    Bilhah Wardy, "Jewish Religion in Pagan Literature during the Late Republic and Early Empire," Pp.592-644
    Meyers, Eric M., "The Cultural Setting of Galilee: The Case of Regionalism and Early Judaism," Pp.686-702
9. Aune, David E., "Orthodoxy in First Century Judaism? A Response to N. J. McEleney," Journal for the Study of Judaism in the Persian, Hellenistic and Roman Period [JSJ], Vol VII, June 1976, No.1, Pp.3
10. "Authority, Rabbinical," The Jewish Encyclopedia, Vol.2, ed. Isidore Singer, Funk & Wagnalls Co., NY, 1909, Pp.337-338
11. Avi Yonah, Michael, The Jews Under Roman and Byzantine Rule, Schocken Books, NY, 1984
12. The Babylonian Talmud, edited by Rabbi Dr. Isidore Epstein, Soncino Press, London, 1978
13. The Babylonian Talmud, edited by Rabbi Dr. Isidore Epstein, Soncino Press, London, 1978 on CD-ROM, Davka Corp.
14. Bader, Gershom, The Jewish Spiritual Heroes, Vol. I,

translated by Solomon Katz, Pardes Publishing House, NY

15. "Bar Kokba and the Bar Kokba War," in The Jewish Encyclopedia, Vol. 2, Edited by Isidore Singer, Funk and Wagnalls, NY & London, 1906

16. Basser, Herbert, "The Development of the Pharisaic Idea of Law as a Sacred Cosmos," JSJ, Vol.XVI, 6/85, no.1, Pp.104-116

17. Baumgarten, J.M., "The Unwritten Law in the Pre-Rabbinic Period," JSJ, Vol.III, no.1, 10/72, Pp.7-29

18. Berkovits, Eliezer, Not in Heaven: the Nature and Function of Halakha, Ktav Publishing Co., NY, 1983

19. Bowersock, G. W., "A Roman Perspective on the Bar Kokhba War," in Approaches to Ancient Judaism, Vol. II, edited by William Scott Green, Scholars Press, Chico, CA., 1980

20. Bowman, John, The Fourth Gospel and the Jews—A Study in Rabbi Akiba, Esther, and the Gospel of John, The Pickwick Press, Pittsburgh, PA., 1975

21. The Canon and Masorah of the Hebrew Bible, ed. by Sid Z. Leiman, Ktav Publishing House, NY, 1974

22. Charlesworth, James H., Jesus Within Judaism, Doubleday, NY, 1988

23. Charlesworth, James H., "Reinterpreting John," Bible Review, P.19-25, 54

24. Cohen, Norman J., "Shekhinta ba-Galuta: A Midrashic Response to Destruction and Persecution," JSJ, Dec. 1982, Pp.147-171

25. Cohen, Shaye J.D., "The Significance of Yavneh: Pharisees, Rabbis, and the End of Jewish Sectarianism," Hebrew Union College Annual 55, 1984, Pp.27-53

26. Cohen, Stuart A., The Three Crowns: Structure of Communal Politics in Early Rabbinic Jewry, Cambridge U. Press, Cambridge, 1990

27. Collins, J.J., The Apocalyptic Imagination: An Introduction to the Jewish Matrix of Christianity, Crossroad Publishing Co., NY,1984

28. Dalman, Gustaf, Jesus Christ in the Talmud, Midrash, Zohar and the Liturgy of the Synagogue, Arno Press, NY, 1973 (1893)

29. Daniel to Paul, edited by Gaalyahu Cornfeld, MacMillan, NY, 1962

30. Daube, David, "Rabbinic Methods of Interpretation and Hellenistic Rhetoric," HUCA, XXII, 1949

31. Davies, W.D., Torah in the Messianic Age and/or the Age to Come, Society of Biblical Literature, Philadelphia,1952

32. Davies, W.D., Paul and Rabbinic Judaism; Some Rabbinic Elements in Pauline Theology, SPCK, London, 1948

33. Dio Cassius, Dio's Rome, trans. Herbert B. Foster, Fifth Vol., Pafraets Book Co.,Troy, NY, 1906
34. Donin, Hayim Halevy, To Be a Jew, Basic Books, 1991
35. Early Judaism and its Modern Interpreters, ed. by Robert A. Kraft, & George W.E. Nickelsburg, Fortress Press, Phila., 1986
36. Edersheim, Alfred, The Life and Times of Jesus the Messiah, Anson D.F. Randolph and Company, New York, 1883, Vol. I, Pp.371-2
37. Ehrhardt, Arnold A.T., "Birth of the Synagogue and R. Akiba," Studia Theologica: Scandinavian Journal of Theology, v.9, No.2, Pp.86-111, 1955
38. Elman, Yaakov, "R. Zadok HaKohen on the History of Halakha," Tradition: A Journal of Orthodox Jewish Thoughts, Vol.21, No.4, Pp.1-26
39. Finkelstein, Louis, "Akiba", in Great Jewish Personalities in Ancient and Medieval Times, Bnai Brith Great Books Series: Vol.1, edited by Simon Noveck, 1973
40. Finkelstein, Louis, Akiba: Scholar, Saint and Martyr, Atheneum, NY, 1978
41. Gerhardson, Birger, Memory and Manuscript: Oral Tradition and Written Tranmission in Rabbinic Judaism and Early Christianity, trans. E.J. Sharpe, Lund, Gleerup, 1961
42. Ginzburg, Louis, "Akiba ben Joseph" & "Aquila", in The Jewish Encyclopedia, Vols. 1 & 2, Edited by Isidore Singer, Funk and Wagnalls, NY & London, 1906
43. Goldenberg, R. "Early Rabbinic Explanations of the Destruction of Jerusalem," JJS, Vol.33, 1982, Pp.517-525
44. Goldstein, R. Morris, Jesus in the Jewish Tradition, The Macmillan Co., NY, 1950
45. Goodblatt, D., "The Place of the Pharisees in First Century Judaism: The State of the Debate," JSJ, Vol.XX, no.1, 6/89, 26-27,
46. Gordon, Cyrus, "Jewish Reaction to Christian Borrowings," Pp.685-690
47. Greek and Latin Authors on Jews and Judaism, Vol. 2, edited by Menahem Stern, The Israel Academy of Science and Humanities, Jerusalem, 1980
48. Gruber, Mayer I., "The Mishnah as Oral Torah: A Reconsideration," JSJ, Vol.XV, 1984, Pp.112-122
49. Guttmann, Alexander, Rabbinic Judaism in the Making, Wayne State U. Press, Detroit, 1970
50. Harkabi, Yehoshaphat, The Bar Kochba Syndrome—Risk and Realism in International Politics, Rossel Books, Chappaqua, NY, 1983
51. Herford, R. Travers, Judaism in the New Testament Period,

The Lindsey Press, London, 1928

52. Herford, R. Travers, <u>Christianity in Talmud and Midrash</u>, Reference Book Publishers, Clifton, NJ, 1966

53. Himmelfarb, Gertrude, <u>The New History and the Old</u>, The Belknap Press of Harvard U. Press, Cambridge, MA, 1987

54. <u>The Holy Scriptures</u>, The Jewish Publication Society, Philadelphia, 1917

55. Horsley, Richard A., "High Priests and the Politics of Roman Palestine: A Contextual Analysis of the Evidence in Josephus," <u>JSJ, 17</u>, 1986, Pp.23-55

56. A.Z. Idelsohn, Jewish Liturgy and Its Development, Schocken Books, NY, 1967, P.xix

57. Isaac, Benjamin, and Oppenheimer, Aharon, "The Revolt of Bar Kokhba: Ideology and Modern Scholarship," <u>Journal of Jewish Studies</u>, Vol.XXXV, No.1, Spring 1985, Pp.33-60

58. Jagersma, Henk, <u>A History of Israel from Alexander the Great to Bar Kokhba</u>, Fortress Press, Philadelphia, 1986

59. Josephus, Flavius, <u>The Works of Josephus</u>, translated by William Whiston, Hendrickson Publishers, Peabody, MA., 1985

60. <u>Judaisms and Their Messiahs at the Turn of the Christian Era</u>, ed. J Neusner et al., Cambridge U. Press, Cambridge, 1987

61. Kirschner, R., "Apocalyptic and Rabbinic Responses to the Destruction of 70," <u>Harvard Theological Review 78</u>, 1985, Pp.27-46

62. "Lamentations" and "Ecclesiastes", translated by A. Cohen, in <u>Midrash Rabbah, Vol. 4</u>, edited by H. Freedman & Maurice Simon, Soncino Press, London, 1977

63. Lehman, Marcus, <u>Akiba: The Story of Rabbi Akiba and His Times</u>, translated by Joseph Leftwich, Phillip Feldheim Inc., NY, 1956

64. Levine, Etan, The Aramaic Version of the Bible, de Gruyter, NY, 1988

65. Levine, Lee I., "The Nature and Origin of the Palestinean Synagogue Reconsidered," Journal of Biblical Literature, 115/3, 1966, Pp.425-448

66. Longenecker, Richard N., <u>The Christology of Early Jewish Christianity</u>, Alec R. Allenson Inc., Naperville, IL, 1970

67. Longenecker, Richard N., <u>Biblical Exegesis in the Apostolic Period</u>, Wm. B. Eerdmans Pub. Co., Grand Rapids,1975

68. Maimonides, Moses, "The Epistle to Yemen [to Jacob al-Fayyumi]," <u>Crisis and Leadership: Epistles of Maimonidies</u>, trans. by Abraham Halkin, Jewish Publication Society, Philadelphia, 1985

69. Maimonides, Moses, <u>Mishneh Torah</u>, (Yad Hazakah), Ed. by Philip Birnbaum, Hebrew Publishing Co., NY, 1985

70. Mantel, Hugo, "The Causes of the Bar Kochba Revolt", in The Jewish Quarterly Review, Vol. 58, #3 & #4, Philadelphia, 1968

71. Mantel, H.D., Studies in the History of the Sanhedrin, Harvard U. Press, Cambridge, 1961

72. Matar, N.I., "The Idea of the Restoration of the Jews in English Protestant Thought, 1661-1701", Harvard Theological Review 78, 1985, Pp.115-148

73. Mendels, Doron, The Rise and Fall of Jewish Nationalism, Jewish and Christian Ethnicity in Ancient Palestine, Doubleday, NY, 1992

74. The Messiah, ed. J. H. Charlesworth, Fortress Press, Minn., 1992

75. Midrash Rabbah, Exodus, trans. by S. M. Lehrman, Soncino, London, 1939

76. Midrash Rabbah, Leviticus, trans. by Judah Slotki, Soncino, London, 1939

77. Midrash Rabbah, Soncino Press, London, on CD-ROM, Davka Corp.

78. Moore, G.F., Judaism in the First Centuries of the Christian Era, Vols. 1-3, Harvard U. Press, Cambridge, 1927-40

79. New American Standard Bible, The Lockman Foundation, Holman Bible Publishers, Nashville, TN, 1981

80. Neusner, Jacob, Early Rabbinic Judaism: Historical Studies in Religion, Literature, and Art, E.J. Brill, Leiden, 1975

81. Neusner, Jacob, Our Sages, God, and Israel: An Anthology of the Talmud of the Land of Israel, Rossel Books, Chappaqua, NY, 1984

82. Neusner, Jacob, "The Use of the Mishnah for the History of Judaism Prior to the Time of the Mishnah," JSJ, Vol.11, No.2, 12/80, pp.177-185

83. New International Version, with Biblia Hebraica Stuttgartensia, 1983 and Greek New Testament, 1993, MacBible 3.0

84. Niditch, Susan, "Merits, Martyrs, and 'Your Life as Booty', JSJ, Dec. 1982

85. Oberman, Heiko, The Roots of Anti-Semitism in the Age of Renaissance and Reformation, Fortress Press, Phila., 1983

86. Oppenheimer, Aharon, "The Bar Kokhba Revolt," translated by N. Handelman, Immanuel: A Bulletin of Religious Thoughts and Research in Israel, Vol.14, 1982, Pp.58-72

87. Parkes, James, The Conflict of the Church and the Synagogue, Atheneum, NY, 1969

88. The Pentateuch and Haftorahs, edited by Dr. J. H. Hertz, Soncino Press, London, 1958

89. <u>The Pentateuch and Rashi's Commentary, Numbers</u>, edited by Abraham Ben Isaiah and Benhamin Sharfman, S.S.& R. Pub. Co., Brooklyn, 1949

90. <u>Rabbinic Authority and Personal Autonomy</u>, edited by Moshe Sokol, Jason Aronson Inc., Northvale, NJ, 1992

Lawrence Kaplan, "Daas Torah: A Modern Conception of Rabbinic Authority," Pp.1-60

Aaron Kirschenbaum, "Subjectivity in Rabbinic Decision-Making," Pp.61-91

Michael Rosensweig, "Eilu ve-Eilu Divrei Elohim Hayyim: Halakhic Pluralism and Theories of Controversy," Pp.93-122

Jonathan Sacks, "Creativity and Innovation in Halakhah," Pp.123-168

Moshe Sokol, "Personal Autonomy and Religious Authority," Pp.169-216

I. Waxman, "Toward a Sociology of Pesak," Pp.217-237

91. Reznick, Liebel, <u>The Holy Temple Revisited</u>, Jason Aronson, Inc., Northvale, NJ, 1993

92. Roth, Sol, <u>Halakhah and Politics: The Jewish Idea of the State</u>, Ktav Publishing House, NY, 1988

93. Sanders, Dr. E. P., "Rabbi Akiba's View of Suffering", in <u>The Jewish Quarterly Review, Vol. 63, #4</u>, 1973

94. Sandmel, Samuel, "The Jewish Scholars and Early Christianity", in the <u>75th Anniversary Volume of The Jewish Quarterly Review</u>, edited by Abraham A. Neuman & Solomon Zeitlin, Philadelphia, 1975

95. Schafer, P., "Rabbi Akiba and Bar Kokhba," in <u>Approaches to Ancient Judaism, Vol. II</u>, edited by William Scott Green, Scholars Press, Chico, CA., 1980

96. Schafer, Peter, review of Martin Goodman, State and Society in Roman Galilee, A.D. 132-212, <u>JJS</u>, Vol.XXXV, No.1, Pp.103-105

97. Schaff, Philip, <u>History of the Christian Church, Vol.II</u>, Charles Scribners' Sons, NY, 1883

98. Schiffman, Lawrence H., <u>Who Was a Jew—Rabbinic and Halakhic Perspectives on the Jewish Christian Schism</u>, Ktav Publishing, Hoboken, NJ, 1985

99. Schurer, Emil, <u>The History of the Jewish People in the Age of Jesus Christ</u>, revised and edited by Geza Vermes and Fergus Millar, T & T Clark Ltd., Edinburgh, 1973

100. Schurer, Emil, <u>A History of the Jewish People in the Time of Jesus</u>, edited by Nahum Glatzer, Schocken Books, NY, 1967

101. Schwartz, Daniel R., "Josephus and Nicolaus on the Pharisees," <u>JSJ</u>, Vol.XIV, 12/83, no.2

102. Shimoff, Sandra R., "Hellenization among the Rabbis:

Some Evidence from Early Aggadot concerning David and Solomon," JSJ, XVIII, no.2, Dec. 1987

103. Silberman, Neil Asher, "Searching for Jesus," Archaelogy, Nov-Dec. 1994, Pp.31-40

104. Silverstone, A. E., Aquila and Onkelos, Manchester U. Press, Manchester, 1931

105. Smallwood, E. Mary, The Jews Under Roman Rule, E. J. Brill, Leiden, 1976

106. Stone, M.E., "Reactions to Destructions of the Second Temple," JSJ, 12, 1981, Pp.195-204

107. The Talmud of the Land of Israel, Vol. 2, Peah, Trans. by Roger Brooks, U. of Chicago Press, Chicago, 1990

108. Touger, Eliyahu, As A New Day Breaks, S.I.E., Brooklyn, 1993

109. Vanderkam, J.C., "2 Maccabees 6, 7A and Calendrical Change in Jerusalem," JSJ, Vol.XII, No.1, 7/81, pp.52-74

110. Williams, A. Lukyn, Adversus Judaeos: A Bird's Eye View of Christian Apologiae until the Renaissance, Cambridge U. Press, London, 1935

111. Williams, A.Lukyn, Talmudic Judaism and Christianity, SPCK, London, 1933

112. The World History of the Jewish People, Vol. 8, Society & Religion in the Second Temple Period, edited by Michael Avi Yonah & Zvi Baras, Jewish History Publishers Ltd., Jerusalem, 1976

113. Yadin, Yigael, Bar Kokhba: The Rediscovery of the Legendary Hero of the Last Jewish Revolt Against Imperial Rome, Random House, NY, 1971

114. Zeitlin, Solomon, The Rise and Fall of the Judean State, Vol.3, Jewish Publication Society, Philadelphia, 1978

115. Zeitlin, Solomon, Solomon Zeitlin's Studies in the Early History of Judaism, Vol.II, Ktav, NY, 1974